Out of his definitive six-volume work on Lincoln and his times, Carl Sandburg has written this superb 430,000 word biography. These volumes have sold over 1,200,000 copies in high-priced editions. Now for the first time they are published in an inexpensive three-volume paperback edition. Here is Volume I, *The Prairie Years*. Volume II contains *The War Years (1861-1864)*; Volume III, *The War Years (1864-1865)*.

CARL SANDBURG was born in Galesburg, Illinois, on January 6, 1878. He graduated from Lombard College in Galesburg, and has since received honorary degrees from Harvard, Yale, New York University, Northwestern, Knox College, Wesleyan University, Syracuse University, Lafayette, Rollins, Augustana and Dartmouth. At thirty he married Lillian Steichen, sister of the great photographer. He has been Secretary to the Mayor of Milwaukee, private in the U.S. Army, newspaper correspondent, editorial writer, film writer, folk song recitalist, poet and Lincoln biographer. In addition to the Pulitzer Prize for Poetry (1950) and the gold medal for history given by the American Academy of Arts and Letters (1952), Sandburg has won several literary awards. His published works begin with *Chicago Poems* (1915) and are still appearing. *Remembrance Rock,* his only novel, appeared in 1948. ABRAHAM LINCOLN: THE PRAIRIE YEARS was first published in 1926, and THE WAR YEARS in 1939.

VOLUME II

THE WAR YEARS, 1861-1864

CARL SANDBURG

Abraham Lincoln

THE PRAIRIE YEARS *and* THE WAR YEARS

in three volumes

A Laurel Edition

Published by
DELL PUBLISHING CO., INC.
750 Third Avenue
New York 17, N.Y.

Reprinted by arrangement with
Harcourt, Brace and Company, Inc.
New York, N. Y.

First Dell printing—October, 1959
Second Dell printing—January, 1960
Third Dell printing—April, 1960
Fourth Dell printing—October, 1960
Fifth Dell printing—December, 1960
Sixth Dell printing—August, 1963
Seventh Dell printing—August, 1964
Eighth Dell printing—July, 1965

Printed in U.S.A.

CONTENTS

Chapter 1

America Whither? —
Lincoln Journeys to Washington

"America whither?" was the question, with headache and heartache in several million homes, as Lincoln began his winding journey to Washington. There Congress had not yet, after canvass of electoral votes, declared and certified him President-elect. There coming events were yet to unlock a box of secrets. In the hair-trigger suspense General Scott was saying to an aide, "A dog fight now might cause the gutters to run with blood." And he was putting guards at doorways and vantage points to make sure of order when the electoral vote for President would be canvassed February 13.

The high-priced lawyer, Rufus Choate, listening to foreign language opera in New York had told his daughter, "Interpret for me the libretto lest I dilate with the wrong emotion." In the changing chaos of the American scene, people were dilating with a thousand different interpretations. Lincoln was to be, if he could manage it, the supreme interpreter of the violent and contradictory motives swaying the country, the labor pains of the nation.

Only tall stacks of documents recording the steel of fact and the fog of dream could tell the intricate tale of the shaping of a national fate; of many newspapers North and South lying to their readers and pandering to party and special interests; of Southern planters and merchants $200,000,000 in debt to the North, chiefly to the money controllers of New York City; of the jealousy of Virginia and Kentucky slave breeders whose market was interfered with by the African slave traders; of the race question, one thing in the blizzard region of New England, where a Negro on the streets was a rare curiosity, and something else again in the deep drowsy tropical South, where in many areas Negroes outnumbered whites; of Southern slave traders who flouted the Constitutional law prohibiting the delivery of naked cargoes in the Gulf Coast canebrakes and everglades; of the law as to fugitive slaves mocked at by abolitionists stealing slave property and running it North to freedom; of abolitionists South and North hanged, shot, stabbed, mutilated; of the Northern manufacturer able to throw out men or machines no longer profitable while the Southern planter could not so easily scrap his production apparatus of living black men and women; of a new quantity production intricately organized in firearms and watch factories; of automatic machinery slightly guided by human hands producing shoes, fabrics, scissors, pins and imitation jewelry sold by a chain of Dollar Stores; of a wilderness of oil derricks sprung up in western Pennsylvania; of balloons soaring 23,000 feet and predictions of passenger balloons to Europe; of microscopically exact gauges to measure one ten-thousandth of an inch; of the far western State of Iowa having double the population of South Carolina; of the persistent national vision of a railroad to the Pacific; of covered wagons heading west with signs "Ho for California," "Oregon or Death"; of 500 westbound wagons a day passing through Fort Kearney, Nebraska; of horse stages taking passengers across plains, deserts, mountains, in a regular 23-day run from St. Louis to San Francisco; of the pony express running mail from St. Joseph, Missouri, to San Francisco in 11 days, using 500 horses and 80 riders, each taking the sacks an average of 133⅓ miles; of farming machinery almost exclusively in the North that doubled and tripled crop land one man could handle; of woman's household work lightened by labor-saving sewing machines, churns, egg-beaters and the like; of Abraham Lincoln reading in his personal copy of *Blackwood's Magazine* that in 30 years the U.S. population would double and in 1940 reach 303,000,000; of immense stretches of the Great Plains where sod might yet be broken for unnumbered millions to come; of new empires of production and trade in the prospects of practical men who had in the past ten years spent $400,000,000 on railroads and canals between the Midwest and the Atlantic seaboard; of lands, homesteads and vast exploits waiting out yonder where the railroad whistle would shatter old solitudes; of backbreaking labor by Irish construction gangs on railroads and canals; of dog-eat-dog rivalries among merchants, manufacturers and other interests battling for customers and trade areas; of customers haggling over retail-store prices and the sensational announcement of A. T. Stewart's big store in New York that goods had one price only, as marked; of the clean and inexplicably mystic dream in many humble hearts of an indissoluble Federal Union of States; of the Mississippi River system draining 1,000,000 square miles of rich farm land, floating $60,000,000 worth of steamboats, hauling from 12 states North and South; of the certainty that the new Republican party power at Washington would aim to limit extension of slavery and put it in the course of "ultimate extinction"; of the 260,000 free Negroes of the South owning property valued at $25,-000,000, one being the wealthiest landowner in Jefferson County, Virginia; of at least one in every hundred free Negroes owning one or two slaves, a few owning 50 or more; of the Southern poor white lacking slaves, land and the decent creature comforts of the Negro house servant, and often clutching as a dear personal possession the fact that he was not born black; of Northern factory hands and garment-trade workers paid a bare subsistence wage, out of which to guard against accident, sickness, old age, unemployment; of the vague hope across the South that Northwestern States might join their confederacy or form a confederacy of their own; of the one-crop Cotton States' heavy dependence on the Border Slave States and the North for food supplies, animal fodder, implements and clothing; of the Cotton States' delusion that New England and Europe were economic dependents of King Cotton; of the American system having densely intricate undergrowths, shot through from the growths of oncoming modern capitalism moderated and offset by an immense domain of cheap land absorbing otherwise disturbing and antagonistic elements.

Thus might run a jagged sketch of the Divided House over which Lincoln was to be Chief Magistrate.

The journey from Springfield to Washington brought Lincoln face to face with the governors and legislators of five states. He set foot in key cities; spoke with important men controlling politics, money, transportation, supplies; delivered more than 20 speeches; shook the hands of thousands of people; took his own look at immense crowds who wanted their look at the pivotal figure of the American scene.

Persons on board the Wabash Railroad train carrying the President-elect over the Indiana cornlands included press correspondents, old Eighth Circuit lawyers Ward Hill Lamon, Orville H. Browning, Jesse K. Dubois, Judge David Davis, Norman B. Judd of Chicago, four uniformed Regular Army officers, and 24-year-old Colonel Elmer Ephraim Ellsworth, whose Zouaves had swept the country, won championship colors, performed at West Point for Regular Army officers, and on the White House lawn. Crowds, one of 70,000, had seen their "lightning drill" with musket, bayonet, knapsack, in scarlet baggy trousers, red caps, blue jackets with orange and yellow trimmings. Later Ellsworth had gone to Springfield, had made the Lincoln & Herndon office his headquarters and delivered stump speeches for the Lincoln ticket.

The Wabash train drew into Indianapolis at five o'clock. To Governor Oliver P. Morton and "Fellow Citizens of the State of Indiana," Lincoln spoke of himself as "a mere instrument, an accidental instrument" of a great cause. Later in a speech from the balcony of the Bates House, he agreed with Solomon there is a time to keep silence and was quoted as saying: *"When men wrangle by the mouth with no certainty that they mean the same thing while using the same words, it perhaps would be as well if they would keep silence."*

On Lincoln's 52d birthday he set foot in Cincinnati, stepped into a carriage drawn by six white horses, and rode in a procession that included brass bands, fife-and-drum corps, La Fayette Guards, Rover Guards, German Yagers, Zouaves, Guthrie Greys, Washington Dragoons, citizens on horseback, in carriages, afoot.

The mayor introduced the President-elect. To Kentuckians just across the Ohio River he would say, "We mean to treat you, as near as we possibly can, as Washington, Jefferson, and Madison treated you," that "under the Providence of God, who has never deserted us . . . we shall again be brethren, forgetting all parties—ignoring all parties." As to Germans and other foreigners, "I esteem them no better than other people, nor any worse." This brought laughter. "It is not my nature, when I see a people borne down by the weight of their shackles—the oppression of tyranny— to make their life more bitter by heaping upon them greater burdens; but rather would I do all in my power to raise the yoke, than to add anything that would tend to crush them." This brought cheers and was too grave for laughter.

Not yet had Congress declared Lincoln President. Excitement ran high in Washington February 13. Crowds climbed Capitol Hill for gallery seats, at every doorway finding armed guards. "No one could pass except Senators and Representatives, and those who had the written ticket of admission signed by the Speaker of the House or the presiding officer of the Senate," wrote L. E. Chittenden. "Even members of Congress could not pass in their friends." A Washington militia colonel in civilian clothes said his men and their rifles were within easy call. Pennsylvania Avenue, "choked with a howling angry mob," saw much street fighting and many arrests.

Tellers read the certificates state by state. John C. Breckinridge, the Vice-President, a Kentuckian whose heart lay deep with the secession cause, pronounced:

> Abraham Lincoln, of Illinois, having received a majority of the whole number of electoral votes, is elected President of the United States for four years, commencing the 4th of March, 1861 . . .

Lincoln that day rode on his special train on the Little Miami Railroad to the capital of Ohio. To the state legislature at Columbus that night Lincoln made a speech peculiar from several angles: "I cannot but know what you all know, that, without a name, perhaps without a reason why I should have a name, there has fallen upon me a task such as did not rest even upon the Father of his Country . . . I turn, then, and look to the American people and to that God who has never forsaken them . . ." He spoke sentences that brought inquiry, derision, belittlement of him; he had his own purpose in the calm, deliberate words: "I have not maintained silence from any want of real anxiety. It is a good thing that there is no more than anxiety, for there is nothing going wrong. It is a consoling circumstance that when we look out there is nothing that really hurts anybody . . ."

The Lincoln special reached Pittsburgh February 14. He thanked Mayor Wilson and the citizens for a "flattering reception," again said he would speak on the country's "present distracted condition" when the time arrived, hoped that when he did finally speak he would say nothing to disappoint the people generally throughout the country, and once more threw out soothing words of a bright outlook, further baffling the better-informed philosophers.

At the town of Freedom, a coal-heaver yelled from the crowd, "Abe, they say you're the tallest man in the United States, but I don't believe you're any taller than I am." Lincoln replied, "Come up here and let's measure." The dusty shoveler in work clothes pushed through the crowd, stood back to back with the President-elect and they were exactly the same height. The crowd cheered. The two tall men grinned and shook hands. And here and there earnest people said it was no way for a public man to act with a coal-heaver, and what was the country coming to?

Into Ohio again and up to Cleveland chugged the special train. Artillery roared salutes. Through rain and mud two miles marched the procession of honor to the Weddell House. Again Lincoln spoke to his own purpose: ". . . Why all this excitement? Why all these complaints? As I said before, this crisis is all artificial. It has no foundation in facts. It was not argued up, as the saying is, and cannot, therefore, be argued down. Let it alone and it will go down of itself."

Thus from city to city, and no day of rest, and again six milk-white horses, or eight glossy blacks, with red plumes on their heads and flags in the harness, festoons and bunting of red, white and blue in the roaring streets, and packed human sidewalks.

Lincoln remembered a little girl who had written suggesting his face should have whiskers. He had answered it might look like a piece of "silly affec[ta]tion." Her town was Westfield, New York, and there he told the crowd, "I have a correspondent in this place, and if she is present I would like to see her." No one came forward. "Who is it? Give us her name," came from the crowd. "Her name is Grace Bedell." And Grace was led and carried to the platform, Lincoln saying, "She wrote me that she thought I would be better looking if I wore whiskers." He looked down at the little girl, "You see, I let these whiskers grow for you, Grace." Then he kissed her. Far and wide went the press item. The New York *Tribune* headlined "Old Abe Kissed by Pretty Girl." The St. Louis *Republican,* under the head of "Whiskers and Kisses," jibed: "If kissing pretty girls is a Presidential privilege, Mrs. Lincoln, who knows her rights and knowing dares maintain them, ought to insist on a veto power for herself."

Trying to stem the human surges around the President-elect in Buffalo, Major David Hunter of the Regular Army had his collarbone dislocated. A German Sängerbund offered songs. The crowd made merry over a man at a sawbuck sawing away to pay an election bet that Lincoln would lose. Again Lincoln said he knew the demonstration was not to him personally, and he would speak on national difficulties when he had all the light possible.

Eastward into the Erie Canal zone moved the Lincoln train in the morning. At Rochester he confessed to being overwhelmed "with this vast number of faces at this hour of the morning." The handsome platform rigged up for him at Syracuse was too much of a platform for such a speech as he would make, he said. At Utica he said he had no speech but appeared to see and be seen. So far as the ladies were concerned, he said, "I have the best of the bargain in the sight."

To governors and to key men, speaking in confidence, he counseled as he had written Governor Curtin: "I think you would do well to express, without passion, threat, or appearance of boasting, but nevertheless, with firmness, the purpose of yourself, and your state to maintain the Union at all hazzards. Also, if you can, procure the Legislature to pass resolutions to that effect."

While Lincoln crossed the Empire State from west to east February 18, news came over the wires that down in Montgomery, Alabama, amid thundering cannon and cheers from an immense crowd, Jefferson Davis took his oath as President of the Confederate States of America, six today and more tomorrow. For the first time since leaving home, Lincoln publicly admitted weariness, ending a short speech from the steps of the capitol at Albany, "I have neither the voice nor the strength to address you at any greater length."

The personal humility he had spoken in five states reached its lowest shrinking-point in the Hall of Assembly of the New York capitol: ". . . It is true that while I hold myself without mock modesty, the humblest of all individuals that have ever been elevated to the Presidency, I have a more difficult task to perform than any one of them. When the time comes I shall speak as well as I am able for the good of the present and future of this country—for the good both of the North and the South . . ."

Down the Hudson River, with greetings at Troy, Hudson, Peekskill. Then New York, the Front Door to America, where tall ships came in from the seven seas to one of the great world ports; where the 35,000 votes for Lincoln for President were a third of the total ballots; where had grown up the financial center of the country, with vast controls over trade, manufacture, transportation; where Mayor Fernando Wood had declared that New York should establish itself as a free city, separate from the Union, sovereign in itself like the seceded states of the South, thereby holding its trade and continuing "uninterrupted intercourse with every section" of the country; where bribe money had passed in franchise and city land deals; where the Mayor, as a party boss, had taken $5,000 apiece from two lawyers for nominations for Supreme Court judgeships; where the Mayor and his aldermen awarded a street-cleaning contract for $279,000 when another bid was $84,000 less; where the Mayor's personal fortune had risen to at least $250,000 out of politics; where only the corruption of the courts of justice had saved the Mayor from conviction of forgery, perjury and other crimes; where the Mayor and his brother Ben owned lotteries and were licensed as professional gamblers through charters from Southern States; where they owned the New York *Daily News* and openly advocated the rights of the Confederate States.

Lincoln rode in a procession of 30 carriages led by a platoon of mounted police. His open carriage, a barouche, had accommodated the Prince of Wales a few months before. At the Astor House 500 policemen held the crowds in line. For the first time on his journey Lincoln faced a crowd of peculiar curiosity, its silence having a touch of the sinister. The cheers and shouts were not like Buffalo, Columbus, Indianapolis.

In the City Hall next morning, surrounded by aldermen and writers for the press, Lincoln faced Mayor Wood, spoke thanks for the reception "given me . . . by a people who do not by a majority agree with me." And "in reference to the difficulties . . . of which your Honor thought fit to speak so becomingly, and so justly as I suppose, I can only say that I fully concur in the sentiments expressed." He was talking past Wood and to the country in saying: "This Union should never be abandoned unless it fails and the probability of its preservation shall cease to exist without throwing the passengers and cargo overboard."

White kid gloves were then in style for wear at opera but Lincoln, in a box at the new and sumptuous Academy of

Music on Fourteenth Street and Irving Place, wore *black* kids on his large hands contrasting with the red-velvet box front. In a box opposite, a Southern man remarked to the ladies of his party, "I think we ought to send some flowers over the way to the Undertaker of the Union." The word spread, and the press commented on the one pair of black gloves in the packed house.

Mrs. Lincoln the same evening was holding a fairly successful reception in the parlors of the Astor House. Newspapers mentioned Mrs. August Belmont as among those present, which caused Mrs. Belmont to send a note to the newspapers saying she wished it known that she was not present. Tad and Willie went with a nursemaid and saw a play at Laura Keene's Theatre. With mother and father they saw Barnum's museum and its mammoth monstrosities and concatenated curiosities.

"Abe is becoming more grave," said the partly humorous weekly *Vanity Fair*. "He don't construct as many jokes as he did. He fears he will get things mixed up if he don't look out."

Greeley was saying in his morning *Tribune* that the questions were plopped at Lincoln: "What is to be the issue of this Southern effervescence? Are we really to have civil war?" And Greeley printed a version of a Lincoln fable:

"When I was a young lawyer, and Illinois was little settled, I, with other lawyers, used to ride the circuit. Once a long spell of pouring rain flooded the whole country. Ahead of us was Fox River, larger than all the rest, and we could not help saying to each other, 'If these small streams give us so much trouble, how shall we get over Fox River?' Darkness fell before we had reached that stream, and we all stopped at a log tavern, had our horses put up, and resolved to pass the night. Here we were right glad to fall in with the Methodist Presiding Elder of the circuit, who rode it in all weather, knew all its ways, and could tell us all about Fox River. So we all gathered around him, and asked him if he knew about the crossing of Fox River. 'Oh yes,' he replied, 'I know all about Fox River. I have crossed it often, and understand it well. But I have one fixed rule with regard to

Fox River: *I never cross it till I reach it!*'" The earnest Greeley found this "characteristic of Lincoln and his way of regarding portents of trouble."

A second fable was offered New York political thinkers. "I once knew a good, sound churchman, whom we'll call Brown," Lincoln was quoted, "who was on a committee to erect a bridge over a dangerous and rapid river. Architect after architect failed, and at last Brown said he had a friend named Jones who had built several bridges and could build this. 'Let's have him in,' said the committee. In came Jones. 'Can you build this bridge, sir?' 'Yes,' replied Jones, 'I could build a bridge to the infernal regions, if necessary.' The sober committee were horrified, but when Jones retired Brown thought it fair to defend his friend. 'I know Jones so well,' said he, 'and he is so honest a man and so good an architect that, if he states soberly and positively that he can build a bridge to Hades—why, I believe it. But I have my doubts about the abutments on the infernal side.'" "So," Lincoln added, "when politicians said they could harmonize the Northern and Southern wings of the democracy, I believed them. But I had my doubts about the abutments on the Southern side."

The New York reception of the President-elect was the most elaborate, pretentious, detailed, expensive—and yet the coldest—of all on the Lincoln journey toward inauguration.

Before the New Jersey Assembly at Trenton he referred to himself again as of no personal importance and thanked them for receiving him as "the representative, for the time being, of the majesty of the people of the United States . . . The man does not live who is more devoted to peace than I am. None who would do more to preserve it. But it may be necessary to put the foot down firmly. [Here the audience broke out in cheers so loud and long that for some moments it was impossible to hear Mr. Lincoln's voice.] And if I do my duty, and do right, you will sustain me, will you not?" Loud cheers, and cries of "Yes, yes, we will." He closed saying in effect that he might be the last President of the United States: "If it [the ship of state] should suffer attack now, there will be no pilot ever needed for another voyage."

He arrived in Philadelphia at four o'clock. In the hotel parlor Lincoln stood handshaking that night for an hour or two. Later in Norman B. Judd's room Lincoln met Allan Pinkerton, a railroad detective in the service of the Philadelphia, Wilmington & Baltimore Railroad, to guard trains and bridges and circumvent threatened explosions and fires. Pinkerton opened: "We have come to know, Mr. Lincoln, and beyond the shadow of a doubt, that there exists a plot to assassinate you. The attempt will be made on your way through Baltimore, day after tomorrow. I am here to help in outwitting the assassins." Lincoln sat with legs crossed, a good-natured curiosity on his face fading to a sober look. "I am listening, Mr. Pinkerton."

A barber named Fernandina was foremost among the conspirators, according to Pinkerton's spies, who, he said, had been at work for weeks and had become "bosom friends and inseparable companions" of the plotters. A melodramatic, maudlin speech by Fernandina at a secret meeting of the military company he captained was described by Pinkerton to Lincoln, the barber waving "a long glittering knife" over his head and crying: "This hireling Lincoln shall never, never be President. My life is of no consequence in a cause like this, and I am willing to give it for his. As Orsini gave his life for Italy, I am ready to die for the rights of the South and to crush out the abolitionist."

Pinkerton went personally to Baltimore, purporting to be a Georgia secessionist, and "Fernandina cordially grasped my hand, and we all retired to a private saloon." Fernandina was asked if there was no other way to save the South than by killing Lincoln. He replied, in the Pinkerton report: "No, as well might you attempt to move the Washington Monument yonder with your breath, as to change our purpose. He must die—and die he shall." With another drink by this time, he was asked about the police. He had fixed that, too: "They are all with us. I have seen the Chief Marshal of Police, and he is all right. In a week from today,

Lincoln will be a corpse." Also it seemed that Pinkerton detected another conspirator named Hill, who also drank heavy and often, and also was ready, in his talk, to kill Lincoln. He said, in the Pinkerton report, "I shall immortalize myself by plunging a knife into Lincoln's heart."

Lincoln interrupted with many questions. Supporting Pinkerton's viewpoint were the practical Judd and the equally practical Samuel M. Felton, a railroad president who considered the evidence positive of a plot to burn railroad bridges, blow up trains, "and murder Mr. Lincoln on his way to Washington." Pinkerton gave details of a wild-eyed plot. The police chief at Baltimore was arranging to send only a small force to the railroad depot, where a gang of toughs would start a fight to draw off the policemen. Then the Fernandina assassins would close round the President-elect and deliver the fatal shot or knife thrust. "We propose," said Pinkerton, "to take you on to Washington this very night, Mr. President, and steal a march on your enemies."

Lincoln deliberated, then: "Gentlemen, I appreciate the suggestions, and while I can stand anything essential in the way of misrepresentation, I do not feel I can go to Washington tonight. Tomorrow morning I have promised to raise the flag over Independence Hall, and after that to visit the legislature at Harrisburg. Whatever the cost, these two promises I must fulfill. Thereafter I shall be ready to consider any plan you may adopt."

From Washington that night arrived Frederick W. Seward, son of Lincoln's announced Secretary of State. He found Chestnut Street and the Continental Hotel gay with a serenade to the President-elect, music, flowers, flags, buzzing conversations, and "brilliantly lighted parlours filled with ladies and gentlemen who had come to 'pay their respects.'" Lamon took Seward to Lincoln's bedroom. "Presently Colonel Lamon called me," wrote Seward of that night, "and we met Mr. Lincoln coming down the hall . . . After friendly greeting he sat down by the table under the gas light to peruse the letter I had brought." The communi-

cations his father had so secretly and hurriedly sent on,
which Lincoln read deliberately twice, stressed a report of
one Colonel Stone:

> A New York detective officer on duty in Baltimore
> for three weeks past reports this morning that there is
> serious danger of violence to, and the assassination of,
> Mr. Lincoln in his passage through that city, should
> the time of that passage be known. He states that there
> are banded rowdies holding secret meetings, and that
> he has heard threats of mobbing and violence, and has
> himself heard men declare that if Mr. Lincoln was to
> be assassinated they would like to be the men . . . All
> risk might be easily avoided by a change in the travel-
> ing arrangements which would bring Mr. Lincoln and
> a portion of his party through Baltimore by a night
> train without previous notice.

"Did you hear any names mentioned?" Lincoln pressed.
"Did you, for instance, ever hear anything said about such
a name as Pinkerton?" No, Seward had heard no such
name. Lincoln smiled. "If different persons, not knowing of
each other's work, have been pursuing separate clues that
led to the same result, why then it shows there may be
something in it. But if this is only the same story, filtered
through two channels, and reaching me in two ways, then
that don't make it any stronger. Don't you see?" They discussed it further and Lincoln rose, "Well, we haven't got to
decide it tonight, anyway."

In studying what to do Lincoln had to consider the silence of Baltimore and Maryland. Governor Thomas H.
Hicks of that state favored the Union as against secession
and was himself threatened with death by men proclaiming
their volunteer militia would shoot down Northern soldiers
en route to Washington, would burn supply depots and railroad bridges, would if war came march their corps to
Washington and take that city. Governor Hicks had a seething and sensitive public to handle, a people ready to show
what they could do with guns, clubs, stones, bricks, in street

fighting. The marshal of police, George P. Kane, was an open secessionist.

At six o'clock that morning of February 22, Washington's Birthday, Lincoln amid cannon salutes and crowd applause pulled a rope and raised a flag over Independence Hall. Inside Independence Hall he spoke to an audience crowding all corners and overflowing. He had often pondered over the "dangers" incurred by the men who had assembled there and framed the Declaration. Not merely separation from a motherland, but liberty as a hope to all the world, for all future time, was the sentiment guiding them. "It was that which gave promise that in due time the weights should be lifted from the shoulders of all men, and that *all* should have an equal chance . . ." He asked if the country could be saved on that basis. If so he would consider himself one of the happiest men in the world. "But, if this country cannot be saved without giving up that principle—I was about to say I would rather be assassinated on this spot than surrender it." He could see no need of bloodshed and war. "And I may say in advance, there will be no blood shed unless it be forced upon the Government . . ."

Judd had been up nearly the whole night in a conference with Pinkerton and other men. They arranged for Lincoln to journey from Harrisburg on a two-car train that night under conditions they believed would deliver him safely in Washington the next morning. In Harrisburg, amid guns and platoons, Lincoln replied to Governor Curtin's welcome that under the weight of his great responsibility he brought an honest heart, but "I dare not tell you that I bring a head sufficient for it." He would lean on the people. "If my own strength should fail, I shall at least fall back upon these masses, who, I think, under any circumstances will not fail."

That evening Lincoln was at a table in the dining room of the Jones House in Harrisburg. He had made three speeches during the day, listened to other speeches longer than his own, talked with Governor Curtin and men of power in Pennsylvania, and held a conference with members of his party. For the first time others than Judd learned of the change in plans. Judd had told Lincoln these other old friends should know what was afoot, Lincoln approving. "I reckon they will laugh at us, Judd, but you had better get them together."

Lincoln told them, "Unless there are some other reasons besides fear of ridicule, I am disposed to carry out Judd's plan." A. K. McClure, legislative member and a founder of the Republican party, was sure he heard Lincoln say, "What would the nation think of its President stealing into its capital like a thief in the night?" while Governor Curtin declared the question not one for Lincoln to decide.

Close to six o'clock Lincoln was called from the dinner table, went upstairs to his room, changed his dinner dress for a traveling suit, and came down with a soft felt hat sticking in his pocket, and a folded shawl on his arm. A carriage was ready. Then, as Judd told it: "Mr. Lamon went first into the carriage; Col. Sumner of the regular army, was following close after Mr. Lincoln; I put my hand gently on his shoulder; he turned to see what was wanted, and before I could explain the carriage was off. The situation was a little awkward." Judd had tricked Colonel Sumner into a moment of delay, and to the Colonel's furious words Judd replied, "When we get to Washington, Mr. Lincoln shall determine what apology is due you."

Lincoln and Lamon, with a lone car to themselves, drawn by a lone locomotive of the Pennsylvania Railroad, rode out of Harrisburg, no lights on, Lamon carrying two ordinary pistols, two derringers and two large knives. Telegraph linemen had cut the wires; all telegrams into or out of Harrisburg were shut off till further orders.

In Philadelphia shortly aften ten a carriage with Detective Pinkerton and Superintendent Kenney of the P. W. & B. Railroad met Lincoln and Lamon at the Pennsylvania Railroad station and took them to the P. W. & B. station, where they were put on the last car of the New York-Washington train. A woman detective working for Pinkerton had reserved rear berths of a sleeping-car, one for her "invalid brother" to be occupied by Lincoln, who was quickly in his berth with the curtains carefully drawn.

Unknown to Pinkerton or Lamon, on that last car a

powerfully built man, armed with a revolver, slept in a
berth engaged at New York. He was Superintendent John
A. Kennedy of the New York police department, an officer
of valor and integrity, who did not know that his detective,
Bookstaver, had rushed on to Washington and reported his
Baltimore findings to Seward. Kennedy was acting on reports received from his other two men in Baltimore, and
his intention, as he slept in the same car with Lincoln that
night, was to warn the authorities in Washington next morning that Lincoln would require safeguarding in his sched-
uled trip across Maryland the next day.

Baltimore was reached at 3:30 in the morning, and of the
stop there Pinkerton wrote: "An officer of the road entered
the car and whispered in my ear the welcome words 'All's
well' . . ." An hour and more the train waited for a connect-
ing train from the west. A drunken traveler on the train
platform sang "Dixie," sang over and again how he would
live and die in dear old Dixie. Lincoln murmured sleepily,
said Pinkerton, "No doubt there will be a great time in
Dixie by and by." Except for "a joke or two in an under-
tone," Lincoln was not heard from during the night, according to Lamon. At six in the morning the President-elect
stepped off the train in Washington.

Thus ended the night ride of the vanishing and reappear-
ing President-elect. The special train from Harrisburg drew
into Baltimore in the afternoon like a clock with its hour
hand gone, disappointing Mayor George Brown, city officials and an immense crowd. "At the Calvert station were
not less than 10,000 people," wrote I. K. Bowen to Howell
Cobb in Georgia, "and the moment the train arrived, supposing Lincoln was aboard, the most terrific cheers ever
heard were sent up, three for the Southern Confederacy,
three for 'gallant Jeff Davis,' and three groans for 'the Rail
Splitter.' Had Lincoln been there, contrary to my precon-
ceived opinions, he would have met with trouble . . ."

In many variations the tale went world-wide of the long-
shanked Chief Magistrate in flight disguised in a Scotch
plaid cap and a long military cloak. In thousands of journals it was repeated in news items, cartoons and editorial

comment. Who started it? A lone press writer, Joseph Howard, a pathetic rascal who had a habit of getting newspapers
into trouble with his frauds and hoaxes. Howard telegraphed his newspaper, the New York *Times,* a responsible
journal friendly to Lincoln, of Lincoln's arrival in Washington: "He wore a Scotch plaid cap and a very long military cloak, so that he was entirely unrecognizable." The
Times printed it. And the world took to it as a good story.

Lamon wrote that Lincoln "was convinced that he had
committed a grave mistake in listening to the solicitations
of a professional spy and of friends too easily alarmed."
Nevertheless Lincoln's advisers may have saved his life, said
Lamon, believing there was never a moment from then on
during his days in Washington that he was not in danger of
death by violence.

In the swirl of events to come there would be little time
to thresh over the pros and cons of the night ride through
Baltimore. Much other night riding lay ahead.

On February 4, 1861, the Peace Convention in Washington had begun its sessions behind closed doors. Though an
air of secret and important deliberation was desired by
many of the delegates, the main proceedings reached newspapers from day to day. Twenty-one Border and Northern
States sent delegates; Michigan, Wisconsin and Minnesota
let it be known they expected only useless or mischievous
talk.

Mostly the delegates were old men. One day's session
was given to eulogy over an aged and almost blind delegate
who died before presenting his credentials. The presiding
officer was a tottering, ashen ruin, John Tyler, once President of the United States. The record of the convention
noted that nearly every speaker advised short speeches and
then made a long one. The conflict of wills and opinion
over the country was reproduced in the convention. On Lincoln's first evening in Washington the delegates called on
him at nine o'clock in his Willard's Hotel suite, with no
particular result.

Lincoln had breakfast with Seward the morning he arrived and at 11 called with Seward at the White House, chatted with President Buchanan, and shook hands with the Cabinet. In the afternoon he met the Illinois Congressmen and Senators, headed by Stephen A. Douglas. At seven he dined at Seward's home on F Street and at ten o'clock he received "reciprocal" calls from the Buchanan Cabinet members, also plenty of private citizens. Betweenwhiles he had held interviews with General Scott, Francis P. Blair, Sr., Montgomery Blair, many officials and would-be officials. Tomorrow was Sunday. Perhaps he would sleep.

Mrs. Lincoln and the three Lincoln boys took their first Washington breakfast with husband and father next morning. And Lincoln went with Seward to St. John's Church (Episcopal) that Sunday morning.

Two Republican party elements pressed Lincoln: the antislavery extremists Sumner, Chase, Wade, Stevens, and the conciliators Seward, Charles Francis Adams, Tom Corwin. "With which side would Lincoln be allied? That, north and south, was the question," wrote C. F. Adams, Jr., who saw Seward age ten years that winter. "These men had been brooding over the questions at issue and dwelling on them till their minds had lost their tone, and become morbid."

Sumner and Lincoln were getting acquainted. Up to Lincoln, Sumner would stride to tell him this or that *must* be done. The Senator from Massachusetts, the scholar in politics, the most elegantly tailored man in House or Senate, wearing maroon vests, fawn gaiters, blue-violet neckties, high silk hat, cape over shoulders, gold-headed cane, gold watch chain, was born in Boston to money and leisure. He had a handsomely modeled head, wavy locks of hair, sideburns; he was a beau, scholar, zealot, bachelor, 50 years old. His father, Charles Pinckney Sumner, had been named for a South Carolina statesman. His grandfather, Major Job Sumner, had marched through the Revolutionary War in hardship and danger alongside Major John Lucas of Georgia, and these two comrades from Massachusetts and Georgia were buried side by side in St. Paul's churchyard on Broadway, New York. He was the only man of whom

Lincoln would remark, "Sumner thinks he runs me." Lincoln saw early what Henry Adams emphasized in letters of the hour, that Sumner had unaccountable dignity. "He stands six feet two in his stockings—a colossus holding his burning heart in his hand to light up the sea of life," wrote the poet Longfellow.

"I am in morals, not politics," said Sumner. He took it as his mission and role to tell the Senate and thereby the country North and South a series of tragic and horrible facts about slavery. He knew he was telling the truth. But he believed also that any such truth as he might omit was of no importance. The categories of fact always entering into the discussions of Lincoln and Seward as to slavery were out of Sumner's range and beyond his chosen role. Such points of understanding as might have come from association with Southerners were completely absent from his arguments. He mentioned the unmentionable, with a cold wrath and an evenly measured scorn, till at last there were Southern Senators and Representatives who wanted to see him suffer and die.

His own antislavery associates in the Senate had reservations about him, Grimes of Iowa writing to Mrs. Grimes that Sumner was "harsh, vindictive," and a friend of Ben Wade's noting: "For Wade there was a suspicion of arrogance, a flavor of sham, in the grand assumption of the splendid Sumner . . . Most men at each interview with him had to tell him who and what they were."

"The planter will one day take a slave for his harlot, and sell her the next as a being of some lower species, a beast of labor," Sumner quoted from Southey's *History of Brazil* in a Senate speech, Douglas replying, "We have had another dish of the classics served up, classic allusions, each one only distinguished for its lasciviousness and obscenity . . ." By degrees Sumner had come to stand for something the South wanted exterminated from the Union. He was perhaps the most perfect impersonation of what the South wanted to secede from. No other man in the Federal Government so thrust at the sin and guilt of the South while evading the issues of sin and guilt in the North.

In his Senate seat, after a session had closed and nearly all the members had left the chamber, Sumner had been struck on the head with a cane. The blows rained till the cane broke in pieces. Bruised and lacerated without warning or a chance to fight back, he struggled to rise and get at his unseen assailant, nearly wrenching loose his desk from the iron screws that held it to the floor, he was so powerful physically. Several of his enemies stood by with their unspoken wishes, "Let him suffer and die—it would be a blessing to the country," while Sumner lay senseless in an aisle, the blood flowing from his head. As the news of the assault went over the country, it set tongues raging in the North and deepened the sullen defiance of the South.

Then for Sumner had come pain, the sickbed, a wheel chair, years of grinding his teeth day by day as treatments, applications of fire, were given to heal a bruised spine and a partially disordered brain area. The assailant, Congressman Preston Brooks of South Carolina said he had only wanted to half-kill Sumner and watch him live and suffer. He had resigned his seat, had been re-elected by his constituents and presented with more canes and wishes that he would use them as he knew how. He died in bed of strangulation, clutching at his throat as if he would tear it open while he lay a victim of violent croup or acute inflammation of the throat.

In June 1860 Sumner stood up in the Senate for the speech marking his return to active politics. He had spent nearly four years in a wheel chair. What had been his meditations? What would the sick man now well again have to say? The old Sumner spoke: statistics, morals and a finality of doom. He pronounced an excommunication titled "The Barbarism of Slavery," put the slave masters of the South in a class with barbarous African tribal chiefs; he read the Southern people beyond the pale of civilization. He had collected "every instance of cruelty, violence, passion, coarseness, and vulgarity recorded as having happened within the Slave States," said the New York *Times,* which asked: "What general good can be hoped for from such envenomed attacks? Do they aid in the least the solution of what

every sensible man acknowledges to be the most delicate
and difficult problem of this age?" For reasons best known
to himself he omitted completely his thought on the ways
and means by which slave property valued at $3,000,000,-
000 could somehow be made nonproperty, could somehow
be devalued to zero, and whether he favored forcible subju-
gation of Southern society toward that end.

In five campaign addresses Sumner had endorsed Abraham Lincoln, and later inquired as to the election, "What
victory of the cartridge-box ever did so much?" and said of
the crisis, "Happily, Abraham Lincoln [Prolonged cheers.]
has those elements of character needed to carry us through
. . . he is calm, prudent, wise, and also brave . . . the Union
shall be preserved and made more precious by consecration
to Human Rights."

Then came weeks that harassed Sumner, when old friends
saw him as "morbid" and "crazy." The winds of doctrine
roared in the caverns of his mind. Before he entered his
career in politics he had been one of the foremost antiwar
advocates in America, six printings having been circulated
of his oration on "The True Grandeur of Nations," saying,
"War crushes with bloody heel all justice, all happiness, all
that is God-like in man," and, "In our age there can be no
peace that is not honorable; there can be no war that is not
dishonorable."

Old and tried friends were tenderly guiding the course of
one possibly not fully recovered in a maimed head and
spine. "Looks well in the face, but is feeble and walks with
an uncertain step," Longfellow had written in his journal,
writing later to Sumner in Europe, "It will not do to go
limping through the remainder of your life with a tangled
brain."

His occasional caution in politics was there in his telling
Lincoln that Cameron was thief, corruptionist and hypo-
crite, and then in so consequential a matter refusing to give
Lincoln one line of writing to that effect. In a scene where
connivance and fraud were so prevalent, where men were
so often controlled by personal material advancement, Sum-

ner's charm and integrity were peculiar and extraordinary
or he could not have held unwaveringly such friendships as
he had with those other men of like integrity in varied
walks, Longfellow the poet, John A. Andrew the politician,
and Wendell Phillips the agitator. They took him as hero
and crusader, Longfellow saying one could understand
Sumner only through seeing what he *was* instead of empha-
sizing what he was *not*.

The gracious Julia Ward Howe asked him to meet some
friends of hers at dinner. He said he wasn't interested and,
"Really, Julia, I have lost all my interest in individuals."
Her quick answer: "Why, Charles! God hasn't got as far as
that yet." Few were aware that long before Lincoln's night
ride into Washington, one of Sumner's wealthy Massachusetts friends, George Luther Stearns, a Medford ship chandler and abolitionist who had supplied John Brown with
money and rifles, paid a bodyguard to watch and protect
Sumner constantly.

"Sumner had never seen Lincoln before he came to
Washington," wrote Carl Schurz. "When he met Lincoln he
was greatly amazed and puzzled by what he saw and heard
. . . Many thought that these two men, being so essentially
different, could not possibly work together. But on the
whole they did, and they were able to do so, because, however great the divergence of their views on some points,
they believed in one another's sincerity."

On Sunday, March 3, Lincoln received in his room at
Willard's the Virginia Congressman A. R. Boteler, who
that afternoon had asked Congressman Benjamin Stanton
of Ohio to withdraw his Force Bill, which would fix on the
President complete authority over all regular and militia
troops of the nation. Boteler said the bill if passed would
force Virginia out of the Union. "The bill must pass the
House this evening," Stanton had replied.

Boteler told Lincoln that the Force Bill was exciting painful anxiety in Virginia and frustrating patriotic efforts to
prevent secession. He wrote of their chat: "It served to

deepen the impression . . . that Mr. Lincoln was a kind-hearted man; that he was . . . by no means disposed to interfere, directly or indirectly, with the institutions of slavery in any of the States, or to yield to the clamorous demand of those bloody-minded extremists, who were then so very keen to cry 'havoc!' and 'let slip the dogs of war' . . ."

The House clock indicated nearly ten that night when Stanton called up his Force Bill for consideration. After two attempts to move adjournment, by Illinois Republican Washburne and Pennsylvania Republican Hickman, the floor was obtained by New York Republican John Cochrane, who before taking his seat renewed the motion to adjourn. By a vote of 77 to 60 the House adjourned and, wrote Boteler, "the Thirty-Sixth Congress expired on the following Monday of March 4, without having given to Mr. Lincoln the power to call out the militia and to accept the services of volunteers."

In those closing hours of Congress a bill was passed to forbid the Federal Government forever from interfering with slavery in any manner whatsoever in any Slave State— requiring three-fourths of the states of the Union to approve the measure as an amendment to the Constitution. This was as far as Congress could go within its powers to guarantee the South that whatever it intended to do as to slavery extension in the Territories, its policy was to let slavery alone in the Slave States. The act was in line with the Republican party platform and Lincoln's public and private declarations.

Chapter 2

Lincoln Takes the Oath as President

March 4 dawned with pleasant weather that later turned bleak and chilly for the 25,000 strangers roving Washington. With hotels and rooming houses overcrowded, hundreds had slept on the porches of public buildings and on street sidewalks. Thousands filled the street around Willard's as the forenoon wore away. General Scott and Colonel Stone had arranged for riflemen in squads to be placed in hiding on the roofs of certain commanding houses along Pennsylvania Avenue. From windows of the Capitol wings riflemen were to watch the inauguration platform.

President Buchanan drove with Senator Baker of Oregon and Senator Pearce of Maryland from the White House to Willard's in an open carriage. Buchanan stepped out and soon returned arm in arm with Lincoln as police kept a path for them. Then the procession moved down Pennsylvania Avenue with representations from all branches of the Government. A new procession was formed to escort the President-elect to the east portico and the platform outdoors, where a crowd of at least 10,000 that had waited long gave its applause and scattering cheers.

Senator Douglas took a seat and looked over the crowd. One comment ran that rather than a sea of upturned faces it was a sea of silk hats and white shirt bosoms. Lincoln in a new tall hat, new black suit and black boots, expansive white shirt bosom, carrying an ebony cane with a gold head the size of a hen's egg, had the crowd matched.

Ned Baker's silver-bell voice rang out: "Fellow-citizens, I introduce to you Abraham Lincoln, the President-elect of the United States." The applause was a slight ripple. Then came the inaugural address; Lincoln drew the papers from an inside pocket, slowly pulled spectacles from another pocket, put them on, and read deliberately the fateful document.

Then stepped forward Chief Justice Taney, worn, shrunken, odd, with "the face of a galvanized corpse," said Mrs. Clay of Alabama. His hands shook with age, emotion, both, as he held out an open Bible toward the ninth President to be sworn in by him. Lincoln laid his left hand on the Bible, raised his right hand, and repeated after the Chief Justice the oath prescribed by the Constitution: "I do solemnly swear that I will faithfully execute the office of President of the United States, and will, to the best of my ability, preserve, protect, and defend the Constitution of the United States."

The artillery over on the slope boomed with all its guns a salute of thunder to the 16th President of the United States. That was all. The inauguration was over.

The inaugural address itself, as a state paper from the first administration of a new party, as a definition of policy and viewpoint, as a breaking of Lincoln's long silence, was the high point of the day. Beyond the immediate hearers was the vast unseen audience that would read the address in cold print. Never before in New York had such crowds waited at newspaper offices and jammed and scrambled for the first sheets wet from the press. In its week of delivery it was the most widely read and closely scrutinized utterance that had ever come from an American President. No previous manuscript from Lincoln's hand had been so carefully written by him, rearranged, modified. The draft made in Springfield underwent important changes, mainly deletions, under the suggestions of Seward and Browning, with Lincoln's added light as he traveled and events shifted.

The two closing sentences of Lincoln's original draft were too warlike, Seward believed. They read: "You can forbear the assault upon it [the Government]; I can not shrink from the defense of it. With you, and not with me, is the solemn question of 'Shall it be peace, or a sword?' " Lincoln dropped them. Seward believed "some words of affection, some of calm and cheerful confidence," should close the address and Lincoln revised a paragraph submitted by Seward.

The finished address Lincoln gave the world went to readers who searched and dug into every line and phrase. Reason and emotion wove through it—and hopes, fears, resolves. Parts of it read:

> . . . Apprehension seems to exist among the people of the Southern States, that by the accession of a Republican Administration, their property, and their peace, and personal security, are to be endangered. There has never been any reasonable cause for such apprehension. Indeed, the most ample evidence to the contrary has all the while existed, and been open to their inspection. It is found in nearly all the published speeches of him who now addresses you. I do but quote from one of those speeches when I declare that "I have no purpose, directly or indirectly, to interfere with the institution of slavery in the States where it exists. I believe I have no lawful right to do so, and I have no inclination to do so." Those who nominated and elected me did so with full knowledge that I had made this, and many similar declarations, and had never recanted them . . .
>
> There is much controversy about the delivering up of fugitives from service or labor. The clause I now read is as plainly written in the Constitution as any other of its provisions:
>
> "No person held to service or labor in one State, under the laws thereof, escaping into another, shall, in consequence of any law or regulation therein, be discharged from such service or labor, but shall be delivered up on claim of the party to whom such service or labor may be due." . . .
>
> There is some difference of opinion whether this clause should be enforced by national or by state authority; but surely that difference is not a very material one . . .

A disruption of the Federal Union heretofore only menaced, is now formidably attempted.

I hold, that in contemplation of universal law, and of the Constitution, the Union of these States is perpetual. Perpetuity is implied, if not expressed, in the fundamental law of all national governments. It is safe to assert that no government proper, ever had a provision in its organic law for its own termination . . .

The Union is much older than the Constitution. It was formed in fact, by the Articles of Association in 1774. It was matured and continued by the Declaration of Independence in 1776. It was further matured and the faith of all the then thirteen States expressly plighted and engaged that it should be perpetual, by the Articles of Confederation in 1778. And finally, in 1787, one of the declared objects for ordaining and establishing the Constitution, was *"to form a more perfect Union."* . . .

It follows from these views that no State, upon its own mere motion, can lawfully get out of the Union— that *resolves* and *ordinances* to that effect are legally void; and that acts of violence, within any State or States, against the authority of the United States, are insurrectionary or revolutionary, according to circumstances.

I therefore consider that, in view of the Constitution and the laws, the Union is unbroken; and, to the extent of my ability, I shall take care, as the Constitution itself expressly enjoins upon me, that the laws of the Union be faithfully executed in all the States. Doing this I deem to be only a simple duty on my part; and I shall perform it, so far as practicable, unless my rightful masters, the American people, shall withhold the requisite means, or, in some authoritative manner, direct the contrary. I trust this will not be regarded as a menace, but only as the declared purpose of the Union that it *will* constitutionally defend, and maintain itself.

In doing this there needs to be no bloodshed or violence; and there shall be none, unless it be forced upon the national authority. The power confided to me, will be used to hold, occupy, and possess the property, and places belonging to the government, and to collect the duties and imposts; but beyond what may be necessary for these objects, there will be no invasion—no using of force against, or among the people anywhere . . .

If a minority, in such case, will secede rather than acquiesce, they make a precedent which, in turn, will divide and ruin them; for a minority of their own will secede from them, whenever a majority refuses to be controlled by such minority. For instance, why may not any portion of a new confederacy, a year or two hence, arbitrarily secede again, precisely as portions of the present Union now claim to secede from it. All who cherish disunion sentiments are now being educated to the exact temper of doing this . . .

Plainly, the central idea of secession, is the essence of anarchy . . .

One section of our country believes slavery is *right,* and ought to be extended, while the other believes it is *wrong,* and ought not to be extended. This is the only substantial dispute . . .

Physically speaking, we cannot separate. We cannot remove our respective sections from each other, nor build an impassable wall between them. A husband and wife may be divorced, and go out of the presence, and beyond the reach of each other; but the different parts of our country cannot do this . . . Suppose you go to war, you cannot fight always; and when, after much loss on both sides, and no gain on either, you cease fighting, the identical old questions as to terms of intercourse, are again upon you.

This country, with its institutions, belongs to the people who inhabit it. Whenever they shall grow weary of the existing government, they can exercise their *constitutional* right of amending it, or their *revolutionary* right to dismember, or overthrow it. I cannot be ignorant of the fact that many worthy, and patriotic citizens are desirous of having the national constitution amended. While I make no recommendation of amendments, I fully recognize the rightful authority of the people over the whole subject, to be exercised in either of the modes prescribed in the instrument itself . . . I understand a proposed amendment to the Constitution—which amendment, however, I have not seen, has passed Congress, to the effect that the federal government, shall never interfere with the domestic institutions of the States, including that of persons held to service. To avoid misconstruction of what I have said, I depart from my purpose not to speak of particular amendments, so far as to say that, holding such a provision to now be implied constitutional law, I have no objection to its being made express, and irrevocable . . .

Why should there not be a patient confidence in the ultimate justice of the people? Is there any better, or equal hope, in the world? In our present differences, is either party without faith of being in the right? If the Almighty Ruler of nations, with his eternal truth and justice, be on your side of the North, or on yours of the South, that truth, and that justice, will surely prevail, by the judgment of this great tribunal, the American people . . .

While the people retain their virtue, and vigilence, no administration, by any extreme of wickedness or folly, can very seriously injure the government, in the short space of four years.

My countrymen, one and all, think calmly and *well*, upon this whole subject. Nothing valuable can be lost by taking time . . . Intelligence, patriotism, Christianity, and a firm reliance on Him, who has never yet forsaken this favored land, are still competent to adjust, in the best way, all our present difficulty.

In *your* hands, my dissatisfied fellow countrymen, and not *mine*, is the momentous issue of civil war. The government will not assail *you*. You can have no conflict, without being yourselves the aggressors. *You* have no oath registered in Heaven to destroy the government, while *I* shall have the most solemn one to "preserve, protect and defend" it.

Thus flowed the reasonings, explanations, watchwords that ended Lincoln's long silence. He finished: "I am loth to close. We are not enemies, but friends. We must not be enemies. Though passion may have strained, it must not break our bonds of affection. The mystic chords of memory, stretching from every battle-field, and patriot grave, to every living heart and hearthstone, all over this broad land, will yet swell the chorus of the Union, when again touched, as surely they will be, by the better angels of our nature."

Far out in Iowa was a farmer who had written Lincoln not to yield: "Give the little finger and shortly the whole hand is required." Far down in Nolensville, Tennessee, W. N. Barnes had written him that the people there were "overwhelmingly loyal to the flag of their country." Barnes wanted a statement to circulate. Now he had it.

The Montgomery *Advertiser* in Alabama was sure the inaugural meant war, nothing less would satisfy "the abolition chief," and the artfully worded address was written by a pen more skillful than the Rail Splitter wielded.

"To twenty millions of people," said the New York *Tribune* of the address, "it will carry tidings, good or not, as the case may be, that the federal government of the United States is still in existence, with a Man at the head of it." Not one "fawning expression" could be found in it, observed the Boston *Transcript*. "The language is level to the popular mind, the plain, homespun language of a man accustomed to talk with the 'folks' and the 'neighbors,' whose words fit his facts and thoughts."

The New York *Herald* commented, "It would have been almost as instructive if President Lincoln had contented himself with telling his audience yesterday a funny story and letting them go"; however, the inaugural was "not a crude performance," for "it abounds with traits of craft and cunning." The Baltimore *Sun* read in the inaugural that "it assumes despotic authority, and intimates the design to exercise that authority to any extent of war and bloodshed. If it means what it says, it is the knell and requiem of the Union, and the death of hope." The Baltimore *Exchange* believed "the measures of Mr. Lincoln mean war"; while Douglas said publicly, "It is a peace offering rather than a war message."

The Richmond *Enquirer* saw in it "the cool, unimpassioned, deliberate language of the fanatic . . . Sectional war awaits only the signal gun . . . The question, 'Where shall Virginia go?' is answered by Mr. Lincoln. She must go *to war*." The Charleston *Mercury* announced, "It is our wisest policy to accept it as a declaration of war."

A group of Southern leaders meeting in Washington the night of the inauguration sent word to their Government: "We all agreed that it was Lincoln's purpose at once to attempt the collection of the revenue, to re-enforce and hold Fort Sumter and Pickens, and to retake the other places. He is a man of will and firmness. His cabinet will yield to him with alacrity."

Inauguration night saw an attempt at gaiety, the Union Ball, in a new building on Judiciary Square, the hall light-flooded by five large gas chandeliers. Lincoln shook hands from 8:15 till 10:30. The estimate was 25 hands a minute. His gloves were now *white* kids. He looked absent-minded, as young Henry Adams saw him, as though "no man living needed so much education as the new President but all the education he could get would not be enough."

The Marine Band played "Hail to the Chief" at 11. Lincoln entered leading the grand march, arm in arm with Mayor Berret, followed by Mrs. Lincoln arm in arm with Senator Stephen A. Douglas. Lincoln avoided waltz and square dance, but Mrs. Lincoln and Douglas were partners in a quadrille. Hundreds of women in crinoline trod the waltz, schottische, polka, mazurka. Mrs. Lincoln wore a new blue gown, a large blue feather in her hair. Many said it must be her happiest night of life, the realization of dreams long awaited. The ball over, Mr. and Mrs. Lincoln went for the first night in their new house of presences, shadows, ghosts.

As Lincoln slept that night, relays of ponies and men were rushing west from St. Joe, Missouri, with his inaugural address. They would be seven days and 17 hours reaching Sacramento, California, with his plea for the east and west coasts, the Great Lakes and the Gulf, the Rio Grande and the Penobscot, to belong to one common country.

"The President is determined he will have a compound Cabinet," Seward wrote to his wife. Seward objected to Chase in the Cabinet, and on Saturday, March 2, he had notified Lincoln he must "withdraw." Lincoln on Monday wrote to Seward: "I feel constrained to beg that you will countermand the withdrawal. The public interest, I think, demands that you should; and my personal feelings are deeply inlisted in the same direction." Handing the note to John Hay to copy, he said, "I can't afford to let Seward take the first trick." Next morning Seward with a polite note was back in the Cabinet. Thus the struggle between conservatives (Seward) and radicals (Chase) began. Lincoln wrote Seward for "an interview at once."

Thus far Lincoln's Cabinet slate, with two minor exceptions, stood as he had framed it late on election night in the Springfield telegraph office. When told, "They will eat you up," he replied, "They will be just as likely to eat each other up."

At noon on March 5 the Senate received and approved the new President's nominations: Secretary of State, William H. Seward; Secretary of the Treasury, Salmon P. Chase; Secretary of War, Simon Cameron; Secretary of the Navy, Gideon Welles; Secretary of the Interior, Caleb B. Smith; Attorney General, Edward Bates; Postmaster General, Montgomery Blair. The new Cabinet had four old-line Democrats (Chase, Cameron, Welles, Blair) and three old-line Whigs (Seward, Bates, Smith), a wrong balance, Lincoln heard many times, and made clear: "I'm something of an old-line Whig myself and I'll be there to make the parties even." These Cabinet men he would see and hear often; they would be stubborn with him and he with them.

Seward, eight years older than Lincoln, had been, until

Lincoln's nomination and election, leader of the Republican party. As a New York man close to the controlling financial and commercial interests of the country, he sponsored protective tariffs, steamship subsidies, a bill for a railway to the Pacific. He analyzed canals, railroads, trade balances, tariffs, new factors in commerce, the stream of surplus capital and labor arriving from Europe, and foretold their economic role with a surer grasp than Lincoln. Although an Episcopalian, he had for years been close to Archbishop John Hughes of New York, the most influential Roman Catholic prelate in America. His start in politics was with the Anti-Masonic party, which elected him state senator in 1830. His recommendation as governor of New York that public-school funds be allotted to Catholics as well as Protestants had brought the American or Know-Nothing faction clamoring against him within the Republican party.

He had quit snuff for cigars. His beautiful Arabian horses were pictured in *Harper's Weekly*. His five-course dinners at his Washington residence were a topic of smart society, and one of his loyal friends, Charles Francis Adams, Jr., noted: "When it came to drinking, Seward was, for a man of sixty, a free liver; at times his brandy-and-water would excite him, and set his tongue going with dangerous volubility; but I never saw him more affected than that—never anything approaching drunkenness. He simply liked the stimulus, and was very fond of champagne; and when he was loaded, his tongue wagged." Between this man and Lincoln was a friendship that would grow deeper.

Salmon Portland Chase had held off from taking the Treasury portfolio. Wrote Chase to J. T. Trowbridge, "Some rumor of my hesitation got abroad, and I was immediately pressed by the most urgent remonstrances not to decline. I finally yielded to this." He had been governor of Ohio and U.S. Senator, had received 49 ballots for the presidential nomination at Chicago, had expected that Seward's nomination would bring him second place on the ticket. An ambition to be President lay deep.

Tall and portly, Chase was spoken of as "handsome," as

having "a stately figure," a "classic face." At 24 he married Katherine Jane Garniss, three years younger than himself, and within two years she died, leaving him a girl child who lived only four years. At 29 he married Eliza Ann Smith of Cincinnati, a girl of 18, who died six years later, having borne him three children, of whom only one had lived. A year later he married Sarah Bella Dunlop Ludlow of a well-known and propertied Cincinnati family; she died within six years, having borne him two children, of whom one lived. Thus he had across 17 years stood at the burial caskets of three wives and four children.

Out of these accumulated griefs he had two living daughters. One of them was a gleaming, vital creature, Katherine Jane Chase, known as Kate and born under strange stars. She had grown to be his chum and helper, playing chess with him, walking with him to the office, telling him what she got from a newly read book. Her glimpses into politics sometimes went further than his. She was as much a son as a daughter, men said.

Chase had lights for leading, though his gnawing ambition was a chronic personal ailment beyond remedy or easement. In early years in Cincinnati, he had taken without fee so many cases of black people claimed as fugitive slaves that Kentuckians called him "the attorney-general for runaway negroes." He had quit the Democratic party, led in organizing the Liberty party, then the Free-Soil party, ending with the Republicans. On a platform in Cincinnati he was hit with a brick, with rotten eggs. To abolitionists these were credentials. The way had been opened to commercial and corporation law practice; a fortune in money beckoned. He chose to throw his fate with runaway Negroes; also ambition dictated his politics.

When finally named by Lincoln, to refuse might isolate him, with risk to his moving higher. The story was easily half-true that he faced a mirror and bowed to himself, murmuring "President Chase."

Simon Cameron, the new Secretary of War, had proper claims to his portfolio. His white-hatted delegates to the

Chicago convention had on the first presidential nomination ballot voted for him. Cameron's release of those delegates had started the stampede to Lincoln. Lincoln's managers had, without authority from Lincoln, pledged Cameron a Cabinet place.

Politics was a business, a sport, a passion with Cameron. At 62, for 20 years he had been the dominant political manager in Pennsylvania. His mother's father, a German, had fought in the Revolutionary War. His Scotch father was a country tailor, a poor provider, and nine-year-old Simon was adopted by a physician, at ten began typesetting, learned the printer's trade, and before he was 21 edited the Doylestown *Democrat*. On borrowed money Cameron became owner and editor of the Harrisburg *Intelligencer*. With a contract for state printing, his profits grew and more contracts came. He manipulated toward electing Andrew Jackson to a second term; the Federal patronage of Pennsylvania entire came into his hands.

Ten of Cameron's earlier years had been given to bank, railroad and canal building, getting a fortune. His nickname, "the Czar of Pennsylvania," rested on a reputation as the most skilled political manipulator in America. His decision had put Buchanan into the U.S. Senate twice. Then, suddenly seeing Buchanan's power rising to question his own in Pennsylvania, he organized the People's party, had himself elected U.S. Senator in 1856. In the same year he amalgamated Whigs, Know-Nothings, Republicans into the Union party of Pennsylvania, with a unique signed agreement by the national electors to give a solid vote for either Frémont, the national Republican candidate, or Fillmore, the national American or Know-Nothing candidate, if the electoral vote of the state would elect either to the presidency.

Loose gray clothes hung from his tall, slim frame. He was smooth of face, sharp-lipped, with a delicate straight nose, a finely chiseled mask touched with fox wariness. As he pronounced dry and pretendedly forthright decisions Cameron's face was more often mask than face. He wrought effects from behind the scenes. His setup of himself as a presidential possibility at the Chicago convention was one of his effects. He did not care to be President, but he came to Chicago with something to trade and got a pledge from Davis, Swett, Medill and others that with Lincoln elected he would be Secretary of the Treasury.

When it dawned on Lincoln that Cameron as Treasury head would look peculiar and call for dry wit, Lincoln named him for the War Department, took it back, named him again to stay. Cameron did not care deeply about any policies or principles involved in the affair, but when Chase, Sumner, Curtin, McClure and others started out to scalp and gut him politically, he stuck by his guns, brought as many witnesses as they to face Lincoln for him, his best ones Seward and Weed. When at last the opposition refused to prefer any charges against Cameron in writing, and all the accusations were exercises in oral denunciation, Lincoln said his name would stay on the original slate. The Keystone State with its iron and railroad domain was wanted by Lincoln for the national emergency, and Cameron was its leading link of business and politics. Lincoln appointed Cameron, though groaning, according to Whitney, as they talked about it, "How can I justify my title of Honest Old Abe with the appointment of a man like Cameron?"

Gideon Welles, the Connecticut Yankee named for Secretary of the Navy, was, like Cameron, an old Jackson Democrat. His newspaper, the Hartford *Times,* was among the earliest to cry Jackson for President. Lincoln saw Welles as a more than relatively honest Democrat who had quit his party on the slavery-extension issue, who as a Republican made a losing run for the governorship in 1855 and was chairman of his state's delegation to the Chicago convention. Fifty-eight years old, his short, thickset body had a massive head surmounted by a patriarchal wig, which with his white prophet's beard gave him a Neptune look. A smooth-shaven upper lip, and eyes kindly in repose, told those who met him not half what he could put into his diary. Lincoln put him at the head of all of Uncle Sam's seagoing vessels, and later made jokes about Uncle Gide-

on's not knowing bow from stern. His opinions and prejudices would run free, wide and faulty in the diary, but in
recording fact as to what he saw and heard he would be a
competent witness. Not all was going on that he believed or
guessed, but what he put down as seeing and hearing was
usually there.

Edward Bates, the new Attorney General, born in 1793,
was a sergeant of volunteers in the War of 1812, going
west and studying law in 1814 in St. Louis, then a settlement of 2,000 people. He had been attorney general of
Missouri, a state senator, a Congressman. Events slowly
piloted him to where he had no place to go but the Republican party. As a Free-Soil Whig from a Border State, it
was argued that he was the man who as President could
soften the shocks between the sections. His 48 votes on the
first ballot at the Chicago convention sank to 22 on the
third ballot and finally went to Lincoln. His course had
been even and consistent. Most of his life Bates had been
first a lawyer and secondly a politician. President Fillmore's offer to appoint him Secretary of War he had refused. He was quaint, old-fashioned, of a school that was
passing. "An Old-Line Whig," said Bates, "is one who takes
his whiskey regularly, and votes the Democratic ticket occasionally."

Caleb B. Smith of Indiana, Secretary of the Interior, was
Boston-born, 1808, and taken to Ohio when six years old.
Lawyer, editor, orator, at Connersville, Indiana, he became
a Whig Congressman, held appointive Federal office, took
up the practice of law in Cincinnati in 1850, and moved to
Indianapolis in 1858. Of the new Cabinet members he was
nearest the class of ordinary professional politician.

Montgomery Blair, Postmaster General, was viewed as a
sign that among Lincoln's chosen advisers was the Blair
family, headed by Old Man Blair, Francis Preston Blair,
born in 1791 of a Scotch-Irish line, graduate of Transylvania University, a volunteer in the War of 1812, a fighting Jackson man through both of Jackson's stormy presidential terms, editing at Washington the *Globe,* which told

Jackson's friends and enemies where to get on or off as to current issues.

His influence among Border State delegates joined to Montgomery's control of Maryland delegates, plus his son Frank's sway over Missouri delegates, were thrown to Lincoln on the third ballot at Chicago. His cordial relations with Lincoln, many feared, might grow into the same important intimacy he had held with Presidents Jackson and Van Buren. This fear was grounded partly on his tangible strength in having his first choice for President in 1860, Bates, as Attorney General, his old fellow Democrat, Welles, as Navy Department chief, his son-in-law, Gustavus Vasa Fox, slated to be Assistant Secretary of the Navy, another son-in-law, S. P. Lee, as a ranking admiral in the Navy, and finally his son Montgomery as Postmaster General. Subtle, cadaverous, bald, poised he was— persistent and silken in spinning his webs, delicately sensitive to political trends. Lincoln sought the views of this skilled professional politician. Often the views came unsought. The elder Blair was one of the few to whom Lincoln confidentially loaned a copy of the inaugural address for comment and suggestion.

Montgomery, born in 1813, had been district attorney for Missouri, mayor of St. Louis, judge of the court of common pleas. He had moved to Maryland to be near his large Federal Supreme Court practice. As counsel for Dred Scott, the fugitive slave, he won friends among antislavery men. He had helped get a lawyer to defend John Brown. He represented in Maryland the moderate wing of the Republican party as against the Henry Winter Davis radical faction. The Blair appointment resulted in protests to Lincoln nearly as furious as in the case of Cameron.

The man who would inherit this Cabinet and sit at the head of it in the event of Lincoln's death, Hannibal Hamlin, had been consulted about the Cabinet several times by Lincoln. At their meeting in Chicago, Lincoln said, "Mr. Hamlin, I desire to say to you that I shall accept, and shall always be willing to accept, in the very best spirit, any advice that you, the Vice President, may give me." This was unusual. Hamlin said so. Except for Jackson and Van Buren, the relation between the Vice-Presidents and the Presidents had not as a rule been friendly. Hamlin pledged himself to be a friend and to render his humble advice as best he could.

Hamlin had been elected to Congress twice as a Democrat, had then been elected U.S. Senator as a Democrat, and on the slavery-extension issue had resigned as U.S. Senator, joined in organizing the Republican party in Maine, was elected governor of Maine, and resigned as governor to take a seat as one of the first Republicans in the U.S. Senate, later resigning as U.S. Senator to make the run for Vice-President on the Republican ticket. He was 52, tall and powerfully built, saying he did not need a revolver to guard against assassination, showing two fists that he said would take care of trouble. His face was swarthy, of a complexion so dark that many Southerners said and believed he was a mulatto and that his blood accounted for his radical antislavery sentiments. His recorded ancestors were of the pure English stock that settled the colony of Massachusetts. In college when he was 18 word came that his father was dead and he went back home to work the farm. Later he bought a country weekly paper, learned typesetting, studied law and oratory, and convinced the hardheaded, slow-going people of Maine that he should be their leading public servant.

Later in March Lincoln and his Cabinet gave a state dinner. William Howard Russell of the London *Times* wrote of being "surprised to find a diversity of accent almost as great as if a number of foreigners had been speaking English."

The new President had to give more hours daily to the Federal patronage, and applicants for places, than to all other items on the day's program. For 30 years, except eight Whig years, the thousands of Federal jobs had been the Democratic spoils of victory. The custom was for the new party to sweep out the old and put in new postmasters, port collectors, marshals, superintendents, paymasters, each having deputies, assistants, clerks. Thousands of the applicants had given time and money toward Republican victory, often with a clear promise of jobs.

At Willard's the main-floor corridors surged with office seekers, overflowing up the staircases into halls, reading room, barbershop, writing room, out on the porch and steps. From all over the North "the triumphant Republicans had winged their way to the prey." Many wore the new paper collars, some had linen. They crowded the Willard bar morning and night. Target cuspidors were circled with miss-shots. One excited pilgrim ordering breakfast for a crucial day called for black tea, toast, scrambled eggs, fresh spring shad, wild pigeon, pig's feet, two robins on toast, oysters, breads and cakes. One rushed out of the Willard barbershop, his face half-lathered, a towel under his chin, calling to a Senator about the place promised him. One stopped Lincoln in a hack at a street crossing and handed up his recommendation papers toward Lincoln, who frowned, burst out, "No! no! I won't open shop in the street," and rode on.

Of a visit of several days in Washington Herndon wrote that Lincoln could scarcely cease from referring to the persistence of office seekers. They slipped in, he said, through half-opened doors; they edged their way through crowds and thrust papers in his hands when he rode. Herndon quoted Lincoln in one outburst: "If our American society and the United States Government are demoralized and overthrown, it will come from the voracious desire for office, this wriggle to live without toil, work, and labor, from which I am not free myself."

The humorist Orpheus C. Kerr (Office Seeker) in April wrote: "Every soul of them knew old Abe when he was a child, and one old boy can even remember going for a doctor when his mother was born. I met one of them the other day (he is after the Moosehicmagunticook post-office), and his anecdotes of the President's boyhood brought tears to my eyes, and several tumblers to my lips."

Advice and philosophy crept into Lincoln notes to department heads. "This man wants to work—so uncommon a want that I think it ought to be gratified," began one note, and another: "The lady bearer of this says she has two sons who want to work. Set them at it if possible. Wanting to work is so rare a want that it should be encouraged." Not often was the tone so peremptory as in one note: "You must make a job for the bearer of this—make a job of it with the collector and have it done. You *can* do it for me and you *must*." A rebuke might go, as in a note to "Hon. Sec. of Interior": "How is this? I supposed I was appointing for register of wills a *citizen of this District*. Now the commission comes to me 'Moses Kelly, of *New Hampshire!*' I do not like this." One disgruntled place hunter snorted, "Why, I am one of those who made you President." And Lincoln started to dig into a pile of papers on his desk. "Yes, and it's a pretty mess you got me into!"

The President reached for friends he did not want to lose, writing to Senator Jacob Collamer of Vermont: "God help me! It is said I have offended you. Please tell me how."

In mid-March Senator John Sherman of Ohio introduced to Lincoln his brother William Tecumseh Sherman who, having just resigned as head of the Louisiana Military Academy, seeing war ahead, "may give you some information you want." Lincoln asked, "How are they getting along down there?" On Sherman fiercely replying, "They are preparing for war," the President said, "Oh, well, I guess we'll manage to keep house." And Sherman said no more to Lincoln, went away to take a job as street-railway superintendent in St. Louis at $40 a week, telling his brother what he had to tell politicians in general, Lincoln included: "You have got things in a hell of a fix, and you may get them out as best you can." Undoubtedly Sherman offered his services to the President in no ordinary office seeker's manner; he was asking no fat job, nor an easy life. Had Lincoln known of the steeled loyalty of this Ohio man, he would have met Sherman with a different greeting. However, the President was in a mood when he chose to show no anxiety, and this worried Sherman.

Seward heard from the President that John C. Frémont

and William L. Dayton, Republican candidates for President and Vice-President in 1856, were to have respectively appointments as Ministers to France and England. This arrangement, proposed by Lincoln without consulting Seward, was "scarcely courteous" to his Secretary of State, and in the case of Frémont was "obnoxious" to Seward, who was no admirer of Frémont, according to C. F. Adams, Jr. "The President did not yield the point readily," and only persistent effort by Seward brought about the transfer of Dayton to Paris, and the naming of Charles Francis Adams, Sr., as Minister to the Court of St. James, London.

Carl Schurz was to be Minister to Spain and his case was argued up and down in the Cabinet. Seward declared that Schurz's record in insurrectionary, red-republican movements in Germany in 1848 would be frowned on by the Spanish monarchy. Lincoln replied that Schurz would be discreet; it ought not to be held against the man that he had made efforts for liberty; and it might be well for European governments to realize this. Chase and Blair agreed with Lincoln. Seward yielded, but didn't like it.

In the Cabinet, Chase, Cameron and Blair had their friends and allies to take care of in about the same proportion as Seward, a hundred asking an office that could go to only one. "Blair is nearly run to death with office seekers," wrote G. V. Fox to his wife. "They left him at 2 this morning and commenced at 8 this morning. The President is equally beset. I have seen Abe often." Among many wanting office was a belief that either money or influence could bring it, while Lincoln guessed he had "ten pegs where there was but one hole to put them in." Often his salutation to a White House caller was, "Well, sir, I am glad to know that you have not come after an office."

In some quarters was a constant murmuring, such as that of Senator Sumner writing to an applicant for a foreign post: "Nobody who wishes to succeed should hail from Massachusetts or New York. Their claims are said to be exhausted." The New York complications got worse as Greeley and other anti-Seward Republicans worried in fear that Seward and Weed, getting control of Lincoln, would dictate all appointments. They called at the White House with a delegation, men who, as Lincoln well knew, had for years fought Seward and Weed for Republican party control in New York. They had gone to the Chicago convention hoping to stop the nomination of Seward. Lincoln said to the New Yorkers: "One side shall not gobble up everything. Make out a list of the places and men you want, and I will endeavor to apply the rule of give and take."

Seward on April 1 laid before Lincoln as odd a document as ever came from a department secretary to a chief magistrate, headed: "Some Thoughts for the President's Consideration." Seward numbered his thoughts. "First, we are at the end of a month's administration, and yet without a policy, either domestic or foreign." Second, "the need to meet applications for patronage" had prevented "attention to more grave matters." Third, "further delay . . . would not only bring scandal on the administration, but danger upon the country." Fourth, leave "foreign or general" appointments "for ulterior and occasional action." Fifth, "Change the question before the public from . . . slavery . . . to Union or disunion." (As though Lincoln had not for years lost sleep over how to do that very thing.) "I would terminate it [the occupation of Fort Sumter] as a safe means for changing the issue . . . This will raise distinctly the question of union or disunion." Yet the next sentence read, "I would maintain every fort and possession in the South."

Next Lincoln's eyes met weird proposals from his Secretary: "If satisfactory explanations are not received from Spain and France, [I] Would convene Congress and declare war against them. But whatever policy we adopt . . . it must be somebody's business to pursue and direct it incessantly. Either the President must do it himself, and be all the while active in it, or Devolve it on some member of his Cabinet . . . It is not in my especial province. But I neither seek to evade nor assume responsibility."

This was saying nearly straight out that Lincoln had fumbled and bumbled as a President and he, Seward, knew how to be one. And there in black ink on white paper was

the strange and wild advice that by starting wars with Spain
and France, the Union would be saved. The seceded Southern States would move back into the Union and fight under
the Old Flag. Lincoln wrote in reply, "I have been considering your paper," pointed to his inaugural and quoted
to show how definitely he had announced policies as to
Sumter and union or disunion. "Upon your closing propo-
sitions," he wrote, ". . . I remark that if this must be done,
I must do it." His closing words were soft, as though soothing a mind under strain. "When a general line of policy is
adopted, I apprehend there is no danger of its being
changed without good reason, or continuing to be a subject
of unnecessary debate; still, upon points arising in its progress, I wish, and suppose I am entitled to have the advice
of all the cabinet."

The Union was weaker than a month before because the
administration had exhibited "a blindness and a stolidity
without a parallel in the history of intelligent statesman-
ship," said the New York *Times*. Lincoln had "spent time
and strength in feeding rapacious and selfish politicians,
which should have been bestowed upon saving the Union,"
and "we tell him . . . that he must go up to a higher level
than he has yet reached." This lent support to the *Herald*'s
repeated jabs: "the Lincoln Administration is cowardly,
mean, and vicious," the blame resting on "the incompetent,
ignorant, and desperate 'Honest Abe.' "

William Cullen Bryant in a New York *Evening Post* editorial took the *Tribune* and *Times* outbursts as nervous and
peevish. To frame in 30 days a clear policy for so complex
a national situation was a hard matter, as Bryant saw it,
and furthermore, how could the facile critics know that
Lincoln had not fixed upon his policy, with a decision to
make it known to the world by action instead of a windy
proclamation?

Henry J. Raymond of the *Times* later went down to
Washington, talked with Lincoln, and got his viewpoint: "I
am like a man so busy in letting rooms in one end of his
house, that he can't stop to put out the fire that is burning
in the other."

Chapter 3

*Sumter and War Challenge —
Call for Troops*

The morning after inauguration Lincoln had studied dispatches from Major Robert Anderson, commander of Fort Sumter in Charleston Harbor, reporting that his food supplies would last four weeks or by careful saving perhaps 40 days. The Confederates stood ready to batter Fort Sumter and run down its flag whenever the word came from their Government at Montgomery.

When the Senate on March 25 requested from the President the Anderson dispatches to the War Department, the President replied, "I have, with the highest respect for the Senate, come to the conclusion that at the present moment the publication of it would be inexpedient." The Senators from Virginia, North Carolina, Tennessee, Arkansas, Texas, were in their seats answering roll call from day to day, their states not having officially and formally seceded.

Lincoln had called his Cabinet for its first meeting March 9 and put a written question, "Assuming it to be possible to now provision Fort Sumter, under all the circumstances, is it wise to attempt it?" The Cabinet members went away, returning March 16 with written answers. Seward advised No: it was not a time for the use of force. Chase advised Yes and No; Yes if it meant peace, No if the attempt was to bring on civil war, armies, million-dollar budgets. Cameron advised No, seeing that "no practical benefit will result to the country." Welles advised No: "I entertain doubts." Smith advised No: giving up Fort Sumter would cause "surprise and complaint" but it could be "explained and understood." Bates advised No: "I am willing to evacuate Fort Sumter." Blair was the only one with an unmodified Yes: Buchanan had hesitated and failed; Jackson had acted and won; provisioning the fort would "vindicate the hardy courage of the North, and the determination of the people and their President to maintain the authority of the Government." Thus the seven new counselors stood five against sending food to Anderson, one for it, and one neither for nor against it.

The President called in Assistant Secretary of the Navy Gustavus Vasa Fox, 39 years old. Born in Saugus, Massachusetts, a Naval Academy graduate of 18 years' service in coast survey, of Mexican War experience, commander of U.S. mail steamers, he resigned in 1856 to become agent of woolen mills in Lawrence, Massachusetts. On March 21, acting as Lincoln's messenger and observer, Fox had arrived in Fort Sumter under escort of a former friend, a Confederate captain formerly of the U.S. Navy, who stood within earshot while Major Anderson and Fox talked. Fox reported back to Lincoln that no time was to be lost; Anderson's final scraping of flour and last slab of bacon would be used up at noon April 15. On March 28 Lincoln instructed Fox to prepare a short order detailing the ships, men, supplies required for his plans to provision Fort Sumter. Lincoln kept a memorandum of this order for use in a day or two.

Lamon had arrived from a trip to Charleston. From the Governor of South Carolina he brought the message to Lincoln: "Nothing can prevent war except the acquiescence of the President of the United States in secession . . . Let your President attempt to reinforce Sumter, and the tocsin of war will be sounded from every hilltop and valley in the South."

The President on March 28 met his Cabinet in secret session. He read to them a memorandum from General Scott discouraging attempts to reinforce Sumter and advising, "The giving up of Forts Sumter and Pickens may be justified." This amazed several members. Blair was first to find his tongue and blurted out that the head of the Army was more than military, was "playing politician." Blair indicated that he blamed Seward's intrigue for this move. All agreed, however, that the advice of the head of the Army was not to be taken. The President asked the Cabinet to meet next day. And that night, said his secretaries, "Lincoln's eyes did not close in sleep." All night long his mind sought the realities behind multiple mirrors.

At noon next day the Cabinet met to discuss going to war. Bates wrote he would reinforce Fort Pickens, and "As to Fort Sumter, I think the time is come to either evacuate or relieve it." The President asked the others to write their views. Seward wrote: "I would at once, and at every cost, prepare for a war at Pensacola and Texas" and "I would instruct Major Anderson to retire from Fort Sumter forthwith." Chase would maintain Fort Pickens and provision Fort Sumter. Welles would make Fort Pickens impregnable, and as to Sumter, the Government was justified in "a peaceable attempt to send provisions to one of our own forts." Smith seemed to believe he would defend Fort Pickens and evacuate Fort Sumter, recognizing it as risky politically. Blair would hold Fort Pickens and fight "the head and front of this rebellion" at Fort Sumter. Cameron was absent. So the Cabinet stood three for and three against the evacuation of Sumter.

The Cabinet meeting over, the President brought out the memorandum of Captain Fox's order and at the bottom wrote an order on the Secretary of War: "Sir: I desire that an expedition, to move by sea, be got ready to sail as early as the 6th. of April next, the whole according to memorandum attached; and that you co-operate with the Secretary of the Navy for that object." This with a signed duplicate to the Secretary of the Navy was delivered, and Captain Fox started for New York to get ready the expedition.

A messenger went from Lincoln that week to Richmond, where a convention of delegates, debating over secession and voting against secession, had been sitting since February 13. The messenger gave to Judge George W. Summers Lincoln's request to come to Washington for a conference. Summers consulted other delegates and chose for the errand John B. Baldwin, who in a closed carriage arrived April 4 at the White House, and later wrote: "Mr. Lincoln received me very cordially . . . and said he desired to have some private conversation with me. He started through to a back room, opening into another room, but we found two gentlemen there engaged in writing; he seemed to think that would not do, and we passed across the hall into a small room opposite, and through that into a large front room . . . He locked the door, and . . . drew up two chairs and asked me to take a seat."

Precisely what Lincoln said in the interview was not clear in Baldwin's later recollections. Lincoln did vaguely say "something about a withdrawal of troops from Sumter on the ground of military necessity," and whatever the point was, Baldwin replied: "That will never do under heaven . . . Mr. President, I did not come here to argue with you . . . I tell you before God and man, that if there is a gun fired at Sumter, war is inevitable." Also Baldwin offered his surmise that if the Virginia convention did dissolve and its members did go home, another convention would be called in short order.

Efforts at peace were going on the rocks. Baldwin returned to Richmond declaring he had received from Lincoln "no pledge, no undertaking, no offer, no promise of any sort." Hay, Nicolay, Whitney, believed Lincoln gave Baldwin a message he failed to deliver. At a later time Lincoln, through a letter of Hay's, confirmed statements of Baldwin, as written, though having no corroboration then or since. Delegate Tarr of the Virginia convention later wrote Hay of hearing Baldwin say that he [Lincoln] "had sent for Mr. Baldwin, a member of the convention, and had him in the White House with him alone, and told him that if they would pass resolutions of adherence to the Union, then adjourn and go home, he, the President, would take the responsibility at the earliest proper time to withdraw the troops from Fort Sumter and do all within his line of duty to ward off. collision." Hay replied that the President "directs me to state . . . that your first statement is substantially correct, but that for the present he still prefers that you withhold it from the public."

On April 1, 1861, Nicolay brought to Willard's a pack-

age of papers which he handed to Secretary Welles, who
lived there. Welles read the papers; then, as Welles told it:
"Without a moment's delay I went to the President with the
package in my hand. He was alone in his office and, raising
his head from the table at which he was writing, inquired,
'What have I done wrong?' "

Then came the unraveling of a tangled affair. In Welles'
hands were two papers signed by Lincoln, who after reading them said he was surprised he had sent such a document
to the Secretary of the Navy. He had signed the papers without reading them, he told Welles; Seward with two or three
young men had been at the White House through the day
on a subject Seward had in hand. "It was Seward's specialty,
to which he, the President, had yielded, but as it involved
considerable details, he had left Mr. Seward to prepare the
necessary papers."

Thus Welles heard Lincoln's explanation. "These papers
he had signed, many of them without reading—for he had
not time, and if he could not trust the Secretary of State
he knew not whom he could trust. I asked who were associated with Mr. Seward. 'No one,' said the President, 'but
these young men were here as clerks to write down his plans
and orders.' I then asked if he knew the young men. He said
one was Captain Meigs, another was a naval officer named
Porter . . . He seemed disinclined to disclose or dwell on
the project, but assured me he never would have signed
that paper had he been aware of its contents, much of
which had no connection with Mr. Seward's scheme . . .
The President reiterated they were not his instructions, and
wished me distinctly to understand they were not, though
his name was appended to them—said the paper was an im-
proper one—that he wished me to give it no more consideration than I thought proper—treat it as canceled—as if
it had never been written."

Next day the tangle of orders and countermands became
worse. Something of Navy Department feeling was reflected
in Gustavus Vasa Fox's writing to his wife: "Mr. Seward
got up this Pensacola expedition and the President signed

the orders in ignorance and unknown to the Department. The President offers every apology possible and will do so in writing."

Among the papers Nicolay brought to Willard's for Welles to sign were instructions to the Secretary of the Navy, in the handwriting of Captain Meigs of the War Department, with a concluding sentence, "Captain Samuel Barron will relieve Captain Stringham in charge of the Bureau of detail," and the signature "Abraham Lincoln." Attached was a postscript in the handwriting of Lieutenant Porter, also signed "Abraham Lincoln," requesting of the Secretary of the Navy "that you will instruct Captain Barron to proceed and organize the Bureau of detail in the manner best adapted to meet the wants of the navy, taking cognizance of the discipline of the navy generally, detailing all officers for duty, taking charge of the recruiting of seamen, supervising charges made against officers, and all matters relating to duties which must be best understood by a sea officer."

The request proceeded: "You will please afford Captain Barron any facility for accomplishing this duty, transferring to his department the clerical force heretofore used for the purposes specified. It is to be understood that this officer will act by authority of the Secretary of the Navy, who will exercise such supervision as he may deem necessary."

Lincoln did not know when signing this appointment, nor Seward when advising Lincoln to sign it, that the man thereby appointed, Captain Samuel Barron, supposedly of the U.S. Navy, had five days before accepted a commission as a commodore in the Confederate States Navy! Nor could Lincoln or Seward under the circumstances have guessed that two weeks later Captain Barron would go to Richmond, take the oath of Confederate loyalty, and enter actively into building coast fortifications to defend Virginia and North Carolina against ships whose officers would have been detailed by him had he managed to get into the place to which Lincoln appointed him and from which Lincoln removed him the day Welles entered Lincoln's office in such anger that Lincoln's greeting was, "What have I done wrong?"

A naval lieutenant, Gwathmey, arrived in Secretary Welles' office and took from a belt strapped around his body under his shirt a letter from Captain Adams, senior naval officer in command of Fort Pickens. Welles learned that Adams was operating in obedience to an armistice negotiated by the Buchanan administration by which the U.S. Government was not to reinforce Fort Pickens provided the Confederate forces did not attack it.

Taking the letter to Lincoln, they decided to send word back to Adams to forget the armistice and to land troops. This message, however, could not be carried by Lieutenant Gwathmey. He was requesting that his resignation from the Navy be accepted; he was going to join the Confederates; he had been sufficiently loyal to his oath as an officer. So John Worden, a naval lieutenant whose loyalty to the Union was vouched for, received from the Secretary of the Navy a dispatch and was advised to memorize it, burn it, and on arriving in Florida make a certified copy as he remembered it. Worden did this, and Fort Pickens was reinforced the night of April 12.

The New York *Herald* spoke for a variety of powerful interests April 10: "Our only hope now against civil war of an indefinite duration seems to lie in the over-throw of the demoralizing, disorganizing, and destructive [Republican] sectional party, of which 'Honest Abe Lincoln' is the pliant instrument." "The new pilot was hurried to the helm in the midst of a tornado," wrote Emerson of Lincoln's first weeks in office. As yet, however, the tornado was merely beginning to get under way.

Fort Sumter, three miles out from Charleston, rising almost sheer with the rock walls of its island, was being ringed round with batteries, guns and 5,000 recruits under General P. G. T. Beauregard, constantly in touch with Governor F. W. Pickens of South Carolina and Secretary L. P. Walker of the Confederate War Department at Montgomery. Visitors to the U.S. Army officers or soldiers at Fort Sumter were challenged by Confederate pickets, had to show passes from Governor Pickens.

Three commissioners from the Confederate Government had arrived in Washington, instructed to "play with" Seward, which they did. And Seward had "played with" them. What to say to those commissioners, and how to say it without recognizing their Government, Seward took as his own problem. He carried on furtive, indirect negotiations with them without consulting the President, whom he saw as lacking plan and decision, which was the view of the New York *Tribune,* the New York *Times,* the New York *Herald.*

The Confederate commissioners wrote and telegraphed their Government that the Lincoln administration would give up Sumter. Days passed. On March 30 the Governor of South Carolina was telegraphing the Confederate commissioners in Washington asking why Sumter was still flying the Stars and Stripes. April 2, the Confederate commissioners telegraphed their Government: "The war wing presses on the President; he vibrates to that side . . . Their form of notice to us may be that of the coward, who gives it when he strikes."

Week by week the country had watched the emergence of Major Robert Anderson into a national figure. "Bob Anderson, my beau, Bob," ran a song line. He had kept a cool head and held on amid a thousand invitations to blunder. Even the Charleston *Mercury* complimented him as a gentleman whose word was good. He was a West Pointer, a sober churchman, born and raised in Kentucky. He had married a Georgia girl, had owned a plantation and slaves in Georgia and sold the slaves. He could see that his immediate duty was to obey orders from the U.S. Government but, according to one of his officers, if war came between the South and the North, and if his State of Kentucky seceded, he would go to Europe.

By now the Sumter garrison was stopped from getting fresh meat and vegetables at the Charleston market. By now there had arrived in Charleston a War Department clerk from Washington, Robert S. Chew, who on April 8 read to Governor Pickens a notification from President Lincoln:

Washington, April 6. 1861

Sir—You will proceed directly to Charleston, South Carolina; and if, on your arrival there, the flag of the United States shall be flying over Fort-Sumpter, and the Fort shall not have been attacked, you will procure an interview with Gov. Pickens, and read to him as follows:

"I am directed by the President of the United States to notify you to expect an attempt will be made to supply Fort-Sumpter with provisions only; and that, if such attempt be not resisted, no effort to throw in men, arms, or ammunition, will be made, without further notice, or in case of an attack upon the Fort"

After you shall have read this to Governor Pickens, deliver to him the copy of it herein inclosed, and retain this letter yourself.

But if, on your arrival at Charleston, you shall ascertain that Fort-Sumpter shall have been already evacuated, or surrendered, by the United States force; or, shall have been attacked by an opposing force, you will seek no interview with Gov. Pickens, but return here forthwith.

The doubts of long months were at an end. Thus Lincoln framed an issue for his country and the world to look at and consider. Sumter was a symbol. Jefferson Davis called his advisers into session at Montgomery to consider Lincoln's message to Governor Pickens, which had been telegraphed on. Robert Toombs, Secretary of State, read Lincoln's letter, and said, "The firing on that fort will inaugurate a civil war greater than any the world has yet seen; and I do not feel competent to advise you . . . You will wantonly strike a hornet's nest which extends from mountains to ocean; legions, now quiet, will swarm out and sting us to death . . ." President Davis, however, decided in favor of attacking the fort, leaving to Beauregard the choice of time and method.

On April 10 Governor Andrew Curtin of the great iron and coal State of Pennsylvania read a note from Lincoln: "I think the necessity for being ready increases. Look to it."

Beauregard on April 11 sent a little boat out to Sumter. A note to Anderson from Beauregard, his old-time affectionate pupil in artillery lessons at West Point, read: "I am ordered by the Government of the Confederate States to demand the evacuation of Fort Sumter . . . All proper facilities will be afforded for the removal of yourself and command . . ." Major Anderson wrote in answer: ". . . It is a demand with which I regret that my sense of honor, and of my obligations to my Government, prevent my compliance . . ." As Major Anderson handed this note to Beauregard's aides, he made the remark, "Gentlemen, if you do not batter us to pieces, we shall be starved out in a few days."

Now four men from Beauregard went in a boat out to Sumter. Past midnight they handed Major Anderson a note saying there would be no "useless effusion of blood" if he would fix a stated time for his surrender. Anderson called his officers; from one till three they consulted. And at 3:15 that morning Anderson gave his answer: "Cordially uniting with you in the desire to avoid the useless effusion of blood, I will, if provided with the proper and necessary means of transportation, evacuate Fort Sumter by noon on the 15th instant, and I will not in the meantime open my fire on your forces unless compelled to do so by some hostile act against this fort or the flag of my Government . . . should I not receive prior to that time controlling instructions from my Government or additional supplies."

Within five minutes they gave Anderson a written answer:

> Fort Sumter, S. C., April 12, 1861—3:20 A.M.
>
> Sir:
>
> By authority of Brigadier-General, commanding the

Provisional Forces of the Confederate States, we have the honor to notify you that he will open the fire of his batteries on Fort Sumter in one hour from this time.

We have the honor to be, very respectfully, your obedient servant,

JAMES CHESNUT, JR.
Aide-de-Camp.
STEPHEN D. LEE,
Captain, C. S. Army, Aide-de-Camp.

The four men got into their boat, with Chesnut musing over Major Anderson's parting words, "If we do not meet again on earth, I hope we may meet in Heaven."

Old Edmund Ruffin—a farmer from Virginia, soil expert, farm paper editor, ally of Rhett, 67 years old, his face framed in venerable white ringlets of hair—pulled the first gun of the war, and swore he would kill himself before he would ever live under the U.S. Government.

Mrs. James Chesnut, Jr., whose husband had helped get the guns going, wrote in her diary April 12 as the shooting began: "I do not pretend to go to sleep. How can I? If Anderson does not accept terms at four, the orders are he shall be fired upon. I count four, St. Michael's bells chime out and I begin to hope. At half-past four the heavy booming of a cannon. I sprang out of bed, and on my knees prostrate I prayed as I never prayed before."

Encircling batteries let loose all they had. The mortars and howitzers laughed. Wood fires on hulks at the inner harbor entrance and daybreak lighted one lonesome relief ship from Lincoln; it and two others arriving later could be of no help. Through daylight of the 12th and through the rain and darkness of the night of the 13th, the guns pounded Sumter with more than 3,000 shot and shell. Smoke, heat, vapor, stifled the garrison; the men hugged the ground with wet handkerchiefs over mouths and eyes till they could breathe again. The last biscuit was gone; they were down to pork only for food. The storm and dark of the early morning on the 13th ended with clear weather and a red sunrise.

Again offered the same terms of surrender as before, Anderson, after 33 hours of bombardment, gave up the fort. On Sunday, the 14th, he marched his garrison out with colors flying, drums beating, saluting his flag with 50 guns. They boarded one of the relief ships and headed north for New York Harbor. They had lost one man, killed in the accidental explosion of one of their own cannon. In their last glimpse of Fort Sumter they saw the new Confederate flag, Stars and Bars, flying. In his trunk Major Anderson had the flag he had defended; he wished to keep this burnt and shot flag and have it wrapped round him when laid in the grave.

On that Sunday of April 14, the White House had many visitors in and out all day. Senators and Congressmen came to say their people would stand by the Government, the President. The Cabinet met. A proclamation was framed. It named the States of South Carolina, Georgia, Alabama, Florida, Mississippi, Louisiana and Texas as having "combinations too powerful to be suppressed" by ordinary procedure of government.

"Now therefore, I, Abraham Lincoln, President of the United States, in virtue of the power in me vested by the Constitution and the laws, have thought fit to call forth, and hereby do call forth, the militia of the several States of the Union, to the aggregate number of seventy-five thousand, in order to suppress said combinations, and to cause the laws to be duly executed."

He called on "all loyal citizens" to defend the National Union and popular government, "to redress wrongs already long enough endured." The new army of volunteer soldiers was to retake forts and property "seized from the Union." Also, "in every event, the utmost care will be observed, consistently with the objects aforesaid, to avoid any devastation, any destruction of, or interference with, property, or any disturbance of peaceful citizens."

Also the proclamation called both Houses of Congress to meet at noon on the Fourth of July. The war of words was over and the naked test by steel weapons, so long foretold, was at last to begin.

From day to day since Lincoln was sworn in as President he had been moved toward war, saying casually to John Hay one day in April, "My policy is to have no policy." Day to day events dictated. How did he explain Sumter? "The assault upon and reduction of Fort Sumter was in no sense a matter of self-defense on the part of the assailants," he wrote later. "They well knew that the garrison in the fort could by no possibility commit aggression upon them. They knew—they were expressly notified—that the giving of bread to the few brave and hungry men of the garrison was all which would on that occasion be attempted."

The dilemma of a divided country Lincoln and Douglas discussed at the White House that Sunday of April 14, just after the flag came down at Sumter. Now Lincoln could be thankful that across the years of political strife between him and Douglas, the two had so spoken to and of each other that their personal relations had never reached a breaking point. The two foremost American political captains were closeted for a two-hour confidential talk, with only Congressman Ashmun in the room. Douglas read the proclamation to be published next morning, gave it his approval, though advising that he would call for 200,000 rather than 75,000 troops.

Douglas, at Willard's, wrote out a dispatch which next day went to the country through the Associated Press. He had called on the President and had "an interesting conversation on the present condition of the country," the substance of which was, on the part of Mr. Douglas, "that while he was unalterably opposed to the administration in all political issues, he was prepared to fully sustain the President in the exercise of all his constitutional functions, to preserve the Union, maintain the Government, and defend the capital. A firm policy and prompt action was necessary. The capital was in danger, and must be defended at all hazards, and at any expense of men and money." He added that he and the President "spoke of the present and future without any reference to the past." Douglas was a hoarse and worn man of dwindling vitality, but he struck with decisive words that sank deep in every one of his old loyal followers. He knew he had trumpets left, and he blew them to mass his cohorts behind Lincoln's maintenance of the Union.

Now came the day of April 15, 1861, for years afterward spoken of as "the day Lincoln made his first call for troops." What happened on that day was referred to as the Uprising of the People; they swarmed onto the streets, into public squares, into meeting halls and churches. The shooting of the Stars and Stripes off the Sumter flagstaff—and the Lincoln proclamation—acted as a vast magnet on a national multitude.

In a thousand cities, towns and villages the fever of hate, exaltation, speech, action, followed a similar course. Telegrams came notifying officers and militiamen to mobilize. Newspapers cried in high or low key the war song. Then came mass meetings, speeches by prominent citizens, lawyers, ministers, priests, military officers, veterans of the War of 1812 and the Mexican War, singing of "The Star-spangled Banner" and "America," fife-and-drum corps playing "Yankee Doodle." Funds were subscribed to raised and equip troops, resolutions passed, committees appointed to collect funds, to care for soldiers' families, to educate or trouble the unpatriotic. Women's societies were formed to knit and sew, prepare lint and bandages. Women and girls saw their husbands and sweethearts off to camp. Nearly every community had its men and boys marching away to the fifing of "The Girl I Left Behind Me." In churches and saloons, in city crowds and at country crossroads, the talk was of the War and "What will the President do next?"

In the large cities military units of the foreign-born were formed. Irishmen of New York made up four regiments: the 69th, Irish Zouaves, Irish Volunteers, St. Patrick Brigade. The Italian Legion made ready, also the Garibaldi Guards. Germans supplied the Steuben Volunteers, the German Rifles, the Turner Rifles, the De Kalb Regiment. The

English and Irish Home Guards were proposed for men of former service in the British Army and Irish constabulary, while the British Volunteers were to recruit from British subjects in New York.

Bishop Matthew Simpson of the Methodist Episcopal church in a talk with the President gave his opinion that 75,000 men were but a beginning of the number needed; that the struggle would be long and severe. The New York *Herald*, shifting its outlook, voiced the new viewpoint of powerful business interests in declaring: "The business community demand that the war shall be *short;* and the more vigorously it is prosecuted the more speedily will it be closed. Business men can stand a temporary reverse. They can easily make arrangements for six months or a year. But they cannot endure a long, uncertain and tedious contest." Astor, Vanderbilt, Aspinwall, A. T. Stewart, Belmont of the House of Rothschild, the millionaires who had been at the breakfast to Lincoln when he came through New York, they and their cohorts and lawyers were now for war. Senator Douglas at Bellaire, Ohio, in Chicago at the Wigwam, in Springfield before the Illinois Legislature, was saying that the shortest way to peace would be stupendous and unanimous preparation for war.

None leaped so eagerly as the abolitionists at the ways now open for a war with slaveholders. "I was a Disunionist," said Wendell Phillips. "I did hate the Union, when Union meant lies in the pulpit and mobs in the streets, when Union meant making white men hypocrites and black men slaves . . . The only mistake I made was in supposing Massachusetts wholly choked with cotton dust and cankered with gold."

Gerrit Smith, abolitionist of means who had given 120,000 acres of land to 3,000 colored men, who had spent $16,000 on the Kansas civil war, told an audience at his home town of Peterboro, New York, that the last fugitive slave had been returned. "A few weeks ago I would have consented to let the slave states go without requiring the abolition of slavery . . . But now, since the Southern tiger has smeared himself with our blood, we will not, if we get him in our power, let him go without having drawn his teeth and claws." Gerrit Smith was offering to equip a regiment of colored troops, and was sending his only son, Greene Smith, into the army, insisting it be without soldier's pay.

Cheers and applause greeted the public reading of a letter of Archbishop John Hughes declaring for the Stars and Stripes: "This has been my flag and shall be till the end." At home and abroad, the Archbishop would have it wave "for a thousand years and afterward as long as Heaven permits, without limit of duration." On April 20, 50,000 people made their way to a Union mass meeting at Union Square in New York City. As William H. Appleton, publisher of books, stood at Broadway and Fourteenth Street watching the human swarm, he remarked to a friend, "We shall crush out this rebellion as an elephant would trample on a mouse."

Far from Union Square, in a cornfield near Iowa City, the farmer Governor Samuel J. Kirkwood saw an earnest man on a spent and foam-flecked horse. This corn-fed courier had been riding hours from Davenport on the Mississippi with a telegram he handed the Governor from the Secretary of War: "Call made on you tonight's mail for one regiment of militia for indefinite service." The Governor wrinkled his brow and gazed across a slope of cut cornstalks: "Why! The President wants a whole regiment of men! Do you suppose I can raise as many as that?" Yet a few days later, ten Iowa regiments were offered and Governor Kirkwood was telegraphing Washington: "For God's sake send us arms! We have the men."

At a Western religious conclave jubilant hosannas came from a bishop of the Methodist Episcopal church, the Reverend Edward R. Ames: "There has been held a grand Union convention amid the fortresses of the everlasting hills. The Rocky Mountains presided, the mighty Mississippi made the motion, the Allegheny Mountains seconded it and every mountain and hill, valley and plain, in this vast country, sent up a unanimous voice; Resolved, that we are one and inseparable and what God has joined together, let no man put asunder." It was a week of distinguished and inflammatory oratory.

Nathaniel Hawthorne wrote to his wife, "It was delightful to share in the heroic sentiment of the time, and to feel that I had a country . . . Though I approve the war as much as any man, I don't quite understand what we are fighting for." More distinct was Parson Brownlow, an editor in Knoxville, Tennessee, at the peril of his neck telling the world that though he was against abolition, he was for the Union and he would "fight the Secession leaders till Hell froze over and then fight on the ice."

Three delegates came to the White House as a special committee from the Virginia convention which in secret session had voted 60 to 53 against seceding from the Union. They politely inquired of Lincoln as to his intentions. He replied politely that his intentions were still the same as reported in his inaugural. He read over part of his inaugural, as though they had not read it carefully enough, and as though by patience they might find new clues in it: "The power confided to me will be used to hold, occupy, and possess the property and places belonging to the government . . ." They reported back to their convention—and Virginia, the Old Dominion, the Mother of Presidents, went out of the Union.

On April 17 when Virginia seceded, her troops were set in motion for a surprise march on the U.S. fort and arsenal at Harpers Ferry, the most dramatic point northward for raising her new flag. They arrived April 18 and took the fort and arsenal without fighting. The barrels and locks of 20,000 pistols and rifles were sent to Richmond to be remade. Two days later the U.S. navy yard at Norfolk, Virginia, was threatened, or the commander was afraid it was, and guns, munitions, ships and war property valued at $30,000,000 went up in smoke.

Robert E. Lee, Virginian, resigned from the U.S. Army, gave up his stately home on Arlington Heights overlooking Washington, to take command of the Army of Virginia. Long ago he had opposed slavery. He favored the Union but couldn't fight against his native state. Before resigning he was interviewed by Francis P. Blair, Sr., who said later: "I told him what President Lincoln wanted him to do; he wanted him to take command of the army . . . He said he could not, under any circumstances, consent to supersede his old commander [General Scott]. He asked me if I supposed the President would consider that proper. I said yes . . . The matter was talked over by President Lincoln and myself for some hours on two or three different occasions . . . The President and Secretary Cameron expressed themselves as anxious to give the command of our army to Robert E. Lee." Now Lee had gone to Richmond.

Lincoln had lost a commander that General Scott reckoned as worth 50,000 men. "Save in the defense of my native State I never again desire to draw my sword," Lee wrote to Scott. Two months before, in Texas, he had told army associates: "I fear the liberties of our country will be buried in the tomb of a great nation . . . If Virginia stands by the old Union, so will I. But if she secedes (though I do not believe in secession as a constitutional right, nor that there is sufficient cause for revolution) then I will still follow my native State with my sword, and, if need be, with my life." The break came hard for Lee.

The seething of propaganda began. Southern newspapers reported elaborate plans in the North to stir up insurrections of slaves, with robbery, arson, rape, murder. Northern newspapers reported a Northern woman teacher in a New Orleans grammar school as being stripped naked and tarred and feathered in Lafayette Square "for abolition sentiments expressed to her pupils." North and South, horrors were exaggerated or fabricated. The Petersburg, Virginia, *Express* told readers, "Old Abe has his legs in perfect readiness to run. He does not so much as take off his boots."

A volunteer White House Guard gathered under Cassius M. Clay, who would delay sailing as the new Minister to Russia, and Senator James H. Lane, the new Senator from the new State of Kansas. Both men had commanded troops in the Mexican War, had faced mobs in their antislavery careers. Both expected the war to begin in Washington and were ready for a last-ditch fight at the White House doors.

"The White House is turned into barracks," wrote Hay. Alarmists and cranks flitted into the halls and corridors, demanded to see the President or whispered they had information of plots, of attacks planned, of suspicious-looking steamers coming up the Potomac, of a mob that was to overwhelm the Executive Mansion, with picked men to seize and carry off the President. Washington was hemmed in.

From the governors of Border States came warlike answers to Lincoln's dispatch asking for quotas of troops: "Kentucky will furnish no troops for the wicked purpose of subduing her sister Southern States," replied Governor Beriah Magoffin. "Your requisition, in my judgment," replied Claiborne Jackson of Missouri, "is illegal, unconstitutional and revolutionary in its objects, inhuman and diabolical, and cannot be complied with."

President Davis at Montgomery announced that his Government would issue "letters of marque" giving authority to ships joining the Confederacy to seize U.S. vessels of commerce. Lincoln replied by proclaiming a blockade of ports of the seceded states.

Each day in bureaus and departments at Washington came new resignations, Southerners leaving to go south to fight. On all sides were spies interthreading North and South. Lincoln later sketched the situation that week: "A disproportionate share of the Federal muskets and rifles had somehow found their way into these [seceded] States, and had been seized to be used against the government . . . Officers of the Federal army and navy had resigned in great numbers; and of those resigning a large number had taken up arms against the government."

On April 18 arrived 532 Pennsylvania boys from Pottsville, Lewistown, Reading, Allentown, whom Hay noted as "unlicked patriotism that has poured ragged and unarmed out of Pennsylvania." They had passed through Baltimore safely. Not so the 6th Massachusetts regiment the next day. As they marched from one station to another, changing trains, they met stones, bricks, pistols, from a crowd of Southern sympathizers. They answered with bullets. Four soldiers were killed, and 12 citizens. Two by two the 6th Massachusetts marched up Pennsylvania Avenue that evening to the Capitol, their 17 wounded on stretchers.

Now came word that the telegraph wires leading to the North were cut. The Baltimore telegraph office was in the hands of secessionists. The War Office said, "This stops all." With mails stopped, railroads crippled, bridges down, telegraph wires dead, it was not easy in Washington to laugh away the prediction of the New Orleans *Picayune* that Virginia's secession would result in "the removal of Lincoln and his Cabinet, and whatever he can carry away, to the safer neighborhood of Harrisburg or Cincinnati."

At what moment would some free-going body of Southern troops ride into the capital, seize the city, and kidnap the Government? These questions were asked in Washington. Then and later this was regarded as an easy possibility. There were Southerners eager for the undertaking.

More than idle wish or bluster lay back of the Richmond *Examiner*'s declaring: "There is one wild shout of fierce resolve to capture Washington City, at all and every human hazard. The filthy cage of unclean birds must and will be purified by fire . . . Our people can take it, and Scott the arch-traitor, and Lincoln the Beast, combined, cannot prevent it. The just indignation of an outraged and deeply injured people will teach the Illinois Ape to retrace his journey across the borders of the Free negro States still more rapidly than he came."

To Hay that week Lincoln talked about what seemed to him the key point of the hour: "For my own part, I consider the first necessity that is upon us, is of proving that popular government is not an absurdity. We must settle this question now,—whether in a free government the minority have the right to break it up whenever they choose. If we fail, it will go far to prove the incapability of the people to govern themselves."

Impatience was heard in the President's Cabinet. Chase wrote a belief that the President in lieu of any policy had "merely the general notion of drifting, the Micawber policy of waiting for something to turn up." Lincoln, however, was taking to himself one by one the powers of a dictator. He authorized a raid whereby at three o'clock the afternoon of April 20 U.S. marshals entered every major telegraph office in the Northern States and seized the originals of all telegrams sent and copies of all telegrams received during 12 months. Also the President dug into the Treasury of the United States for millions of dollars—without due and required authority of Congress. At a meeting held Sunday, April 21, in the Navy Department, away from any spies and all observers in the White House, the Cabinet members joined with Lincoln in the placing of immense funds.

"It became necessary for me to choose," said Lincoln later, "whether I should let the government fall at once into ruin, or whether . . . availing myself of the broader powers conferred by the Constitution in cases of insurrection, I would make an effort to save it." Government money orders for million-dollar amounts Lincoln sent by private messengers, who went by way of Wheeling and Pittsburgh to New York.

In the Treasury building now were howitzers. At the Mint were howitzers. In the marble corridors of the Capitol were howitzers, muskets, provisions, munitions of war. In the Senate chamber slept the 6th Massachusetts boys. In the House of Representatives slept the Pennsylvania boys. At each Capitol doorway was a ten-foot barricade of sandbags, cement barrels, iron plate. The Georgetown flour mills' supply, 25,000 barrels, was seized as a war necessity.

Newspaper items in the North were creating impressions: "President Lincoln said to a Baltimore deputation that if the passage of U.S. troops was again obstructed he would lay their city in ashes. One of the deputation said that 75,000 Marylanders would contest the passage of troops over her soil. To this the President said that he supposed there was room enough in her soil to bury 75,000." One news writer reported Lincoln saying to a pair of the delegation, by way of illustration. "You have all heard of the Irishman who, when a fellow was cutting his throat with a blunt razor, complained that he *haggled* it. Now, if I can't have troops direct through Maryland, and must have them all the way round by water, or marched across out-of-the-way territory, I shall be *haggled*."

On April 23 a little mail arrived—and newspapers. Anderson and his garrison had arrived in New York and the town had gone wild over them! A Union Square mass meeting with 50,000 people shouting for the Union! Processions, speeches, enlistments of more men than the President called for! Million-dollar appropriations for the war! The famous crack regiment, the dandy 7th of New York, had marched down Broadway between vast walls of cheering crowds, heading south for Washington! The Governor of Rhode Island sailing with troops and guns for Washington!

So the news ran. And out of it all nothing had reached Washington except the few boys now sleeping on their guns in the Capitol building. "I saw the President repeatedly," wrote Henry Villard, "and he fairly groaned at the inexplicable delay of help." "I think I saw three vessels go up to the Navy Yard just now," the President scribbled to the Secretary of the Navy. "Will you please send down and learn what they are?"

The afternoon of April 23 Lincoln was alone in his office in the White House—or believed he was alone, though John Hay, quiet and unobtrusive, was there. And Hay saw Lincoln "after walking the floor alone in silent thought for nearly half an hour," stop at a window and gaze long and wistfully down the Potomac in the direction of the expected ships. And as he gazed he broke out with irrepressible anguish in the repeated exclamation "Why don't they come! Why don't they come!"

Schurz reported of a bad hour Lincoln had in that lonely time: "He told me of an incident which I wish I could repeat in his own language. One afternoon after he had issued his call for troops, he sat alone in this room, and a feeling came over him as if he were utterly deserted and helpless. He thought any moderately strong body of secessionist troops might come over the 'long bridge' across the Potomac, and just take him and the members of the Cabinet

—the whole lot of them. Then he suddenly heard a sound like the boom of a cannon. 'There they are!' he said to himself. He expected every moment somebody would rush in with the report of an attack. The White House attendants whom he interrogated, had heard nothing. But nobody came, and all remained still.

"Then he thought he would look after the thing himself. So he walked out, and walked, and walked, until he got to the Arsenal. There he found the doors all open, and not a soul to guard them. Anybody might have gone in and helped himself to the arms. There was perfect solitude and stillness all around. Then he walked back to the White House without noticing the slightest sign of disturbance. He met a few persons on the way, some of whom he asked whether they had not heard something like the boom of a cannon. Nobody had heard anything, and so he supposed it must have been a freak of his imagination."

On April 24, when as yet no troops had arrived, when Seward's messengers sent out by the dozen had not returned, soldiers and officers of the 6th Massachusetts, wounded in Baltimore street fighting, came to see the White House and the President. Lincoln spoke thanks to them for brave service, and wandered in his talk into the mystery of why the North allowed its Government to be isolated, imprisoned. It was a sad, ironic tone, noted Hay, in which he told them: "I don't believe there is any North! The Seventh Regiment is a myth! Rhode Island is not known in our geography any longer! You are the only Northern realities!"

A locomotive whistle shrieking hallelujah the next day, April 25, was followed by the marching—left, right, left, right—up Pennsylvania Avenue of the 7th New York. Then came 1,200 Rhode Islanders and a brigade of 1,200 from Massachusetts. A crippled locomotive at Annapolis had been repaired by Massachusetts mechanics; volunteer tracklayers put the road from Annapolis in running order again. A troop route to the North had been found. In a few days Washington had 10,000 defense troops. Now, for a time, Lincoln knew that the capital would still be at Washington.

Chapter 4

Jefferson Davis — His Government

The Confederate Government, strengthened by the finally seceded States of Arkansas, Tennessee, North Carolina and Texas, moved the last week in May from Montgomery, Alabama, to Richmond, Virginia, to be nearer the Border States and the expected heavy fighting. Into Richmond streamed regiments from all parts of the South. The cry in the South, "On to Washington!" snarled straight into the cry from the North, "On to Richmond!"

From the Potomac River to the Gulf Coast and the Rio Grande ran the recruiting ground of this Confederate Army. Its line zigzagged 1,500 miles from Chesapeake Bay through Kentucky and out to the corners of Kansas. Its brain and will centered in the capitol, the executive mansion, the departments, at Richmond. Its chief weapon of defense was an army of 100,000 troops. The controls of this Government were out of the hands of those who had first given it breath and fire. Rhett of the True Perpetual Separationists was now only a member of the Confederate Congress with no executive authority; the efforts to appoint him Secretary of War had failed. Yancey was shelved as a commissioner to European nations, with no power to act and no special instructions.

Russell of the *Times* of London wrote in Charleston: "Both sexes and all ages are for the war. Secession is the fashion here. Young ladies sing for it; old ladies pray for it; young men are dying to fight for it; old men are ready to demonstrate it." Russell heard of a Mobile gentleman having a letter from his daughter: "She informs him she has been elected vivandière to a New Orleans regiment, with which she intends to push on to Washington and get a lock of Abe Lincoln's hair."

A new and a young Government it was at Richmond. "Where will I find the State Department?" an Englishman asked Robert Toombs, Secretary of State. "In my hat, sir," replied Toombs, "and the archives in my coat pocket." The impulsive Toombs was soon to resign and take to the camp and battlefield. He should have been Secretary of War, said many, but that place went to Leroy Pope Walker of Alabama, a lawyer and politician, harassed by technical matters of how a people with ports restricted or closed, and with no gun or arms factories or powder mills, should create those requisites. He was soon to step from office to field service, and this Confederate War Department at Richmond took on as Acting Assistant Secretary of War one Albert Taylor Bledsoe, a West Point graduate who had become a Protestant Episcopal clergyman, later a professor of mathematics, though part of his ten years as a practicing lawyer was spent in Springfield, Illinois, with an office adjoining that of Lincoln & Herndon.

The Secretary of the Treasury, Christopher Gustavus Memminger, an orphan-asylum boy, a German Lutheran born in Württemberg, a lawyer, businessman, and politician of exceptional integrity, founder of the public-school system in Charleston, was the one South Carolina name in the Cabinet. He arranged with Gazaway B. Lamar, the Southern secessionist president of the Bank of the Republic in New York, for a contract with the American Bank Note Company to engrave and print in New York the bonds and treasury notes of the Confederacy. "The work was handsomely executed on the best of bank note and bond paper," wrote Memminger, "but with all the precaution taken by Mr. Lamar, the entire issue fell into the hands of the Federal Government and was seized as contraband of war." Engravers rushed from Europe were therefore to direct the printing of Confederate money on paper brought from Baltimore by agents who ran the Federal picket lines.

The Navy head was Stephen R. Mallory of Florida, once

chairman of the Committee on Naval Affairs of the U.S. Senate, and having, as President Davis wrote, "for a landsman much knowledge of nautical affairs." Mallory was the one Roman Catholic of the Cabinet. The one Jew was Judah P. Benjamin of New Orleans, whose wife was a French Roman Catholic. Twice elected U.S. Senator from Louisiana, in his advocacy of the legal grounds for slavery, he once came close to a duel with Jefferson Davis. Once when defending slavery Benjamin was classified by Senator Wade of Ohio as "a Hebrew with Egyptian principles." He had a rare legal mind, and as Attorney General and later as Secretary of State was one of the few trusted helpers of President Davis; he toiled in his Richmond office from eight in the morning till past midnight, and was sometimes referred to as "the brains of the Confederacy." The one Texan in the Cabinet was the Postmaster General, J. H. Reagan, former Congressman, Indian fighter, and Southwestern pioneer.

Heading this Cabinet was a figure chosen as a military authority; he stood in the public eye as a moderate rather than a radical secessionist, having integrity and distinctively Southern qualities. This was the Mississippi cotton planter, West Point graduate, Black Hawk War lieutenant, Mexican War veteran wounded in service, U.S. Senator, Secretary of War under the Pierce administration, orator, horseman, man of fate—Jefferson Davis. He and Lincoln were both born in Kentucky, Davis a year earlier than Lincoln, one as a child carried north to free soil, the other as a suckling babe taken to the lower South.

Lincoln's army of 75,000 volunteers Davis termed a "posse comitatus" to round up 5,000,000 outlaws, and in the "singular document" calling for that army "the President was usurping a power granted exclusively to Congress." Davis would coldly and with studied politeness at intervals point to Lincoln as an ignorant usurper and a bloodthirsty despot, while Lincoln must speak and write as though Davis had no existence legal or personal, a nameless nobody, the invisible ghost of a glimmering hope.

When 17, Davis had replied to a sister's letter telling him of his father's death: "The intelligence contained in yours was more than sufficient to mar the satisfaction of hearing from anyone . . ." This formal manner, this icy perfection, was to stay with him. One of the rare times he dropped it was in his love letters to Sarah Knox Taylor, the 16-year-old daughter of Colonel Zachary Taylor at Fort Crawford, Wisconsin. "By dreams I have been lately almost crazy, for they were of you," he wrote to her, and again: "Kind, dear letter! I have kissed it often and often, and it has driven many mad notions from my brain." She was too young to marry, the father frowned. But Miss Taylor visited a Kentucky aunt, the young Lieutenant resigned from the Army, the couple were married in Kentucky and went to Mississippi near Vicksburg, to Brierfield, an 800-acre planation given them by his brother, Joseph Davis, with 14 Negro slaves on credit. Malarial fever brought both of them down. In six weeks the bride of three months died in a delirium, singing an old hymn, "Fairy Bells," that she had from her mother.

An older brother brought to the plantation Miss Varina Howell, a 17-year-old girl from a well-to-do planter family at Natchez; she had soft liquid eyes, large curved eyebrows, with grace of speech and swift decisions. She was saved from mere prettiness by angular cheekbones and a full-lipped mournful mouth. She was 19 and he 37 when they married, and testimonies ran that she was the perfect helpmeet of a difficult man. When he was away she could write him that it was lonely for her "and I wish you had never loved me, and then I should not have encouraged myself to thinking of you . . . if you cannot come at least write more often . . . have more charity for me, dearest, and set me a better example." She was health to him physically and mentally, in loyalty a tigress.

His national reputation in politics began with his service in the U.S. Senate in 1847, his clashes with Douglas, his denials of secession purposes clouded by arguments that states had a Constitutional right to secede. Sam Houston of Texas briefly set forth that Davis was "ambitious as Lucifer and cold as a lizard." Another Southerner had it Davis "could not forget what ought not to be remembered." His wife wrote, "If anyone differs with Mr. Davis, he resents it and ascribes the difference to the perversity of his opponent." When for nothing much he challenged Senator Benjamin to a duel, it was called off, with Davis saying, "I have an infirmity of which I am heartily ashamed: when I am aroused in a matter, I lose control of my feelings and become personal." He lacked the skill to manage other men, but he was too positive a character to let others manage him, nor would he, as Lincoln did on occasion, let others believe they were managing him.

While Lincoln and Douglas were debating he said he wished they would tear each other to pieces like the Kilkenny cats. When on November 6 Lincoln, though lacking a majority vote, had carried the electors of every Northern State except New Jersey, Davis on November 10 had sent a letter to Rhett: "If South Carolina has determined to secede, I advise her to do so before the Government passes into hostile hands." On a sickbed racked by neuralgia, his left eye lost, Senator Davis talked with Seward, and the news came that Lincoln had declared he would concede almost every point at issue with the South except that no more Slave States could be made from Territories. Mississippi seceded January 9, and 11 days later Davis told the Senate he was officially notified of the secession of his state and must resign.

Tears were in many eyes at his saying they parted "not in hostility to others, not to injure any section of the country, not even for our own pecuniary benefit, but from the high and solemn motive of defending and protecting the rights we inherited, and which it is our duty to transmit unshorn to our children . . . It only remains for me to bid you a final adieu." At night, said his wife, in his restless tossing came often the prayer, "May God have us in his holy keeping, and grant that before it is too late peaceful counsels may prevail."

On February 10, with a warm spring sun pouring down on leaf and petal, he and Varina were in a rose garden trimming and cutting, as though blood-red roses carry ministrations. A messenger threaded his way through the bushes and handed Jefferson Davis a telegram. His wife tried to read his face while he read the telegram. His face took on grief and she was afraid evil news had arrived. "After a few minutes' painful silence he told me, as a man might speak of a sentence of death." The Montgomery delegates to the convention of the Confederate States of America had elected him provisional President, when so definitely he preferred campaign and battlefield to an administrative desk.

She wept a good-by and he rode to Montgomery, sleeping in his clothes, routed from the train by crowds roaring for their new President, calling for speeches, "bonfires at night, firing by day." After inauguration he wrote to her: "I thought it would have gratified you to have witnessed it, and have been a memory to our children."

Davis was a chosen spear of authority heading 11 states committed to him as against 23 states formally still in the Union with Lincoln, one side reckoned as having 9,000,000 people (including 3,900,000 slaves) as against 22,000,000 Northern people.

In the event of his death President Davis' place would be taken by a man who could himself have been President of the Confederate States by saying Yes to one condition. On the evening of February 8 delegates from six states came to Alexander Hamilton Stephens' room, their spokesman Robert Toombs, ever a warm personal friend of Stephens no matter how they disputed over politics.

"Aleck," said Toombs, "you are the choice of every man in Congress, and all of us are ready to pledge to help you form your Cabinet. There is only one point—those fellows from Virginia and the Border States want you to promise to strike the first blow. Those fellows say their States are hanging in the balance, ready to turn with the first blow. They know Buchanan will never dare to strike. They believe Lincoln will be as cowardly. Now they want the question settled in their States, and they want you, when the first opportunity offers—say, if the administration should attempt to re-enforce or provision Fort Sumter—to strike the first blow."

The massive and bulking Toombs had spoken his portentous message to the little frail Stephens. And there was silence. The shrunken and dwarfish figure sat composed, in his slow-burning hazel eyes a touch of clairvoyance and communion. Then slowly and distinctly, "No, I will never strike the first blow." Toombs roared, "Aleck!" and with a long look into the unflinching eyes of Stephens turned on his heel and with the other men strode from the room to where nightlong caucuses were picking another man for President.

"He had the look of being born out of season," said a woman of this Aleck Stephens, who had fought the Know-Nothings and the anti-Catholic movements of Georgia with an unequivocal hostility, under warnings that he was wrecking the Whig party; who had thrice challenged tall heavy men to duels and had the reply in substance, "Pick some man your size."

Stephens wanted retirement, peace, poetry, philosophy, time for friendly talks, time at his home in Liberty Hall to bathe the sore eyes of his old blind dog Rio. Yet Toombs and the others made him Vice-President of the Confederacy. He understood the North and its Lincoln, once writing of old friendships in Congress, "I was as intimate with Mr. Lincoln as with any other man except perhaps Mr. Toombs."

Chapter 5

Turmoil — Fear — Hazards

The Lincoln administration hammered away at shaping a new and huge war establishment. On May 3 the President issued a proclamation calling into service 42,034 three-year volunteers, 22,714 enlisted men to add ten regiments to the regular U.S. Army, 18,000 seamen for blockade service— bringing the total of the Army to 156,861 and the Navy to 25,000. Day and night the President and other anxious officers worked on grand strategy and petty details.

From the windows of the White House Lincoln's spyglass caught the Confederate flag flying over the town of Alexandria eight miles down the Potomac River, where several heavy guns and 500 troops had been forwarded from Richmond.

After May '61, the U.S. mail service no longer ran into the seceded states. In this month too the Confederate Congress authorized all persons owing debts in the United States (except in Delaware, Maryland, Kentucky, Missouri and the District of Columbia) to pay the amount of those debts into the Confederate Treasury. According to R. G. Dun & Company, the South owed Northern merchants about $211,000,000, of which $169,000,000 was due in New York City.

By May 9 some 20,000 troops were in Washington. They included Colonel Elmer E. Ellsworth and the regiment of Fire Zouaves he had recruited in ten days from New York City fire-department men. New Yorkers had raised a fund of $60,000 for uniforms and arms. Ten different patterns of rifles were carried by Ellsworth's red-trousered ranks.

In bright moonlight on May 24 at two o'clock in the

morning, squads of cavalry crossed the bridges leading from Washington across the Potomac into Virginia, and were followed by infantry and by engineers, who began crowning every hill for miles with defense trenches for the protection of the ten-mile-square District of Columbia surrounded by Slave States.

While a Michigan regiment marched toward the rear of Alexandria, Colonel Ellsworth's Fire Zouaves were to sail on transports down to that town of 10,000 and capture it. A Union sloop of war had preceded the transports and under a flag of truce had sent a message giving the Confederate troops one hour to leave town. Ellsworth was told the Confederate force of 500 had agreed to evacuate and, with a few straggling picket shots, they had done so.

Ellsworth started for the telegraph office to stop communication southward, taking a squad with him. They came to the Marshall House, a second-class hotel, flying at the top of its flagpole the secession flag. Ellsworth threw open the front door and walked in to ask a barefoot man in shirt and trousers what sort of flag was over the roof. The man said he was only a boarder and knew nothing of it. Ellsworth sprang up the stairs, followed by his friends, to the third story, where with a ladder he mounted to the roof and cut down the secession flag.

Then, as the New York *Tribune* man told it: "We turned to descend, Corporal Brownell leading the way, and Ellsworth immediately following with the flag. As Brownell reached the first landing-place, after a descent of some dozen steps, a man jumped from a dark passage, and hardly noticing Brownell, leveled a double-barrelled gun square at the Colonel's breast. Brownell made a quick pass to turn the weapon aside, but the fellow's hand was firm, and he discharged one barrel straight to its aim, the slugs or buckshot entering the Colonel's heart, and killing him at the instant. I think my arm was resting on poor Ellsworth's shoulder at the moment; at any rate, he seemed to fall almost from my grasp. He was on the second or third step from the landing, and he dropped forward with that headlong weight which comes of sudden death." Brownell sent his own rifle slug into the face of Ellsworth's killer, "and before the man dropped, he thrust his saber-bayonet through and through the body."

Ellsworth's body was laid on a bed in a room nearby, the secession flag wrapped about his feet. The *Tribune* man left to make sure of the seizure of the telegraph office. "When I returned to the hotel, there was a terrible scene enacting. A woman had run from a lower room to the stairway where the body of the assassin lay, and cried aloud with an agony so heart-rending that no person could witness it without emotion. She flung her arms in the air, struck her brow madly, offered no reproaches, appeared almost regardless of our presence, and yielded only to her own frantic despair. It was her husband that had been shot—James W. Jackson, proprietor of the hotel"—the partly-dressed man who had told Ellsworth, "I am only a boarder here."

The body of Ellsworth arrived in Washington and was placed in a navy yard building. The tolling of bells went on, the flags of public buildings at half-mast. In the White House a New York *Herald* man, with Senator Wilson of Massachusetts, saw the President standing at a window looking out across the Potomac: "He did not move until we approached very closely, when he turned round abruptly, and advanced toward us, extending his hand: 'Excuse me, but I cannot talk.' . . . to our surprise the President burst into tears, and concealed his face in his handkerchief . . . 'I will make no apology, gentlemen,' said he, 'for my weakness; but I knew poor Ellsworth well and held him in high regard. Just as you entered the room, Captain Fox left me, after giving me the painful details of his unfortunate death.'"

Mrs. Lincoln visited the navy yard in the afternoon, left flowers, and talked with Corporal Brownell. An hour later, the embalming completed, she came again with the President, and they looked on the still face of Ellsworth, Lincoln moaning: "My boy! my boy! Was it necessary this sacrifice should be made?" Lincoln invited the Zouave guards to take the body to the White House for the funeral services.

They brought the body into the East Room, where Ellsworth lay in state and was viewed by thousands, had escorts with muffled drums and reversed arms. Then home at last to Mechanicsville, New York, for burial, arriving in a gale of wind and wild rain. Addressing a letter "To the Father and Mother of Col. Elmer E. Ellsworth," the President wrote: "In the untimely loss of your noble son, our affliction here, is scarcely less than your own . . . May God give you that consolation which is beyond all earthly power."

So Ellsworth became a legend identified with patriotic valor, the image of youth moving to drums and banners for the sake of emblems and a sacred, mystic cause.

In the Chicago Wigwam, Stephen A. Douglas had told an immense audience, "Before God it is the duty of every American citizen to rally around the flag of his country," and then gone home, to die. At his Oakenwald estate, overlooking Lake Michigan, in hearing of the Illinois Central locomotives, in a place that had always rested him, he argued stubbornly against the final adversary. Once in a delirium he called, "Telegraph to the President and let the column move on." The afternoon of June 3 his wife, holding his hand, asked if he had any last word for his boys and he answered, "Tell them to obey the laws and support the Constitution of the United States." These were telegraphed and generally recorded as his last words, though Chicago and New York newspaper accounts agreed in substance with that of the New York *Herald:* "When a few moments before his death, his wife leaned lovingly over him and sobbingly asked, 'Husband, do you know me? Will you kiss me?' he raised his eyes and smiled, and though too weak to speak, the movements of the muscles of his mouth evinced that he was making an almost dying struggle to comply with her request. His death was calm and peaceful; a few faint breaths after 9 o'clock; a slight rattling of his throat; a short, quick convulsive shudder, and Stephen A. Douglas passed into eternity."

His 48 years of life had taken his short, massive body through enough spectacular tumults, quarrels and dramas to fill a life of many more years. Northern Democrats mourned the lost giant of their party, while Republicans paid tribute to a leader who in a crisis had hushed mutiny among his followers.

Roll call of the Todd family of Lexington, Kentucky, found Mary Todd Lincoln's eldest brother Levi, and her half-sister Margaret Kellogg for the Union, while her youngest brother George and her three half-brothers Samuel, David and Alexander had joined the Confederate Army, and her half-sisters Emilie Helm, Martha White and Elodie Dawson were the wives of Confederate officers.

To the White House on Lincoln's invitation had come Ben Hardin Helm, West Pointer, son of a former governor of Kentucky, a Democrat, and the husband of Mary Todd Lincoln's "Little Sister" Emilie. During those few days the White House guest talked with old West Point comrades, some of them resigned and packing to go South. He was still undecided when as he left the White House Lincoln handed him an envelope holding a major's commission in the U.S. Army, saying: "Ben, here is something for you. Think it over for yourself and let me know what you will do." Mary Lincoln gave him a kiss to carry to Emilie and said, "Good-by, we hope to see you both very soon in Washington." After a long handclasp with Lincoln, Helm walked slowly down the stairs and out the door and was gone. Days passed and word came that he would wear the Confederate gray.

The fierce old Kentucky preacher and Union man, Robert Jefferson Breckinridge, could not get personal with his opposition. It included two of his own sons who were going into Confederate gray, one of them organizing a company for service under the Stars and Bars, and such kinsmen as his nephew John C. Breckinridge, and such illustrious Kentuckians as James B. Clay, the son of Henry Clay. Of his three sons only one was choosing the Stars and Stripes to fight under.

The Kentucky Legislature, after almost continuous session since January '61, adjourned sine die, proclaiming neutrality but still in the Union, and slowly drifting away from her sister Slave States to the south, who occasionally taunted Kentucky with "hesitation and cowardice." Joshua Speed and his brother James at Louisville had been allies of Dr. Breckinridge. Commissioned a brigadier general by Lincoln, Robert Anderson, who had said at Fort Sumter that if Kentucky seceded he would go to Europe, had set up headquarters in Cincinnati and given his best efforts to keep Kentucky in the Union. A naval lieutenant, William Nelson of Kentucky, had asked Lincoln to send him to his native state to stop secession. Nelson and others had distributed 10,000 rifles among Union men and Union military organizations. By stealth in the nighttime many a homeguard Unionist took to his arms his "Lincoln rifle" for use in emergency. Across the Ohio River on Ohio soil recruiting camps were set up, and some Ohio regiments had a fourth of their enrolled men from Kentucky. In the June balloting for members of the Congress Lincoln had called to meet July 4, Kentucky elected antisecessionists in nine out of the ten districts, the Union majority in the state being 54,700.

At the Baltimore election of April 24, 1861, only one ticket had been in the field, "States' Rights." Of 30,000 voters in the city, only 9,244 went to the polls and they all voted for secessionist members of the Maryland Legislature, which was to assemble two days later.

What with Union regiments increasing daily at Annapolis, Governor Hicks could have pleased the secessionist element by calling the legislature to Baltimore. Instead he convened it at the town of Frederick, a Unionist community but without Union troops. Such decisions favoring the Unionists came regularly from Governor Hicks. His message to the legislature reported his personal interviews with the President and the Cabinet, and the President's insistence that while he wished to avoid collisions through bringing troops across Maryland, military necessity required that such troops be brought to the defense of the national capital.

Slowly it became clear that the strength of secession in Maryland lay chiefly in a furiously active minority in

Baltimore. William Rollinson Whittingham, Episcopal bishop of Maryland, was not of this minority. He rebuked clergymen who omitted the prayer for the President of the United States, and admonished them that the offense must not continue. A commission appointed by the Maryland Legislature reported May 6 that they had been courteously received by the President at Washington. They had differed as to fact, but on the general principle at issue, said the report, "The President concurred in the opinion that so long as Maryland had not taken, and was not taking, a hostile attitude toward the Federal Government, that the exclusive military occupation of her ways of communications, and the seizure of the property of her citizens, would be without justification."

Day by day the boiling point in Maryland receded as it became more evident that secession would result in devastating trade losses to Baltimore. Charleston at her distance could more easily be defiant. The days passed till 10, 20, 30 regiments had crossed Maryland to Washington. A military department under Brigadier General Benjamin F. Butler was set up at Annapolis.

In rain, darkness and thunder Butler moved 1,000 troops to Baltimore May 13, stacked arms on Federal Hill overlooking Baltimore, issued a proclamation that they were there to enforce respect and obedience to the laws of the United States. The North cheered Butler. He was continuing in the national scene his Massachusetts record for ingenuity and expedients, for sheer nerve and audacity, for the calculated exhibitions of a careerist, for the chameleon shifts of a wily criminal lawyer suspected by his own clients of a shaded and always partly defensible treachery. Heavy of body, with a well-rounded paunch, bald, sleepy-eyed with cunning, a cast in one eye, he was at every moment an actor with ready answers fitting his favorite combined role of the Man of the People and the Man Who Knows How. His militia troops in Massachusetts had elected him colonel, then brigadier general. To Carl Schurz passing through Annapolis, the chunky-shaped Butler was a little grotesque, was most evidently enjoying his power, and "keenly appreciating its theatrical possibilities."

As between two lawyers, Butler had told Lincoln that the order for him to leave with his brigade for Washington arrived when he was trying a case before a jury. He had quit his argument to the jury and got his case continued. It woke Lincoln to muse slowly, "I guess we both wish we were back trying cases."

Butler when removed from Maryland and put in charge of Fortress Monroe in Virginia protested personally to Lincoln; the treatment of him implied reproaches. The President, according to Butler's report, said very kindly and courteously, "The administration has done everything to remove every thought of reproach upon you."

They shook hands and Butler left to spread word that they were "the warmest personal friends." Not yet had Butler discredited himself. His performances in Maryland had heartened the North, and he was on form worth the high commission Lincoln handed him. Yet he was basically an actor, a political general, and a military politician, so that eventually when John Hay should say to Lincoln he believed Butler was the only man in the Army to whom power would be dangerous, Lincoln would reply: "Yes, he is like Jim Jett's brother. Jim used to say that his brother was the damndest scoundrel that ever lived, but in the infinite mercy of Providence he was also the damndest fool."

The Butler gift for expedients rang across the country again when in May fugitive slaves flocked by hundreds into his camp. The legal question Butler disposed of by his decision, "The negro must now be regarded as *contraband*" (like smuggled goods or anything forbidden to be supplied by neutrals to belligerents). The country picked up this word "contraband" as often untying knots of the Fugitive Slave Law. Many a runaway slave, after starving in timber and swamp, arrived in the Union lines to say with jubilation, "I'se contraband."

The next flare-up in Maryland ended with the Chief Justice of the U.S. Supreme Court tangled in dispute with the

President. General George Cadwalader, in command of Fort McHenry near Baltimore, sent a squad of soldiers who at two o'clock the morning of May 25 roused one John Merryman from bed in his home at Hayfields and took him to Fort McHenry and locked him up "in close custody." Lawyers for Merryman appeared the same day before Roger B. Taney, who made his home in Baltimore. They denied that Merryman was guilty of reported charges of treason, prayed for a writ of habeas corpus. Chief Justice Taney issued the writ and commanded that General Cadwalader appear before him "and that you have with you the body of John Merryman."

General Cadwalader's response to Taney was brought by a staff member, Colonel Lee, who explained that the General was busy with pressing matters and then read a statement from the General that the aforesaid John Merryman was charged with treason, was publicly known to be holding a commission as lieutenant in a company having in their possession arms belonging to the United States, and avowing his purpose of armed hostility against the Government. "He has further to inform you that he is duly authorized by the President of the United States in such cases to suspend the writ of *habeas corpus* for public safety." After various proceedings neither Merryman nor Cadwalader appeared in court as ordered by Taney. The Chief Justice transmitted to the President a long written opinion on the ancient Anglo-Saxon custom of issuing writs of habeas corpus, with reminders and admonitions that the Executive himself should not violate law.

Police Marshal George P. Kane, whose methods clearly allied him with the Confederacy, was arrested at dawn June 27 and locked up at Fort McHenry. Four police commissioners, who were avowed secessionists, met and protested this action, and disbanded the city police force. So on July 1 the four police commissioners were also arrested and locked up in Fort McHenry. The secessionist trend in Maryland was definitely checked in June, when railroad schedules were re-established, Unionists were elected to Congress in the six districts of Maryland, and Governor Hicks was having no difficulty enlisting four regiments of men to serve within the limits of Maryland or for the defense of the national capital.

Lincoln's reply to Chief Justice Taney was given to the country in a message to Congress on July 4:

> Soon after the first call for militia, it was considered a duty to authorize the Commanding General, in proper cases, according to his discretion, to suspend the privilege of the writ of habeas corpus; or, in other words, to arrest, and detain, without resort to the ordinary processes and forms of law, such individuals as he might deem dangerous to the public safety . . . Of course some consideration was given to the questions of power, and propriety, before this matter was acted upon . . . Are all the laws, *but one,* to go unexecuted, and the government itself go to pieces, lest that one be violated? Even in such a case, would not the official oath be broken, if the government should be overthrown . . . It was not believed that any law was violated . . . It was decided that we have a case of rebellion . . . Now it is insisted that Congress, and not the Executive, is vested with this power. But the Constitution itself, is silent as to which, or who, is to exercise the power . . .

Seward was still playing lingeringly with his old idea that a war with Great Britain might bring the Southern forces behind the old American flag in a solid Union. He believed nothing was to be lost by using a menacing tone to the British Government. His good friend in London, Minister Adams, took his reckless threats and turned them into well-measured reproaches and courteous arguments. Adams was English-blooded and had instincts that were at home in London, one saying his face could "outfreeze" that of any English gentleman with whom he had to dicker.

Queen Victoria's proclamation of May 13, 1861, took

notice of hostilities "between the government of the United States of America and certain States styling themselves the Confederate States of America" and declared the "royal determination to maintain a strict and impartial neutrality in the contest between said contending parties." The Queen and her consort, Prince Albert, the political liberals and the masses of the English people leaned to the North in sympathy, while Prime Minister Palmerston and the officials and imperialistic cliques voiced by the London *Times* favored the South and in various technical rulings deviated far from strict neutrality. To the New York Rothschild agent, August Belmont, Palmerston said, "We do not like slavery, but we want cotton, and we dislike very much your Morrill tariff." A queer obstacle, not easily defined yet definitely operating, known as British Public Opinion, was about all that stopped Palmerston from giving complete recognition to the Southern Confederacy and lending it the British fleet.

To Carl Schurz departing for Spain Lincoln spoke about foreign affairs "with the same nonchalance with which he might have discussed an everyday law case at Springfield, Illinois." He told Schurz that if the administration had so far "stumbled along," as was said, it had, on the whole, "stumbled along in the right direction."

When the captain and crew of the privateer *Jefferson Davis* were convicted in Philadelphia of piracy, the decision was finally put up to Lincoln whether they should hang as pirates, in which event an equal number of Federal officers in Southern prisons, chosen by lot, would likewise be hanged, announced the Confederate Secretary of War. And Davis went so far as to name the 13 Union officers, selected by drawing of numbers, who would go to the gallows. Lincoln refused to begin a competition in hanging.

The President and the Cabinet through the new and often bungling personnels of their old departments were wrestling with crazy patterns of military organization, red tape, confusions of counsels, inpouring brigades, telegrams exchanged daily or hourly with governors recruiting troops, the direction of four grades of troops: (1) regulars; (2) three-month volunteers; (3) state militia; (4) three-year volunteers; besides independent troop units in Border States still neutral.

In the furious, complex and driving labors of shaping effective armies for grand strategic campaigns, General Scott was slow and fussy, his dropsy and vertigo pathetic afflictions of an aged hero. In many cases Lincoln and Secretary Cameron went directly over Scott's head and ordered action on political grounds, if not military.

The new consul to Paris, John Bigelow, heard a conversation between Lincoln and a Senator on army and field operations. "I observed no sign of weakness in anything the President said," noted Bigelow. "What did impress me, however, was what I can only describe as a *certain lack* of *sovereignty*. He seemed to me, nor was it in the least strange that he did, like a man utterly unconscious of the space which the President of the United States occupied that day in the history of the human race . . . This impression was strengthened by Mr. Lincoln's . . . frequent avowals of ignorance, which, even where it exists, it is as well for a captain as far as possible to conceal from the public."

In commissioning major generals of volunteers the President seemed to rest chiefly on the judgment of Scott, who favored John E. Wool, John A. Dix, Henry W. Halleck, Don Carlos Buell. The appointment of John C. Frémont as a major general was mainly political, as were the appointments of Benjamin F. Butler and Nathaniel P. Banks. David Hunter, Edwin V. Sumner and John Pope, who had accompanied Lincoln from Springfield to Harrisburg, were commissioned as brigadiers. Among the May and June appointees as brigadiers nearly all had West Point training and Mexican War service records.

William Tecumseh Sherman came again to the White House and left with a colonel's commission. Sherman had amazed the President and given him a healthy laugh by refusing a brigadier's commission and saying he would rather work up from colonel. Sherman sent the St. Louis horsecar street railways a word of good-by as superintendent; he would do his best for the war, though he was storm-tossed and haunted with impressions that men North and South were blind and crazy, that greedy politicians had too large a sway at Washington, and the war would end in a hundred years rather than the hundred days many people were predicting. Another West Pointer, Joseph E. Johnston of Virginia, of much the same feeling, in grief and tears had just resigned as quartermaster general of the U.S. Army to go into Confederate gray.

Sherman had said to Lincoln, "Why don't you nominate Thomas?" meaning George H. Thomas, a Virginian and a West Pointer of long army experience. Lincoln replied that Thomas was born in Virginia and there were doubts as to his loyalty. Sherman protested, "Mr. President, Old Tom is as loyal as I am, and as a soldier he is superior to all on your list." Lincoln inquired, "Will you be responsible for him?" Sherman snapped, "With the greatest pleasure." And Lincoln sent the nomination of Thomas as brigadier general to the Senate that day.

Of a total of 1,108 U.S. Army officers, 387 had resigned to go South. These resigned Southerners, 288 of them West-Point-trained, included promising officers, of actual field and battle service. Among West Pointers in Northern service were 162 born in Slave States. Among West Pointers gone South for service were 19 Northern-born men. Lincoln was writing in a message to Congress: "It is worthy of note, that while in this, the government's hour of trial, large numbers of those in the Army and Navy, who have been favored with the offices, have resigned, and proved false to the hand which had pampered them, not one common soldier, or common sailor is known to have deserted his flag. Great honor is due to those officers who remain true . . ."

In May and June '61 Lincoln was stressing popular government and maintenance of the Union above all issues. If the slavery issue was to come up front it would be through force of circumstances, through "yielding to partial and temporary departures, from necessity." This necessity had begun to work the moment the secession movement gained headway. It thrust the slavery issue forward for discussion and required that the millions of Negroes in the South be considered as a war factor, to be used by one side or both.

The South had a secret the North knew little of; the South had many doubts about slavery. Over the South not yet did they dare speak this secret. As to white-race superiority the South had no doubts. While it defended black-race slavery as a living institution, the South was not sure but that the institution was dying of some inherent malady.

Up in Maine the little woman who had written *Uncle Tom's Cabin* received in the mail one day a pair of Negro ears sent by someone who loathed her race-equality ideas.

In his message to Congress Lincoln was writing no line or word dealing with any phase of the Negro and slavery. The President kept an official loyalty to the Fugitive Slave Act. It seemed that fugitive slaves from Virginia, owned by secessionist Virginians, who fled into Butler's camp at Fortress Monroe were easily held as "contraband," having no intercessors for their owners at Washington. But Maryland slaves who drifted into District of Columbia and Virginia camps of the Union Army were immediately and hotly spoken for by Maryland Unionist members of Congress, sometimes for slaveowners who could not be shown as disloyal. So Lincoln began slowly evolving a policy of letting commanders and localities develop their own method of treating fugitive slaves, military necessity always to govern the method.

On July 6, 1861, Secretary of War Cameron notified Lincoln that 64 volunteer regiments of 900 men each, besides 1,200 Regulars, were in readiness around Washington, and the troops enrolled elsewhere over the North made a total of 225,000. Of this army, one of the largest the earth had ever seen, Lincoln was Commander in Chief. And he wrote his high pride of these volunteers in his message to Congress, for the world to know: "So large an army as the government has now on foot, was never before known, without a soldier in it, but who has taken his place there, of his own free choice. But more than this: there are many single Regiments whose members, one and another, possess full practical knowledge of all the arts, sciences, professions, and whatever else, whether useful or elegant, is known in the world . . ."

Pierre Gustave Toutant Beauregard, superintendent of the West Point Military Academy before he resigned the previous winter, a Mexican War veteran, was now commanding an army of 20,000 Confederate troops near Washington at Manassas Junction. As the hero who had shot away the flag at Fort Sumter, he was called to Virginia to check Northern invasion. He began June 1 with a proclamation: "A reckless and unprincipled tyrant has invaded your soil. Abraham Lincoln, regardless of all moral, legal, and constitutional restraints, has thrown his Abolition hosts among you . . . All rules of civilized warfare are abandoned . . . Your honor and that of your wives and daughters, your fortunes, and your lives are involved in this momentous contest."

On July 4 when Congress assembled it was in the air that soon a battle would be fought near Washington. Greeley's *Tribune* clamored in headlines: "Forward to Richmond! Forward to Richmond! The Rebel Congress must not be allowed to meet there on the 20th of July! By that date the place must be held by the National Army!"

Business was worse, money scarce, loans slow. A short war was wanted. Everybody agreed on that. The time was already up for some three-month troops; the 4th Pennsylvania Volunteers and the 8th New York Artillery were calling for their discharges.

In his message to Congress the President gave a miniature history of the Fort Sumter affair, of how the fort was bombarded to its fall "without even awaiting the arrival of the provisioning expedition." It forced the questions: "Is there, in all republics, this inherent, and fatal weakness? . . . Must a government, of necessity, be too *strong* for the liberties of its own people, or too *weak* to maintain its own existence?" No choice was left but "to call out the war power of the Government." Applause swept the House at the recommendation "that you give the legal means for making this contest a short and decisive one" and for the work at least 400,000 men and $400,000,000.

The President then queried whether the Southern movement should be called "secession" or "rebellion," saying that the instigators of the movement understood the difference. "They knew they could make no advancement directly in the teeth of these strong and noble sentiments [of their people]. Accordingly they commenced by *an insidious debauching of the public mind.* [Italics added.] They invented an ingenious sophism . . . that any state of the Union may, *consistently* with the national Constitution, and therefore *lawfully,* and *peacefully,* withdraw from the Union, without the consent of the Union, or of any other state. The little disguise that the supposed right is to be exercised only for just cause, themselves to be the sole judges of its justice, is too thin to merit any notice. With rebellion thus *sugar-coated,* they have been *drugging the public mind* [italics added] of their section for more than thirty years; and, until at length, they have brought many good men to a willingness to take up arms against the government the day *after* some assemblage of men have enacted the farcical pretense of taking their State out of the Union, who could have been brought to no such thing the day *before* . . . To be consistent they must secede from one another, whenever they shall find it the easiest way of settling their debts, or effecting any other selfish, or unjust object."

The message was a brief for a client, a letter to the American people. The Northern press gave it greater approval than any utterance hitherto from Lincoln. The editor of *Harper's Weekly,* George William Curtis, vented his enthusiasm in a letter: "I envy no other age. I believe with all my heart in the cause, and in Abe Lincoln. His message is the most truly American message ever delivered . . . Wonderfully acute, simple, sagacious, and of antique honesty! I can forgive the jokes and the big hands, and the inability to make bows. Some of us who doubted were wrong. This people is not rotten. What the young men dream, the old men shall see."

The Senate confirmed the President's appointments. A new army bill gave the President more than he asked, authorizing 500,000 three-year volunteers. A joint resolution to make legal and valid the extralegal, dictatorial and pro-scriptive acts of the President in the emergencies since his proclamation of war in April met little direct opposition, but was held up and laid away amid unfinished business from day to day. He had gone out of his way to do so many things without the required authority from Congress. Now Congress politely refused to sanction all he had done. Some of the murmuring took the form that he should have called Congress earlier and day by day asked its Yes or No.

Senator Baker of Oregon rang out: "I want sudden, bold, forward determined war; and I do not think anybody can conduct war of that kind as well as a Dictator."

Chapter 6

Bull Run — McClellan —
Frémont — The Trent Affair

The President on June 29 had called a Cabinet meeting be-fore which General Irvin McDowell laid his plans. His army of 30,000 was to fight the 21,900 Confederates at Manassas under General Beauregard. Another Confederate army over in the Shenandoah Valley was to be held by a Union army under General Robert Patterson, also in the valley, and stopped from joining Beauregard. General Scott approved McDowell's battle plan but favored waiting till a larger army, better trained and prepared, could win victories that would be destructive.

Lincoln and his Cabinet, as political authorities yielding to the demand of the country for fighting, and considering that the time of the three-month troops was almost run out, overruled Scott. On McDowell's asking for more time to drill and discipline his troops, Lincoln remarked, "You are green, it is true, but they are green also."

The Battle of Bull Run, Sunday, July 21, 1861, was to a

large and eager public a sort of sporting event, the day and place of combat announced beforehand, a crowd of spectators riding to the scene with lunch baskets as though for a picnic. On horseback, in buggies and gigs, Senators Trumbull, Wade, Chandler, Grimes, Wilson, McDougall, besides Congressmen with emergency navy revolvers and pretty ladies in crinoline gowns, rode out to gaze on a modern battle. The word was that the Northern Shovelry would make Southern Chivalry bite the dust.

Lincoln went as usual that Sunday morning to the New York Avenue Presbyterian Church. During the afternoon he read telegrams from the battlefield, one every 10 or 15 minutes. A messenger from Scott arrived. All seemed favorable. The President went for a drive in his carriage, as usual of evenings. At six o'clock came Seward, pale, worn, hoarse, asking Nicolay and Hay, "Where is the President?" He had gone to drive, they told Seward, showing telegrams indicating victory. "Tell no one," came the words from Seward. "That is not true. The battle is lost." He had news that McDowell's army was retreating and calls were coming for General Scott to save Washington.

The President returned a half-hour later. Nicolay and Hay told him the news. "He listened in silence, without the slightest change of feature or expression, and walked away to army headquarters." There a dispatch from a captain of engineers read: "The day is lost. Save Washington and the remnants of this army. The routed troops will not re-form." General Scott refused to believed it. The Cabinet was called. Now came a telegram from McDowell. His army had gone to pieces, and was "a confused mob."

That night Lincoln lay on a lounge in the Cabinet room and heard eyewitnesses tell what they had seen from saddle, buggy or gig on the 20-mile ride from the battlefield. Strewn along roadways for miles were hats, coats, blankets, haversacks, canteens, rifles, broken harness, wagons upside down—the evidence of thousands of soldiers in panic and retreat to Washington.

At three that afternoon McDowell thought he had the battle won. An hour later his army was going to pieces. Yet back of the enemy lines there was panic; and as Jefferson Davis came from Richmond toward the battle lines, he saw many runaways and asked an old man how the battle had gone. "Our line was broken," was the answer. "All was confusion, the army routed and the battle lost."

McDowell's staff man, James B. Fry, recorded 16 officers and 444 men killed, 78 officers and 1,046 men wounded, 50 officers and 1,262 men missing, not including Congressman Alfred Ely of New York captured and sent to Libby Prison in Richmond. General Johnston officially reported Confederate losses at 378 killed, 1,489 wounded, and 30 missing.

After the hot, sweltering Sunday of the battle came a Monday of drizzling rain. Across Long Bridge over the Potomac, from daylight on, came lines of bedraggled men. Hour by hour these silhouettes of defeat trod the bridge to the capital. Thousands were taken into homes and fed.

Congress, the press, the pulpit, politicians, talkers, began fixing the blame. The regulars were to blame for driving their caissons at top speed through the regimental ranks when heading to the rear for ammunition. The three-month troops were to blame; two of their regiments, claiming their time of service was over, marched off the field as the cannons began to sing. The shoulder-straps, political brigadiers, colonels, majors, were only tin soldiers good for sham battles; at four o'clock, as the rout was developing, more than 12,000 volunteers had lost their regimental organization. The Senators, Congressmen, politicians, correspondents, civilians, hack drivers, ladies in crinoline, who had come to see the show, ran like sheep first of all and started the stampede. Thus ran talk, alibis, explanations.

But more than any other General Robert Patterson was blamed; if he had smashed at Johnston's army in the Shenandoah Valley, then Johnston's fresh regiments wouldn't have marched in and started the panic. To Lincoln he read orders, telegrams, letters, which he believed cleared him of failure. He must have a trial by his peers in order to stop the daily abuse laid on him. "The President replied that he would cheerfully accede to any practicable measure to do me justice, but that I need not expect to escape abuse as long as I was of any importance or value to the community, adding that he received infinitely more abuse than I did, but he had ceased to regard it, and I must learn to do the same."

"As for blame and causes," wrote George William Curtis in a private letter, "they are in our condition and character. We have undertaken to make war without in the least knowing how." And from this public calamity Curtis turned to the private grief of Henry Wadsworth Longfellow's wife burned to death in the tragic swift blazing of a crinoline gown.

In a letter to Lincoln from Greeley in New York, the foremost American editor was ready for an armistice, a national convention, peace, disbandment of forces. "The gloom in this city is funereal—for our dead at Bull Run were many, and they lie unburied yet. On every brow sits sullen, scorching, black despair." He would support any compromise Lincoln believed right. He closed, "Yours, in the depths of bitterness." Lincoln made no reply. To Hay later he spoke of the letter as "pusillanimous." Greeley, having helped bring on the tornado, was terrified at its first chaotic howlings.

Probing, analyzing, approving of Lincoln but more often scolding, were Horace Greeley and his newspaper. Among the 50,000 subscribers of the New York *Tribune* were nearly all the editors and news writers of America. Greeley had arrived in New York 20 years old, with $10 in his pocket, a greenhorn from Vermont farms who had picked up the trade of printer. He edited the *New Yorker*, the *Jeffersonian*, the *Log Cabin*, and in 1841 started his penny morning paper, the New York *Tribune*, which for 21 years was at the forefront reporting, if not advocating, every reform, radical idea and "ism" that came to view. "I have been branded aristocrat, communist, infidel, hypocrite, demagogue, disunionist, traitor, corruptionist, and so forth and so forth," he once declared in urging a friend not to class him also a poet. A half-myth the country talked about, he was fair, pink-skinned, baby-faced, blue-eyed with a stare of innocence. His cherubic face rose out of an under-chin beard, the voice a high squeal. He shuffled rather than walked, wore his cravat in disorder, one pant leg stuffed in one boot. He owned a farm at Chappaqua, 33 miles from New York, and liked to call himself a farmer. "Go West, young man" was his repeated advice, and in the westward flow of settlers a famous slogan.

Once, making a denial, he declared: "I never said all Democrats were saloon-keepers. What I said was that all saloon-keepers were Democrats." His office door was open, and when a man came in and bawled at the *Tribune*'s sins and errors, Greeley quietly scratched away at his two daily columns. Once a caller had used up his profanity and vituperation and was leaving; Greeley squeaked, "Come back, my friend, come back and relieve your mind."

Beggars and borrowers knew he was easy. He classified them as casual, chronic, or systematic, and usually let them know he knew they were lying about paying back the loan. To one borrower who paid back $20 he said, "You are the first one that has disappointed me."

At 25 he married Mary Y. Cheney, a Connecticut schoolteacher whom he met at a vegetarian boardinghouse in New York. She was slight, girlish-looking, a brunette with long curls falling below her shoulders. Their first child was fair, with notable complexion and hair that fell as "a shower of ruddy gold" to his shoulders; he died at five in an Asiatic cholera plague that infected New York in 1848. Another boy died at six from croup. One girl died at six months of age. Two infants died at childbirth. Of the seven Greeley children two daughters were alive.

"I didn't raise my children for this world but for the next," said the mother. Her freezing manners and sharp words kept many from making a second visit to the Chappaqua farm. They spoke of Mrs. Greeley snatching manuscripts from her husband's hand and throwing them in the fire so that he took to hotels occasionally to finish his editorials. And they spoke of him as being patient and not answering back.

Thousands of "self-made men" echoed his saying, "Of all horned cattle the most helpless in a printing office is a college graduate." Junius Henri Browne, of many years' service under Greeley, noted him wayward, moody, undisciplined. "His friends could not be certain of him, for he could not be certain of himself. He was not only unlike other men—he was unlike himself often."

Greeley recalled having seen Lincoln at the White House about two weeks after inauguration. And he had felt that Lincoln was too bland, too easygoing. His moaning letter to Lincoln just after Bull Run beginning "This is my seventh sleepless night" reflected his fear that Lincoln was not losing enough sleep over the war.

Lincoln gave his personal attention to the camps around Washington, kept close to men and officers, mixed with them. He rode in an open hack with Seward one day across the Potomac. Colonel William Tecumseh Sherman at a roadside asked if they were going to his camp. "Yes," said Lincoln. "We heard that you had got over the big scare, and we thought we would come over and see the boys." He asked Sherman into the hack. At the camp, noted Sherman, "Mr. Lincoln stood up and made one of the neatest, best, and most feeling addresses I ever listened to, referring to our disaster, the high duties that still devolved on us, and the brighter days to come."

When Lincoln had finished a speech to the 79th New York regiment, with his usual appeal that they should present grievances to him, one Highlander stepped forward, "Mr. President, we don't think Colonel Sherman has treated us very well," and rehearsed their being driven out of a barn to make room for the Colonel's horses. "Well, boys," said the President, "I have a great deal of respect for Colonel Sherman and if he turned you out of the barn I have no doubt it was for some good purpose. I presume he thought you would feel better if you went to work and tried to forget your troubles."

At the camp of the 69th New York (Irish), who had fought with impetuous valor and whose Colonel Michael Corcoran was taken prisoner in the thick of the fighting, "Mr. Lincoln made to them the same feeling address," wrote Sherman, "with more personal allusions, because of their special gallantry in the battle under Corcoran." Lincoln again made his offer to hear willingly the grievance of any man. An officer stepped forward who that morning had tried to quit the service and leave camp, saying, "Mr. President, this morning I went to speak to Colonel Sherman, and he threatened to shoot me." Lincoln: "Threatened to shoot you?" "Yes, sir, he threatened to shoot me." Lincoln looked at the officer, looked at Sherman, and then, stooping toward the officer as if to give a confidential message, and speaking in a stage whisper that could be heard for yards around, "Well, if I were you, and he threatened to shoot, I would not trust him, for I believe he would do it." The officer turned and vanished. The men whooped.

On the night of Bull Run, noted his secretaries, Lincoln did not go to bed, stayed on the lounge in the Cabinet room all night. The next night, having heard more accounts of the lost battle, he lay on a sofa in his office and penciled an outline of what must be done, a program for immediate action.

On Friday, July 26, the President had a call from Henry C. Whitney, fresh from Illinois. Whitney suggested, "Everything is drifting into the army, and I guess you will have to put me in." Lincoln said in a day or two he would make Whitney a quartermaster. The afternoon wore on. Congress was in session. War and revolution surged. Conversation between the two old friends ran from early afternoon till near sunset. The President needed a short holiday and took it. He "didn't care a cornhusk," according to Whitney, for those "who think that a statesman, like a blind horse in a treadmill, needs no rest, or that, like the conventional whitewashed statue of justice, he must always *pose* for dignified effect."

The Senate resolution to approve the President's unconstitutional acts done without approval of Congress during the emergency weeks, when Congress was not in session and could not then approve, was introduced the third day of the session. It would declare legal and valid the President's first call for state militia troops, his proclamation of blockade and action therein, his call for three-year volunteers and his increase of the Regular Army and the Navy, and not least of all his suspension of the ancient Anglo-Saxon writ of habeas corpus.

For weeks this resolution lay amid unfinished business. On August 5, the day before Congress adjourned, a bill to increase army pay came up for action and to this was added a rider declaring "that all the acts, proclamations, and orders of the President" relating to the militia and volunteers "are hereby approved and in all respects legalized and made valid, to the same intent and with the same effect as if they had been issued and done under the previous express authority and direction of the Congress of the United States." By a vote of 37 to 5 it passed the Senate, and by 74 to 19 the House, the Nays being Border State votes, with help from Ohio and Indiana. Thus the President failed of full approval, was not yet by Congress whitewashed of guilt as a usurper in what he did with the Regular Army, with closing ports by blockade, and with the hoary and precious right of the writ of habeas corpus.

Senator Preston King of New York made clear that he approved "the vigorous measures" of the Executive, "but I have a disinclination to pass upon a question the whole length and breadth and extent of which I do not entirely comprehend." John Sherman of Ohio presented his opinion: "I do not believe the President of the United States has the power to suspend the writ of *habeas corpus,* because that power is expressly given to Congress, and to Congress alone. I do not believe the President of the United States has the power to increase the regular army, because that power is expressly given by the Constitution to Congress alone. Still I approve of the action of the President. I believe the President did right. He did precisely what I would have done if I had been in his place—no more, no less; but I cannot here, in my place, as a Senator, under oath, declare that what he did do was legal."

When Congress adjourned August 6, it had given the

President nearly all the practical measures he needed to proceed with the war. He was more of an executive than most of them had expected.

To his wife John Lothrop Motley was writing: "A grim winter is before us. Gather you rosebuds while you may. The war is to be a long one." In the blouse of a dead Confederate soldier at Fairfax Court House was a letter from a girl begging him to watch his own "precious life" while remembering "kill a Yankee for me."

The Army of the Potomac grew into 168,000 in November from 50,000 on July 22, when Washington had received its new commander, General George Brinton McClellan. McClellan was appointed by Lincoln by reason of an overwhelming weight of public and private opinion. He looked the part, with a well-modeled head, mustache and goatee, sat his saddle as a trained Man on Horseback, issued commands with authority, published proclamations modeled on Napoleon. Washington adopted him, the Army took to him, correspondents nicknamed him "Little Mac" and "the Young Napoleon."

Only the year before, he had married Ellen Mary Marcy, the daughter of a Regular Army officer, to whom he was now writing, "Who would have thought, when we were married, that I should so soon be called upon to save my country?" He had left her and a $10,000-a-year job as president of the Ohio & Mississippi Railroad at Cincinnati. He had been chief engineer and then vice-president of the Illinois Central Railroad, entertained Douglas in his Chicago home, and the only ballot he had ever cast was for Douglas. His *Manual on the Art of War,* his translation of a French book on bayonet exercises, were reputable. Commanding an army of 18,000 in West Virginia, he had overcome about two-thirds that number, giving the North the only actions thus far having semblance of military victories.

Not quite 35 now, he had entered West Point when only 15 years and seven months old; the regulation as to age was suspended in his case because of his superior health and physique and high standing in mental examinations; he had graduated second in a class of 59.

He was riding 12 hours a day and toiling till three in the morning organizing his army. On August 8, however, he wished his wife to know he had been "pestered to death with senators, etc." and had "a row with General Scott," and later, "I have scarcely slept one moment for the last three nights, knowing well that the enemy intend some movement."

One daily bulletin home read: "On Sunday, instead of going to church, was sent for by the President immediately after breakfast, and kept busy until midnight, when I returned from a long ride too tired to talk even. Yesterday in the saddle from ten to five, and then persecuted until after midnight. Today the President sent for me before I was up; have been at work ever since, and soon start out to receive a brigade and some batteries." When he had an army twice the size of the enemy camped near Manassas, he wrote his wife that he was sleeping with one eye open at night "looking out sharply for Beauregard, who, I think, has some notion of making a dash in this direction."

An illusion that the enemy outnumbered him kept growing. Day by day in personal interviews, in notes and letters, he called on the President, on Scott and others, for more and more men. "I am here in a terrible place; the enemy have from three to four times my force," he wrote his wife August 16, adding a few days later, "I do not *live* at all; merely exist, worked and worried half to death."

One day in late September when hazy gray folded the blue hills, and slashes of yellow and scarlet stood out on woodlands, McClellan rode with the President, the Secretary of War and Governor Curtin to a ceremonial of presenting flags to 15 Pennsylvania regiments. At a luncheon afterward McClellan invited the party to ride around his army and have a look at it. At one point they halted to view a Confederate flag on Munson's Hill, when McClellan "somewhat disturbed the equanimity of most of the party by saying we were just at that time outside of the Union lines." McClure noted Lincoln on a horse, "legs halfway between the under part of the girth and the ground, his long arms could have guided his horse by the ears," while the high silk hat somehow didn't belong. They drew rein before regiments that lifted genuine cheers for McClellan. Lincoln was impressed.

In November General Winfield Scott was retired on pay, with honors, and with tributes from the President and others. McClellan was now commissioned General in Chief, and at the White House Lincoln said to him, "I should be perfectly satisfied if I thought this vast increase of responsibility would not embarrass you." "It is a great relief, Sir!" said McClellan. "I feel as if several tons were taken from my shoulders today. I am now in contact with you, and the Secretary. I am not embarrassed by intervention." "Well," said Lincoln, as John Hay heard him, "draw on me for all the sense I have, and all the information. In addition to your present command, the supreme command of the army will entail a vast labor upon you." "I can do it all," McClellan said quietly.

When Lincoln had suggestions for McClellan which he did not care to put in writing, he took another course. He dated and signed a card September 30, 1861, reading, "Will Gen. McClellan please see Pay-Master Whitney a moment?" Whitney saw this as "an old habit Mr. Lincoln had of sending a verbal message on any subject he did not wish to put down in writing. He frequently sent verbal messages by those he could trust."

One night as they parted at McClellan's house the General said to Lincoln: "I intend to be careful and do as well as possible. Don't let them hurry me, is all I ask." "You shall have your own way in the matter, I assure you," replied Lincoln as he and John Hay started on their walk to the White House. Two nights later, on October 12, a telegram was handed Lincoln from McClellan saying the enemy was before him in force and would probably attack in the morning. "If they attack," he added, "I shall beat them." This expected attack, like others expected, failed to arrive.

In November Lincoln, Seward and John Hay went to

McClellan's house one evening. The General was at a wedding, said the servant, and would soon return. "We went in," wrote Hay in his diary, "and after we had waited about an hour, McC. came in and without paying any particular attention to the porter who told him the President was waiting to see him, went upstairs, passing the door of the room where the President and Secretary of State were seated. They waited about half-an-hour, and sent once more a servant to tell the General they were there; and the answer coolly came that the General had gone to bed."

Hay considered this deliberate snub the first sign of military authorities overriding the civil government. "Coming home I spoke to the President about the matter, but he seemed not to have noticed it, specially, saying it was better, at this time, not to be making points of etiquette & personal dignity." And the President said another day, "I will hold McClellan's horse if he will only bring us success."

Sometimes the President sent for McClellan to come to the White House. More often Lincoln called at McClellan's house. Once they met at Seward's house and McClellan's daily letter told his wife: "The President is honest and means well. As I parted from him on Seward's steps he said that it had been suggested to him that it was no more safe for me than for him to walk out at night without some attendant. I told him that I felt no fear; that no one would take the trouble to interfere with me. On which he deigned to remark that they would probably give more for my scalp at Richmond than for his."

A few days later, however, McClellan felt the President, pressing for action, was bothering him too much. At the home of Edwin M. Stanton he wrote, "I have not been at home for some three hours, but am concealed at Stanton's to dodge all enemies in shape of 'browsing' Presidents, etc."

McClellan's army now numbered more than 160,000; he had at least three times as many troops as the enemy at Manassas. Twice in that autumn of 1861 the spick-and-span platoons of the Army of the Potomac had passed in grand review before President Lincoln, the Cabinet, gov-

ernors of states and ladies in silken crinoline. There had
been autumn weather on which many commented—mild,
pleasant days and cool nights, perfect weather for an army
movement to redeem Bull Run, to end the war. Thus ran
hope and talk.

On "a lovely, a rare October day" at Ball's Bluff, on
high ground overlooking the Potomac, a few hundred
Union soldiers were cornered, killed, captured. Their commander went down, a picked target of marksmen who sent
several bullets into him as he came into the open calling
to his troops to follow. Near sunset that day Lincoln, entering McClellan's headquarters, "spoke of the beauty of
the afternoon" to a correspondent, who noted "the lines
were deeper in the President's face than when I saw him
in his own home, the cheeks more sunken." The telegraph
was clicking off the minor battle of Ball's Bluff. The name
of the killed commander, General Edward D. Baker, Lincoln's "Ned" Baker, came through. "Five minutes passed,"
wrote a correspondent, "and then Mr. Lincoln, unattended,
with bowed head and tears rolling down his furrowed
cheeks, his breast heaving, passed through the room. He
almost fell as he stepped into the street. We sprang from
our seats to render assistance, but he did not fall."

Gone now forever from Lincoln was a trumpet, a shield,
an intimate companion and a bright light of loyalty, namesake of his second-born boy, his choice of all men to introduce him for a presidential inaugural address.

Driving snow came with the last week in November.
Winter weather was on. Wool coats, heavy blankets fire-
wood, tents, huts, were the need. The war was costing
more than $1,000,000 a day. A hazard was in the air.
Would the Young Napoleon slog through in a winter cam-
paign and take Richmond? If he should, said men of the
South at Richmond, he would find it as Napoleon did
Moscow, a city in ashes.

The war had not really set in as yet. Only that summer
of '61 squads of Union recruits had marched down one
side of a street in Louisiville while recruits on the other side

headed for the Confederate Army. On a railroad train in central Kentucky one car held a company of troops going to a Union camp while in another car was a company of Confederates.

The Kentucky Senator, John P. Breckinridge, once a Vice-President of the United States, had called at the White House to bid good-by to his kinswoman, Elizabeth Todd Grimsley. He was resigning as U.S. Senator and joining the Confederate Army as a brigadier general.

Secretary Cameron returned from a trip west in November to say that Sherman, now a brigadier general in Kentucky, insisted 200,000 troops would be required to hold his 300-mile line and move that line southward. Sherman was "insane," related a Cincinnati newspaper item widely reprinted in the North. He was ordered removed from command; the order was recalled. There was confusion and worse.

In a few cases Lincoln made colonels and brigadiers of politicians, "to keep them from fighting against the war with their mouths," said Whitney. Lincoln commissioned his old-time dueling challenger, James Shields, a brigadier general; he was one of several commissioned Democrats who were to make bright records. Illinois Republican editors complained that 40 out of 70 Illinois regiments had Democratic colonels.

In many cases Lincoln commissioned politicians and adventurers because they could raise troops; they had followings. One was Illinois Congressman John A. McClernand, a Douglas Democrat; another was John A. Logan, also a Douglas Democrat and a southern Illinois Congressman. In Logan's district a Pope County mass meeting declared for secession, and a mass meeting in Williamson County pledged itself to attach southern Illinois to the Confederacy. Lincoln had to gauge communities where uprisings die down and flare up again. The war thermometer varied.

One dark night Lincoln with four other men climbed up the tower of the Smithsonian Institution. Toward hills encircling Washington they flashed signals. Next day an army officer marched into Lincoln's office with a prisoner, Professor Joseph Henry, secretary and director of the Smithsonian Institution, the most eminent man of learning in the employ of the U.S. Government. "Mr. President," said the officer, "I told you a month ago Professor Henry is a rebel. Last night at midnight he flashed red lights from the top of his building, signaling to the Secesh. I saw them myself."

Lincoln turned. "Now you're caught! What have you to say, Professor Henry, why sentence of death should not immediately be pronounced upon you?" Then, turning to the army officer, Lincoln explained that on the previous evening he and others had accompanied Henry to the Smithsonian tower and experimented with new army signals. The officer thereupon released from his custody a physicist of international repute.

In Missouri during the summer and fall of '61 the warfare had raw bones, pointed a sinister forefinger toward the future, and had its weight in moving Lincoln to write in a message to Congress: "In considering the policy to be adopted for suppressing the insurrection I have been anxious and careful that the inevitable conflict for this purpose shall not degenerate into a violent and remorseless revolutionary struggle."

Nathaniel Lyon, short, bearded, with dark-red hair and fiery temperament, drove himself hard, some of his raw volunteer troops saying he talked to them as if they were mules. The son of a Connecticut Yankee farmer, a West Pointer, Indian fighter in Florida, shot in the leg entering Mexico City with the American Army, Lyon handled regulars on the West Coast, at Forts Riley and Kearney, and came to St. Louis from Prairie Dog, Kansas. Congressman Frank Blair knew Lyon as a Union man and saw to it early that Lincoln appointed him commandant of the St. Louis arsenal. Lyon and Frank Blair had worked out their plans, which made it impossible for Missouri to secede from the Union. The Germans of St. Louis, who were mainly Union and antislavery, gave their help as valuable allies.

Lyon threw his army of 6,000 at more than twice that number of Confederates August 10, 1861, at Wilson's Creek. Bullets struck him near the ankle, on the thigh; one cut his scalp to the bone; his horse was shot. Mounting another horse, his face white from loss of blood, he ordered a bayonet charge and led it, tumbling off his horse into the arms of his orderly with a bullet hole close to the heart. His army retired, the enemy not following. The losses were about 1,200 killed and wounded on each side. Missouri boys of both armies lay dead in the cornfields alongside Kentucky, Iowa and Illinois boys. The Confederates gave over the body of Lyon. Crowds came to view the coffin as it journeyed to Connecticut, where the general assembly mourned its "beloved son."

An outcry arose when Congressman Frank Blair and others put the blame for Lyon's death, Wilson's Creek and other losses on General John Charles Frémont, commander of the Department of the West, with headquarters, troops and munitions at St. Louis. Frémont, in 1856 the first Republican party candidate for President, was born in Savannah, Georgia. Expelled from college in Charleston, South Carolina, for "continual disregard of discipline," he was an instructor of mathematics on a U.S. war sloop, a railroad surveyor in the Tennessee mountains, and became a lieutenant in the U.S. Topographical Corps. In Washington he fell in love with 15-year-old Jessie Benton, daughter of Senator Thomas H. Benton of Missouri. The Senator had him sent west of the Mississippi River on a surveying trip. He came back and ran away with Jessie; they were married, and thereafter the Benton home in St. Louis was his too, but he used it little. He led expeditions west, exploring the Rocky Mountains, South Pass, winning the first recorded climb up the highest point in the Wind River Mountains. Fremont Peak was named for him.

He clashed with the Spanish rulers of California, took a hand in overthrowing them and setting up the State of California, of which he was the first U.S. Senator. Then came land, gold mines, money pouring in at the rate of $75,000 a month, and Frémont's Mariposa estate of 46,000 acres, which had cost him $3,000, was estimated at $10,000,000. Then too came squatters, rival claims and the details of management and finance. He was in Paris trying to sell half of his estate when news came of Sumter. He offered his services and Lincoln with no waiting commissioned him a major general. At the White House he had talked with Lincoln of the plan for him to organize an army in the Northwest and go down the Mississippi and split the Confederacy in two.

Though he was head of the Western Department on July 3, Frémont lingered in Washington, delayed in New York, arrived in St. Louis on July 25; he directed entrenchments thrown around St. Louis, wore out relays of telegraphers with messages to governors and troop commanders. Many days he worked from five in the morning till midnight.

From the southwest corner of Missouri had come a messenger from Lyon begging Frémont to send him men. Frémont answered, "If he fights it will be on his own responsibility." Frémont had urged Lyon to retreat to Rolla, which would be falling back about halfway to St. Louis. And he started two regiments toward Lyon. But Lyon never saw them. For him war was fighting; he sought out the enemy. Lyon died in the drawn battle at Wilson's Creek. The memory rankled with men like Frank Blair.

"I will neither lose the state nor permit the enemy a foot of advantage," Frémont wrote Lincoln. "I have infused energy and activity into every department." Frémont addressed a telegram to "The President of the United States" inquiring, "Will the President read my urgent dispatch to the Secretary of War?" He received the reply on August 15: "Been answering your messages ever since day before yesterday. Do you receive the answers?"

Lincoln's anxiety about Frémont and Missouri grew as the mail brought stories of extravagance, blunders, favoritism, corruption. Frank Blair called on Frémont with General John M. Schofield, who wrote, "To my great surprise, no questions were asked, nor mention made, of the bloody field from which I had just come, where Lyon had been killed." Instead of wanting to learn any possible lessons from a tried soldier, Frémont led Schofield to a table and pointed out on maps the triumphant line of march his army would take. Blair and Schofield left Frémont's office. "We walked down the street for some time in silence. Then Blair turned to me and said, 'Well, what do you think of him?' I replied in words rather too strong to print. Blair said, 'I have been suspecting that for some time.'"

Frémont through the night of August 29 and far into the morning of August 30 worked on a proclamation. In pompous terms and with threats he didn't have power to enforce, he declared "martial law throughout the State of Missouri." Drawing the line of the Union Army across half the state, he promised that all persons north of this line caught "with arms in their hands" would be courtmartialed and "if found guilty will be shot." Also "the property, real and personal, of all persons in the State of Missouri who shall take up arms against the United States, or who shall be directly proven to have taken an active part with their enemies in the field, is declared to be confiscated to the public use, and their slaves, if any they have, are hereby declared freemen."

Lincoln, along with the country, first heard of the proclamation through the newspapers. After getting an authentic text he wrote Frémont September 2: "Should you shoot a man, according to the proclamation, the Confederates would very certainly shoot our best man in their hands in retaliation; and so, man for man, indefinitely. It is therefore my order that you allow no man to be shot, under the proclamation, without first having my approbation or consent . . . The confiscation of property, and the liberating slaves of traiterous owners, will alarm our Southern Union friends, and turn them against us—perhaps ruin our rather fair prospect for Kentucky." He asked Frémont to modify the proclamation.

Frémont took six days to reply. And this letter to Lincoln was carried by a special messenger—Mrs. Frémont herself.

She left St. Louis September 8 with her English maid, sitting two days and nights in a hot, overcrowded car, arriving in Washington the third day. She sent from Willard's a written request to know when she might deliver Frémont's letter to the President. A White House messenger brought back a card: "Now, at once. A. Lincoln."

Near nine in the evening she walked to the White House with Judge Edward Coles of New York, met the President in the Red Room and wrote of it: "I introduced Judge Coles, who then stepped into the deep doorway leading to the Blue Room—and there he remained walking to and fro, keeping in sight and hearing . . . He was struck at once, as I was, by the President's manner, which was hard . . . Nor did he offer me a seat. He talked standing, and both voice and manner made the impression that I was to be got rid of briefly . . . In answer to his question, 'Well?' I explained that the general wished so much to have his attention to the letter sent, that I had brought it to make sure it would reach him. He answered, not to that, but to the subject his own mind was upon, that 'It was a war for a great national idea, the Union, and that General Frémont should not have dragged the negro into it,—that he never would if he had consulted with Frank Blair. I sent Frank there to advise him.' He first mentioned the Blairs, in this astonishing connection. It was a *parti pris,* and as we walked back Judge Coles, who heard everything, said to me, 'This ends Frémont's part in the war. Seward and Montgomery Blair will see to that, and Lincoln does not seem to see the injustice, the wrong of receiving secret reports against him made by a man authorized to do so, and as everyone knows, with his mind often clouded by drink and always governed by personal motives' [meaning Frank Blair]."

When Mrs. Frémont began talking about the difficulty of conquering by arms alone, how England and the wide world would welcome a blow struck against slavery, she thought there was "a sneering tone" in the President's voice as he remarked, "You are quite a female politician." And Jessie Benton Frémont returned to St. Louis with contempt for Lincoln, hate for the Blairs and a sharper eye for conspirators against her husband. As Congressman J. B. Grinnell of Iowa reported Lincoln's version of the Jessie Frémont interview, she came "opening her case with mild expostulations, but left in anger flaunting her handkerchief before my face, and saying, 'Sir, the general will try titles with you! His is a man and I am his wife.'"

Lincoln's reply to Frémont September 11 pointed to the clause relating to confiscation of property and liberation of slaves, which "appeared to me to be objectionable, in its non-conformity to the Act of Congress passed the 6th. of last August." He had therefore written his wish to Frémont that the clause be modified and now, "Your answer, just received, expresses the preference on your part, that I should make an open order for the modification, which I very cheerfully do."

From antislavery quarters rose a sure breeze of hostile criticism. Press, pulpit, men and women of antislavery fervor, spoke and wrote their scorn of Lincoln. Even Bill Herndon was writing to a friend: "Does the war go on to suit you? It does not suit me. Frémont's proclamation was right. Lincoln's modification of it was wrong."

Lincoln wrote in one letter: "Our adversaries have the power, and will certainly exercise it, to shoot as many of our men as we shoot of theirs. I did not say this in the public letter, because it is a subject I prefer not to discuss in the hearing of our enemies."

General Jeff Thompson, Confederate commander of the First Military District of Missouri, had issued a proclamation to meet Frémont's, announcing "most solemnly" that for every soldier of the state guard or of the Southern Army put to death as ordered by Frémont he would "hang, draw, and quarter a minion of said Abraham Lincoln."

It was a saying, "When the Blairs go in for a fight they go in for a funeral." Frémont, once their protégé, they had marked to be destroyed. Frémont fought back. Mrs. Frémont joined. Congressman Washburne headed a committee which investigated Frémont's department. Judges David

Davis and Joseph Holt were appointed to direct an audit of accounts. War Secretary Cameron, with an adjutant general, went personally to St. Louis.

They all found extravagance, mismanagement, blunders, but no specific outstanding corruption. The total of contracts for food, guns, steamboats, uniforms, supplies, fortifications, ran to about $12,000,000. Nothing could be fastened on Frémont. He came through the search with a record for personal honesty. He let it be told that Frank Blair had asked him to give a contract for 40,000 uniforms to a friend of Blair and he had refused. He threw Blair into jail, let him go, arrested him a second time, and let him go. He suppressed the St. Louis *News*.

The Chicago Irish Brigade under Colonel James A. Mulligan defended Lexington eight days against 20,000 of the enemy and surrendered 1,600 men September 20. Blamed for this fresh loss of good troops, Frémont had notified General Scott at Washington: "I am taking the field myself . . . Please notify the President immediately." General Scott replied, "The President is glad you are hastening to the scene of action; his words are, 'he expects you to repair the disaster at Lexington without loss of time.' " Yet Frémont went on losing time.

And while Frémont sat with his dreams of war and glory, a man wearing clothes like a Southern planter got off a horse at the Frémont picket lines just beyond Springfield and told the pickets he was a messenger with information from the rebel lines. They let him in, the officer of the day taking him to the chief of staff. No, he couldn't see General Frémont, but they would pass in anything he wanted to tell Frémont. The man in the Southern-planter clothes refused this offer. Hours went by. And late in the evening the chief of staff took him to the office where General Frémont sat at the end of a long table.

The man ripped from his coat lining a paper and handed it to Frémont, who nervously unfolded it, read the name "A. Lincoln" signed to it, slammed the document down on the table, and frowned. "Sir, how did you get admission into my lines?" The man said he came in as a messenger bearing information from the "rebel" lines. Frémont waved him out. "That will do for the present."

Thus on November 2 Frémont was removed from command. Lincoln's removal order, dated October 24, had gone to General S. R. Curtis at St. Louis with instructions that the order was not to be handed Frémont if when reached by messenger "he shall then have, in personal command, fought and won a battle, or shall then be actually in a battle, or shall then be in the immediate presence of the enemy, in expectation of a battle." Curtis made copies of Lincoln's order and sent three messengers by separate routes with it. Curtis had heard of Frémont's arrangements for no removal order to be delivered. General Hunter temporarily took command. Other plans for reaching New Orleans were under way.

Frémont had lasted in Missouri just 100 days. In that time he made himself a hero in the eyes of nearly all the antislavery elements of the Northern States and of Europe. Sober citizens pulled the portraits of Lincoln from their walls and trampled under foot the face of the President, according to the Cincinnati *Gazette*. Wendell Phillips estimated Lincoln as "not a man like Frémont, to stamp the lava mass of the nation with an idea." Honoring Frémont in person, Henry Ward Beecher in his Brooklyn church said, "Your name will live and be remembered by a nation of freemen." James Russell Lowell, Greeley and Bryant spoke deep offense at Lincoln's treatment of Frémont. The Chicago *Tribune* denounced the President's action and predicted grave humiliation unless the administration took a more vigorous policy.

The Springfield, Massachusetts, *Republican* editor, Samuel Bowles, wrote, "It is gratifying to know that we have a President who is loyal to law—when that is made to meet an emergency—as he is to meet an emergency for which no law is provided." The New York *Herald* said: "The President, who has always been known as an upright man, of late months, has justly earned the reputation of a wise and energetic statesman . . . The moderate and effective rebuke contained in his letter to Major-General Frémont is eminently worthy of admiration, both for the dignified and courteous language in which it is couched, and the death blow it strikes at all attempts of badly advised local commanders to overstep the legitimate sphere of their military duties."

Not for long could any man be the hero of the New York *Herald*. The foremost innovator in the journalism of his time, James Gordon Bennett, was studied by Lincoln as one of the powers to be kept on the Union side as far as possible. Brilliant and even bawdy in its endless chatterings, the *Herald* was generally acknowledged to have circulation, resources and prestige surpassing any other American journal. Daily printing 84,000 copies, the *Herald* rated itself on April 9, 1861, as "the most largely circulated journal in the world." Two days before the bombardment of Fort Sumter the *Herald* said the only hope against civil war seemed to lie "in the overthrow of the demoralizing, disorganizing, and destructive sectional party, of which 'Honest Abe Lincoln' is the pliant instrument."

The *Herald* was concededly the only American newspaper of considerable circulation and influence in Europe. Its insolent anti-British tone, and its arrogant policy in general, misrepresented America, and Lincoln in his anxiety about foreign good will picked Thurlow Weed to approach Bennett. Weed pointed out that he and Bennett for 30 years had been political and personal enemies, but narrowed down to a choice from several proposed emissaries, Lincoln decided on Weed. At dinner and in a long conversation Bennett and Weed threshed over the issues. Bennett went on and on in bitter denunciation of Greeley, Garrison, Seward, Sumner, Wendell Phillips and Weed himself as having exasperated the South into the war. Weed returned to Washington, reported the interview, believed the President and the Cabinet were "gratified" over his diplomacy. The results were slender, if any. The *Herald* went on harpooning the British Empire.

Self-announced as "daily daguerreotype of American manners and thought" the *Herald's* 66-year-old owner and editor, born of Roman Catholic parents in Keith, Scotland, had trained for priesthood at Aberdeen, had starved as a bookseller in Boston, had lived shabbily as a hack writer in New York. He issued his first four-page penny New York *Herald* in 1835, doing all the work except the printing himself, writing and shaping the whole paper on an editorial desk of one board slung over two dry-goods boxes, "one poor man in a cellar against the world," as he phrased it.

Then with years of toil from five in the morning till ten at night, scrambling, scandalizing, dramatizing, playing with a scale of shrieks and whispers delicately manipulated, Bennett built a world-famed newspaper. "The newspaper's function," he said, "is not to instruct but to startle."

He was first to print financial news on a large scale, regularly to expose stock-market frauds, to publish lists of bankrupts, to mock at "high society," and to give large spreads to bawdyhouse murders.

Four times in public places Bennett was beaten with canes, each time giving his readers a full report of the event as he saw and felt it. In the baffling human whirlpool of New York, Bennett was playing with paradoxical forces that were to be a heavy anxiety to the Lincoln administration. He kept close to the needs of business expansion and the widening streams of Northern capital that sought new fields and larger earnings.

After Bull Run the *Herald* counseled fresh determination and further preparations, almost in the tone of Lincoln's memoranda for immediate action; no panic, no bewilderment, as in the case of Greeley. Then on Lincoln's revoking Frémont's personal proclamation of Negro emancipation had come the *Herald's* encomiums for Lincoln, praise in heaping measure, compliments that like fresh roses must soon wither and fade, petal by petal. With no cessation Bennett would continue putting the blame for the war on "nigger worshippers," sprinkling his editorial page with that phrase, and steadily maintaining that antislavery agitators were hypocrites rather than heroes.

To friends of Sumner who in September '61 urged Lincoln to issue a proclamation giving freedom to the slaves, he said, "It would do no good to go ahead any faster than the country would follow," Sumner's author friend, Charles Edwards Lester, writing that he heard the President add to this, "You know the old Latin motto, *festina lente.* How do the Italians, those bastard Romans, say the same thing now?" "They have improved on it, Mr. President. They say, *'Andante adagio, perchè ho premúra'*—'Go slow, because I am in a hurry.'" "That's it, exactly. I think Sumner and the rest of you would upset our applecart altogether, if you had your way. We'll fetch 'em; just give us a little time. We didn't go into the war to put down slavery, but to put the flag back."

In November '61 came a dramatic clash of English-speaking nations. The *Trent,* a British Royal Mail packet, one day out from Havana, was steaming serenely along the Bahama Channel. At noon November 8 she came to where the channel narrows to a width of 15 miles. There the *San Jacinto,* a screw sloop of the American Navy, was waiting.

The *Trent* hoisted the British colors. The *San Jacinto* ran up the Union flag. Also the *San Jacinto* fired a shot across the bow of the *Trent.* And as the British steamer showed no signs of slowing down, the American sloop sent a shell that burst in front of the bow of the *Trent.* This brought her to. Captain Moir of the *Trent* lifted a trumpet to his lips, and sang out, "What do you mean by heaving my vessel to in this way?" No answer came.

Three boats were leaving the *San Jacinto* with officers, sailors, marines. They rowed to the *Trent* in a few minutes, and Lieutenant D. MacNeill Fairfax, speaking for the commander of the *San Jacinto,* asked for the passenger list of the *Trent.* He had information that James M. Mason and John Slidell, newly appointed Confederate commissioners to Great Britain and France respectively, were on board.

Mr. Slidell standing near stepped up to Lieutenant Fairfax. "I am Mr. Slidell; do you want to see me?" Mr. Mason, also being near, stepped up, and as he and Lieutenant Fairfax had been introduced years before there was no need for him to say who he was. Next the Lieutenant asked for the secretaries to Messrs. Mason and Slidell and they were lined up. At this point the American Lieutenant informed the British Captain that he had been sent by his commander to arrest Messrs. Mason and Slidell and take them as prisoners on board the U.S. vessel nearby.

Among those with spyglasses on the *San Jacinto* was a heavy-jawed man with a dangerous eye and wavy locks of hair—Charles Wilkes, 63 years old, scientist, experimenter in astronomical observation, explorer of south-polar ice fields, authority on meteorology, author of 11 volumes and atlases.

Mrs. Slidell inquired who was the commander of the *San Jacinto*. "Your old acquaintance, Captain Wilkes," said Fairfax, which surprised Mrs. Slidell. She had sipped tea with him in Washington. "He is playing into our hands!" said Mrs. Slidell spunkily.

"Good-by, my dear, we shall meet in Paris in sixty days," said Mr. Slidell as he bade farewell to his wife. Lieutenant Fairfax went with him to his cabin for his luggage. There Slidell's daughter clung to him and begged to go with him. She wept as he was rowed with the three other prisoners to the *San Jacinto*. The two ships moved away toward different horizons and soon each was alone in the silence of the sea.

When the *Trent* passengers reached London November 27, they found themselves accepted heroes and heroines who had undergone severe tests. Commander Williams, the royal naval agent, told of "the marines rushing with the points of their bayonets at Miss Slidell," how she screamed, and it was then that he, Commander Williams, had just time "to put his body between her and the bayonets of the marines." England went into an uproar. The London *Times* fastened on Captain Wilkes: "He is an ideal Yankee. Swagger and ferocity, built on a foundation of vulgarity and cowardice, these are his characteristics, and these are the most prominent marks by which his countrymen, generally speaking, are known all over the world." The London *Morning Chronicle* tore its hair and gave the war party its cues: "Abraham Lincoln, whose accession to power was generally welcomed on this side of the Atlantic, has proved himself a feeble, confused and little-minded mediocrity. Mr. Seward, the firebrand at his elbow, is exerting himself to provoke a quarrel with all Europe."

On the intervention of Queen Victoria and Prince Albert, the severe instructions to Lord Lyons from Lord Palmerston, the Prime Minister, and Lord John Russell, Secretary for Foreign Affairs, were softened, and instead they framed a note for Seward and Lincoln to read. Mainly it asked whether Captain Wilkes had done what he did by his own wish and whim or at the command of his Government. If it was a Government order and in line with U.S. policy—then war! The ships of the best and biggest navy in the world were made ready. Eight thousand picked troops were put on transports and set sail for Canada.

By this time the United States had gone into an uproar. Yankee Doodle tore his shirt. The eagle was brought out to scream. "The Star-Spangled Banner" blared its sonorous patriotism from multitudinous brass instruments. Captain Wilkes arrived at the port of New York with his prizes, marched down Broadway for a City Hall reception. Banquets were spread for him; in New York, Boston, he was dined, wined, toasted.

That the U.S. Government had in its clutches John Slidell was exciting to antislavery men, for Slidell had led in repealing the Missouri Compromise, was an author of the Fugitive Slave Law, had lengthily examined John Brown in jail, seeking information that might convict New England financial backers of Brown. Mason's record ran close to that of Slidell. The two of them personified the doctrines justifying slavery. America trembled with war fever. Famous lawyers such as Caleb Cushing and Edward Everett justified Wilkes as having the law with him, though other good lawyers like Charles Sumner and Charles Francis Adams were sure he was in the wrong.

Near midnight December 18 the Queen's messenger delivered to the British Minister in Washington the note from Her Majesty's Government. The London *Times* correspondent met Seward at a cotillon party "in very good humor and inclined to talk." Seward without a doubt was feeling extra good. "We will wrap the whole world in flames!" he told W. H. Russell, Prince de Joinville and others. "No power so remote that she will not feel the fire of our battle and be burned in our conflagration." Russell asked one of the guests if Seward was showing fight. "That's all bugaboo talk," was the explanation. "When Seward talks that way, he means to back down."

During the weeks of this fury Lincoln gave no inkling of what he would do. In his December message to Congress he made no reference to the matter. Galt, the Canadian financial Minister, in a White House visit asked the meaning of fortifications and depots of arms on the Great Lakes, Lincoln replying, "We must say something to satisfy the people." And what about the Mason and Slidell case? Galt inquired. "Oh, that'll be got along with," was the brief and equivocal response. Minister Lyons treasured the anecdote, and it was rehearsed in many legations that to a portentous diplomatic inquiry the American President had answered, "Oh, that'll be got along with."

So often the White House callers were asking, "Is it to be peace or war?" The President could ease the public mind by speaking just a few words, he was reminded. One politician kept pressing and received a Lincoln parable: "Your question reminds me of an incident which occurred out west. Two roughs were playing cards for high stakes, when one of them, suspecting his adversary of foul play, straightway drew his bowie-knife from his belt and pinned the hand of the other player upon the table, exclaiming: 'If you haven't got the ace of spades under your palm, I'll apologize.'"

Sumner showed Lincoln letters from Bright and Cobden

of the British House of Commons, and wrote to Bright: "The President is much moved and astonished by the English intelligence. He is essentially honest and pacific in disposition, with a natural slowness. Yesterday he said to me, 'There will be no war unless England is bent on having one.'"

"One war at a time," was Lincoln's word to Seward. Blair was the only Cabinet member with Lincoln from the first. "The English didn't give us time to turn around," was a later comment of Lincoln's. "It was very humiliating, but we had one big war on hand and we didn't want two at the same time. England in the end will be the only one hurt."

Notes from the French, Austrian and Prussian governments were read to the Cabinet, advising the release of Mason and Slidell. Yet the tone of the press and of public opinion over the North was decidedly for war rather than a "backdown" to Britain.

Minister Adams put up a brave front and told the British government he was sure his Government was not responsible for Captain Wilkes' act. From week to week Adams was helpless till one day the mail brought Seward's note calling for arbitration and saying the captured Southern commissioners "will be cheerfully liberated." Discussion of this note had run two days in Lincoln's Cabinet, and Bates wrote: "There was great reluctance on the part of some of the members of the cabinet—and even the President himself"—to give up the Southern commissioners. However, it was so ordered. The British reply later took exception to minor points and acknowledged satisfaction as to "the reparation which Her Majesty and the British nation had a right to expect." Mason and Slidell were let out of their comfortable jail in Boston and placed on board a British war vessel to cross the Atlantic.

Lincoln had mixed feelings over the affair. To Horace Porter and others, on their request, he later gave what he regarded as the essentials. "It was a pretty bitter pill to swallow, but I contented myself with believing that England's triumph in the matter would be short-lived, and that after

ending our war successfully we would be so powerful that
we could call her to account for all the embarrassments she
had inflicted on us. I felt a good deal like the sick man in
Illinois who was told he probably hadn't many days longer
to live, and that he ought to make peace with any enemies
he might have. He said the man he hated worst of all was a
fellow named Brown in the next village and he guessed he
had better begin on him. So Brown was sent for, and when
he came the sick man began to say, in a voice 'as meek as
Moses,' that he wanted to die at peace with all his fellow
creatures, and he hoped he and Brown could now shake
hands and bury all their enmity. The scene was becoming
altogether too pathetic for Brown, who had to get out
his handkerchief and wipe the gathering tears from his eyes.
It wasn't long before he melted and gave his hand to his
neighbor, and they had a regular love-feast. After a parting that would have softened the heart of a grindstone,
Brown had about reached the room door, when the sick
man rose up on his elbow and said, 'But, see here, Brown, if
I *should* happen to get well, mind *that old grudge stands.*' "

Chapter 7

The Politics of War —
Corruption

The war cost was mounting toward $1,500,000 a day as
the winter of '61 set in. Money was pouring in and out in
larger aggregates, bigger numbers, than Federal bookkeep-
ing ever before recorded. A long-drawn battle, with money
as ammunition, had been fought between the North and
the South in Great Britain and on the continent of Europe.
The fighting—with gold, moneybags, credit—was over war
supplies. The North outbid and outbought the South.

On the revolutionary advances in communication a magazine writer had noted, "Today newspapers multiplied by millions whiten the whole country every morning like the hoar frost." Lincoln's message to Congress in December '61 swept the national horizons. Westward from Omaha gangs of linemen had strung wires to the coast. "The President's message," said a dispatch, "read in Congress at 12 o'clock on Tuesday, was received by telegraph at San Francisco, and published early on Wednesday morning."

The message maintained in austere tone throughout that the Union was intact and its Government would ride the crisis and enforce its will. Lincoln opened with "great gratitude to God for unusual good health, and most abundant harvests." Kentucky "is now decidedly, and, I think, unchangeably," ranged on the side of the Union. Missouri had passed beyond seizure by the insurrectionists. The three states of Maryland, Kentucky and Missouri, "neither of which would promise a single soldier at first, have now an aggregate of not less than forty thousand in the field, for the Union."

In this message Lincoln changed from referring to himself as "he" or "the executive." After nine months as President he was "I." Where before he had written, "The executive deems it of importance," he now wrote, "I deem it of importance."

Three territories created by the last Congress, Colorado, Dakota, Nevada, had been organized, with civil administrations inaugurated. In this, and in other gestures, the President gave the impression of a young pioneer country striding into a vast and irreckonable future. He could see, with the Union maintained, promises for the future. "There are already among us those, who, if the Union be preserved, will live to see it contain 250 millions. The struggle of today, is not altogether for today—it is for a vast future also." One argument read:

Labor is prior to, and independent of, capital. Capital is only the fruit of labor, and could never have existed if labor had not first existed. Labor is the superior of capital, and deserves much the higher consideration. Capital has its rights, which are as worthy of protection as any other rights. Nor is it denied that there is, and probably always will be, a relation between labor and capital, producing mutual benefits. The error is in assuming that the whole labor of the community exists within that relation . . . Men with their families—wives, sons, and daughters—work for themselves, on their farms, in their houses, and in their shops, taking the whole product to themselves, and asking no favors of capital on the one hand, nor of hired laborers or slaves on the other. It is not forgotten that a considerable number of persons mingle their own labor with capital—that is, they labor with their own hands, and also buy or hire others to labor for them; but this is only a mixed, and not a distinct class . . .

Again: as has already been said, there is not, of necessity, any such thing as the free hired laborer being fixed to that condition for life. Many independent men everywhere in these States, a few years back in their lives, were hired laborers . . . This is the just, and generous, and prosperous system, which opens the way to all—gives hope to all, and consequent energy, and progress, and improvement of condition to all . . .

Declaring friendship for two Negro national governments the President could see no good reason for "withholding our recognition of the independence and sovereignty of Hayti and Liberia."

Five vessels being fitted out for the slave trade had been seized and condemned. Two mates of vessels engaged in the trade had been convicted. One captain "taken with a cargo of Africans on board his vessel" had been convicted of the highest grade of offense, punishable by death.

The Confiscation Act, by which Negroes belonging, as property, to disloyal slaveholders became freemen, was scrupulously recited in terms of law. "The legal claims of certain persons to the labor and service of certain other persons have become forfeited." In such numbers had these liberated Negroes come into the Union army lines and become Federal dependents, and so sure was it that more of them would arrive for disposal, that it now became necessary to have a permanent policy for their disposal.

The message drew more approval and perhaps less hostile comment in general than either the first inaugural or the July 4 message to Congress. Its most original feature concerned Negro freedom. Delicately, tentatively, and in the strictest of legal terms pertaining to the management of property, Lincoln projected his policy of gradual compensated emancipation. In substance his proposal was that the Border Slave States might enact laws for selling their slaves to the U.S. Government, which in turn should free the slaves and then take steps to colonize them.

Though the President had reported progress in suppression of the African slave trade, the New York *Times* estimated that 30,000 Africans were landed in Cuba the current year. Corruption, bribery, secret influence bought and paid for, marked each step of a slave ship's cruise from its first port clearance to the purchase of Negro tribesmen at the African Gold Coast on to permissions to sell in Cuba and later to smuggle the slaves into the Cotton States on the Gulf of Mexico.

The organized abolitionists expected little from the President. The executive committee of the American Anti-Slavery Society in its 28th annual report scored Lincoln as "under the delusion that soft words will salve the nation's sore." They analyzed him: "A sort of bland, respectable middle-man, between a very modest Right and the most arrogant and exacting Wrong . . . He thinks slavery wrong, but opposes the immediate abolition of it; believes it ought to be kept out of the Territories, but would admit it to the Union in new States . . . affirms the equality of white men and black in natural rights, but is 'not in favor of negro citizenship.' "

Wendell Phillips held that Lincoln was honest but "as a pint-pot may be full, and yet not be so full as a quart, so there is a vast difference between the honesty of a small man and the honesty of a statesman." Governor John Andrew with Mrs. Andrew, Julia Ward Howe and James Freeman Clarke talked with the President "mostly on indifferent topics." They took leave and "were out of hearing," as Julia Ward Howe wrote, when Clarke said of Lincoln, "We have seen it in his face; hopeless honesty—that is all!" This almost tallied with Attorney General Bates' writing in his diary, "The President is an excellent man, and in the main wise, but he lacks will and purpose, and I greatly fear he has not the power to command."

There came before Lincoln the case of Nathaniel Gordon of Maine, captain of a ship which had sailed to Africa and at the mouth of the Congo River had taken on board some 900 Negroes. Captured on the high seas and convicted as a slave trader, Gordon was sentenced to death by a judge declaring, "You are soon to pass into the presence of that God of the black man as well as the white man." Lincoln read the evidence, scrutinized many respectable names on a petition for pardon. Then he wrote a death sentence giving the doomed man an extra two weeks to live. It recited:

> . . . Now, therefore, be it known, that I, Abraham Lincoln, President of the United States of America, have granted and do hereby grant unto him, the said Nathaniel Gordon, a respite of the above recited sentence, until Friday the 21st day of February, A.D. 1862, between the hours of twelve o'clock at noon and three o'clock in the afternoon of the said day, when the said sentence shall be executed.
>
> In granting this respite it becomes my painful duty to admonish the prisoner that, relinquishing all expectation of pardon by Human Authority, he refer himself alone to the mercy of the common God and Father of all men.

Thus was sent to death the first and only slave trader in the history of the United States to be tried, convicted and hanged in accordance with the Constitution and Federal law. One of the prosecuting attorneys, Ethan Allen, told of extraordinary pressure on Lincoln to pardon Gordon.

From day to day as Congress met and in discussion, inquiry, report, touched every living and immediate question shaking the American people, the President had no special collaborator and spokesman in that body. Owen Lovejoy of Illinois and Albert Gallatin Riddle of Ohio were the only radical antislavery Congressmen—and Isaac N. Arnold of Chicago the only moderate—who spoke faith in the President.

When in December Congress appointed a Committee on the Conduct of the War, Lincoln saw it as one extreme intended to check another. Among its members were D. W. Gooch of Massachusetts, George W. Julian of Indiana, John Covode of Pennsylvania and Moses F. Odell of New York. Chiefly radical antislavery Republicans, they were headstrong men of brains, courage, ability, of long training in politics and the antislavery struggle; of the group the gadfly was Julian. Nothing less than genius shone and coruscated from some facets of this committee. They were to help Lincoln, and more often to interfere with him, for a long time. They sniffed out waste and corruption; they cleared away stenches; they muddled, accused men wrongly, roused fear and suspicion, and left ranklings; they wrangled and bombinated; they played with the glory and despair of democracy.

The chairman of the committee, Benjamin Franklin Wade, strode into the White House one day and stormily told Lincoln he must throw McClellan overboard. Lincoln asked who should then be put in McClellan's place. Snorted Wade, "Anybody!" Lincoln, coolly: "Wade, *anybody* will do for you but I must have *somebody*."

Short, deep-chested, defiant-looking Ben Wade was 61, of Puritan stock, his father a Revolutionary War soldier. Day laborer on the Erie Canal, farm hand, cattle-driver, schoolteacher, prosecuting attorney of Ashtabula County, he entered the Ohio Legislature and put through a bill forbidding that body to grant divorces. He fought against passage of the Fugitive Slave Law and then fought against its enforcement. He entered the U.S. Senate in 1851 as one of the small group of antislavery men who first dared, on broad policy grounds, to challenge the Southerners.

Senator Zachariah Chandler of Michigan, another member of the committee, had driven from the Bull Run battlefield to the White House, told of the battle, and urged the President to call for a half-million more troops to show the country that the Government was "just beginning to get mad." Detroit millionaire dry-goods merchant and landowner, "Zach" Chandler was of the breed of restless, rawboned New England Yankees who had pushed west, settled up the country, made money, and were restless to make history and more money.

Lyman Trumbull, another member, who had outplayed Lincoln for election to the U.S. Senate from Illinois in 1856, was cold, shrewd, scholarly, humanitarian though no friendly mixer, accurate in statement, no demagogue, a clean politician whose word was dependable. He often suspected Lincoln as cunning if not Machiavellian. An intangible factor in the relationship of Trumbull and Lincoln was the unrelenting hatred of Mrs. Lincoln for Julia Jayne Trumbull.

The Southern Union man on the committee was Senator Andrew Johnson, whose hammer-and-tongs oratory had rung across Tennessee in loyalty to the Lincoln administration. With never a day of regular school in his life, it was said, he had learned to read while sitting cross-legged at his trade of tailor in Greenville. Marrying the 16-year-old Eliza McCardle in 1827 turned out to be one of the blessings of his life. Supporting the Breckinridge ticket in 1860, he had fought secession tooth and nail and flaunted the Union banner in a Slave State nearly encircled by Slave States. More than once he had brought out his loaded revolver facing crowds ready to lynch him.

The Republican floor leader of the House of Representatives, chairman of the Committee on Ways and Means, a gnarled thorn tree of a man, "the master mind of the House," was not a member of the Committee on the Conduct of the War, but he had helped create it. And who could read Thaddeus Stevens' heart? He was as impenetrable as Abraham Lincoln, and as lonely and incessant in his broodings on the fate of man on the cold planet Earth. His mother was the high priceless memory of his life. He talked of her often. "She worked day and night to educate me." And when he became a lawyer with practice and money, he said, "I really think the greatest gratification of my life resulted from my ability to give my mother a farm of 250 acres, and a dairy of fourteen cows."

Though Stevens limped with a clubfoot, he was a horseman and a swimmer. His tongue was often sharp and, men said, malicious and arrogant. In the Pennsylvania Legislature he had put through bills that won him the name of father of the free-school system of the state. In law practice, investments, iron and furnace projects, Thaddeus Stevens had made one fortune of $200,000, lost it, made another, and had a reputation for paying his debts to the last dollar. His recreation was gambling. An old-timer said he lost and won and didn't seem to care. "He played with consummate coolness, never lost his temper, and never increased the amount of his bet." While his fellow players "were eating and drinking with the voracity of cormorants, he never indulged in anything more stimulating than a cracker and a sip of water."

His home people liked Stevens to the extent that his re-election to Congress in 1860 was by a vote of 12,065 to his opponent's 470. Meeting a Lancaster lawyer who had double-crossed him, he stood still, leaned on his cane and slowly clipped his words: "You must be a bastard, for I knew your mother's husband and he was a gentleman and an honest man!"

When in 1842 he had moved from Gettysburg to Lancaster, he had brought with him one who became the most talked-of woman in Lancaster. Lydia Smith was the widow of a Gettysburg Negro barber, by whom she had two children. She was a comely quadroon with Caucasian features and a skin of light-gold tint, a Roman Catholic communicant with Irish eyes, her maiden name Hamilton. For 20 years she was the clean, efficient, careful housekeeper of the bachelor attorney Thaddeus Stevens, herself quiet, discreet, retiring, reputed for poise and personal dignity. Some newspapers referred to her as "Mrs. Stevens," insisting that that title was used by some who had speaking acquaintance with her.

Stevens was a familiar of the hearts of murderers and at home in the chicanery of courts and the skulduggery of evidence. After Daniel Webster's famous speech on the Compromise of 1850, Stevens' quiet wrath found words: "As I heard it, I could have cut his damned heart out." And after a neutral soothing speech of Seward in early '61, "I listened to every word and, by the living God, I haven't heard a thing."

He flashed with unexpected sarcasm; even Southern members laughed with him. Giving the floor to another member, he closed: "I now yield to Mr. B. who will make a few feeble remarks." Entering the House when a vote was being taken in a contested election case, and hearing from a party member that it was a case of "two damned rascals," he asked, "Which is *our* damned rascal?"

When Lincoln had declared a blockade of the seceded states, Stevens in a White House call made the point that a nation did not blockade its own ports and therefore the declaration of blockade was a tacit acknowledgment of Southern independence. According to Stevens, Lincoln said mildly: "Yes, that's a fact. I see the point now, but I don't know anything about the Law of Nations and I thought it was all right."

Born in 1793, Stevens had seen Jackson, Clay, Calhoun, Webster and Douglas rise and pass out. Nearly 70 now, he was bald and wore a heavy wig of black hair. An emphatic shake of the head sometimes jiggled the wig over one ear. When an abolitionist woman asked him for a lock of hair, he took off the wig and offered it to her. Scholar, wit, zealot of liberty, part fanatic, who could read the heart of limping, poker-faced old Thaddeus Stevens?

Early he had gone to warn Lincoln that Cameron had taking ways and might not be the man for War Department head. "You don't mean to say you think Cameron would steal?" Lincoln asked. "No," was the reply, "I don't think he would steal a red-hot stove." Lincoln repeated this to Cameron as good wit and perhaps a warning to be careful. Cameron insisted that Stevens must retract. So Stevens at the White House said, "Mr. Lincoln, why did you tell Cameron what I said to you?" "I thought it was a good joke and didn't think it would make him mad." "Well, he is very mad and made me promise to retract. I will now do so. I believe I told you he would *not* steal a red-hot stove. I now take that back."

In January '62 it was six months since McClellan had been put at the head of the Army of the Potomac. Money, men, bread, beef, gunpowder, arms, artillery, horses, had been given McClellan on a colossal scale. The army under him in the public prints and in common talk was rated the largest and finest known in modern history. And with this well-trained force of fresh troops he settled into winter quarters, the enemy army only two days' easy march away.

His army was made up mainly of boys in the early 20's, thousands of them 19 and under. They wrote home about their winter huts, pork and beans, coffee and soup from tin cups, epidemics of measles and mumps, digging trenches, putting up telegraph wires, clearing range for artillery with pick and shovel, throwing up earthworks, driving beef to camp, hauling military stores, dysentery, sore feet, roaches in hardtack, target practice, washing shirts and underwear in creeks and rivers.

In November McClellan wrote to his friend Barlow: "The President is perfectly honest and is really sound on the nigger question—I will answer for it now that things go right with him." Early in December Lincoln had handed McClellan a carefully worked-out memorandum asking specific and technical questions about a forward movement. McClellan kept the memorandum ten days and

sent it back with replies scribbled in pencil and a note
dismissing all of Lincoln's suggestions: ". . . I have now
my mind actively turned towards another plan of campaign." When officers of other armies called for more
troops McCellan was surprised, sometimes shocked. General Sherman wired for 75,000 men to help the Western
forces drive south; McClellan handed the dispatch to Lincoln, then at his headquarters, with the remark, "The man
is crazy."

From week to week the contact grew worse between the
political power, as embodied in Lincoln and Congress, and
the military branch that asked for what it wanted. The political power tried to give it but the military branch did not
seem to know this process was getting tiresome to the political end of the Government, which was closer to the people and the taxpayers.

Late in December McClellan fell sick with typhoid fever
and took to his bed for three weeks. During those weeks
he ran his armies, from the Atlantic to the Mississippi and
beyond, from his bed. Lincoln wrote Chase a card January 2, 1862: "I have just been with General McClellan;
and he is very much better." Days followed, however, when
others came to McClellan's bedside and did business—but
the President was kept outside, and failed to get polite
entry.

What flitted through Lincoln's mind at this time was
merely hinted at in an entry in the diary of Senator Browning: "Sunday Jany 12 A very warm day. Went to Dr. Gur-
leys Church in A.M. with dress coat & no overcoat . . . Had
long talk with the President about the war—He told me he
was thinking of taking the field himself, and suggested several plans of operation." Lincoln had been reading military
treatises drawn from the Library of Congress, had held
long conversations with officers widely versed in the theory
of war, and considered himself as having grasped a few of
the essentials.

In the Department of Missouri, General Halleck wrote
Lincoln, mutinous "foreign" regiments calling for Frémont

to command them had been disarmed; high officers were in
the plot with the soldiers, Halleck believed; public property
was robbed and plundered; discipline was going to pieces.
Lincoln wrote on Halleck's letter: "It is exceedingly discouraging. As everywhere else, nothing can be done." Lincoln gave Gustave Koerner to Halleck, saying that Koerner
could be made a brigadier general. "He is an educated and
talented German gentleman, as true a man as lives. With
his assistance you can set everything right with the Germans."

In memoranda kept by General McDowell were glimpses
of Lincoln at the time McClellan lay sick and directing his
armies. McDowell wrote of January 10, 1862: "Repaired
to the President's house at eight o'clock, P.M. Found the
President alone. Was taken into the small room in the north-
east corner. Soon after we were joined by Brigadier-General
Franklin, the Secretary of State, Governor Seward, the Secretary of the Treasury, and the Assistant-Secretary of War.
The President was greatly disturbed at the state of affairs
. . . said he was in great distress, and as he had been to
General McClellan's house, and the General did not ask
to see him; and as he must talk to somebody, he had sent
for General Franklin and myself to obtain our opinion as
to the possibility of soon commencing operations with the
Army of the Potomac. To use his own expression, 'If something was not soon done, the bottom would be out of the
whole affair; and if General McClellan did not want to
use the army, he would like to borrow it provided he could
see how it could be made to do something.'"

Two nights later somewhat the same group met—with
McClellan present, up and out of bed. He refused to discuss
proposed movements of the army. "Much conversation ensued, of rather a general character," ran McDowell's memorandum. "The Secretary of the Treasury then put a direct
question to General McClellan to the effect as to what he
intended doing with his army, and when he intended doing
it?" After a long silence McClellan said a movement in
Kentucky was to precede any from Washington. "After

another pause he said he must say he was very unwilling to develop his plans, always believing that in military matters the fewer persons who were knowing them the better; that he would tell them if he was *ordered* to do so. The President then asked him if he counted upon any particular time; he did not ask what that time was, but had he in his own mind any particular time a movement could be commenced. He replied he had. Then, rejoined the President, I will adjourn this meeting."

Now that McClellan was up and they could get at him, the Committee on the Conduct of the War called him for a consultation. Senator Chandler spoke bluntly: "General McClellan, if I understand you correctly, before you strike at the rebels you want to be sure of plenty of room so that you can run in case they strike back." And this was seconded by Wade's sneer, "Or in case you get scared." McClellan then went into an explanation for the Senators of how wars are fought and how necessary it is for generals to have always available lines of retreat as well as lines of communication and supply.

Lincoln, while refusing to remove McClellan from command, as urged by radicals, was getting ready to let McClellan know who held authority. He issued on January 27 his General War Order No. 1, fixing February 22, 1862, as "the day for a general movement of the Land and Naval forces of the United States against the insurgent forces." He named the army "at & about, Fortress Monroe," the Army of the Potomac, the Army of Western Virginia, the army near Munfordville, Kentucky, the army and flotilla of gunboats at Cairo, Illinois, and a naval force in the Gulf of Mexico as ordered to be ready to move on that day. Department heads, commanders and subordinates "will severally be held to their strict and full responsibilities, for the prompt execution of this order." Four days later he followed this with "President's Special War Order No. 1" commanding that the Army of the Potomac, after providing for the defense of Washington, move on February 22 to seize and occupy Manassas Junction, "all details to be in the discretion of the general-in-chief." To this last he added a note to McClellan on February 3 urging his plan for a land attack on the Confederate army near Washington rather than an expedition by water for a peninsular attack on Richmond:

> ... If you will give me satisfactory answers to the following questions, I shall gladly yield my plan to yours. Does not your plan involve a greatly larger expenditure of *time,* and *money* than mine? Wherein is a victory *more certain* by your plan than mine? Wherein is a victory *more valuable* by your plan than mine? In fact, would it not be *less* valuable, in this, that it would break no great line of the enemie's communications, while mine would? In case of disaster, would not a retreat be more difficult by your plan than mine?

McClellan replied on the same day with a long letter showing his belief that by rapid enveloping movements on the peninsula near Richmond he could take the Confederate capital. A direct land attack on the Confederate army near Washington he could not approve. But he did have a mental picture of what he was going to do, for, wrote Secretary Chase, he came February 13 and said, "In ten days I shall be in Richmond . . . The ten days passed away; no movement, and no preparation for a movement, had been made."

McClellan gave consent to Lincoln's plucking Frémont from his retirement. There was created the Mountain Department in West Virginia, where Frémont took command of 25,000 men, later reinforced by 10,000. He was to follow a pet plan of Lincoln's, which he approved. The idea was to march over the mountains into East Tennessee, lend strength to the Unionist sentiment which dominated there, and seize the railroad at Knoxville. McClellan had no objections. And for the time being Lincoln had found a niche for the political and military figure about whom there clung such an aura of romance that thousands of boy babies in antislavery families were named Frémont.

A jobber from Vermont, Jim Fisk, twisted his swagger mustache and grinned with a cock of his eye, "You can sell anything to the government at almost any price you've got the guts to ask." His suite at Willard's welcomed Congressmen to a Havana cigar, a favorite drink and any kind of a dicker that would pay.

A report to Congress in December by the Committee on Government Contracts threw light on curious commissions and special favors, exorbitant prices charged the Government, and low-quality goods and articles delivered to the Army and Navy. Corruption so underlay the Government, wrote General Sherman in a private letter, that "even in this time of trial, cheating in clothes, blankets, flour, bread, everything, is universal."

To a resolution directing that the Secretary of War furnish the Senate with information as to contracts, amounts, names of contractors, dates, payments of money, Cameron made no reply. Months passed and Cameron sent neither information nor excuses nor regrets nor acknowledgments to the Senate.

Part of the clamor that arose was political and aimed at smearing the administration. Part of it traced to the jealousy of contractors and special interests not in favor with Cameron. Of this Lincoln was keenly aware. A delegation of New York and Boston bankers called on him and urged the removal of Cameron. "They talked very glibly," said Lincoln later to the portrait painter Frank B. Carpenter. Lincoln finally had to tell them: "Gentlemen, if you want General Cameron removed, you have only to bring me *one proved* case of dishonesty, and I promise you his 'head.' But I assure you I am not going to act on what seems to me the most unfounded gossip."

Firearms scandals were disposed of in a single sentence that, coming from Cameron with no facts or data, might be read in several ways: "Combinations among manufacturers, importers, and agents, for the sale of arms, have, in many cases, caused an undue increase in prices."

The catalogue of frauds and extortions was, said several journals, sickening. In the speeches of Holman, Trumbull,

Dawes, Van Wyck, was no tone of persecution or of political maneuvering. They were Republican party men who wanted to get on with the war and win it, and they were sickened by the job of having first of all to combat men of their own party within the administration whom they termed "public enemies." They said they were well aware that disturbers, gossips, spies, informers, disgruntled competitors, jealous rivals in politics and business, not to mention newspaper sensationalists, were spreading exaggerated stories and rumors; it was no time for idle chatter but one for sticking strictly to the documentary record. Interruptions of their speeches were usually requests for further information. The methods and findings of the Committee on Government Contracts were almost universally accepted. The longer addresses of Representative Charles H. Van Wyck of New York had lamentation, depth of woe. He said, "The mania for stealing seems to have run through all the relations of Government—almost from the general to the drummer-boy; from those nearest the throne of power to the merest tide-water. Nearly every man who deals with the Government seems to feel or desire that it would not long survive, and each had a common right to plunder while it lived."

Van Wyck called the roll of rascals, gave cases and names, with the amounts stolen or the extortionate profits garnered, and alluded to them as the equivalents of incendiaries, horse thieves, dancing harlots. Was it a truth or a masked traitor's lie that every star of the sky stands as a sentinel over the graves where the patriot dead sleep? "The pirates who infest the ocean are not more deserving the execration of mankind than the gang who, on land, are suffered to feast upon the sweat of the poor and the blood of the brave."

To Nicolay, Lincoln said one day amid the furor: "It is a good thing for individuals that there is a Government to shove their acts upon. No man's shoulders are broad enough to bear what must be."

In the War Department Cameron personally was slovenly as to method, seemed to have no files or records in his office, and according to Representative Riddle, "in any official matter he would ask you to give its status and what he had last said about it." On being informed, "he would look about, find a scrap of paper, borrow your pencil, make a note, put the paper in one pocket of his trousers and your pencil in the other." Once a caller had to tell him, "The last thing you did in this case, Mr. Secretary, was to put my pencil in your pocket." After fussing with the often vague and indirect Cameron it was a relief, said Riddle, to go to Assistant Secretary Thomas A. Scott and meet an "electric brain and cool quiet manner."

Slowly the President had arrived at his appraisal, given to Nicolay, that Cameron was utterly ignorant and, regardless of the course of things, obnoxious to the country, selfish, incapable of organizing details, and—least of all—"openly discourteous to the President." To Sumner, A. B. Ely was writing: "Thaddeus Stevens said Cameron would add a million to his fortune. I guess he has done it."

The first open break between Lincoln and Cameron came in December '61 when the Secretary issued his annual report. Without having consulted the Executive, Cameron was thrusting himself forward as a spokesman of administration policy. The slave property of rebels should be confiscated, declared the paragraph that surprised and offended the President: "It is as clearly a right of the Government to arm slaves, when it may become necessary, as it is to use gunpowder taken from the enemy. Whether it is expedient to do so is purely a military question . . . If it shall be found that the men who had been held by the rebels are capable of bearing arms and performing efficient military service, it is the right, and may become the duty of the Government to arm and equip them, and employ their services against the rebels."

As Lincoln first glanced at the copy from the public printer placed in his hands, and his eye rested on the passage about arming the slaves, he was instantly aroused. And as the incident later came to the painter Carpenter, Lincoln spoke decisively: "This will never do! General Cameron must take no such responsibility. That is a question which belongs exclusively to me!" Telegrams went to the postmasters of the leading cities. The Cameron report was mailed back to Washington. A new edition was printed with the closing paragraph of the first edition omitted and a new paragraph substituted.

Newspapers had easily gotten copies of the Cameron report and published the suppressed paragraph alongside the final official one. The difference between the two was that the first sounded as though the administration was about ready to throw Negro troops into the war, while the later one suggested that the administration was still hesitating. Bursts of approval came from the antislavery ranks for Cameron, though it seemed on the part of Cameron too sudden a conversion to the cause of the Negro, in which he had hitherto been no radical. In the crusader's mantle he was a comic.

Both Lincoln and Cameron knew they had come to the parting of the ways. "Having corrected his minister's haste and imprudence," wrote Nicolay and Hay, "the President indulged in no further comment . . . They met in Cabinet consultations, or for the daily dispatch of routine business, with the same cordial ease as before." Cameron began to hint that his War Department duties wearied him and he would prefer a foreign mission. Lincoln said nothing for several weeks. Then a note of January 11, 1862, written by Lincoln to Cameron was made public: "As you have, more than once, expressed a desire for a change of position, I can now gratify you, consistently with my view of the public interest. I therefore propose nominating you to the Senate, next Monday, as minister to Russia."

In a private letter of the same date Lincoln wrote to Cameron that Cassius Marcellus Clay was returning from the post of Minister to Russia to fight for his country as a major general, and therefore the President could now offer that post to Mr. Cameron. "Should you accept it, you will bear with you the assurance of my undiminished confidence, of my affectionate esteem . . ." This letter, subscribed "Very sincerely Your friend, A. Lincoln," could be used by Cameron either at the court of the Czar or in

Pennsylvania political circles for the information of any who wished to know how matters stood between him and the President. Cameron's reply of the same date "with profound respect" acknowledged the "kind and generous tone" of the President's letter.

Four days the Senate wrestled behind closed doors on the President's naming Cameron Minister to Russia. Cameron was confirmed January 17 by a vote of 28 to 14.

No other member of Lincoln's Cabinet seemed to have the complete approval accorded Edwin McMasters Stanton to replace Cameron. A Jackson Democrat replacing an ousted secessionist in President Buchanan's Cabinet as the Cotton States were seceding, he confidentially advised Seward and other Unionists of what went on in Cabinet meetings. Since then Stanton had been legal adviser to McClellan, to Cameron, John Dix and others. As the days passed he wrote letters to Buchanan, to Dix, to others, referring to "the painful imbecility of Lincoln," mentioning "distrust in the sincerity of Lincoln." He heard this and that and sped it onward in letters. "It is said that Lincoln takes the precaution of seeing no strangers alone." Bull Run was "another imbecility of the administration"; it was "the result of Lincoln's running the machine for five months." McClellan wrote as though amused and somewhat baffled by Stanton's frequently referring to Lincoln as to the "original gorilla."

Often in handling people Stanton seemed to manage a fierce glare and a domineering, tempestuous manner. He was crazy or sick, more often just plainly difficult, according to various people. In fact, asthma was the lesser of his afflictions. Before Cameron sent to Lincoln his report favoring the arming of Negroes for Union service, he called in his legal adviser, Stanton. And Stanton gave approval to this clause and wrote an additional paragraph which Cameron adopted and inserted. By a tortuous path this nervous, asthmatic, strong man of many contradictions had come to be head of a War Department having authority over 600,000 soldiers. Moderates or conservatives like Seward, Cameron and McClellan endorsed him while in the same moment the radicals Chase, Wade and Sumner were saying, "He is one of us."

Stanton, the son of a widowed mother, at 13 years of age took care of her and a family of five. Working his way through Kenyon College, clerking in a bookstore in Columbus, Ohio, he met Mary Lamson, daughter of an Episcopal clergyman, carefully educated and, like himself, poor. They took their honeymoon in a 125-mile sleigh ride from Columbus to Cadiz, Ohio, where he began law practice, made money from the start, was known as stiff and proud rather than sociable, on occasion designated as "cheeky."

"He is accounted the first lawyer in America," said the Chicago *Tribune* of Stanton. That, however, took no account of the moody and hectic Stanton, of the weird undergrowth of behavior swarming behind his black whiskers and black bushy hair, his spectacled nearsighted eyes with a vehement stare, his stocky and deep-chested body. As a boy he trained snakes, and once horrified a quiet family of women and children by entering their home with two large wriggling snakes around his neck. When his child Lucy died, after her body had been buried a year he had it exhumed, cremated, and placed the ashes in a metal box which he kept in his own room.

The wife of his youth died in childbirth in 1844 and Stanton insisted she must wear her wedding clothes for burial. For years he went twice a week to decorate her grave, on Sundays always going alone, "to meet her," he said. Twelve years passed before he married the daughter of a wealthy merchant in Pittsburgh.

Stanton's favorite relaxation was to leave home of a morning with a market basket on his arm, walk slowly along to the grocer's and huckster's, and shop for the home pantry and icebox. He knew the Constitution and the price of eggs and was solemn about both. Born of a Quaker strain, he was raised a Methodist and became a devoted communicant of the Episcopal church. In odd intervals he was writing a book to be called *Poetry of God,* he told Donn Piatt. A vortex of action called. He sat in Buchanan's Cabinet across a table from John B. Floyd, secessionist and Secretary of War, as Floyd urged withdrawal of troops from Charleston Harbor. Stanton exploded with wrath, declaring that the surrender of Fort Sumter would be a crime equal to treason and all who took a hand in it should be hanged. Then months had passed with history in a whirligig, events seen in a mist, and he sat in Donn Piatt's room in Washington replying to a query from Mr. and Mrs. Piatt. "Yes, I am going to be Secretary of War to Old Abe." "What will you do?" was asked. "Do? . . . I will make Abe Lincoln President of the United States. I will force this man McClellan to fight or throw up."

At the War Department, at ten o'clock in the morning a room 15 by 20 feet began to fill up with claim agents, contractors, relatives of soldiers, Senators and Congressmen, all unable to get a private interview with the department head. At 11 there was a buzz and a stir and Stanton walked in, speaking to no one till he reached a high desk opposite the entrance. Then he picked out one by one those he would do business with. To a gushing office seeker he might say, "Sit down, sir, I'll attend to you by-and-by." He might roar at an officer, even a major general in brass buttons and gold stars: "Come, sir, what are you doing in Washington? You are not needed here. I'll see about mustering you out."

Some were troubled over the new titan who might go too far and try to run away with the whole concern, they told Lincoln. He drawled: "We may have to treat him as they are sometimes obliged to treat a Methodist minister I know of out West. He gets wrought up to so high a pitch of excitement in his prayers and exhortations, that they are obliged to put bricks in his pockets to keep him down. We may be obliged to serve Stanton in the same way, but I guess we'll let him jump awhile first."

Every day Stanton had his errands at the White House. At any hour he might be seen walking from the War Office taking telegrams, letters, official business, to the President. And Lincoln stepped over to the War Office nearly every day, sometimes during large troop movements or battles spending hours with his War Secretary over the latest wire news. The President gave wide and free play to Stanton's capacity for hard work and Stanton's enjoyment of personal power. In office less than two weeks, Stanton ordered the arrest of General Charles P. Stone in the Ball's Bluff disaster.

On Stanton's announcing to him the news of the arrest, the President said, "I suppose you have good reasons for it; and having good reasons, I am glad I knew nothing of it until it was done." Willie Lincoln lay sick with fever, and later in connection with the Stone affair the President wrote, "Owing to sickness in my family, the Secretary of War made the arrest without notifying me that he had it in contemplation." To a Senate request for information three months later the President answered: "In relation to Brigadier General Stone . . . he has not been tried because in the state of military operations, at the time of his arrest and since, the officers to constitute a court-martial, and for witnesses, could not be withdrawn from duty without serious injury to the service. He will be allowed a trial without any unnecessary delay; the charges and specifications will be furnished him in due season; and every facility for his defence will be afforded him by the War Department." And Stone was held in Fort Lafayette prison 189 days, released without trial and without charges having been preferred against him, then again restored to his brigadier shoulder straps.

Lincoln's response to a formal record of censure of Cameron was unexpected and took the form of a long message to Senate and House. The House had not struck at him; its language implied Lincoln had been betrayed by men he had trusted. Yet Lincoln defended those men. He reviewed the outbreak of the war, treason in all departments, and Washington beleaguered, and then gave Congress extended statements of what he had before told Congress in explanation of why he had assumed dictatorial powers.

He closed with a paragraph of explanatory comment which took all censure off Cameron and placed it on the entire administration, and which seemed to assume the situation had been so chaotic and the action so furious that it was a time to let some bygones be bygones: "Congress will see that I should be wanting equally in candor and in justice if I should leave the censure expressed in this resolution to rest exclusively or chiefly upon Mr. Cameron ... It is due to Mr. Cameron to say that, although he fully approved the proceedings, they were not moved nor suggested by himself, and that not only the President but all the other heads of departments were at least equally responsible with him for whatever error, wrong, or fault was committed in the premises."

Nicolay and Hay noted: "Cameron gratefully remembered this voluntary and manly defense of his official integrity. He remained one of the most intimate and devoted of Lincoln's personal friends."

The great industrial State of Pennsylvania—with its iron and coal—nearest to Washington and most liable to invasion, was not to be torn by the political warfare and disruption that would have followed the particular sort of degradation Cameron's enemies would have put on him. The unblemished abolitionist Congressman Owen Lovejoy, with a curiously steady light of conscience for a lamp to his feet, might have dropped the word to Lincoln to try Cameron longer.

Yet the unremitting quest of individual profits and personal fortunes, behind war fronts where men were dying for proclaimed sacred causes, made a contrast heavy for the human mind to hold and endure.

Chapter 8

Donelson — Grant — Shiloh — Monitor *and*
Merrimac — *"Seven Days" — The Draft*

Lincoln called to Washington James B. Eads, a St. Louis man who had spent many days on the bottom sand and mud of the Mississippi River, salvaging ships with a diving bell he invented. Eads, back in St. Louis and under Government contract, got 4,000 men over the country working on his plans. In 100 days he had ready eight iron-plated, steam-propelled gunboats. These and more made up a flotilla com-manded by Andrew H. Foote, a Connecticut Yankee Puri-tan sea dog, who in 1856 had lost 40 of his own men and killed 400 Chinese in the Canton River of China, who never swore nor drank nor allowed intoxicating liquor on ship-board; his prayer meetings and sermons among seamen were a topic in naval and other circles.

On February 6, 1862, Commodore Foote's gunboats es-corted steamboats down the Tennessee River carrying 18 regiments under Brigadier General Ulysses S. Grant. They crowded the decks watching the scenery, 18,000 troops—cornhuskers, teamsters, rail splitters, shopmen, factory hands, college students, from Iowa, Nebraska, Illinois, In-diana, Ohio, Missouri, many of them not yet old enough to vote.

The gunboats stopped at Fort Henry, shelled it, and troops marched in and took its flag. The Confederate gar-rison had left for Fort Donelson on the Cumberland River. Grant marched his army 12 miles across country to Fort Donelson in fair weather, warm and balmy.

Foote took his gunboats up to the Mississippi, down to Cumberland, and exchanging shots with the Fort Donelson guns was disabled so that he had to steam upriver. This left Grant with 27,000 troops, counting new arrivals, to contest with 18,000 troops inside a fort. Before the fighting began a cold wind came, snow fell, the roads froze. In ten-above-zero weather men fired and loaded their muskets, and in the night huddled and shivered, seeking fences, brush, trees, logs, to keep off the wind. Neither side dared light a bivouac fire. Men and boys were found next morning frozen stiff.

On Sunday, February 16, telegrams began trickling into the War Department in Washington. General Simon B. Buckner, commanding Fort Donelson, had sent a messen-ger to Grant asking for "terms of capitulation" and Grant replied: "No terms except an unconditional and immediate surrender can be accepted. I propose to move immediately upon your works." And the Confederate commander was surrendering the fort and 13,828 prisoners. The battle losses were: Union, 500 killed, 2,108 wounded, 224 missing; Confederate, 231 killed, 1,534 wounded. The victory clinched Kentucky to the Union, gave a foothold in Tennessee, sent Union armies 200 miles forward into enemy territory. It lighted up the gloom of the North and the hopes of Lincoln.

Ulysses S. Grant, an Ohio boy, graduated at West Point as number 21 in a class of 39. At West Point he rode a horse over a hurdle six feet six, a new record. At Monterey in the Mexican War he went for ammunition relief, riding under fire in Comanche style, clinging to the saddle with one leg while holding his head and body close to the side of the horse away from the enemy. He was five feet eight in height, wore a full beard, was nearly always a little disheveled, even sat for his picture with coat or hair in disorder. He had quiet manners, gravity, gray eyes, and a face with economy of expression.

At Fort Vancouver on the West Coast in 1854 no works or projects challenged him. He was homesick, carried in his inside coat pocket a worn pack of letters from his wife. Grant had married her without a regular proposal; they were buggy-riding across a flooded bridge when she cried, "I'm going to cling to you no matter what happens," and safely over, he asked, "How would you like to cling to me for the rest of your life?"

One day there came to Fort Vancouver a locket holding a long thin braid of a woman's hair interwoven with a little curl of a child's hair; this Grant wore around his neck. Why did he drink harder at this time? Was it loneliness for home? For he was warned that as a captain his drunkenness was bad for the regiment. He wrote out a blank resignation and gave it to the colonel; it was to be dated and sent to the War Department if whisky again got the best of him, which it did. He quit the Army.

Grant cleared land on 80 acres near St. Louis left to him by his wife's father. He became accustomed to two slaves given to his wife by her father, a slaveholder. He hauled wood ten miles into St. Louis at $10 a cord. He built himself a two-story house of logs, a masterpiece of simple design and craftsmanship, and named the place Hardscrabble. They traded Hardscrabble for a house and lot in St. Louis. As a real-estate salesman Grant failed. Friends said ague and rheumatism still held him; chills shook him on spring afternoons, weakened him so that he was dizzy and had to be helped to the omnibus he rode home in. He looked glum and felt useless. The family moved to Galena, Illinois, where he was selling hides to shoemakers and harness- and saddlemakers, his income $800 a year, when the war commenced. He went to Springfield, Illinois, was made colonel, and took a regiment to Missouri.

Chaplain James B. Crane, bringing him the *Missouri Democrat* one day in August, said, "I see that you are made brigadier-general." "Well, sir," said Grant, "that's some of Washburne's work. I knew Washburne in Galena. He was a strong Republican and I was a Democrat, and I thought from that he never liked me very much."

The country had now nicknamed him "Unconditional Surrender" Grant. Halleck wired McClellan, "His army seems to be as much demoralized by the victory of Fort Donelson as was that of the Potomac by the defeat of Bull Run." McClellan believed he understood the case, and wired back, "Do not hesitate to arrest Grant at once if the good of the service requires it."

Against intrigue, connivance and slander, Lincoln gave to Grant the stars of a major general. The President was more than interested in this plain fighter who had given the Union cause its first victories worth mentioning. Lincoln saw among the driving motives in the Fort Donelson victory the passion of the Northwest, his own region, for nationalism, for an unbreakable Union of States.

The laughter at McClellan was now wry, bitter. The Western forces had battled and won big points sooner than commanded in Lincoln's order setting February 22 as the day for a general movement of land and sea forces. Washington's Birthday came while McClellan's colossal Army of the Potomac kept to its tents and winter huts around Washington. Johnston nearby at Manassas had in his Confederate army less than one man for McClellan's three.

A clerk who handled much of the White House mail, William O. Stoddard, noted that Lincoln was "intensely, absorbingly interested" in the February 22 advance he had ordered. A staff officer from McClellan came and began explanations of why the advance could not be made February 22. "Why?" asked the President. The officer murmured, "The pontoon trains are not ready," and was interrupted, "Why in hell and damnation *ain't* they ready?" And as Stoddard saw it: "The officer could think of no satisfactory reply, but turned very hastily and left the room. Mr. Lincoln turned to the table and resumed the work before him."

Lincoln now stepped publicly into the handling of the Army of the Potomac, to the extent of publishing on March 7 and 8 his General War Orders No. 2 and No. 3. One directed McClellan to organize his army for active field operations into four corps, Lincoln naming the generals to command. The second ordered that whatever the field operations might take, enough troops should be left in and about Washington to leave the capital secure. This and other matters brought McClellan to the White House. On Sunday, March 9, while McClellan sat in conference with Lincoln and Stanton, a message came with news that Johnston's army at Manassas had moved out of its entrenchments, broken from winter quarters, and moved southward, leaving as mementoes many "Quaker guns"—logs on wheels, painted to look like cannon.

McClellan, shocked into action, that very Sunday ordered his army to march. At three the next morning he telegraphed Stanton, "The troops are in motion." He arrived at Bull Run Creek, at Manassas, and found it as reported— empty. Then he marched his army back again to Washington. To those asking why he did not push on, find the enemy and attack, he let it be known he was giving his troops a practice maneuver.

Among powerful financial, transportation and industrial

interests gathered around such individuals as August Belmont, William H. Aspinwall, Cyrus McCormick, James Gordon Bennett, there was still faith in McClellan. Slowly too the impression grew in some circles that McClellan was interfered with too much by Stanton, by War Office bureaucrats, by the suspicious antislavery radicals.

Browning asked Lincoln if he still had confidence in McClellan and wrote: "He assured me he had . . . That he [McClellan] had now gone to Fortress Monroe with his Command, with orders to move on Richmond without delay, and that only on yesterday when McClelland came to take leave of him preparatory to marching, he shed tears when speaking of the cruel imputations upon his loyalty, and defending himself against them The President added that Genl Scott, and all the leading military men around him, had always assured him that McClelland possessed a very high order of military talent, and that he did not think they could all be mistaken . . . that he had studied McClelland . . . that he thought he had the capacity to make arrangements properly for a great conflict, but as the hour for action approached he became nervous and oppressed with the responsibility and hesitated to meet the crisis, but that he had given him peremptory orders to move now, and he must do it."

Eight days later Browning wrote of seeing the President and "He told me he was becoming impatient and dissatisfied with McClellan's sluggishness of action."

Lincoln had ordered McDowell with 40,000 troops to stay in and near Washington. The capture of the national capital would probably bring Britain and France to recognize the Confederate Government, the blockade would be broken, arms and supplies would pour into the South. Lincoln wrote McClellan: "My explicit order that Washington should, by the judgment of *all* the commanders of Army corps, be left entirely secure, had been neglected. It was precisely this that drove me to detain McDowell."

Then came bickering. McClellan was to claim he must have more troops. The War Office would ask why he did not have more than he claimed. "There is a curious mystery about the *number* of troops now with you," wrote Lincoln. "When I telegraphed you on the 6th. saying you had over 100,000 with you, I had just obtained from the Secretary of War, a statement, taken as he said, from your own returns, making 108,000 then with you, and *en route* to you. You now say you will have but 85,000 when all *en route* to you shall have reached you. How can the discrepancy of 23,000 be accounted for?" He tried gently to prod McClellan into moving forward and fighting. "Once more let me tell you, it is indispensable to *you* that you strike a blow. *I* am powerless to help this."

McClellan wrote his wife: "I have raised an awful row about McDowell's corps. The President very coolly telegraphed me . . . that he thought I had better break the enemy's lines at once! I was much tempted to reply that he had better come and do it himself." It also troubled McClellan that the President issued an order limiting his command to that of the Army of the Potomac. He wrote his wife of "rascality" and "traitors" in Washington.

In such a mood McClellan in April '62 headed the Army of the Potomac, on the peninsula before the Confederate entrenchments at Yorktown. Moving this army from Washington by water had required 113 steamers, 188 schooners, 88 barges, hauling for three weeks 121,500 men, 14,592 animals, 1,150 wagons, 44 batteries, 74 ambulances, besides pontoon bridges, telegraph materials, equipage, cattle, food, supplies.

McClellan kept his army at Yorktown for weeks while he threw up entrenchments, built batteries, installed big guns. "Do not misunderstand the apparent inaction here," he wrote to Lincoln. "Not a day, not an hour has been lost. Works have been constructed that may almost be called gigantic." And when at last McClellan's big guns were set to blow the enemy off the map, when finally Union troops moved out to capture the foe, they found nobody to fight. Again he had not heard Lincoln's warning: "the present hesitation to move upon an intrenched enemy, is but the story of Manassas repeated."

When at last after a month of siege the empty Confederate entrenchments were captured, McClellan telegraphed: "Yorktown is in our possession . . . No time shall be lost . . . I shall push the enemy to the wall." The total force under Johnston, who had evacuated, numbered 55,633 men, about one to two of McClellan's. They had waited till McClellan had finished building elaborate batteries, till McClellan was perfectly satisfied that he could shell and shatter all opposition. Then they drew off.

Other actions were staged elsewhere and with different results. Three days' fighting went on at Pea Ridge in the northwest corner of Arkansas between Missouri, Iowa, Illinois and Ohio regiments against Missouri, Arkansas and Texas regiments along with three Red Indian regiments. The Union forces lost 203 killed, 972 wounded, 174 missing, as against 800 to 1,000 killed, 200 to 300 missing, of the Confederates. The battle clinched Missouri deeper into the Union.

An action came as "a thrust into the vitals of the Confederacy." The sea dogs Commodore David Glasgow Farragut and Commodore David Dixon Porter, with battleships and mortar boats, along with Major General Ben Butler heading an army of land troops, ran and battered their way through the forts and batteries at New Orleans and captured the largest seaport and the most important metropolitan center of the South, a city of 168,000. An army of 10,000 Confederates left the city, their torches lighting 15,000 bales of cotton, a dozen large ships, several fine steamboats, unfinished gunboats and property worth millions of dollars.

In charge of the city as its military governor came Ben Butler, the former Breckinridge proslavery Democrat who had at one time striven to nominate Jefferson Davis for the Presidency of the United States. Butler tried to regulate newspapers, the food supply, money, flags permitted or prohibited. Regulating the women was no simple affair. They drew aside their skirts when they met Union officers and soldiers. They grimaced and taunted. They spat on the

Union flag. They stepped off the sidewalk rather than pass a Yankee. Butler arrested the mayor, the chief of police and others, and put them in the guardhouse of a captured fort. In time the new governor was to be known among Southerners as "Beast Butler" or "Butler the Beast," or in token of stolen silverware, "Spoons Butler."

On the Tennessee River near the Mississippi State line at Shiloh Church and Pittsburg Landing, General Albert Sidney Johnston had hurled 40,000 Confederate troops in attack on 36,000 under Grant. The Union lines were steadily forced back. Would night find them driven to the bank of the wide Tennessee River and no bridge to cross? Sherman had three horses shot under him, got a bullet in the hand, another through his hat; a third grazed his shoulder. One tree about as thick as a lean man received 90 bullets, another tree 60. In a clearing between woodlands men lay so thick that careful walking was required not to step on the dead.

Toward evening Grant sat his horse, watching the Confederates try to take a hill guarded by a battery and Union gunboats. Someone asked him if things looked gloomy. He answered: "Delay counts for everything with us. Tomorrow we shall attack them with fresh troops, and drive them, of course." Darkness fell on the Sabbath slaughter. Rain came in torrents on the tentless soldiers of the two armies. In the gray of dawn the Union troops moved in attack and that day, reinforced by 20,000 under Buell and 6,000 under Lew Wallace, drove the enemy to retreat. Albert Sidney Johnston, counted one of the most brilliant of Confederate commanders, was killed the day before, it was learned. The Union army lost 13,047 in killed, wounded and missing, the Confederates 10,694.

The President issued a proclamation: "It has pleased Almighty God to vouchsafe signal victories to the land and naval forces engaged in suppressing an internal rebellion, and at the same time to avert from our country the dangers of foreign intervention and invasion." He recommended to the people that "at their next weekly assemblages in their accustomed places of public worship" they should "especially acknowledge and render thanks to our Heavenly Father for these inestimable blessings." He spoke of hope for peace, harmony and unity in his own country, and beyond that "the establishment of fraternal relations among all the countries of the earth."

At first the joy over victory ran high in the North. Then this was modified by a widely spread story that Grant was drunk at Shiloh. Lincoln received at the White House one night at 11 o'clock his friend A. K. McClure, who as spokesman for a number of Republicans talked for nearly two hours on how "the tide of popular sentiment" was against Grant and Grant should be dismissed from the service so that the President could retain the confidence of the country. Lincoln let McClure talk with few interruptions. Then, as McClure reported it: "When I had said every thing that could be said from my standpoint, we lapsed into silence. Lincoln remained silent for what seemed a very long time. He then gathered himself up in his chair and said, in a tone of earnestness that I shall never forget, 'I can't spare this man—he fights!' "

In Richmond on February 22, 1862, Jefferson Davis had taken his inauguration oath for a six-year term of office. Heavy rain fell while President Davis under a canvas cover addressed a big crowd holding umbrellas: "After a series of successes and victories . . . we have recently met with serious disasters." He was referring to Fort Donelson. Pale, worn, resolved, and around him men also resolved, they would consecrate their toil, property, lives, to a nation of their own. Tears trickled down the faces of gray-headed men of the planter aristocracy. They joined in silence in the prayer of Davis spoken across the rain: "Acknowledging the Providence which has so visibly protected the Confederacy during its brief but eventful career, to Thee, O God! I trustingly commit myself, and prayerfully invoke Thy blessing on my country and its cause."

And in the White House the President was hit hard by a personal grief. The boys Tad and Willie, joined by two playmates from Cincinnati, Bud and Holly Taft, were often a comfort to him. Once they took rags and old clothes and made a doll they named Jack. In red baggy trousers, with a tight blue jacket and a red fez on his head, this Jack was a Zouave. And they sentenced Jack to be shot at sunrise for sleeping on picket duty. They were burying Jack when the head gardener asked, "Why don't you have Jack pardoned?" Into the White House chased the four boys, upstairs to a desk where a man dropped his work, heard them, and soberly wrote on a sheet of Executive Mansion stationery:

> The doll Jack is pardoned.
> By order of the President
>   A. LINCOLN

To Julia Taft, sister of Bud and Holly, Tad gave this pardon paper, saying there would be no burying of Jack. In a week, however, Jack was hanging by the neck, dangling from the branch of a big bush in the garden, Tad saying, "Jack was a traitor and a spy."

Tad was dashing, valorous, often impudent; Willie more thoughtful and imaginative. All the main railroad stations from New York to Chicago were in Willie's memory and at his tongue's end. He could call them off, including Troy, Schenectady, Utica, Rome, including Ashtabula, Cleveland, Sandusky, Toledo. He spent hours drawing up timetables and would conduct an imaginary train from Chicago to New York with perfect precision. Also Willie spent hours curled up in a chair enjoying books, a grave, delicate boy. In his diary Attorney General Bates wrote that Willie was too much "idolized" by his parents. The boy had rare lights —and the father and mother made much of him.

Willie Lincoln went riding on his pony in a chilly rain and fell sick with a cold and fever in February '62, at a time when a White House ball was planned. The President spoke of the ball to Miss Dorothea Dix, wanted to stop it, had it announced officially there would be no dancing. "But the Marine band at the foot of the steps filled the house with music while the boy lay dying above," wrote one woman. "A sadder face than that of the President I have rarely seen.

He was receiving at the large door of the East Room, speaking to the people as they came, but feeling so deeply that he spoke of what he felt and thought, instead of welcoming the guests. To General Frémont he at once said that his son was very ill and he feared for the result . . . The ball was becoming a ghastly failure."

During the next few days Willie called for Bud Taft, who came and held his hand. The President would come in, lean over and stroke Willie's hair. "Better go to bed, Bud," he said one night. Bud answered, "If I go he will call for me." Still another night Lincoln came in, found Bud asleep, picked him up and carried him off to another room.

A few days later Willie lay still and cold. Elizabeth Keckley, the mulatto seamstress and Mrs. Lincoln's trusted companion, wrote, "The light faded from his eyes, and the death-dew gathered on his brow." She had been on watch but did not see the end, telling of it: "I was worn out with watching, and was not in the room when Willie died, but was immediately sent for. I assisted in washing and dressing him, and then laid him on the bed, when Mr. Lincoln came in." He lifted the cover from the face of his child, gazed at it long, and murmured, "It is hard, hard, hard to have him die!" The mother wept long hours, moaned and shook with grief.

They closed down the lids over the blue eyes of the boy, parted his brown hair, put flowers from his mother in his pale, crossed hands, and soldiers, Senators, Cabinet officers, foreign Ministers, came to the funeral. The mother, too far spent, could not come. The body was later sent west to Illinois for burial. And the mother clutched at his memory and if his name was mentioned her voice shook and the tears came. "She could not bear to look upon his picture," said Mrs. Keckley. "And after his death she never crossed the threshold of the Guest's Room in which he died, or the Green Room in which he was embalmed."

The grief over Willie was hard to shake off; a month later in answering a letter which should have had an earlier reply the President wrote of "a domestic affliction" which "has delayed me so long." Among letters of condolence that had come was one, softhearted and sincere, from ex-President Pierce, mentioning that he too had once lost a boy he loved and could understand the grief.

On Sunday, March 9, 1862, news came that sent Secretary Welles hurrying to the President, who at once called the Cabinet. A U.S. 40-gun frigate, the *Merrimac,* had been fitted by the Confederates with a cast-iron ram, and covered with four-inch iron plates. On Saturday afternoon, she had met two Union war vessels, the *Congress* and the *Cumberland,* and shot and rammed their wooden hulls till they were helpless. Another Union war vessel, the *Minnesota,* also wooden, had been run aground. And the news was that the *Merrimac* would on Sunday morning be free to move on Washington or New York.

Welles told of one hope; the *Monitor,* a new type of seafighting craft, had arrived at Hampton Roads the night before. When Welles mentioned to Stanton that the *Monitor* carried only two guns, "his mingled look of incredulity and contempt cannot be described," wrote Welles. ". . . To me there was throughout the whole day something inexpressibly ludicrous in the wild, frantic talk, action, and rage of Stanton as he ran from room to room . . . swung his arms, scolded, and raved."

Stanton got Admiral Dahlgren to make ready 60 rock-laden canalboats to be sunk in the Potomac and obstruct the *Merrimac.* But Dahlgren refused to take further orders from the Secretary of War; he was in the Navy and that department had its own Secretary. According to Welles: "Stanton claimed that, instead of consulting and asking, the military could order naval assistance, and that it was the duty of the Secretary of the Navy and of naval officers to render it. President Lincoln would not, however, lend himself to this view of the subject."

Towed by a tug out of New York Harbor three days before, the little *Monitor* met rough weather; water broke over the engines, down the blower pipes and smokestacks;

hand pumps were rigged and worked. Then the wind and high waves went down, or the *Monitor* would have gone to sea bottom. Once again fighting rough sea in shoals the captain and crew wondered if the hawser running to the tug would hold. It did and they rode out two storms.

They were a tired crew on the *Monitor*, twice nearly sunk, no food but hard sea biscuit on a storm-soaked vessel, and no sleep in 48 hours. Their commander, Lieutenant John Worden, said no captain ever had a better crew; the crew swore their captain was the best that ever walked a deck. As the Confederate *Merrimac* came on toward the *Minnesota* next morning, the little *Monitor* made straight for her, a David against a Goliath, ten guns on the *Merrimac* against two on the *Monitor*. "A cheesebox on a raft," "a tin can on a shingle," that was the *Monitor*, equipped with a revolving steel tower or turret, so that she could shoot from any position; and her raftlike deck was so low that it would be difficult for the big *Merrimac* to ram her.

The tiny *Monitor* moved around the giant *Merrimac* like a fast bantamweight circling a ponderous heavyweight. The big one crashed its ten guns against the little one. And the little one did not move except to answer with its two guns. A deep thrill went round the hearts of the men handling the guns in the *Monitor* turret when the first heavy slugs of the *Merrimac* thundered their impact on the outside of the turret. Sometimes it was hard to start the turret revolving. They hoped it would not snarl. "Once the *Merrimac* tried to ram us," wrote S. Dana Greene, lieutenant commander, "but Worden avoided the direct impact by skillful use of the helm, and she struck a glancing blow which did no damage."

The *Monitor* turret ran out of shells and she drew off for 15 minutes to bring up fresh ammunition. The *Merrimac*, drawing 22 feet, could not follow the *Monitor*, which could steam into water a little over 12 feet deep. The *Monitor* came back; again the two guns against ten trying to cripple or kill each other. "Again she came up on our quarter and fired twice," said a Confederate on the *Merrimac* after the fight. "The impact forced the side in bodily two or three inches. All the crews of the after guns were knocked over by the concussion, and bled from the nose or ears. Another shot in the same place would have penetrated."

The *Merrimac* ceased firing, and a gunnery officer was asked by his superior, "Why are you not firing, Mr. Eggleston?" "Why, our powder is very precious," called the lieutenant, "and after two hours' incessant firing I find that I can do her about as much damage by snapping my thumb at her every two minutes and a half."

At ten yards' distance a shell from the *Merrimac* hit the sighthole of the pilothouse, stunning Lieutenant Worden, filling his eyes with powder and blinding him, his face covered with blood. The *Monitor* drew off to care for its commander and to examine how badly the pilothouse was wrecked. The *Merrimac* drew off and steamed to Norfolk.

After six hours it was a drawn battle. Each side had made its mistakes. If the *Merrimac* had concentrated its entire fire on the *Monitor* pilothouse from the first, it would have destroyed the *Monitor*'s control. If the *Monitor* had shot at the *Merrimac*'s water line, where the armor was weak, it would have sunk the *Merrimac*. However, the two ships had taught the navies of the world a lesson. London and Paris declared that the era of wooden fighting craft was over. The Washington Government would now begin building a fleet of monitors. The blockade of Southern ports would go on.

In the crews of both ships were men writing home, as did S. Dana Greene, of being worn. "My men and myself were perfectly black with smoke and powder. All my underclothes were perfectly black, and my person was in the same condition . . . My nerves and muscles twitched . . . I lay down and tried to sleep—I might as well have tried to fly."

News of the battle came with pleasure to John Ericsson, the Swede who designed the *Monitor*. He grew up among mines and ironworks in Sweden, became a captain in the Army, resigned, invented an instrument for taking sea soundings, a hydrostatic weighing machine, artificial drafts that decreased smokestack size and economized fuel, a self-acting gunlock for naval cannon, a steam carriage in 1829 which ran 30 miles an hour. He came to the United States in 1839, and two years later furnished designs for a screw warship, "the first vessel having propelling machinery below water-line, out of reach of hostile shot." He improved gun carriages, optical instruments, won medals for innovations "in the management of heat."

His wife came from Sweden, joined him in New York, was as proud of his genius as he was of her beauty. And while she filled her time as best she could, Ericsson worked at the shop all day and stuck to his drawing table till midnight. After a time he found that she was, as he said, "jealous of a steam-engine." So she went to England. Ericsson sent her an allowance; they wrote letters to each other. He sent her passage money to cross the Atlantic and begin over their home life. It arrived to find her on a deathbed, a sister writing to Ericsson her last message for him: "I have always been a trouble to you. Forgive me." She could not quite gather his passion for tools, wheels, progress, man's quest in the material world.

This granitic man of quiet pride had written to the President in August '61 that "steel-clad vessels cannot be arrested in their course by land batteries." He was 58 when in '61 he laid his plans before a naval board of three commodores. They told him his plans had been considered when previously presented by a friend of Ericsson—and they were rejected. He asked why they had been rejected. Mainly, it turned out, they were afraid the *Monitor* as designed would upset; it lacked stability. So Ericsson talked about stability of vessels.

At one session of the naval board Lincoln and Cabinet members were present. All were surprised at the novelty of the plan. Some advised trying it; others ridiculed it. The session closed with Lincoln holding a pasteboard model of the *Monitor* and remarking: "All I have to say is what the girl said when she put her foot into the stocking. It strikes me there's something in it."

Finally they gave Ericsson a contract with a clause saying that if the *Monitor* did not prove "invulnerable" he was to refund all Government money paid him. Croakings were in his ears as he went to New York, drew his final plans, and saw the ship built in exactly 100 days. When she went into action the final Government payment on her had not been made. Now he could read a letter from the chief engineer of the *Monitor* saying: "Thousands have this day blessed you. I have heard whole crews cheer you."

On the day after the *Merrimac-Monitor* battle Lincoln wrote advising Welles the *Monitor* could be easily boarded and captured, her turret wedged, her machinery drowned by pouring water. He passed on the advice from Lieutenant Worden that "she should not go sky-larking up to Norfolk."

A naval lieutenant arrived at a Cabinet meeting to tell the President the wounded Worden was at his house. The President dismissed the Cabinet. Ushering Lincoln into an upstairs room at his house, the naval lieutenant said, "Jack, here is the President come to see you." The President stood gazing down on Worden in bed, the scorched eyes closed, the torn face bandaged. "You do me great honor," murmured Worden. No answer came. The lieutenant turned to see Lincoln in tears with nothing to say for the moment. When he did find words he said: "It is not so. It is you who honor me and your country, and I will promote you." And he made Worden a captain that very day.

A few weeks later Lincoln, with Stanton and others, went down the Potomac in a steamer to Fortress Monroe, commanded by General John E. Wool. Near Kettle Bottom Shoals they saw a long line of boats. "Oh," said the President, as Welles noted it, "that is Stanton's navy. That is the fleet concerning which he and Mr. Welles became so excited in my room. Welles was incensed and opposed the scheme, and it has proved that Neptune was right. Stanton's navy is as useless as the paps of a man to a sucking child. They may be some show to amuse the child, but they are good for nothing for service."

After a long conference with Commodore Louis M.

Goldsborough on his flagship the *Minnesota,* the fleet, by orders of the President, moved to attack Confederate batteries at Sewell's Point. The *Merrimac* came out, wavered, hesitated. Beyond and waiting stood the little *Monitor.* The *Merrimac* retreated and refused to give battle.

Ashore on horseback, the President with General Wool inspected troops, rode through the burned village of Hampton, destroyed by the Confederates when retiring before Union forces.

Commodore Goldsborough was summoned ashore by the President. Again an attack on the Sewell's Point batteries was ordered. The bombardment put one battery out of commission and revealed that a second battery was not as effective as supposed. The *Merrimac* steamed out slowly, paused, stood a while, again turned back, and looked as if she would fight only when she had to.

Lincoln had talked with a pilot, studied a chart, and found a landing place nearer to Norfolk than the one considered by General Wool. The President in a tug was scouting the shore line; Chase was aboard the *Miami.* "Several horsemen who seemed to be soldiers of the enemy, appeared on the beach," wrote Chase. "I sent to the President to ask if we should fire on them, and he replied negatively." Returning to General Wool and discussing plans for taking Norfolk from the Confederates, the President allowed Wool to use the landing the General preferred.

Six regiments were put on shore, marched to Norfolk, found it evacuated by the Confederates, with smoking ruins of large stores of military supplies. The mayor of Norfolk formally surrendered the city to General Wool. The President had been "greatly alarmed for our safety" by the report of General Mansfield, wrote Chase, "and you can imagine his delight when we told him Norfolk was ours. Mr. Stanton came into the President's room and was equally delighted. He fairly hugged General Wool."

The President, with Stanton and Chase, next day rode through the streets of captured Norfolk and gazed on the ruined hulk of the *Merrimac,* which the Confederates had blown up rather than risk another fight with the *Monitor.*

Then the party sailed back to Washington on the steamer *Baltimore*, Chase writing to his daughter Janet: "So ended a brilliant week's campaign by the President; for I think it quite certain that if he had not gone down, Norfolk would still have been in the possession of the enemy . . . The whole coast is now virtually ours."

A curious week it was for Lincoln with his first experience at direct handling of sea and land forces, with fleet and field headquarters under his hat.

McClellan's army after nine months of organization, practice, drill, first went under fire in April '62, fought a rear-guard action at Williamsburg, and moved to White House Landing, 20 miles from Richmond. Meanwhile McClellan renewed his calls on the War Department and the President for more men and guns. Also he continued, with some of his generals, an undiminished political activity.

Long letters passed between McClellan and Lincoln on corps organization. Rain, mud, heavy roads, bogged his army, McClellan complained to Lincoln, who remarked to Hay that "he seemed to think, in defiance of Scripture, that Heaven sent its rain only on the just and not on the unjust."

One McClellan handicap was a fear that enemies among his own officers were leagued with enemies at Washington in plots against him. He wrote his wife May 1: "I shall be very glad when we are really ready to open fire, and then finish this confounded affair. I am tired of public life . . . the rebels on one side, and the abolitionists and other scoundrels on the other."

The wounded Confederate commander Joseph E. Johnston was replaced by Robert E. Lee. Lee sent Stonewall Jackson to the Shenandoah Valley. Jackson with 17,000 men swept the valley region and in 14 days marched his army 170 miles, routed 12,500 Union troops, captured $250,000 worth of supplies and property, took 3,000 prisoners and 9,000 rifles, a raid which threatened Washington so seriously that Lincoln called off McDowell from co-operation with McClellan. Strategy worked out by Lincoln, for bagging Jackson's army in the clutch of three Union

armies, was logical enough. But Jackson was an illogical
phantom, got away with his supplies and prisoners, and
joined Lee at Richmond—as Lee had guessed he would.
McClellan guessed that Lee must have at least 200,000
troops or he would not have dared to detach Jackson for
the Shenandoah Valley operation. Lee had less than 83,000
when reinforced by Jackson.

Lincoln understood with McClellan that if the Army of
the Potomac could smash the enemy army and take Richmond, it would set bells ringing over the North. On the
other hand, the wreck of McClellan's army might mean the
end of the Union cause. The hazards affected McClellan's
mind. Over and again in letters to his wife he told her of his
courage, his resolution, how firm he was. He mentioned his
faith and his fearlessness often enough to show his own
doubt of himself. These phases of McClellan haunted Lincoln, Stanton, Ben Wade, Zach Chandler. "He's got the
slows," was one comment of Lincoln.

Lincoln wrote a letter for Seward to use among men of
financial and political power who were insisting they must
know precisely where the President stood. In this letter was
a manner of oath: "I expect to maintain this contest until
successful, or till I die, or am conquered, or my term ex-
pires, or Congress or the country forsakes me." The President was convincing. Seward and others got the governors
of the North to sign a request that more troops be raised.
Lincoln on July 1 made a call for 300,000 three-year men
—wondering how the country would take it. He wrote to
McClellan, who was calling for 50,000 more soldiers, to be
patient.

The raising of new troops came addedly hard because of
McClellan's handling of his army. The enemy struck at his
White House Landing base of supplies, where food, guns,
powder, wagons, mules, arrived from Washington, and
what came to be known as the Seven Days' battles were on.
McClellan ordered a change of base to Harrison's Landing
on the James River. On McClellan's retreat Lee put in every
last man and gun he had and tried to crumple up McClellan

and capture his army. In the finish, and after bloody fighting, McClellan still held Harrison's Landing and had lost only 16,000 men as against 20,000 Confederate losses.

A complex and weary McClellan, after the first of the Seven Days' battles, telegraphed to Secretary Stanton: "I have seen too many dead and wounded comrades to feel otherwise than that the government has not sustained this army. If you do not do so now the game is lost." Then McClellan used accusing words: "If I save this army now, I tell you plainly that I owe no thanks to you or any person in Washington. You have done your best to sacrifice this army." Of these words, McClellan wrote his wife: "Of course they will never forgive me for that. I knew it when I wrote it."

But Lincoln and Stanton did not see the final accusing words of the telegram till much later. For Colonel E. S. Sanford, supervisor and censor of telegraphic messages, found these words to be outrageous, infamous, treasonable, designed by McClellan "to reach the public as a means of shifting the cause of defeat from his own to other shoulders." And Colonel Sanford took on himself the duty of cutting from the telegram what he regarded as treason. Lincoln replied to the mutilated telegram: "Save your Army at all events. Will send re-inforcements as fast as we can."

At one time, as McClellan came near Richmond, the gold and the archives of the Confederate Government were loaded on railroad cars ready to move in case McClellan reached the city.

On both sides were courage, tenacity. A correspondent saw a Federal soldier brought into a field hospital, "both legs torn off by a shell, both arms broken by bullets, the film of death glazing his eyes," but when spoken to he cried out, "I trust to God we are licking them!" At Malvern Hill a Confederate colonel had shouted: "Come on, come on, my men! Do you want to live forever?"

Gay humor lighted grim incidents. General O. O. Howard's right arm was shattered, and when he met General

Phil Kearney, who had lost his left arm in Mexico, the two men shook hands on Howard's saying, "Hereafter we buy our gloves together."

For all his losses of men and material McClellan had won a victory. His cannon mounted tier on tier at Malvern Hill had mowed down the repeated lines of Confederates ordered up by Lee. Moving from Yorktown toward Richmond, McClellan had killed more of the enemy forces than they had of his. And now, having broken the fiercest blow the enemy could bring against him, he shrank under the protection of his gunboats at Harrison's Landing. The collapse of this campaign staggered Lincoln, who remarked of it later, "I was as nearly inconsolable as I could be and live." In a lighter vein he told Lamon: "It seems to me that McClellan has been wandering around and got lost. He's been hollering for help ever since he went south, wants somebody to . . . get him out of the place he's got into."

McClellan wrote the War Department, "To accomplish the great task of capturing Richmond and putting an end to this rebellion reinforcements should be sent to me rather much over than much less than 100,000 men." Lincoln said, "Sending men to that army is like shoveling fleas across a barnyard—not half of them get there." Still again, when another request came for more men, he said: "If I gave McClellan all the men he asks for they could not find room to lie down. They'd have to sleep standing up."

With Stanton, Lincoln started for Harrison's Landing, spent a day there, talked with McClellan, quizzed his generals, and found McClellan had 86,500 troops present for duty, 34,000 absent by authority, 3,700 absent without authority, his command including more than 120,000.

Lincoln and Stanton rode horseback alongside McClellan reviewing troops. Chaplain Joseph Twichell of a Connecticut regiment wrote his father July 9, 1862: "It did seem as though every moment the President's legs would become entangled with those of the horse he rode and both come down together . . . That arm with which he drew the rein, in its angles and position resembled the hind leg of a grasshopper—the hand before—the elbow away back over the horse's tail. The removal of his hat before each regiment was also a source of laughter in the style of its execution— the quick trot of the horse making it a feat of some difficulty, while from the same cause, his hold on it, while off, seemed very precarious. But, the boys liked him, in fact his popularity with the army is and has been universal. Most of our rulers and leaders fall into odium, but all have faith in Lincoln. 'When he finds it out,' they say, 'it will be stopped.' "

Lincoln returned to Washington carrying a long letter written by McClellan, giving freely his ideas on what policies should guide the Government. The war should be "conducted upon the highest principles known to Christian civilization." Private property should be respected; "radical views, especially upon slavery," would melt away the armies. McClellan was sincere in believing his advice would save the country. His sincerity was incomplete, however, else he would have informed Lincoln that Fernando Wood, the mayor of New York who in '61 tried to get his city to secede from the Union, had called on him in camp to talk politics. With Wood was another Democrat of national influence—and they told McClellan, as between Democrats, that he ought to be his party's candidate for President in the next campaign.

McClellan spoke of "saving" his army almost as though by some slight whim of mind or caprice of heart he might not choose to save it—and what then? His chief of staff and father-in-law, R. B. Marcy, deepened misgivings in Washington when in a talk with Stanton he remarked that he would not be surprised if McClellan's army should be forced to "capitulate." The lingo could mean anything. Browning noted: "This excited Stanton very much, and he went directly to the President and reported what had been said. It also excited the President, whereupon he sent for Marcy and said to him sternly, 'Genl I understand you have used the word "Capitulate"—that is a word not to be used in connection with our army &c.' Marcy blundered out some kind of explanation, excuse or apology."

The habit of blaming others for mistakes, accidents, fate,

had grown on McClellan. He wrote to his wife, "I am tired of serving fools. God help my country!" He saw "incompetents" in Washington doing "injustice" to him. This, that, was "infamous."

Lincoln had called General Halleck from the West to serve as General in Chief of all land forces. Halleck was to puzzle Lincoln. Forty-seven years old, New York born, a West Pointer, an engineer with artillery in the Mexican War, he had written a book, *Elements of Military Art and Science*. When the war opened he was head of the leading law firm of San Francisco and major general of the state militia. After Shiloh he took the field, replacing Grant, moved slowly onward with pick and shovel, entrenching, making sure that his 100,000 would bag the enemy 50,000. After six weeks he had arrived at Corinth when the enemy had slipped out and was 50 miles away again. He reported this to Washington as a victory. But Lincoln was through with gathering more troops for McClellan, saying, reported Browning: "That if by magic he could reinforce McClelland with 100,000 men today he would be in an ecstasy over it, thank him for it, and tell him that he would go to Richmond tomorrow, but that when tomorrow came he would telegraph that he had certain information that the enemy had 400,000 men, and that he could not advance without reinforcements." Halleck was asking McClellan's generals whether they ought to stay before Richmond on the peninsula. Some said No, some Yes.

Slowly, at last, the whole story had to be told to the country of the Seven Days' battles. Out over the country, in homes where had been faith, doubts crept in. The national mood reached the White House, where the President sat in his library writing, "with directions to deny him to everybody." Senator Browning stepped in a moment and in the evening wrote, "He looked weary, care-worn and troubled. I shook hands with him, and asked him how he was. He said 'tolerably well' I remarked that I felt concerned about him —regretted that troubles crowded so heavily upon him, and feared his health was suffering. He held me by the hand, pressed it, and said in a very tender and touching tone—

'Browning, I must die sometime,' I replied, 'your fortunes Mr. President are bound up with those of the Country, and disaster to one would be disaster to the other, and I hope you will do all you can to preserve your health and life.' He looked very sad, and there was a cadence of deep sadness in his voice. We parted I believe both of us with tears in our eyes."

The Army of the Potomac, its sick and wounded, its cannon and horses, its farm hands, shopmen, college boys, store clerks, was brought back from the peninsula to old places on the Potomac River within sight of the Capitol. And McClellan was relieved of command in the field and told to report for orders at Alexandria.

Hate, fear, jealousy, were rampant. To a man who came complaining against his superior officer, rather loose-mouthed, Lincoln merely said, "Go home and read Proverbs xxx, 10." And the man hunted up his Bible and read "Accuse not a servant unto his master, lest he curse thee, and thou be found guilty."

Lincoln had scolded McClellan, drollery ran, for not sending more complete and detailed reports of his army's progress. So McClellan sent a telegram to Lincoln one day: "Have captured two cows. What disposition should I make of them?" And Lincoln: "Milk 'em, George."

On August 4, 1862, Lincoln issued a second call for 300,000 troops. This meant conscription by the states, "the draft." Sheriffs and commissioners took lists of all men between 18 and 45 in counties and cities. Names written on folded ballots were shaken in a revolving wheel or drum-shaped box. A blindfolded man drew the names of those who were to go to war for nine months, or inside of five days pay a substitute to go.

Men who did not want to go to war, by thousands, filed exemption claims—they were physically unfit to go; they were citizens of other countries; they held to a religious belief that war was a sin. In ten days, 14,000 claims were filed in New York City. Thousands were crossing into Canada or buying steamship tickets for Europe One steamer was overhauled at sea and all men passengers were taken back to New York.

Resistance and evasion of the attempts of the state governments to draft soldiers spread so far that the President issued a proclamation that "all persons discouraging volunteer enlistments, resisting militia drafts, or guilty of any disloyal practice, affording aid and comfort to Rebels against the authority of the United States" would come under martial law—and the writ of habeas corpus would be useless in any jail where they were held.

For Lincoln there were decisions—every day hundreds of decisions—Yes or No—take it or leave it—right or wrong.

Governor Andrew telegraphed he could not get "quick work" out of U.S. paymasters delaying transport of regiments. Lincoln wired: "Please say to these gentlemen that if they do not work quickly I will make quick work with them. In the name of all that is reasonable, how long does it take to pay a couple of Regts.?"

To Archbishop John Hughes the President wrote in late '61 with the salutation "Rt. Rev. Sir" and began: "I am sure you will pardon me if, in my ignorance, I do not address [you] with technical correctness." Though he could find no law authorizing his appointment of chaplains for hospitals, "yet the services of chaplains are more needed, perhaps, in the hospitals, than with the healthy soldiers in the field." Therefore he had given "a sort of quasi appointment" to three Protestant ministers and "If you perceive no objection, I will thank you to give me the name or names of one or more suitable persons of the Catholic Church, to whom I may with propriety, tender the same service." The President's personal touch with the Archbishop went into a closing sentence: "Many thanks for your kind, and judicious letters to Gov. Seward, and which he regularly allows me both the pleasure and the profit of perusing."

Some decisions came easy, such as signing the Pacific Railway Bill July 1, 1862. Rails were to be laid from the western Iowa line to San Francisco Bay. The Union Pacific and the Central Pacific corporations were to build the road, getting ten sections of land per mile alongside the right of way, with graduated Government loans on a per-mile basis—$16,000 for level work, $32,000 for desert work (the Great Basin), and $48,000 for mountain work. As the bill stood now, it was under "military necessity" an offer to railroad financiers to push through a job that would tie the two coasts closer.

He signed the Homestead Bill May 20, 1862, giving a farm free to any man who wanted to put a plow to un-broken sod. Immense tracts of land were thrown open in the Western Territories. Anyone a citizen of the United States or taking out first papers declaring intention of citizenship, paying a registration fee of $10 and staying on the same piece of ground five years, could have title papers making him the owner of 160 acres. Tens of thousands of Britons, Irish, Germans, Scandinavians came, many ex-claiming, "What a good new country where they give away farms!" As a war measure touching enlarged food supply, and as an act fulfilling a Republican party pledge, Lincoln found it easy to sign the bill.

Chapter 9

Second Bull Run — Bloody Antietam — Chaos

The popular Orpheus C. Kerr [Robert H. Newell] and his nonsense helped relieve the gloom of some readers, including Lincoln. Kerr, August 9, 1862, set forth: "Notwithstanding the fact that President Lincoln is an honest man, my boy, the genius of Slumber has opened a large wholesale establishment here, and the tendency to repose is general." And three weeks later: "As every thing continues to indicate, my boy, that President Lincoln is an honest man, I am still of the opinion that the restoration of the Union is only a question of time, and will be accomplished some weeks previous to the commencement of the Millenium."

During that desperate, hammering summer of '62 Lincoln revolved often in his mind the curious failure of his 200,000 men in Virginia against half that number. Would he have to try one general, another and still another, and for how long?

Robert Edward Lee, 55 years old, had become the most portentous personality with whom Lincoln would have to contend in the months ahead. Lee had two rare gifts, patience with men and readiness with unforeseen circumstance. His training in handling and understanding men had been long, hard, varied and thorough. The smooth reciprocal functioning of Lee with Davis was almost startling in contrast to Lincoln and McClellan. Militarily Lee and Davis were one head of the Army of Northern Virginia. Where Davis would often fail to read the enemy mind Lee supplied the deficiency. Neither jealousy, envy, nor ambition, in any ordinary sense, gnawed at the heart of Lee.

Lee was a baby when taken in a family coach to Alexandria, Virginia. Growing up he became immersed in the legends of George Washington. Men who studied him closely said that one of his secrets was a grip on the character of Washington as a model, a hope and a light.

His mother, Ann Hill Carter Lee, was the daughter of Charles Carter, in his day reputed the richest man in Virginia except George Washington. Her inheritance had dwindled so far that West Point was the advisable place for her son's education. John C. Calhoun signed his appointment, and after graduation with high standing, he was married to Mary Custis, a frail blonde girl of whom it was said, "She loved wildflowers and old gardens and evening skies." She bore seven children in 14 years, and became a chronic invalid.

Lee had directed engineers and work gangs to cut ditches in Georgia mudbanks, to blast rock from the bed of the Mississippi for river channel improvement at St. Louis, to repair casemates in New York Harbor, to run pile drivers in Baltimore Harbor. His reputation for fair dealing spread far; when he assured an offending soldier, "You shall have justice," the answer was quick—"That is what I am afraid of."

Lee's only leave of absence during 30 years in the Army was an annoying year in which he acted as executor of the tangled estate of his wife's father, about that time writing, "I have no enjoyment in life now but what I derive from my children." Cold and austere he seemed on parade in his official uniform, panoplied for duty, though in the bosom of his family "he was very fond of having his hands tickled, and what was still more curious, it pleased and delighted him to take off his slippers and place his feet in our laps to have them tickled," said one of the sons. They would ask for more stories and he teased them. "No tickling, no story!" With a physical frame "solid as oak," trained to hardships and loneliness, Lee sipped wine occasionally, drank no hard liquor, cared nothing for tobacco.

In Alexandria he read of Virginia's secession. To a druggist in Alexandria he had remarked the day before, "I must say that I am one of those dull creatures that cannot see the good of secession." He sent Secretary Cameron his resignation and wrote to Scott: "I shall carry to the grave the most grateful recollections of your kind consideration, and your name and fame will always be dear to me . . . Save in defence of my native State, I never desire to again draw my sword." He had written a son, "While I wish to do what is right, I am unwilling to do what is wrong, either at the bidding of the South or the North." Of his hope for preservation of the Union he wrote, "I will cling to it to the last." He felt and resented "the aggressions of the North," though "I am not pleased with the course of the 'Cotton States.'" On the South Carolina proposals to legalize and reopen the African slave trade he was decisive, writing a son: "One of their plans seems to be the renewal of the slave trade. That I am opposed to on every ground." To his wife in 1856 from western Texas he wrote his views: "In this enlightened age, there are few I believe, but what will acknowledge, that slavery as an institution, is a moral & political evil in any Country. It is useless to expatiate on its disadvantages. I think it however a greater evil to the white than to the black race, & while my feelings are strongly enlisted in behalf of the latter, my sympathies are more strong for the former."

When offered high command of the Union armies, Lee had said, according to Old Man Blair, "If I owned the four million slaves of the South I would sacrifice them all to the Union," and then asked a question that Blair couldn't answer: "But how can I draw my sword against Virginia?" The very asking of the question included its answer.

"The war may last ten years," Lee had written his wife shortly after arriving in Richmond. He warned soldiers and politicians they were "on the threshold of a long and bloody war," advising that they must plan with that expectation, that he knew the Northern people well, and "they would never yield except at the conclusion of a long and desperate struggle." Riding on a field where one of his sons was fighting, he remarked, "That's right, my son, drive those people back." Or again he would refer to the enemy as "our friends across the river."

Suddenly, when General Joseph Johnston was wounded, Lee had been sent forward to take in hand four different armies, weld them into a unit for action. In a four months' campaign, at times outnumbered two to one, he had stopped McClellan and earned a name as the savior of Richmond and the Confederacy. To a doubting inquirer one of Lee's generals had said his first name was "Audacity," that he would tower head and shoulders above all others in audacity. In a conference with generals just before the Seven Days' battles, one of them, busy with pencil and paper, was showing that McClellan with superior forces could sweep on to Richmond. "Stop, stop!" said Lee. "If you go to ciphering we are whipped beforehand."

Lee knew better than McClellan that war is a conflict of wills, and had imposed his will on McClellan to the extent that McClellan believed he was a loser when he was not, which was why he did not try to push through and take Richmond after Malvern Hill. While Lee was leaving all Southern politics to Jefferson Davis, McClellan concentrated his mind for many hours on the political difficulties of the North and wrote the long letter instructing Lincoln in the matter of Government policy. In one letter to Lincoln, McClellan estimated Lee as "personally brave and energetic to a fault" yet "too cautious and weak under grave responsibility . . . likely to be timid and irresolute in action. I am confident of success. Not only of success but of brilliant success."

Lee's right-hand man Thomas Jonathan Jackson also was born for war. His valley campaign up and down the Shenandoah, in which he captured half of one Union army, beat off three other armies with which Lincoln was trying to trap him, and slipped through for a rapid march to join Lee, had become a shining chronicle of the Confederacy. Lincoln from the White House undertook to direct continuously from day to day the field movements of several armies. To Frémont, to Banks, to McDowell, with forces three times that of Jackson, Lincoln sent telegrams giving the reported movements of Jackson's "foot cavalry." During three weeks in a series of telegrams there glimmered Lincoln's hope that from his assorted varieties of armies in and about the Shenandoah, he might set up one little combination that would cross Jackson's path somewhere and damage or break that adventuring zealot. The opening telegrams on the same day advised Frémont: "Much—perhaps all—depends upon the celerity with which you can execute it. Put the utmost speed into it. Do not lose a minute"; and McDowell, "Every thing now depends upon the celerity and vigor of your movement."

But Jackson was putting on a campaign that for swift troop movement amazed the world. Thirty miles in 24 hours his infantry marched. With 17,000 men in this one month he won five battles, took many prisoners, sent to Richmond great wagon trains of captured muskets, munitions, medicines and supplies, threw Washington into a scare, made McDowell's army of 40,000 hug close to Washington. An order from Lincoln to McDowell that he should detach 20,000 men to reinforce Frémont for fighting Jackson, McDowell termed "a crushing blow" that he obeyed with "a heavy heart."

Why Lincoln at such a distance should have undertaken what he did was not clear, particularly when Frémont was the key and he knew from Missouri experience of Frémont's "celerity." His seriously telegraphing Frémont "Put the utmost speed into it. Do not lose a minute" was not in accord with his usual judgment of men.

Lincoln, advising with McDowell about starting to destroy Jackson, heard McDowell say he could begin marching the next Sunday but he had been excoriated all over the country for fighting Bull Run on a Sabbath. Lincoln hesitated and smiled. "Get a good ready and start on Monday," seemingly unaware that one day might be as decisive as death when hunting Jackson, even one Sabbath day.

Jackson's reverence for the Sabbath went so far that he would not mail his wife a letter to be carried in the mails on a Sunday nor would he open a letter received from her on a Sunday. But "with the blessing of an ever-kind Providence" he would fight, slay and deliver doom to the enemy if on a Sabbath the enemy looked ready for punishment. An orphan boy who managed to get into West Point, Jackson had graduated far below the class leader, George B. McClellan. His Mexican War record bright, he became professor of natural philosophy and artillery tactics in the Virginia Military Institute. Tall, rawboned, with big hands and a peculiar stride, he would walk alone, raise his right hand high over his head and let it down. He was either praying or easing himself physically—onlookers could not tell which. He had many books and two favorites, which he always carried in his mess kit—the Bible and a volume of Napoleon's maxims on war. His spiritual guide was Jesus of Nazareth, his professional and military inspiration the Little Corsican, whose 88 campaigns he had mastered from A to Z.

"His dyspepsia caused drowsiness," said General Daniel H. Hill, "and he often went to sleep in conversation with a friend . . ." His eyes went bad; he was ordered to do no reading by lamplight, and sat one hour, two hours, of an evening in silence with closed eyes or staring at the wall, concentrating on points arisen in his mind during the day. Alongside Negroes on his farm near Lexington he worked with his hands.

Gulping hard to get down whisky ordered by a physician, he said: "I like it; I always did, and that is the reason I never use it." Refusing a glass of brandy, he said to a fellow officer, "I am more afraid of it than of Yankee bullets."

He joined the Presbyterian church in Lexington, became a deacon, conducted a Sunday school for Negroes. He married Eleanor Junkin and a year later saw her and a newborn child to their double grave. Four years afterward he married Mary Anna Morrison, and their household ran like clockwork in its daily program. Letters of Jackson to his wife gushed with little excesses of romance. "When I gave my darling the last kiss" was a moment. He saluted her as "darling," "precious pet," "sunshine," "little jewel of mine," "esposita." He brandished swords about her head in play or leaped from hiding behind a door to take her in his arms.

Of all Southern commanders who had the ear of Lee and of Davis none was more fiercely in favor of defending by taking the offensive, of striking deep into Northern territory. Of his chief he said: "Lee is a phenomenon. He is the only man I would follow blindfold."

A new combination named the Army of Virginia, formed by the three commands of McDowell, Banks and Frémont, was headed by General John Pope. Frémont, however, decided to resign rather than serve under Pope. The new commander was a dashing horseman, his valor in battle impetuous and undisputed. He had been one of Lincoln's military escort en route to inauguration. Kentucky-born, a graduate of Transylvania University, his father a judge whom Lincoln had met in Illinois, a West Pointer, a Mexican War officer promoted for gallantry on the field, an engineer, surveyor, explorer, an 1860 Republican, John Pope had been continuously an army man, soldiering his lifework. His victories had brought in 1,300 prisoners at Blackwater, Missouri, and some 6,000 at Island No. 10 on the Mississippi. He wrote letters from "Headquarters in the Saddle," issued an address to his new command: "I have come to you from the West, where we have always seen the back of our enemies." His overconfidence ran into bombast. For Pope was facing two great proved fighters, two strange captains of men, Lee and Jackson.

In the last week of August '62, Lincoln sat up late every night, and one night through to a bitter dawn. Lee and Jackson were performing around Pope. Lincoln queried Burnside at Falmouth, "Any news from Gen. Pope?" He wired Banks at Manassas Junction, "Please tell me what news." He asked Haupt, "What news?" on August 30 and in a second telegram the same day, "Please send me the latest news." He telegraphed McClellan: "What news from direction of Manassas Junction? What generally?" McClellan replied he was clear that only two courses were open: first, to help Pope with all available forces; "second, to leave Pope to get out of his scrape, and at once use all our means to make the capital perfectly safe."

Lincoln puzzled over such words as "leave Pope to get out of his scrape." Did McClellan possibly mean that if Pope's army could win with men sent from the Army of the Potomac, then such men should *not* be sent? He answered McClellan: "I think your first alternative, towit, 'to concentrate all our available forces to open communication with Pope,' is the right one. But I wish not to control. That I now leave to Gen. Halleck, aided by your counsels."

McClellan was writing his wife: "I fancy that Pope is in retreat, though this is only a guess of mine . . . I don't see how I can remain in the service if placed under Pope, it would be too great a disgrace . . . I shall keep as clear as possible of the President and cabinet; endeavor to do what must be done with Halleck alone; so I shall get on better . . . I have just telegraphed very plainly to the President and Halleck what I think ought to be done . . . I am heart-sick with the folly and ignorance I see around me . . . I have seen neither the President nor the secretary since I arrived here . . ."

John Hay wrote in his diary of a horseback ride from Soldiers' Home to the White House with Lincoln, and of matters that made public would have further torn the country: "We talked about Bull Run and Pope's prospect. The President was very outspoken in regard to McClellan's present conduct. He said that it really seemed to him McC. wanted Pope defeated. The President seemed to think him a little crazy. Envy, jealousy and spite are probably a better explanation of his present conduct. He is constantly sending despatches to the President and Halleck asking what is his real position and command. He acts as chief alarmist and grand marplot of the Army . . ."

Stanton took Lincoln and Hay to his house. "A pleasant little dinner and a pretty wife as white and cold and motionless as marble, whose rare smiles seemed to pain her. Stanton was loud about the McC. business . . . He said that nothing but foul play could lose us this battle & that it rested with McC. and his friends. Stanton seemed to believe very strongly in Pope. So did the President for that matter."

Everything seemed to be going well on Saturday, August 30, as Lincoln and Hay saw it. "We went to bed expecting glad tidings at sunrise. But about eight o'clock the President came to my room as I was dressing and, calling me out, said 'Well, John, we are whipped again, I am afraid. The enemy reinforced on Pope and drove back his left wing and he has retired to Centreville where he says he will be able to hold his men. I don't like that expression. I don't like to hear him admit his men need holding.' "

On Sunday things began to look better. "The President was in a singularly defiant tone of mind. He often repeated, 'We must hurt this enemy before it gets away.' " On Monday when Hay spoke of the bad look of events, the President said: "No, Mr. Hay, we must whip these people now. Pope must fight them. If they are too strong for him, he can gradually retire to these fortifications. If this be not so, if we are really whipped we may as well stop fighting."

What with jealousy, spite, bickering, officialism, politics, pride, sloth, ignorance, large bodies of troops stayed quiet in scattered positions while Pope farther off was outguessed, flanked, surprised, hacked and harassed, and driven off from Bull Run Creek with slaughter. In combat and retreat he lost 14,000 out of 80,000; Lee lost 9,000 out of 54,000.

Stormy tides rocked Washington as the broken pieces of a defeated army straggled in. Outbound railroad trains were packed; thousands fled the national capital. The Federal Treasury building was barricaded with hundreds of barrels of cement. By order of the President clerks in the civil departments enrolled and began military drill. Stanton had important papers gathered into bundles to be carried away on horseback, if necessary.

This was the day that General M. C. Meigs saw Stanton issuing volleys of orders for the safety of the city. And Meigs wrote: "Lincoln, on the other hand, dropped into my room on his weary way to see Stanton, drew himself way down into a big chair, and, with a mingled groan and sigh exclaimed, 'Chase says we can't raise any more money; Pope is licked and McClellan has the diarrhoea. What shall I do? The bottom is out of the tub, the bottom is out of the tub!' I told the President to meet his generals with Stanton, fix the bottom back in the tub, rally the army, and order another advance at once. This seemed to brace him up a little and he went on to the War Department; but for the moment he was completely discouraged and downhearted. Stanton, on the other hand, was more full of power and vehement energy than ever."

The dying colonel of the 1st Michigan Cavalry wrote to his brother and sister: "I die midst the ring and clangor of battle, as I could wish . . . I am one of the victims of Pope's imbecility and McDowell's treason. Tell the President would he save the country he must not give our hallowed flag to such hands." The letter was published, discussed.

Three thousand convalescent soldiers were moved from

Washington to Philadelphia to make room for serious cases from Bull Run. Floors in the Capitol, in the Patent Office building, were cleared for torn and mutilated men.

In this second panic at Bull Run one man satisfied Lincoln in everything, so Hay wrote. Haupt, the railroad man, took on duties outside his particular job, advancing supplies and munitions, rebuilding bridges, watching transport, telegraphing the President, working day and night with little food or sleep. "The President is particularly struck with the business-like character of his despatch, telling in the fewest words the information most sought for." It was some weeks earlier that Lincoln had told of seeing "the most remarkable structure that human eyes ever rested upon," and explained: "That man Haupt has built a bridge across Potomac Creek, about 400 feet long and nearly 100 feet high, over which loaded trains are running every hour, and upon my word, gentlemen, there is nothing in it but bean-poles and cornstalks." From a distance the green, new-cut timbers did look just so.

Pope was relieved of command and assigned to the Northwest to curb Indian tribes. Welles noted that the President "spoke favorably" of Pope and clearly believed he had not had a fair chance. "Pope," said the President, "did well, but there was an army prejudice against him, and it was necessary he should leave. He had gone off very angry, and not without cause, but circumstances controlled us." Lincoln probably told Pope and Halleck, as he did Welles, "We had the enemy in the hollow of our hands on Friday, if our generals, who are vexed with Pope, had done their duty; all of our present difficulties and reverses have been brought upon us by these quarrels of the generals."

Welles also recorded in this week that his convictions joined those of the President "that McClellan and his generals are this day stronger than the Administration with a considerable part of this Army of the Potomac." On a walk with the President, Welles noted the words: "I must have McClellan to reorganize the army and bring it out of chaos, but there has been a design—a purpose in breaking down Pope, without regard of consequences to the country. It is shocking to see and know this, but there is no remedy at present. McClellan has the army with him."

Stanton, Chase, Bates and Smith of the Cabinet had signed a paper in Stanton's handwriting, a remonstrance to be handed the President against McClellan's being once more entrusted with command of the army. Chase argued with Welles to sign. Welles held off, saying that while he wished to get rid of McClellan, it was not exactly fair to the President to be circulating such a paper behind his back. Then this paper disappeared, and Chase came to Welles with a second one, in the handwriting of Bates and with the same four signers as before. Welles said this second one was more reasonable in tone, but he told Chase he could not join with them.

The determination of Stanton and Chase was to remove, and if possible to disgrace, McClellan, as Welles saw it. "Chase frankly stated he desired it, that he deliberately believed McClellan ought to be shot, and should, were he President, be brought to summary punishment." Welles believed that McClellan hesitated in attack, had neither definite plans nor audacity, and was no fighting general. But he could not agree with Stanton and Chase that McClellan was "imbecile, a coward, a traitor." He wrote, "Chase was disappointed, and I think a little chagrined, because I would not unite in the written demand to the President."

Stanton came to see if he could not get Welles to sign. If Welles signed, that would make five out of seven in the Cabinet. "Stanton said, with some excitement, he knew of no particular obligations he was under to the President, who had called him to a difficult position and imposed upon him labors and responsibilities which no man could carry, and which were greatly increased by fastening upon him a commander who was constantly striving to embarrass him in his administration of the Department. He could not and would not submit to a continuance of this state of things." Welles admitted conditions were bad, severe on Stanton. Still he could not sign the paper.

Welles in his diary threw strange crosslights on the half-mutinous figures that sat around Lincoln's Cabinet table. Cabinet discussions went on without order or system, noted Welles, "but in the summing-up and conclusions the President, who was a patient listener and learner, concentrated results, and often determined questions adverse to the Secretary of State, regarding him and his opinions, as he did those of his other advisers, for what they were worth and generally no more."

At one Cabinet meeting Lincoln had all his counselors but one against him. He was reminded of a revival meeting in Illinois when a fellow with a few drinks too many in him had walked up the aisle to a front pew. All eyes were on him, but he didn't care; he joined in the singing, droned amen at the close of prayers, and as the meeting proceeded dozed off in sleep. Before the meeting ended the pastor asked the usual question: "Who are on the Lord's side?" and the congregation arose en masse. When the pastor asked, "Who are on the side of the Devil?" the dozing sleeper came to, heard part of the question, saw the parson standing, arose to his feet to say: "I don't exactly understand the question but I'll stand by you, parson, to the last. But it seems to me," he added reflectively, "that we're in a hopeless minority."

One advantage of Seward was resented. Like the President, he was a storyteller. While other Secretaries were toiling at their duties the Secretary of State "spent a considerable portion of every day with the President, patronizing and instructing him, hearing and telling anecdotes, relating interesting details of occurrences in the Senate, and inculcating his political party notions." And amid these Cabinet jealousies had come one deep cleavage. "Between Seward and Chase there was perpetual rivalry and mutual but courtly distrust . . ."

Before one Cabinet meeting Lincoln had gone with Halleck to McClellan and given him command of the Army again. But the actual words by which authority was once more handed over to him were not spoken by Lincoln. It was left to Halleck, Lincoln explaining to Welles, "I could not have done it, for I can never feel confident that he will do anything effectual." McClellan wrote his wife: "I was surprised this morning, when at breakfast, by a visit from the President and Halleck, in which the former expressed the opinion that the troubles now impending could be overcome better by me than anyone else. Pope is ordered to fall back on Washington, and, as he re-enters, everything is to come under my command again!"

Three days later, as Lincoln and Hay walked over to the telegraph office, Lincoln said: "McClellan is working like a beaver. He seems to be aroused to doing something, by the sort of snubbing he got last week. The Cabinet yesterday were unanimous against him. They were all ready to denounce me for it, except Blair. He [McClellan] has acted badly in this matter, but we must use what tools we have. There is no man in the Army who can man these fortifications and lick these troops into shape half as well as he." Hay spoke of the many letters coming in reflecting a feeling against McClellan. Lincoln commented: "Unquestionably he has acted badly toward Pope. He wanted him to fail. That is unpardonable. But he is too useful just now to sacrifice." And he added later, "If he can't fight himself, he excels in making others ready to fight." He admitted also that calling McClellan to power again was a good deal like "curing the bite with the hair of the dog."

Lincoln had, however, offered command in the field to Burnside, who would not take it, saying to the President, "I do not think that there is anyone who can do as much with that army as McClellan." Also, Lincoln had consented to the dismissal of three major generals, Porter, Franklin and Griffin, who were to have a court-martial on their conduct in the field. And with a heavy heart Lincoln agreed there should be a court of inquiry for McDowell.

"The President," said Chase, ". . . told me that the clamor against McDowell was so great that he [McDowell] could not lead his troops unless something was done to restore confidence; and proposed to me to suggest to him the asking for a Court of Inquiry." Both Chase and Stanton, along with Lincoln, had long ago become convinced that

McDowell was a first-rate, loyal officer, never sulking nor talking loose nor taking a hand in military politics. McDowell went away "very sad," on a 15-day leave of absence, to return for the trial he asked.

A week after the Second Bull Run battle, Lincoln at the War Office referred to "the great number of stragglers he had seen coming into town this morning, and of the immense losses by desertion." Chase noted: "The President said he had felt badly all day." Next day, meeting a committee from New York who urged him to change his policy, "the President became vexed and said, in substance, 'It is plain enough what you want—you want to get Seward out of the Cabinet. There is not one of you who would not see the country ruined if you could turn out Seward.'"

On general policies Chase believed Lincoln had now drifted far out of line with his country and party. "The President," noted Chase, "with the most honest intentions in the world, and a naturally clear judgment and a true, unselfish patriotism, has yielded so much to Border State and negro-phobic counsels that he now finds it difficult to arrest his own descent towards the most fatal concessions."

At one Cabinet meeting, when Lincoln had brought up the matter of shifting and trying new generals, it came to A. K. McClure that the President said: "I think we'd better wait; perhaps a real fighting general will come along some of these days, and then we'll all be happy. If you go to mixing in a mix-up, you only make the muddle worse."

The yellow corn stood ripe in the fields of Maryland. Lee and Jackson knew that corn could help feed their armies. They marched gray and butternut regiments across the Potomac, ragged and footsore men who could fight, as the world knew.

McClellan with an army marched toward Lee. He was feeling better. His three dismissed major generals had been cleared without court-martial and restored to him by the President. McClellan wrote his wife, "The feeling of the government towards me, I am sure, is kind and trusting."

Not in a year had he sent his wife any such pleasant words about the Government. His friend, Lincoln, against a majority of the Cabinet, had again put him at the head of a great army in the field.

Telegrams tumbled into the White House telling of Bragg's Confederate army in Kentucky slipping past Buell's army, which had been set to watch him. Bragg was marching north toward Cincinnati and Louisville, both cities anxious. Also Kirby Smith's men in gray had marched into Kentucky, chased the state legislature out of Frankfort, and captured Lexington, the home town of Mary Todd Lincoln.

"Where is General Bragg?" Lincoln queried in telegrams to several generals in the field. He wired Buell and others, "What degree of certainty have you, that Bragg, with his command, is not now in the valley of the Shenandoah, Virginia?" He wired McClellan, who was calling for reinforcements, that he could have 21,000 under Porter and "I am sending you all that can be spared."

Stonewall Jackson smashed at the Union garrison in Harpers Ferry, trapped them, and took 11,000 prisoners. Four days later, September 17, McClellan's 90,000 troops met Lee's army, about half that of McClellan in troop numbers, at Antietam Creek. Around a cornfield and a little white Dunker church, around a stone bridge, and in a pasture lane worn by cowpaths, surged a human tornado. General Joseph Hooker rode in the worst of the storm, and said of it, "Every stalk of corn in the northern and greater part of the field was cut as closely as could have been done with a knife, and the slain lay in rows precisely as they had stood in their ranks a few moments before." Hooker fell from his saddle with a bleeding foot. An old man with his white hair in the wind, Major General J. K. F. Mansfield, fell dead from his saddle. General Sedgwick was three times wounded, in shoulder, leg, wrist. Four other Union generals fell off their horses with wounds. On the Confederate side, Colonel B. B. Gayle of Alabama was surrounded, drew his revolver, called to his men, "We are flanked, boys, but let's die in our tracks," and fell riddled with bullets. "Don't let your horses tread on me," a wounded man called from a huddle of corpses where officers were picking their way through.

On a golden autumn Sabbath morning three-mile lines of men had faced each other with guns. And when the shooting was over the losses were put at 12,000 on each side. Lee crossed the Potomac, back into the South again. But McClellan did not follow though his chances of wiping out Lee's army were estimated by Longstreet: "We were so badly crushed that at the close of the day ten thousand fresh troops could have come in and taken Lee's army and everything it had. But McClellan did not know it." He had two soldiers to the enemy's one, completely superior cannon, rifles, supplies. He had 93,000 men answering roll call as Lee was fading down the Shenandoah Valley with less than 40,000.

Ten days after the Antietam battle McClellan wrote to his wife: "Not yet have I had a word from any one in Washington about the battle of the Antietam . . . except from the President in the following *beautiful* language, 'Your despatch received. God bless you and all with you! Cant you *bust* them some *even* before they get off?'!!!" Thus for his own purposes and satisfaction, in a highly responsible matter, McClellan could misquote and mangle the President's message, which read: "God bless you, and all with you. Destroy the rebel army, if possible."

Congressman William D. Kelley of Pittsburgh came to the White House and discussed with Lincoln the information that McClellan had held in reserve some 30,000 men, Fitz-John Porter's corps. They did not get into battle, had all their ammunition when the shooting was over. Kelley felt pity and sarcasm in the President's saying, "Whatever the troops and people may think and say of his failure to capture Lee's army and supplies, my censure should be tempered by the consciousness of the fact that I did not restore him to command for aggressive fighting, but as an organizer and a good hand at defending a position."

Lincoln, according to Kelley, was slow and deliberate as he said: "I am now stronger with the Army of the Potomac than McClellan. The supremacy of the civil power has been restored, and the Executive is again master of the situation. The troops know, that if I made a mistake in substituting Pope for McClellan, I was capable of rectifying it by again trusting him. They know, too, that neither Stanton nor I withheld anything from him at Antietam, and that it was not the administration, but their own former idol, who surrendered the just results of their terrible sacrifices and closed the great fight as a drawn battle, when, had he thrown Porter's corps of fresh men and other available troops upon Lee's army, he would inevitably have driven it in disorder to the river and captured most of it before sunset."

In a certain sense Lincoln felt at this time that the war had not really begun. The faults lay deep and were complex. He set forth his view to women attending a national council to organize aid and relief for sick and wounded in the field. Among these devoted workers was Mary A. Livermore, wife of a Universalist clergyman and editor in Chicago. She had lent her strength to raising money and supplies, forming local groups that sent lint, bandages and comforts to the battlefields and hospitals. Before leaving for home they were calling on the President for some word of encouragement.

"I have no word of encouragement to give!" was the slow, blunt reply. The women were silent. They knew he was telling them what he could not well tell the country. The President went on: "The fact is the people have not yet made up their minds that we are at war with the South. They have not buckled down to the determination to fight this war through; for they have got the idea into their heads that we are going to get out of this fix somehow by strategy! That's the word—*strategy!* General McClellan thinks he is going to whip the Rebels by strategy; and the army has got the same notion . . ."

One of the women spoke of the uprisings of hundreds of thousands of volunteers, of valiant behavior at Donelson, Pea Ridge, Shiloh. The President admitted this, and then came back to his theme. "The people *have not* made up their minds that we are at war, I tell you! They think there is a royal road to peace, and that General McClellan is to find it. The army has not settled down into the conviction that we are in a terrible war that has got to be fought out —no; and the officers have not either . . . Whole regiments have two-thirds of their men absent—a great many by desertion, and a great many on leave granted by company officers, which is almost as bad . . . The deserters and furloughed men outnumber the recruits. To fill up the army is like undertaking to shovel fleas. You take up a shovelful but before you can dump them anywhere they are gone. It is like trying to ride a balky horse. You coax, and cheer, and spur, and lay on the whip, but you don't get ahead an inch—there you stick!"

Said one of the women, "Is not death the penalty for desertion? . . . Before many soldiers had suffered death for desertion, this wholesale depletion of the army would be ended." "Oh, no, no!" came the President's reply as he shook his sad head, ". . . if I should go to shooting men by scores for desertion, I should have such a hullabaloo about my ears as I have not heard yet, and I should deserve it. You cannot order men shot by dozens or twenties. People won't stand it and they ought not to stand it. No, we must change the condition of things some other way."

Mrs. Livermore saw his face having ghastly lines, his half-staggering gait like that of a man walking in his sleep.

Chapter 10

The Involved Slavery Issue — Preliminary Emancipation Proclamation

In a rocking chair in a house on F Street in Washington a woman sat knitting. She made her home with her daughter, wife of Missouri Republican Congressman Frank P.

Blair. She was old and blind and had a saying: "Of all things in the world I hate slavery the most—except abolitionism." Thus she carried a double hate, and she could tell which was heavier of the two. Over the country were single, triple and multiple hates. The sum of them made the war.

Lincoln heard the case of a Negro slave who ran away from his master, came to Washington, and was arrested. Chase and Montgomery Blair disputed before Lincoln. Chase would send the captured man into the Union Army; Blair would enforce the Fugitive Slave Law and return the Negro to his legal owner.

The harassed Lincoln said he was reminded of a man in Illinois terribly annoyed by a creditor who kept coming often and pressing him to pay the money he owed. Finally the poor debtor saw nothing to do but to "act crazy" whenever asked for the money. And Lincoln added: "I have on more than one occasion in this room, when beset by extremists on this question, been compelled to appear very mad. I think none of you will ever dispose of this subject without getting mad."

In the hysteria of a changing order, in the drive of forces uprooting a hoary and venerable past, many tongues were let loose and many snap judgments flung into the ears of men. Other extremists were saying the same as Wendell Phillips at a meeting near Boston August 1, 1862: the President "has no mind whatever. He has not uttered a word that gives even a twilight glimpse of any anti-slavery purpose. He may be honest—nobody cares whether the tortoise is honest or not; he has neither insight, nor prevision, nor decision." And, prophesied the agitator, "As long as you keep the present turtle at the head of the Government you make a pit with one hand and fill it with the other."

With a musical voice, with plain words and abrupt thought, Phillips held audiences rapt even when they hated his ideas. Parts of his speeches were splashes of gossip that other platform men could not manage. "The policy that prevails at Washington is to do nothing, and wait for events. I asked the lawyers of Illinois, who had practiced law with Mr. Lincoln for twenty years, 'Is he a man of decision, is hc a man who can say no?' They all said, 'If you had gone to the Illinois bar, and selected the man least capable of saying no, it would have been Abraham Lincoln.' "

Some of the more visionary crusaders believed that with the slaveholders crushed, then would rise a nation of men and women all free, all Christian, "ultimately redeemed." First, however, must be the tragedy of sacrifice and vengeance.

Touched with sorrow yet awful with warning, was Julia Ward Howe's "Battle Hymn of the Republic":

> Mine eyes have seen the glory of the coming of the
>   Lord;
> He is tramping out the vintage where the grapes of
>   wrath are stored;
> He hath loosed the fateful lightning of His terrible
>   swift sword;
>   His truth is marching on.

Published in February '62 her verses had now gone to singing millions. Of her trip to Washington and her visit with Lincoln, Mrs. Howe remembered sharply two things. Lincoln from where she sat was in line with the Gilbert Stuart painting of Washington and she tried to compare them. Also Lincoln remarked, "I once heered George Sumner tell a story." The way he pronounced "heered" fixed it in her memory.

Denunciation poured from abolitionists when the President dealt with a military order issued by his good friend Major General David Hunter, commanding at Port Royal, South Carolina. The General confiscated slaves and declared them free. Also, reasoning that martial law and slavery could not go together, the General declared all slaves in Georgia, Florida and South Carolina "forever free." Chase urged that these orders should stand, that nine-tenths of the country was for them.

Lincoln wrote to Chase, "No commanding general shall do such a thing, upon *my* responsibility, without consulting me." He again urged that the Federal Government co-operate with any Slave State in gradual compensated emancipation of the slaves. To the Border State people, "I do not argue—I beseech you to make arguments for yourselves." Afraid that they were not reading the drift of events, he warned them: "You cannot, if you would, be blind to the signs of the times. I beg of you a calm and enlarged consideration of them, ranging, if it may be, far above personal and partizan politics."

Border State Congressmen at the White House on Lincoln's invitation in July '62 heard him plead for graduated, compensated abolishment of slavery. "I intend no reproach or complaint," he said, "when I assure you that in my opinion, if you all had voted for the resolution . . . of last March, the war would now be substantially ended." He still believed the plan would be swift to end the war. With the slaves freed by purchase in the Border States, the other states farther south would see they could not long keep up the war. In time, as the war dragged on, slavery would be extinguished by mere friction, urged the President. The money spent for buying slaves and setting them free would shorten the war. "How much better to thus save the money which else we sink forever in the war. How much better to do it while we can, lest the war ere long render us pecuniarily unable to do it . . ."

And the Border State men went away, considered and discussed. But nothing came of Lincoln's hope to have the nation buy the slaves and set them free. The hatred of the administration head and his works ran deep among those in Kentucky committed to Jefferson Davis. One wrote for the *Kentucky Statesman:* "This is the man who bids armies rise and fight and commands and dismisses generals at will. This is the man who proclaims (as such could only do) the equality of the races, black and white . . . Kneel down and kiss his royal feet, men of the South!"

Early in August '62 Sumner wrote of Lincoln to John Bright in England: "He is hard to move . . . I urged him on the 4th of July to put forth an edict of emancipation, telling him he could make the day more sacred and historic than ever. He replied, 'I would do it if I were not afraid that half the officers would fling down their arms and three more States would rise.'" Greeley in his *Tribune* of August 19, 1862, issued "The Prayer of Twenty Millions." As the first servant of the Republic, the President was required to execute the laws, declared Greeley, and, "We think you are strangely and disastrously remiss in the discharge of your official and imperative duty." Speaking for 20,000,000 people, as he assumed, Greeley wrote: "You are unduly influenced by the counsels, the representations, the menace of certain fossil politicians hailing from the border slave States." Also: "We complain that a large proportion of our regular army officers with many of the volunteers evince far more solicitude to uphold slavery than to put down the rebellion." Lincoln in a letter dated August 22, 1862, told the country in simple and skillfully wrought sentences what the war was for, as he saw it. Widely reprinted, probably reaching nearly all persons in the country who could read, the letter said:

> . . . I would save the Union. I would save it the shortest way under the Constitution. The sooner the national authority can be restored; the nearer the Union will be "the Union as it was." If there be those who would not save the Union, unless they could at the same time *save* slavery, I do not agree with them. If there be those who would not save the Union unless they could at the same time *destroy* slavery, I do not agree with them. *My paramount object in this struggle is to save the Union, and is not either to save or to destroy slavery.* [Italics added.] If I could save the Union without freeing *any* slave, I would do it, and if I could save it by freeing *all* the slaves I would do it; and if I could save it by freeing some and leaving others alone I would also do that. What I do about slavery, and the colored race, I do because I believe it helps to save the Union; and what I forbear, I forbear because I do *not* believe it would help to save the Union. I shall do *less* whenever I shall believe what I am doing hurts the cause, and I shall do *more* whenever I shall believe doing more will help the cause. I shall try to cor-

rect errors when shown to be errors; and I shall adopt new views so fast as they shall appear to be true views.

I have here stated my purpose according to my view of *official* duty; and I intend no modification of my oft-expressed *personal* wish that all men every where could be free.

The Reverend Moncure Daniel Conway and the Reverend William Ellery Channing, Unitarian antislavery clergymen, called by appointment at the Executive Mansion at eight o'clock one morning. As they waited in the anteroom, noted Conway: "A woman with a little child was waiting. She now and then wept but said nothing. The President saw her first, and she came out radiant. We conjectured some prisoner was that day released." They found the President "gracious." He agreed with Channing on plans for the nation to buy the slaves: compensated abolishment. He had for years favored this plan. He turned to Conway, who said the President could be the deliverer of the nation from its one great evil. What would not that man achieve for mankind who should free America from slavery? "Perhaps," said Lincoln, "we may be better able to do something in that direction after a while than we are now."

He half inquired from Conway whether it was not true that the antislavery people, being in a "movement," naturally met a good many who agreed with them. "You possibly may over-estimate the number in the country who hold such views. But the position in which I am placed brings me into some knowledge of opinions in all parts of the country and of many different kinds of people; and it appears to me that the great masses of this country care comparatively little about the negro, and are anxious only for military successes."

Thus stood the President, Conway reported far and wide. The two clergymen thanked him for his kindly reception. He remarked: "We shall need all the anti-slavery feeling in the country, and more; you can go home and try to bring the people to your views; and you may say any-

thing you like about me, if that will help. Don't spare me!"
This with a laugh. Then gravely: "When the hour comes for
dealing with slavery, I trust I will be willing to do my duty
though it cost my life. And, gentlemen, lives will be lost."

In that summer of '62 Lincoln had to consider such incidents as a Union officer, a Republican, drawing applause at
a mass meeting for recruiting in Terre Haute, Indiana, when
he shouted, "I hate a nigger worse than I hate the devil."

How the Border State men were shifting in degree was
indicated in a Browning diary note: "Garrett Davis Senator from Kentucky, came in whilst I was with the President and in conversation upon the subject of slavery said
that to save the Union he was willing, if necessary, to see
slavery wiped out. Still he is very sensitive upon the subject."

And they were very sensitive, some of the Border State
men, with armies passing to and fro through their cities,
with guerrillas and bushwhackers playing havoc with their
farms, barns, cattle, with informers shifting from one side
to the other, with traders and merchants selling to whichever side would pay high prices. In a letter to a New Orleans man, Lincoln referred to the professed Union men
who would neither help the Government nor permit the
Government to do things without their help. They wished
to stand by without taking sides. "They are to touch neither
a sail nor a pump, but to be merely passengers,—dead-
heads at that—to be carried snug and dry, throughout the
storm, and safely landed right side up." There were true
Union men whose sacrifices were beyond speech to praise.
But there were others whose suggestions could only lead
to a surrender of the Government. Lincoln was not in a
boastful mood. "I shall not do *more* than I can, and I shall
do *all* I can to save the government, which is my sworn
duty as well as my personal inclination." And as if he
might have struggled through tortuous windings to fix for
himself one guiding point amid the intricacies, the President wrote, "I shall do nothing in malice. What I deal with
is too vast for malicious dealing."

Cassius M. Clay, now a major general, had edited the

antislavery *True American*, stumped Kentucky for Lincoln in 1860, and in a debate with a proslavery candidate received a deep stab wound in the left breast over the heart, yet managed to bury his own bowie knife to the hilt in the abdomen of his opponent. This muscular heavyweight, returned from the Russian Legation, came to tell Lincoln to free the slaves, that over Europe he found the governments ready to recognize the Confederacy, anxious to intervene, that an emancipation proclamation now would block these European autocracies. "Kentucky would go against us," said Lincoln, according to Clay. "And we have now as much as we can carry." Clay was decisive, telling the President: "You are mistaken . . ." Lincoln pondered, and at last said: "The Kentucky legislature is now in session. Go down and see how they stand and report to me." And Cash Clay had arrived to find the Kentucky Legislature in flight from approaching Confederate forces.

John Lothrop Motley, the Minister at Vienna, was writing home that having been in London, Paris, Berlin, he was sure that only one of three conditions would stave off European recognition of the Confederacy: (1) a great and conclusive battle crushing the Confederates; (2) the capture of cotton ports and release of large cotton supplies for European factories; (3) a clear-cut policy of emancipation for the slaves. Carl Schurz had reported likewise from Madrid. Lincoln, aware of these points, and at the suggestion of John Bright of the British House of Commons, wrote a resolution suitable for Bright to use:

Whereas, while heretofore States and nations have tolerated slavery, recently, for the first [time] in the world, an attempt has been made to construct a new nation, upon the basis of, and with the primary and fundamental object to maintain, enlarge and perpetuate human slavery; therefore,

Resolved, That no such embryo State should ever be recognized by, or admitted into, the family of Christian and civilized nations; and that all Christian and civilized men everywhere should, by all lawful means, resist to the utmost such recognition and admission.

On August 14, 1862, there came to the Executive Mansion the first committee of free Negroes to arrive by invitation of the President. Greetings and preliminaries over, the President explained that money had been put at his disposal by Congress for the purpose "of colonizing people of African descent," a cause he had long favored. One of those present wrote a memorandum of the words of the President.

"Why," Lincoln asked, "should the people of your race be colonized, and where? Why should they leave this country? . . . Your race suffers very greatly, many of them, by living among us, while ours suffers from your presence . . . Your race are suffering, in my judgment, the greatest wrong inflicted on any people. But even when you cease to be slaves, you are yet far removed from being placed on an equality with the white race . . ." The principal difficulty in the way of colonization, the President suggested to the committee of Negroes, was that "the free colored man cannot see that his comfort would be advanced by it." While slaves would gladly accept freedom on condition of leaving the United States for a colony, the free man would have "nothing to do with the idea . . ." Lincoln unfolded a plan for them to go to a country in Central America, rich in coal mines, farm land, harbors and other advantages. What they could do would depend on themselves. "Success does not as much depend on external help as on self-reliance . . . Could I get a hundred tolerably intelligent men, with their wives and children, and able to 'cut their own fodder,' so to speak? Can I have fifty? If I could find twenty-five able-bodied men, with a mixture of women and children,—good things in the family relation, I think,—I could make a successful commencement. I want you to let me know whether this can be done or not. This is the practical part of my wish to see you."

The President had in view for them to colonize a tract

in the Republic of New Granada. But there were contending factions in the government of New Granada; necessary assurances could not be had of security, and the plan was soon abandoned. The enthusiasm of the free Negroes over such colonization was slight, almost negligible.

Lincoln signed an act ending Negro slavery in the District of Columbia, the Federal Government to buy the slaves at prices not exceeding $200 each. And, the President wishing it, there was provision for steamship tickets to Liberia or Haiti for any freed slaves who cared to go to those Negro republics. This act of Congress and the President was one of many laws, decisions, new precedents, that by percussion and abrasion, by erosion and attrition, were opening gaps in the legal status of slavery, wearing down its props and bulwarks.

Two plans the President struggled with incessantly, like an engineer wrestling to put bridges over a swollen river during a flood rush. One was to make practical the colonization of Negroes to be freed; the other was gradual compensated abolishment. He pointed to Kentucky as a state that recently through legal process had become the owner of slaves, and she sold none but liberated all.

The President asked, and Congress passed, an act recognizing the Negro republics of Haiti and Liberia, though the State Department modified this in announcing that a black man could not be received as a foreign Minister. This in turn was modified informally by the President in a talk with James Redpath, an agent of antislavery societies who had been to Haiti and reported to Lincoln that the Haitian President was profoundly grateful to the American President and so deeply appreciative that he was sending word by Redpath that, if it were the wish of Mr. Lincoln, he would not send to Washington a black man as Haitian Minister. As the Springfield *Republican* correspondent at Washington had it from Redpath, Lincoln hesitated a moment and then drawled, "You can tell the President of Hayti that I shan't tear my shirt if he sends a nigger here!"

When in a few months the Haitian Minister did arrive, C. Edwards Lester wrote of him as having "a finely formed, brilliant face, the complexion being rather dark, but his cheek glowing with the warm tint, and his eye with the liquid beauty of the Creole." Of Mr. Lincoln and the hearty reception accorded him at the White House, the Haitian Minister spoke with veneration, though no name was so dear to the Haitians as that of Charles Sumner. "Signor Carlo il Senatore! why, his picture is in every cottage in Hayti. He has done everything for us."

Congress revised the war regulations so as to forbid any officer of the Army or the Navy to use his forces to capture and return fugitive slaves. Another act provided that such officers could not hear evidence and try cases as to whether a runaway slave should be returned on the claim of an owner. A treaty was negotiated with Great Britain for suppression of the African slave trade. By another act of Congress all slaves in Territories of the United States were declared free. Further legislation provided for the education of Negro children, and Negroes were made admissible as mail-carriers.

These acts of Congress were capped by the Confiscation Act, which the President signed in July '62. Slaves owned by persons convicted of treason or rebellion should be made free, this act declared, and furthermore, slaves of rebels who escaped into Union army lines, or slaves whose masters had run away, or slaves found by the Union Army in places formerly occupied by rebel forces, should all be designated as prisoners of war and set free. Other bills provided that slaves entering Union Army lines could be put to work and earn their freedom; the President could enroll and employ Negroes for camp labor and military service, while the wives, mothers and children of such Negro slaves, if they were the property of armed "rebels," should be set free; the President was authorized "to employ as many persons of African descent as he may deem necessary and proper for the suppression of this rebellion, and for this purpose he may organize and use them in such manner as he may judge best for the public welfare."

Lincoln at first intended to veto the Confiscation Act and have it reframed. Instead he signed it, and returned it with his intended veto message attached, for future record. "It is startling to say that congress can free a slave within a state," ran part of this veto message, "and yet if it were said the ownership of the slave had first been transferred to the nation, and that congress had then liberated him, the difficulty would at once vanish." The slaves of a traitor were forfeited to the Government, which raised the question: "Shall they be made free, or sold to new masters?" He could see no objection to Congress' deciding in advance that they should be free.

Thus far all laws passed by Congress fully protected the ownership of slaves held by men loyal to the Union, or men not partaking in the rebellion. Not many were there of such Unionist slaveowners. All other owners of slaves were under the threat of confiscation of their property if and when the Union armies reached their plantations.

In the midst of these zigzags of public policy, *Harper's Weekly* saw the President as following a midway path, giving in to neither of the extremists. An editorial in May set forth: "In the President of the United States Providence has vouchsafed a leader whose moral perceptions are blinded neither by sophistry nor enthusiasm—who knows that permanent results must grow, and can not be prematurely seized." In a labyrinth of viewpoints Lincoln found himself encircled by groups trying to infiltrate him with their special ideas.

John W. Crisfield, once a fellow member of Congress with Lincoln, and now a member of a House committee to report on gradual compensated emancipation, came to Lincoln's office in July '62 and, according to Lamon, they exchanged remarks. "Well, Crisfield, how are you getting along with your report? Have you written it yet?" "No." "You had better come to an agreement. Niggers will never be cheaper."

On July 22, 1862, as the McClellan campaign for Richmond was fading in mist, mud and disaster, Lincoln called his Cabinet. And as he told it himself at a later time: "I felt that we . . . must change our tactics, or lose the game. I now determined upon the adoption of the emancipation policy . . . I prepared the original draft of the proclamation, and . . . I said to the Cabinet that I . . . had not called them together to ask their advice, but to lay the subject matter of a proclamation before them, suggestions as to which would be in order, after they had heard it read . . . Secretary Seward . . . said in substance, 'Mr. President, I approve of the proclamation, but I question the expediency of its issue at this juncture . . . It may be viewed as the last measure of an exhausted government, a cry for help . . .' His idea was that it would be considered our last *shriek*, on the retreat. 'Now,' continued Mr. Seward, 'while I approve the measure, I suggest, sir, that you postpone its issue, until you can give it to the country supported by military success . . .'

"I put the draft of the proclamation aside . . . Well, the next news we had was of Pope's disaster, at Bull Run. Things looked darker than ever. Finally, came the week of the battle of Antietam . . . The news came, I think, on Wednesday, that the advantage was on our side . . . I finished writing the second draft of the preliminary proclamation . . . called the Cabinet together to hear it, and it was published the following Monday."

At that Cabinet meeting September 22, 1862, the President opened by mentioning that Artemus Ward had sent him a book with a chapter in it titled "High-Handed Outrage at Utica." The President said he would read this chapter, which he thought very funny. It read in part:

In the Faul of 1856, I showed my show in Utiky, a trooly grate sitty in the State of New York . . . 1 day . . . what was my skorn & disgust to see a big burly feller walk up to the cage containin my wax figgers of the Lord's Last Supper, and cease Judas Iscarrot by the feet and drag him out on the ground. He then commenced for to pound him as hard as he cood.

"What under the son are you abowt?" cried I.

Sez he, "What did you bring this pussylanermus cuss here for?" . . .

Sez I, "You egrejus ass, that air's a wax figger . . ."

Sez he, "That's all very well fur you to say, but I tell you, old man, that Judas Iscarrot can't show his-self in Utiky with impunerty by a darn site!" with which observashun he kaved in Judassis hed. The young man belonged to 1 of the first famerlies in Utiky. I sood him, and the Joory brawt in a verdick of Arson in the 3rd degree.

Lincoln enjoyed this clownery. So did other members of the Cabinet, though Seward laughed for fun while Chase smiled rather conventionally. Stanton sat glum and glowering.

Then Lincoln took a grave tone, with a solemn deliberation read the proclamation, commenting as he went along. It began with saying the war would go on for the Union, that the efforts would go on for buying and setting free the slaves of the Border States, and the colonizing of them; that on January 1, 1863, all slaves in states or parts of states in rebellion against the United States "shall be then, thenceforward, and forever free," and the Federal Government would "recognize the freedom of such persons." It was a preliminary proclamation.

Seward suggested adding the words "and maintain" after the word "recognize." Chase joined Seward in this, and it was done. Blair said he was for the principle involved, but the result of the proclamation would be to send the Border States into the arms of the secessionists; also it would give a club to hostile political elements in the North. Seward made another minor suggestion, that colonization should be only with the consent of the colonists; Negroes were to be sent out of the country only as they were willing to go. Lincoln put that in quickly. Then he asked Seward why he had not proposed both of his important changes at once. Seward hedged. And Lincoln said Seward reminded him of a hired man out West who came to the farmer one afternoon with news that one of a yoke of oxen had dropped dead. And after hesitating and waiting a while, the hired man said the other ox in the team had dropped dead too. The farmer asked, "Why didn't you tell me at once that both oxen were dead?" "Because," said the hired man, "I didn't want to hurt you by telling you too much at one time."

Two days later, September 24, on a Monday morning, this preliminary Emancipation Proclamation was published, for the country and the world to read. Serenaders came with a brass band to have music over the proclamation. The President addressed them from a White House balcony: ". . . I can only trust in God I have made no mistake . . . It is now for the country and the world to pass judgment on it, and, may be, take action upon it." He was "environed with difficulties," he soberly wished the crowd to know. "Yet they are scarcely so great as the difficulties of those who, upon the battle field, are endeavoring to purchase with their blood and their lives the future happiness and prosperity of this country." He wanted those soldiers with him. He was privately wondering how many of them now were stronger for him.

On invitation of Curtin a gathering of governors of Northern States met that day in Altoona, Pennsylvania, "to take measures for the more active support of the Government." It was in the minds of Andrew and other anti-slavery governors that they might frame a decision which would bring pressure on the President to remove McClellan from command and to issue some positive declaration against slavery. The ground had been cut from under them by Antietam and the Emancipation Proclamation. Sixteen of them signed an address to the President, pledging loyalty to the Union, endorsing the new emancipation policy, and suggesting that he should call for 100,000 more troops to be organized into a reserve corps for emergencies. Five governors held off from signing. They were from the Slave States Kentucky, Missouri, Maryland and Delaware, and the odd Northern bailiwick of New Jersey. While also pledging loyalty to the Union and support of the President, these five governors could not endorse the Emancipation Proclamation.

To justify their private and rather secretive conference during such a crisis, the governors appointed Andrew and

Curtin a committee to see the President in Washington. They went back home to their state capitals encouraged and refreshed in faith, according to a close friend of Andrew.

The Democratic party, already campaigning for the November elections, raised the issue that the war for the Union had been changed to a war for abolition. McClellan wrote his wife that the President's proclamation, and other troubles, "render it almost impossible for me to retain my commission and self-respect at the same time." Lincoln had now gone over to the radicals, the Louisville *Democrat* and other papers told readers. "The abolitionists have pressed him into their service." John Hay spoke of editorials in the leading newspapers. The President said he had studied the matter so long that "he knew more about it than they did."

Beyond the newspapers and politicians were the People and Lincoln's question was: What were they thinking? In many quarters the proclamation was called grand, historic, and its author an immortal. Lincoln wrote in a letter marked "Strictly private," ". . . while commendation in newspapers and by distinguished individuals is all that a vain man could wish, the stocks have declined, and troops come forward more slowly than ever."

The President's act had been like a chemist tossing a tiny pinch of a powerful ingredient into a seething and shaking caldron. Colors and currents shifted and deepened. New channels cut their way far under the surface. The turmoil and the trembling became unreadable by any man. But below the fresh confusion was heaving some deep and irrevocable change.

The proclamation was aimed at Europe as well as North and South America. London *Punch* cartooned Lincoln with horns and a long tail. London, Henry Adams wrote, ". . . created a nightmare of its own and gave it the shape of Abraham Lincoln." In England, because of the cotton famine, nearly 500,000 men were out of work. In a single textile district of France were 130,000 unemployed. Yet a definite mass opinion favored the North as against the South.

The press and Premier Palmerston and the voices of the ruling class of England could not hope to change the basic instinct of the masses, now deeper in response to the Lincoln Government as against that of Davis at Richmond. In the inner circles of the ruling class it was admitted that now there would be increased difficulty for any European government to recognize the South.

A wave of fury swept the South. Lincoln was breaking the laws of civilized warfare, outraging private-property rights, inviting Negroes to kill, burn and rape, said statesmen, orators, newspapers. The Richmond *Enquirer* fumed, "What shall we call him? Coward, assassin, savage, murderer of women and babies? Or shall we consider them all as embodied in the word fiend, and call him Lincoln, the Fiend?"

Lincoln had warned nearly a year back that the contest might develop into "remorseless, revolutionary warfare." The awful responsibility of carrying on and finishing a war of conquest lay ahead.

Something new was in the writing—but what? Something was dying, something being born—but what?

Toward the end of this sad September Lincoln wrote a riddle that beset his mind, haunted his heart. He left it on his desk. It was not for publication. John Hay made a copy of it: "The will of God prevails. In great contests each party claims to act in accordance with the will of God. Both may be, and one must be, wrong. God cannot be for and against the same thing at the same time. In the present civil war it is quite possible that God's purpose is something different from the purpose of either party; and yet the human instrumentalities, working just as they do, are the best adaptation to effect his purpose. I am almost ready to say that this is probably true; that God wills this contest, and wills that it shall not end yet. By his mere great power on the minds of the new contestants, he could have either saved or destroyed the Union without a human contest. Yet the contest began. And having begun, he could give the final victory to either side any day. Yet the contest proceeds."

Chapter 11

McClellan's "Slows" — Election Losses —
Fredericksburg — '62 Message

Writing from the Paris consulate, John Bigelow asked
Weed, "Why doesn't Lincoln shoot somebody?" From his
pivotal point of observation, however, Lincoln could find
no unanimous opinion as to whom to shoot. In early October '62 Governor Morton of Indiana wrote to the President, "Another three months like the last six and we are
lost—lost."

From day to day political questions interwove with military. At several Cabinet meetings the last week in September '62 came the matter of deporting freed Negroes. Blair
and Bates, the Missouri members, favored forcible depor-
tation, the President holding that only those should go who
wished to go. He laid before Welles the maps, reports,
titles and evidence having to do with the Chiriqui land grant
in Panama, for Welles to make a decision as to whether
the Navy Department should contract to buy coal from
there, the coal to be mined by colonized free Negroes from
the United States. "The President was earnest in the matter," wrote Welles in his diary; "wished to send the negroes
out of the country," was "importunate."

Outside of Cabinet meetings Chase was telling Welles
that Stanton felt useless and deemed it his duty to resign
from the Cabinet. Welles said he was not surprised to hear
it, that sooner or later either Stanton or some of the generals would have to go. "Chase said if Stanton went, he
would go," wrote Welles. "It was due to Stanton and to
ourselves that we should stand by him, and if one goes out,
all had better go, certainly he [Chase] would." Thus Chase

was trying to lay the way for a Cabinet departure, for all of them to quit at once.

Towering over immediate issues stood the sphinx of McClellan's army—how to get it moving. While McClellan "rested" his troops a visitor casually asked Lincoln what number of men he supposed the "rebels" had in the field. And according to *Leslie's Weekly,* he said seriously, "1,200,000 according to the best authority." The visitor turned pale and cried, "My God!" "Yes, sir," went on the President, "1,200,000—no doubt of it. You see, all our generals, when they get whipped, say the enemy outnumbers them from three to five to one, and I must believe them. We have 400,000 men in the field, and three times four makes twelve. Don't you see it?"

On October 1 Lincoln, without notifying McClellan, started for the Army of the Potomac camps. McClellan got word of Lincoln's being on the way, rode to Harpers Ferry, and was pleased to find that no Cabinet members or politicians were with the President, "merely some western officers." "His ostensible purpose," McClellan wrote his wife, "is to see the troops and the battle-field; I incline to think that the real purpose of his visit is to push me into a premature advance into Virginia."

They rode horseback all of one afternoon around the camps. Mathew B. Brady photographed them together sitting in McClellan's tent, Lincoln's right arm resting against a flag draping a table where his tall silk hat stood upside down between two stubs of candles.

The dim gray twilight just before dawn came over the hills of Maryland as Lincoln rose in the tent assigned to him. A few rooster crows drifted on the air from nearby farms. It was a quiet hour. Lincoln stood at the cot of Ozias M. Hatch, once secretary of state in Illinois, saying, "Come, Hatch, I want you to take a walk with me." Hatch got up without a word, the two of them dressed, and left the tent together. Lincoln led Hatch through the streets of a great tented city, amid avenues of little white canvas huts where thousands of soldiers were sleeping. Very little was spoken. "Lincoln seemed to be peculiarly serious," Hatch noted, "and his quiet, abstract way affected me also. It did not seem a time to speak. Nothing was to be said, nothing needed to be said."

They reached a commanding point in the hills where the rising sun spread its moving sheen over the stirring, half-awake army of men at their morning routine. The President waved his hand in a gesture of half-despair, and leaning toward Hatch, said in a husky and almost whispering voice, "Hatch—Hatch, what is all this?" "Why, Mr. Lincoln," said Hatch, "this is the Army of the Potomac." Lincoln hesitated a moment, and then straightening up, in a louder and clearer tone of voice: "No, Hatch, no. This is General McClellan's bodyguard." Nothing more was said. The two men walked slowly back to their tent.

At Frederick, Maryland, the troops were drawn up. The President told them it was not proper for him in his present position to make speeches. He gave thanks to the soldiers for good services, energy shown, hardships endured and blood shed for the Union. He hoped their children, and their children's children for a thousand generations to come, would enjoy the benefits of a united country.

Passing a house in which lay Confederate wounded, Lincoln asked to go in. A correspondent quoted him as saying they were "enemies through uncontrollable circumstances." After a silence, Confederates came forward and without words shook the hand of the President. Some were too sore and broken to walk or to sit up. The President went among these, took some by the hand, wished them good cheer, said they should have the best of care. The correspondent wrote, "Beholders wept at the interview, most of the Confederates, even, were moved to tears."

Lamon and others rode with the President in an ambulance a few miles to Porter's corps. On the way Lincoln said, "Lamon, sing one of your little sad songs." And Lamon sang "Twenty Years Ago," a melancholy Thomas Hood poem of which Lamon said, "Many a time, in the old days on the Illinois circuit, and often at the White House when he and I were alone, have I seen him in tears while

I was rendering, in my poor way, that homely melody."

The song deepened Lincoln's sadness, and, said Lamon: "I then did what I had done many times before; I startled him from his melancholy by striking up a comic air, singing also a snatch from 'Picayune Butler,'" a blackface minstrel comic. Neither Lincoln nor Lamon had any notion that the singing in the ambulance that morning would be interpreted and spread on tongues of hate and malice, to be colored and magnified into an allegation, published and spoken, that while the slain still lay on the battlefield of Antietam, and the wounded were still languishing nearby, the President had called on a boisterous boon companion for a ribald song and had rollicked in laughter over it. So far would the slander spread that the two men were to talk it over in bitterness and prepare a completely detailed statement of what had happened, and then in quiet dignity withhold it from publication.

Two days later Lincoln was in Washington, and a telegram went to McClellan from Halleck, saying: "The President directs that you cross the Potomac and give battle to the enemy, or drive him south. Your army must move now, while the roads are good." No particular results came from this. McClellan may have thought the positive tone of the telegram was due to War Department politics. He believed he had done so well that he was entitled to a rest and asked the President for time. For Lincoln himself were no days off. But he wired McClellan, "You wish to see your family and I wish to oblige you," letting McClellan go to Philadelphia for a visit with wife and daughter.

Three weeks had gone by since Antietam. Yet McClellan stayed north of the Potomac with 100,000 men while Lee not far off in Virginia was recruiting his army from conscripts called up by the Richmond Government.

Repeatedly across months Lincoln remarked of McClellan, "He's got the slows." Like fact was the gossip that a Government official, getting a pass to see McClellan, remarked, "I'll report when I come back if I find the army." "Oh, you will," said Lincoln. "It's there. That's just the difficulty."

By latter October, it seemed, McClellan's dealings at Washington were entirely with Lincoln. "All his official correspondence is with the President direct and no one else," wrote Welles. To Lincoln, McClellan sent his calls for more shoes, mules, horses. To one of these Lincoln replied: "I have just read your despatch about sore tongued and fatiegued horses. Will you pardon me for asking what the horses of your army have done since the battle of Antietam that fatigues anything?" McClellan wrote to his wife, "It was one of those little flings that I can't get used to when they are not merited."

McClellan now slowly moved his army across the Potomac and put it about where Pope's army had lain before Second Bull Run. It was November. Lincoln told John Hay he would make a final judgment of McClellan. If he should permit Lee to cross the Blue Ridge and place himself between Richmond and the Army of the Potomac, Lincoln would remove McClellan from command. When Lee's army reached Culpeper Court House the test of McClellan was over.

The November elections of '62 nearly doubled the number of Democratic Congressmen, raising it from 44 to 75. In five states where Lincoln two years before had won the electoral vote, his party now lost; and the Democrats elected Horatio Seymour as governor of New York. The proadministration New York *Times* said the balloting registered "want of confidence" in the President.

Leslie's Weekly itemized: "When Colonel Forney inquired of him [Lincoln] how he felt about New York, he replied: 'Somewhat like that boy in Kentucky, who stubbed his toe while running to see his sweetheart. The boy said he was too big to cry, and far too badly hurt to laugh.'"

Lincoln wrote to Carl Schurz: "We have lost the elections . . ." and gave three main causes: "1. The democrats were left in a majority by our friends going to the war. 2. The democrats observed this & determined to re-instate themselves in power, and 3. Our newspaper's, by vilifying and disparaging the administration, furnished them all the weapons to do it with. Certainly, the ill-success of the war had much to do with this."

Political confusion of that hour was told in interviews Congressmen had with Lincoln just after the elections. William D. Kelley of Philadelphia came to the White House. Lincoln congratulated him on re-election, saying, as Kelley noted, "Sit down and tell me how it is that you, for whose election nobody seemed to hope, are returned with a good majority at your back, while so many of our friends about whom there was no doubt, have been badly beaten." Kelley said that six months earlier he would have been beaten, but he had been saved by his independent demand for a fighting general to replace McClellan.

J. K. Moorhead, Representative from the Pittsburgh district, heaved through the door, joined with the others in saying the administration had compromised, delayed, held on to McClellan too long. He told of riding to Harrisburg the day before with some of the best and most influential people of his state, including men who had one time been earnest Lincoln supporters. "They charged me," said Moorhead, "to tell you that when one of them said he would be glad to hear some morning that you had been found hanging from the post of a lamp at the door of the White House, others approved the expression."

At this, Kelley noted, the manner of the President changed. He was perfectly calm, and, in a subdued voice: "You need not be surprised to find that that suggestion has been executed any morning. The violent preliminaries to such an event would not surprise me. I have done things lately that must be incomprehensible to the people, and which cannot now be explained."

They talked about who should be named to replace McClellan. Kelley urged trying one general and another till the right man was found, the first change to be made soon. Kelley felt the President thoughtful but evasive in responding to several suggestions, "We shall see what we shall see."

Of the authenticated stories Lincoln used for illustration, one seemed to be reported by callers and visitors more than any other. Often his duties required him to be furtive and secretive beyond what he liked in political affairs. He would tell of the Irishman in Maine where state law prohibits the sale of alcoholic liquor. Having ordered a glass of lemonade and the glass set before him, the Irishman whispered to the druggist, "And now can ye pour in jist a wee drop of the creether unbeknownst to me?" In a public discussion of the use or misuse of presidential powers Lincoln once said, "I am like the Irishman, I have to do some things unbeknownst to myself."

The anti-McClellan group was holding sway. Fitz-John Porter was court-martialed on charges of disobedience, accused of helping to ruin Pope at Second Bull Run. A brave man, a highly competent officer, he was to be cashiered, drummed out of the Army. Don Carlos Buell, in the West, was under investigation by a commission which was to let him out as a major general. Lincoln was keeping hands off, allowing the authorized functionaries to have their way with Porter and Buell.

Old Frank Blair argued with Lincoln against McClellan's removal. Monty Blair told of this interview: "Lincoln . . . at the end of the conference rose up and stretched his long arms almost to the ceiling above him, saying, 'I said I would remove him if he let Lee's army get away from him, and I must do so. He has got the slows, Mr. Blair.'"

Two men traveled in a driving snowstorm near midnight November 7 to find the tent of General McClellan near Rectortown. They stepped in and shook off the snow from their overcoats. They had interrupted him in the writing of a letter to his wife. One of the men was Adjutant General C. P. Buckingham of the War Department. The other was Major General Ambrose Everett Burnside. Buckingham handed McClellan a message relieving him of command of the Army of the Potomac and ordering him to turn it over to Burnside. A second message told McClellan to report to Trenton, New Jersey, for further orders. McClellan finished the letter to his wife: "Alas for my poor country! . . . Do not be at all worried—I am not."

A farewell letter from McClellan read to the army was

cheered. Where McClellan showed himself among the soldiers he was cheered. He had a way with him, a magnetism, and a figure and manner. The man taking his place, Burnside, came near weeping as he told McClellan he had refused to accept command until ordered.

According to Governor Andrew, Lincoln was asked what he would reply to McClellan's earlier advice on how to carry on the affairs of the nation. And Lincoln answered: "Nothing—but it made me think of the man whose horse kicked up and stuck his foot through the stirrup. He said to the horse, 'If you are going to get on I will get off.'"

McClellan's enemies seized on such incidents as one told by Colonel Albert V. Colburn of McClellan's staff— that when the General saw the Emancipation Proclamation in the Baltimore *Sun*, he hurled the paper into a corner, exclaiming: "There! Look at that outrage! I shall resign tomorrow!" McClellan wrote to his wife the last of October, ". . . the good of the country requires me to submit to . . . men whom I know to be vastly my inferiors, socially, intellectually and morally. There never was a truer epithet applied to a certain individual than that of 'Gorilla.'"

No case was ever made out that McClellan was not brave and able. Only politicians, personal enemies, loose talkers, called him coward or sloven. At Malvern Hill and Antietam he performed superbly—and then failed to clinch and use what he had won. If he had been the bold ambitious plotter that Stanton, Chase and others saw, he would have marched his army to Washington and seized the Government there, as he said many urged him to do. His defect was that while he could not have instigated such treason himself, he did allow approaches to such treason to be talked freely in his staff and army without rebuke or repression from him.

His friend Aspinwall, the New York financier, who came to his camp, gave him the keen advice to go along with Lincoln's Emancipation Proclamation, say nothing, and be a soldier. From the way he wrote his wife of what Aspinwall told him, it would almost seem as though this was the first time he seriously considered the gift of silence on politics for a general heading an army given to him by a government wrestling with delicately shaded political questions.

Burnside spent three days with McClellan going over the army organization and plans. He was 39, a log-cabin boy, born at Liberty, Indiana, one of nine sons. His father, a state senator, got him a cadetship at West Point, where he met McClellan, Stonewall Jackson and others who rose in the Army. Burnside's Rhode Island regiment was among the first troops to arrive in Washington, where Lincoln often visited his camp. His chief distinction was in leading a joint naval and military force that early in 1862 captured Roanoke Island with 2,600 prisoners and 32 guns. This won applause, an embellished sword from Rhode Island, and the thanks of the Massachusetts and Ohio Legislatures.

When Burnside called at the White House Lincoln embraced him, and on Burnside's request promoted three of Burnside's brigadiers to major generals. Commanding a corps, he had been with McClellan on the Peninsula and through Antietam. A gathering of generals met him just after his latest promotion and congratulated him. Carl Schurz, now back from Spain and given his commission as major general, for which he had long ago asked Lincoln, wrote that Burnside thanked them "and then, with that transparent sincerity of his nature which made everyone believe what he said, he added that he knew he was not fit for so big a command, but he would do his best." It was touching.

Lincoln took the man who had been a friend of McClellan and who might inherit the good will of the Army for McClellan. Also he had found Burnside free of the plot and intrigue of army politics, exceptional in loyalty and sincerity.

In choosing the Fredericksburg locality for action Burnside was having his own way. "Somewhat to Mr. Lincoln's chagrin," noted Nicolay and Hay, "the first act of the new general was to object to the plan of campaign furnished to McClellan from Washington." Halleck had gone down to

see Burnside about it, returned to Washington, laid the
matter before Lincoln, who said Yes to Burnside's plan
provided he "moved rapidly." Lincoln went down himself
to see the army and Burnside. The President and the General had a long conference.

Now came Fredericksburg, a trap. Lee with 72,000 men
was ready and waiting for Burnside with 113,000. For a
month Burnside had been waiting for pontoons to cross
the river. While the pontoons were on the way Lee made
arrangements. Burnside's columns crossed over. They found
hills spitting flame and metal, a sunken road swarming
with riflemen waiting human prey. "A chicken can not
live on that field when we open on it," a Confederate engineer had told General Longstreet of the plain facing Marye's
Hill. Meagher led his Irish Brigade of 1,315 up the hill and
left 545 in the frozen mud. Hancock's division lost 40 of
each 100 of its men. Between the fog of morning and twilight of evening 7,000 killed and wounded Union soldiers
fell. The wounded lay 48 hours in the freezing cold before
they were cared for. Some burned to death in long, dry
grass set afire by cannon. Total Confederate losses were
5,309; Union, 12,653.

"Oh! those men! those men over there!" cried Burnside at
his headquarters, pointing across the river. "I am thinking
of them all the time." Out of his grief came an idea. He
would take his old corps, the 9th, and lead it against the
stone wall and 300 cannon of the enemy. But his men
would not let him think of it. In a rainy windstorm Burnside drew off his troops from Fredericksburg, back across
the Rappahannock.

The morale of the army was hard hit. The troops had
shown all the courage asked for. But with such commanders above them, what could they do? They asked that. On
review they were called to give a cheer for their general.
They hooted. Some went above Burnside and blamed Lincoln. More officers resigned. More privates deserted.

Lieutenant William Thompson Lusk wrote to his mother:
"Alas, my poor country! It has strong limbs to march, brave
hearts to dare—but the brains, the brains—have we no

brains to use the arms and limbs and eager hearts with cunning? Perhaps Old Abe has some funny story to tell appropriate to the occasion. Alas, let us await the wise words of Father Abraham! . . . I believe Burnside to be brave and honest. The President I doubt not is honest, but 'let the shoemaker stick to his last.' Let Lincoln turn his talents to splitting rails. I prefer George McClellan to Abraham Lincoln, as Commander-in-Chief of the Army."

Burnside gave out a letter to Halleck talking all blame on himself, praising officers and men for gallantry, courage, endurance. "For the failure in the attack I am responsible," he wrote.

The President issued an address to the Army of the Potomac: "Although you were not successful, the attempt was not an error, nor the failure other than an accident. The courage with which you, in an open field, maintained the contest against an entrenched foe, and the consummate skill and success with which you crossed and re-crossed the river in the face of the enemy, show that you possess all the qualities of a great army, which will yet give victory to the cause of the country and of popular government."

Was the President thinking one thing privately and saying something else publicly as to the issues of the battle? Not according to William O. Stoddard of the White House staff, who wrote: "We lost fifty per cent more men than did the enemy, and yet there is sense in the awful arithmetic propounded by Mr. Lincoln. He says that if the same battle were to be fought over again, every day, through a week of days, with the same relative results, the army under Lee would be wiped out to its last man, the Army of the Potomac would still be a mighty host, the war would be over, the Confederacy gone. No general yet found can face the arithmetic, but the end of the war will be at hand when he shall be discovered."

A Department of Interior clerk, T. J. Barnet, wrote in a diary of hearing Lincoln after the Fredericksburg collapse, "If there is a worse place than Hell, then I am in it." And on a later occasion, "I always meant that this war should have a peace in its belly."

A week passed and Burnside made ready for another move, ordered three days' rations in the men's haversacks. He seemed to have another battle in mind. These were hard days for Burnside, for on the same day that Lincoln warned him to make no forward movement, Halleck telegraphed him "to press the enemy," and some of his advisers urged him to win a victory and break the national gloom.

Lincoln now wrote Halleck it was his wish that Halleck go to Burnside, examine Burnside's plan, talk with the officers, get their judgment, notice their temper. "Gather all the elements for forming a judgment of your own: and then tell Gen. Burnside that you *do* approve, or that you do *not* approve his plan. Your military skill is useless to me, if you will not do this."

Halleck took this letter as insinuating. He asked to be relieved of his duties as General in Chief. Lincoln did not want to see Halleck go, as yet, and he did not want to hurt Halleck's feelings. So he "withdrew" the letter, writing the notation on it that it was "considered harsh by General Halleck." This being so, Halleck "withdrew" his request to be relieved.

The President's message to Congress December 1, 1862, opened with reports and comments on miscellaneous affairs and flowed on into discussions of the Union, slavery, the Negro. The argument for the Union mixed logic and sentiment: "A nation may be said to consist of its territory, its people, and its laws. The territory is the only part which is of certain durability." Laws change; people die; the land remains.

He pointed to "that portion of the earth's surface which is owned and inhabited by the people of the United States" as adapted to be the home of "one national family" and not for two or more. With the arrival of "steam, telegraphs, and intelligence," the modern inventions, there was still more advantage in having "one united people."

He pointed to the great interior region bounded by the Alleghenies on the east, Canada on the north, the Rockies on the west, and on the south by the line along which the cultures of corn and cotton meet. Already this region had 10,000,000 people and within 50 more years would have 50,000,000. "And yet this region has no sea-coast, touches no ocean anywhere." With separation of states it would have no outlet and would be cut off by physical barriers and trade regulations.

In previous messages Lincoln had not given so heavy an emphasis to the argument against secession in behalf of the Middle West from which he came. As the war had gone on he had found that the instinct for national solidarity was a deep one with the Midwestern people. Only six weeks before his message was delivered it was announced that Iowa was the first state to fill her quota under the call for 600,000 men; she had put every man into the field by voluntary enlistment, and all for three years of the war. The President was voicing Iowa, Ohio, Kansas and other states in declaring that "outlets, east, west, and south, are indispensable."

He pleaded: "Our strife pertains to ourselves—to the passing generations of men; and it can, without convulsion, be hushed forever with the passing of one generation." From this almost mystic appeal for the saving of the Union he passed to a concrete proposal, the Constitution of the United States to be amended to provide that every state which abolished slavery at any time before January 1, 1900, should be paid for its freed slaves in U.S. bonds at a rate of interest and in sums to be agreed upon for each slave. Congress would be given express power to set aside money and otherwise provide for colonizing free colored persons. "Without slavery the rebellion could never have existed; without slavery it could not continue."

Each state could work out its own plan, and no two states were obliged to proceed alike. Before the end of the 37 years in which the proposed emancipation could be accomplished, the country would have probably 100,000,000 people instead of 37,000,000 to pay the cost. "The proposed emancipation would shorten the war, perpetuate peace, insure this increase of population, and proportionately the wealth of the country."

As to sending freed Negroes out of the country, he made his view clear again. "I cannot make it better known than it already is, that I strongly favor colonization. And yet I wish to say there is an objection urged against free colored persons remaining in the country, which is largely imaginary, if not sometimes malicious." It was insisted Negroes would injure and displace white laborers. On this he gave warnings. "If there ever could be a proper time for mere catch arguments, that time surely is not now. *In times like the present, men should utter nothing for which they would not willingly be responsible through time and in eternity*." [Italics added.]

Every device of the art of persuasion that Lincoln had ever learned was put into this appeal. "The plan would, I am confident, secure peace more speedily, and maintain it more permanently, than can be done by force alone." It was the only way to end the war without victory, with something like permanent justice to all concerned. "All it would cost, considering amounts, and manner of payment . . . would be easier paid than will be the additional cost of the war, if we rely solely upon force. It is much—very much—that it would cost no blood at all."

Permanent constitutional results would be achieved. First, two-thirds of Congress, and afterwards three-fourths of the states, would have to concur in the plan. This would assure emancipation, end the struggle and save the Union for all time.

Was he getting too personal with the Senators and Congressmen? Did it seem too simple that he should assure them of a straight and clear way to cut through the vast labyrinth of interests back of the war? Perhaps so. For he felt it necessary to meet them on personal ground, as man to man. A gesture of true respect was required: "I do not forget the gravity which should characterize a paper addressed to the Congress of the nation by the Chief Magistrate of the nation. Nor do I forget that some of you are my seniors, nor that many of you have more experience than I, in the conduct of public affairs. Yet I trust that in view of the great responsibility resting upon me, you will perceive no want of respect to yourselves, in any undue earnestness I may seem to display."

He pleaded further that whatever objection might be made, still the question would recur, "Can we do better?" An old chapter in national life was over and another begun. "The dogmas of the quiet past, are inadequate to the stormy present. The occasion is piled high with difficulty, and we must rise with the occasion. As our case is new, so we must think anew, and act anew. We must disenthrall ourselves."

Possibly never before had Lincoln used that word "disenthrall." It was not a familiar word with him. He seemed almost to imply that though men might give physical emancipation to others who were oppressed, each individual must achieve his own disenthrallment, rise out of his old into a new self. A subtlety of philosophic thought was in the added suggestion, "In *giving* freedom to the *slave,* we *assure* freedom to the *free*—honorable alike in what we give, and what we preserve."

In his last paragraph he struck for motives to move men. "Fellow-citizens, *we* cannot escape history. We of this Congress and this administration, will be remembered in spite of ourselves. No personal significance or insignificance can spare one or another of us. The fiery trial through which we pass, will light us down, in honor or dishonor, to the latest generation."

He flung out sentences edging on irony. "We *say* we are for the Union. The world will not forget that we say this. We know how to save the Union. The world knows we do know how to save it. We—even *we here*—hold the power, and bear the responsibility . . . Other means may succeed; this could not fail. The way is plain, peaceful, generous, just —a way which, if followed, the world will forever applaud, and God must forever bless."

Thus ended the lesson. What came of it? No action at all except a faint groping toward compensated abolishment in the Slave State of Missouri. The Border States were too divided in viewpoint to act decisively. They were not yet cemented back into the Union. Lexington, Kentucky, on

December 18 again fell into Confederate hands when Bedford Forrest's raiders drove off Illinois cavalry commanded by Colonel Robert G. Ingersoll of Peoria, Illinois.

The President's message was a compromise affair, aimed to throw sops of satisfaction into camps too hostile to be brought together for action. So said some. Others said he was riding a hobby, that as a Border State man he could not see that slavery must be destroyed root and branch first of all. Yet even to many who differed from him, who could not agree that his plan was practical, he delivered an impression of sincerely struggling to lift before men's eyes a banner worth sacrifice.

This December message prepared the way for the Emancipation Proclamation to be issued January 1, 1863—*if* the President should decide to issue it. The question was in the air whether he would. Radical antislavery men were saying the President would not dare issue the proclamation. Certain Border State men were saying he would not dare confiscate and destroy $1,000,000,000 in property values. Army men were not lacking to pronounce the judgment that such a proclamation would bring wholesale desertions, that entire companies and regiments would throw down their arms.

Senator Browning wrote in his diary of ". . . the hallucination the President seems to be laboring under that Congress can suppress the rebellion by adopting his plan of compensated emancipation."

Chapter 12

Thunder over the Cabinet — Murfreesboro

When Chase told Senator Fessenden there was "a backstairs influence" controlling the President, he knew Fessenden understood no one else was meant but Seward. That

Seward with his cigars, cynicism, wit and nonsense, was the most companionable human being in the Cabinet had no bearing.

The Republican Senators in secret caucus December 15, 1862, discussed a letter written by Seward to Minister Adams six months before. Senator Sumner had taken the letter to Lincoln and asked if he had approved it. Lincoln said he had never seen the letter before. The newspapers got hold of this and raked Seward. The radicals claimed one more proof that Seward was a backstairs influence paralyzing the President's best intentions. Seward's offending letter had these words: "It seems as if the extreme advocates of African slavery and its most vehement opponents were acting in concert together to precipitate a servile war—the former by making the most desperate attempts to overthrow the Federal Union, the latter by demanding an edict of universal emancipation as a lawful and necessary, if not, as they say, the only legitimate way of saving the Union."

Senator Fessenden's memorandum of the secret caucus noted: "Silence ensued for a few moments, when Mr. Wilkinson [of Minnesota] said that in his opinion the country was ruined and the cause lost . . . The Secretary of State, Mr. Seward, exercised a controlling influence upon the mind of the President. He, Mr. Seward, had never believed in the war, and so long as he remained in the Cabinet nothing but defeat and disaster could be expected." Ben Wade followed, "particularly censuring the Executive for placing our armies under the command of officers who did not believe in the policy of the government and had no sympathy with its purposes." Senator Collamer found the difficulty in the fact that the President had no Cabinet in the true sense of the word. Fessenden said a duty was upon the Senate in the crisis at hand. It should, however, proceed cautiously and with unanimity or its action would alarm the country and weaken the hands of the Executive.

Browning noted in his diary that "old Ben Wade made a long speech in which he declared that the Senate should go in a body and demand of the President the removal or dismissal of Mr. Seward . . . he would never be satisfied until there was a Republican at the head of our armies."

The next day's caucus appointed a committee of nine to wait upon the President "and urge upon him changes in conduct and in the Cabinet which shall give the administration unity and vigor." The secret caucus was not yet over when Senator Preston King hurried to Seward's house, found his old colleague sitting in the library, and remarked: "I did not stay for the last vote, but just slipped out to tell you, for I thought you ought to know. They were pledging each other to keep the proceedings secret, but I told them I was not going to be bound."

Seward chewed a cigar and said, "They may do as they please about me, but they shall not put the President in a false position." He called for pen and paper and wrote to the President: "Sir, I hereby resign the office of Secretary of State, and beg that my resignation be accepted immediately." Five minutes later King put the note in the hands of Lincoln, who read it, looked up with surprise, and said, "What does this mean?" King told of the day's events. Later in the evening Lincoln stepped over to Seward's house, spoke his regrets to Seward, who remarked that it would be a relief to be free from official cares. "Ah, yes, Governor," said Lincoln, "that will do very well for you, but I am like the starling in Sterne's story, 'I can't get out.' "

Congressman Charles B. Sedgwick, a Syracuse, New York, lawyer wrote to his wife: "I went to the President's with Thad. Stevens & Conklin to urge him to accept Seward's resignation. With his usual adroitness & cunning Seward, soon as he had tendered his resignation, began to send in his friends to the President to frighten him into refusing to accept it & I wanted to do what I could to counteract it . . . I fear the President needs strengthening . . . I think you had better not show this letter at present."

Browning wrote of the next evening. ". . . the President . . . asked me if I was at the caucus yesterday. I told him I was and the day before also. Said he 'What do these men want?' I answered 'I hardly know Mr. President, but they

are exceedingly violent towards the administration . . .'
Said he 'They wish to get rid of me, and I am sometimes
half disposed to gratify them . . . We are now on the brink
of destruction. It appears to me the Almighty is against us,
and I can hardly see a ray of hope.' I answered 'Be firm
and we will yet save the Country. Do not be driven from
your post. You ought to have crushed the ultra, impracti-
cable men last summer . . .' He then said 'Why will men believe a lie, an absurd lie, that could not impose upon a child,
and cling to it and repeat it in defiance of all evidence to the
contrary.' I understood this to refer to the charges against
Mr. Seward."

The committee of Senators was to call on him at seven
that night, Lincoln told Browning—and added, "Since I
heard last night of the proceedings of the caucus I have
been more distressed than by any event of my life." The
committee came that December night of '62, Collamer,
Wade, Grimes, Fessenden, Trumbull, Sumner, Harris, Pomeroy and Howard. "The President received us with his usual
urbanity," Fessenden noted, though Browning had seen
Lincoln only a few minutes earlier wearing a troubled face
and saying he was "more distressed" than by any event of
his life.

Collamer rose and read his carefully prepared paper. Its
main points were that the war for the Union must go on;
the President should employ the combined wisdom and deliberation of his Cabinet members, who in turn should be
unwaveringly for the war; it was unwise and unsafe to commit military operations to anyone not a cordial believer
and supporter of the war as patriotic and just, rendered
necessary by "a causeless and atrocious rebellion."

Ben Wade stood up to say the war had been left in the
hands of men who had no sympathy with it or with the
cause. Grimes and Howard rose to say confidence in Seward was gone. Fessenden began with saying the Senate believed in the patriotism and integrity of the President, dis-
claiming any wish to dictate to him as to his Cabinet. He
dwelt on the public belief that the Secretary of State was
not in accord with a majority of the Cabinet. Again, in the

conduct of the war almost every officer known as an anti-slavery man had been disgraced. The Democrats were using General McClellan for party purposes.

Sumner rose to say that Seward in official correspondence had made statements offensively disrespectful to Congress, and had written dispatches the President could not have seen or assented to. The President replied that it was Seward's habit to read the dispatches to him before they were sent, but they were not usually submitted to a Cabinet meeting. He did not recollect the letter to which Sumner referred.

"Some three hours were spent in conversation with the President," Fessenden noted, "but no definite action was discussed. The President said he would carefully examine and consider the paper submitted, expressed his satisfaction with the tone and temper of the committee, and we left him in apparently cheerful spirits, and so as far as we could judge, pleased with the interview."

The actions against Seward had now taken three days. Tuesday and Wednesday the Republican Senators had caucused. Thursday their committee had organized and had gone to Lincoln for their evening interview. Lincoln called a Cabinet meeting for half-past ten Friday morning, December 19. All the members came except Seward.

Welles wrote in his diary, "The President says the evening was spent in a pretty free and animated conversation. No opposition was manifested towards any other member of the Cabinet than Mr. Seward . . . Him they charged, if not with infidelity, with indifference, with want of earnestness in the War . . . with too great ascendency and control of the President."

One of Lincoln's secretaries noted his telling the Cabinet of the Senate committee members: "While they seemed to believe in my honesty, they also appeared to think that when I had in me any good purpose or intention Seward contrived to suck it out of me unperceived." The President wished the Cabinet to know that he had told the committee he was shocked and grieved at "this movement."

After various remarks from Cabinet members, the Presi-

dent requested that the Cabinet should, with him, meet the
committee of Senators. "This," noted Welles, "did not receive the approval of Mr. Chase, who said he had no knowledge whatever of the movement, or the resignation, until
since he had entered the room." The President named half-
past seven that evening for the interview.

Rumors were spreading that Seward had resigned. "On
Thursday morning," wrote Fessenden, "I received information from a sure quarter that this rumor was well founded,
but the fact was not generally known. The President, my
informant stated, was much troubled about it." Wrote
Browning, ". . . in the course of the afternoon I met him
[the President] between the White House and the War Department, and remarked to him that I had heard that Mr.
Seward had resigned, and asked him if it was so. He replied
that he did not want that talked about at present, as he was
trying to keep things along. This was all that passed. He
cant 'keep them along.' The cabinet will go to pieces." Visitors at his house saw Seward packing up books and papers
preparing to go home to Auburn, New York.

When the committee of Senators came to the White
House that Friday night they did not know that Lincoln had
arranged for them to meet the Cabinet, to sit face to face in
a three-cornered session. The President told them he had
invited the Cabinet, with the exception of Seward, to meet
the committee for a free and friendly conversation in which
all, including the President, should be on equal terms. He
wished to know if the committee had any objection to talking over matters with the Cabinet. "Having had no opportunity for consultation, the committee had no objection,"
noted Fessenden.

The President opened by admitting that Cabinet meetings
had not been very regular, excusing that fact for want of
time. He believed most questions of importance had received reasonable consideration, was not aware of any divisions or want of unity. Decisions, so far as he knew, had
general support after they were made. Seward, he believed,
had been earnest in prosecution of the war, had not im-
properly interfered, had generally read to him the official

correspondence, had sometimes consulted with Mr. Chase. The President then called on members of the Cabinet to say whether there had been any want of unity or of sufficient consultation.

Secretary Chase now protested earnestly, a little hotly, that he certainly would not have come to the meeting if he had known he was going to be arraigned before a committee of the Senate. He went on to say that questions of importance had generally been considered by the Cabinet, though perhaps not as fully as might be desired, that there had been no want of unity in the Cabinet but a general acquiescence on public measures; no member opposed a measure once decided on.

Fessenden was listening; Chase was not now saying in the three-cornered conference what he had been saying in private chats with Senators nor what he had been writing in letters. So Fessenden rose to repeat what he had two nights before told the President, that the Senators came with a desire to offer friendly advice and not to dictate to the President. Collamer said united counsels were needed. Grimes said again he had lost confidence in Seward. Sumner dragged out Seward's foreign correspondence again. Trumbull pointed to the President's own admissions that important questions were decided without full consideration. Bates cited the Constitution to show that the President need not consult his Cabinet unless he pleased. More talk followed. The hours were passing. "The President made several speeches in the course of the evening," wrote Fessenden, "and related several anecdotes, most of which I had heard before."

After hours of threshing over the issues and getting better acquainted, the President asked the Senators to give him their opinions as to whether Seward ought to leave the Cabinet. Collamer said he did not know how his constituents felt and he would not go beyond the paper he had handed the President. Grimes, Trumbull, Sumner, said Seward should go. Harris said No, that Seward's removal would be a calamity to the Republican party of New York. Pomeroy said he had once studied law in Seward's office but his confidence in Seward was gone. Howard said he had not spoken during the evening and would not. Chase suggested, "The members of the Cabinet had better withdraw." They did so. It was midnight. Senators Collamer and Harris took their hats and also went away. Fessenden then noted this conversation:

FESSENDEN: You have asked my opinion about Seward's removal. There is a current rumor that Mr. Seward has already resigned. If so, our opinions are of no consequence on that point.

THE PRESIDENT: I thought I told you last evening that Mr. Seward had tendered his resignation. I have it in my pocket, but have not yet made it public or accepted it.

FESSENDEN: Then, sir, the question seems to be whether Mr. Seward shall be requested to withdraw his resignation.

THE PRESIDENT: Yes.

The Senators left the White House. One of them, Trumbull, turned before going out, walked rapidly back to the President, and told him rather hotly that the Secretary of the Treasury had talked in a different tone the last time they had spoken. Fessenden wrote in his memorandum as to this Friday evening conversation: "It struck me that Mr. Chase seemed to have very much modified his opinions, often previously expressed to me, as to Mr. Seward's influence on the mind of the President and the want of unity in the Cabinet."

Browning asked Senator Collamer how Secretary Chase could venture to tell the committee that the Cabinet got along fairly well when he had been saying the opposite to the Senators privately. "He lied," answered Collamer.

It was one o'clock Saturday morning. The session had lasted five and a half hours. "It was observed by the Senators," wrote Fessenden, "that the President did not appear to be in so good spirits as when we left him on the preceding evening, and the opinion was expressed that he would make no change in his Cabinet. He said he had reason to fear 'a general smash-up' if Mr. Seward was removed."

Lincoln and Welles agreed next morning that while Seward's resignation should not be accepted by the President, neither should Seward get up on his dignity and press for immediate acceptance. Welles said he would go over and see Seward. Lincoln "earnestly" desired him to do so. Lincoln had a messenger sent to notify Chase that the President wished to see him.

Seward was pleased at Welles' report of his interview with the President. He said that "if the President and country required of him any duty in this emergency he did not feel at liberty to refuse it . . ." Back at the White House, Welles met Chase and Stanton in the President's office. Welles told them he was decidedly against accepting Seward's resignation. Neither would give a direct answer. The President came in, asked Welles if he "had seen the man." Welles said Yes and the man was agreed. The President turned to Chase. "I sent for you, for this matter is giving me great trouble."

Chase said he had been painfully affected by the meeting last evening, which was a total surprise to him. Then after some vague remarks he told the President he had written his resignation as Secretary of the Treasury. "Where is it?" asked Lincoln, his eyes lighting up. "I brought it with me," said Chase, taking the paper from his pocket. "I wrote it this morning." "Let me have it," said the President, reaching his long arm and fingers toward Chase, who held on to the paper and seemed to have something further to say before giving up the document. But the President was eager, did not notice Chase, took the letter, broke the seal and read it.

"This," said Lincoln, holding up the letter toward Welles with a triumphal laugh, "cuts the Gordian knot." He face of worry had changed to satisfaction. "I can dispose of this subject now without difficulty," he added as he turned on his chair. "I see my way clear."

Stanton was sitting with Chase, facing the fireplace. Stanton rose to say: "Mr. President, I informed you day before yesterday that I was ready to tender you my resignation. I wish you, sir, to consider my resignation at this time in your possession." "You may go to your Department," said Lincoln. "I don't want yours. This," holding out Chase's letter, "is all I want; this relieves me; my way is clear; the trouble is ended. I will detain neither of you longer." All three left the room, and Lincoln was alone.

When Senator Harris called soon after, Lincoln was beaming and cheerful. "Yes, Judge, I can ride on now, I've got a pumpkin in each end of my bag." (When farmers rode horseback to market two pumpkins in the bag thrown over the horse made a balanced load.) As the anecdote reached Senator Fessenden, the President had said: "Now I have the biggest half of the hog. I shall accept neither resignation."

The President sent polite notes to Seward and Chase that he could not let them quit and must ask them to take up again their duties. Seward replied that he had "cheerfully resumed" his functions. Chase held off. "I will sleep on it." Something rankled in Chase's bosom. He was afraid Lincoln had a sinister cunning that had outguessed and outwitted him. His pride was hurt. He wrote to the President: "Will you allow me to say that something you said or looked, when I handed you my resignation this morning, made on my mind the impression that having received the resignations both of Governor Seward and myself, you felt that you could relieve yourself from trouble by declining to accept either, and that this feeling was one of gratification?" However, after a Sunday of deep thinking Chase decided he would go back to his old place.

The Republican Senators caucused Monday, December 22, and heard the report of their committee, whose duty was over. Browning, however, felt called on to go to the President that night and suggest a new Cabinet be formed. The President said he believed he would rather try to get along with the Cabinet he had than try a new one.

Lincoln said later: "If I had yielded to that storm and dismissed Seward the thing would all have slumped over one way, and we should have been left with a scanty handful of supporters. When Chase gave in his resignation I saw that the game was in my hands, and I put it through."

Fessenden ended a letter to his family: "Yet such is the anomalous character of the President that no one can tell

what a day may bring forth." Uneven, irregular, rather
baffling, so Fessenden found the President; he could not
read what was coming next from Lincoln, and it troubled
him. Fessenden had clean hands and a rare sense of justice
in politics, owning himself with a decency, with a spotless
record. Yet the evils of gossip, greed, jealousy and personal
ambition, amid furious and rushing events, had created
various unfavorable impressions of the President. Fessenden
had his and wrote to John Murray Forbes, who wanted to
see Fessenden in the Cabinet: "No friend of mine should
ever wish to see me there," for in the Cabinet no man could
honestly be himself because of the interference of the President, and "You cannot change the President's character or
conduct, unfortunately; he remained long enough at Springfield, surrounded by toadies and office-seekers, to persuade
himself that he was specially chosen by the Almighty for
this crisis, and well chosen. This conceit has never yet been
beaten out of him . . ."

Forbes began his letter: "I must differ from you about
the President. He has been in the hands of a vacillating, undecided man like Seward!"

Seward and Chase had a daily grasp of special and shifting situations. In diplomatic matters the President often
told callers, "You'll have to see Seward about that," or on
a financial detail, "That is for Chase to say—you go over
and see him." Chase sat daily in conference on money, cash
available, credit balances, the war cost of $2,000,000 a day.
Chase was reporting in December '62 that the Government
would have to borrow $600,000,000 the next year. By a
single act of Congress that year, wherein the views of Chase
were met, the "greenbacks" came, paper money to the
amount of $150,000,000. Gold was hoarded, sent into hid-
ing by paper money. The same act of Congress authorized
a $500,000,000 bond issue, the Government to sell to the
people, investors, banks, that amount of its promises to pay.
Lincoln did not pretend to grasp of it; long ago he had said
he had "no money sense."

Armies of men marching in mud and sleeping on frozen

ground, fighting bloody pitched battles, waited for back pay. Joseph Medill wrote: "Money cannot be supplied much longer to a beaten, demoralized and homesick army. Sometimes I think that nothing is left now but to fight for a boundary." Enigmas of cash and credit, of how paper money chases coin into hiding places, of bond issues to coax money out of hiding places and strongboxes, of the wish for money worth the same next week as this week— under these both Lincoln and Chase writhed.

The future was in bigger debt figures. Spaulding in the House said that $1,000,000,000 at least must be borrowed in the next 18 months. Expenses of the Government reached $2,500,000 a day, Sundays included. Government income from customs tariff, taxes and elsewhere was not over $600,000 a day, which left $1,900,000 to be pried loose from the banks and from the people by manipulation of bonds, notes, appeals to patriotic duty.

Lincoln met more with Seward than with Chase. His advice to Chase on how to raise money for the war was not needed by Chase; it was a special field, with no history of money ever having been written and no unquestionable handbook of finance supplied for such amateurs as Lincoln. His advice to Seward on problems of state was more needed. They were affairs seething and warm in human relationships. Here, working with Seward, Lincoln more often knew precisely what he was doing.

Seward informed him of how the Spanish, British and French governments were joining hands to collect money due from Mexico; so they gave diplomatic explanations. They announced they were not seeking new territory; they asked the United States to join their scheme. Slowly Seward and Lincoln had seen it become reasonably clear that Emperor Napoleon III of France was planning to beat the armies of Mexico, overthrow their republican government, and set up a royal throne, whereon would sit the Archduke Maximilian of Austria.

Throughout many conversations Seward made clear the view of the President that he did not question the right of the three European powers to join hands and seek redress of their grievances, even to war in Mexico, also that the President felt satisfaction in the assurance given by the powers that they would not seek to impair the right of the Mexican people to choose and freely to constitute the form of their government.

Intervention in America was a leading topic of diplomatic conversations in Europe. Leaders in England and France who favored recognition of the Confederacy found Russia a hindrance. Late in '62 a personal letter from President Lincoln was transmitted to the Russian Foreign Minister, Gorchakov, at St. Petersburg, by Acting American Minister Bayard Taylor. Their conversation was published by order of Congress, though Lincoln's letter to Gorchakov was not made known.

"Russia alone has stood by you from the first, and will continue to stand by you," said Gorchakov. "Proposals will be made to Russia to join in some plan of interference. She will refuse any invitation of the kind. You may rely upon it, she will not change." From none of the Great Powers of Europe had the United States been able to win so positive a declaration. In this decision Russia was aligning herself against England and France, who had fought her so recently in the war in the Crimea. Also Russia had no such textile industries as England and France, suffering from cotton famine.

Across Europe ran two extremes of opinion, with many moderate views intermingled. The liberal John Bright of England favored a united country in America, sent a letter to the Chamber of Commerce of New York. Bright wished it known that "there is no other country in which men have been so free and so prosperous as in yours, and that there is no other political constitution now in existence, in the preservation of which the human race is so deeply interested." The conservative London *Dispatch* phrased its view: "The real motives of the civil war are the continuance of the power of the North to tax the industry of the South, and the consolidation of a huge confederation to sweep every other power from the American continent, to enter into the politics of Europe with a Republican propaganda, and to bully the world."

An international world opinion favoring the North was Seward's steady objective. Often he brought to Lincoln's desk designs and schemes for approval on matters of broad policy. The President and his State Minister spent more and more time together, grew in respect and affection. "The President is the best of us," Seward had written to his wife. Often on Sunday mornings they had long talks, came nearer being cronies than any other two of the Cabinet.

Congress passed an act making West Virginia a state, seceding her from Virginia. Blair, Bates and Welles were against the act. Seward, Chase, Stanton, favored it, recommended that the President sign the bill. He did so, urging in a written opinion that her brave and good men regarded her admission into the Union as a matter of life and death. They had been true to the Union through severe trials. "We have so acted as to justify their hopes; and we can not fully retain their confidence, and co-operation if we seem to break faith with them."

Then Lincoln presented the quixotic phase of the matter. "The division of a State is dreaded as a precedent," he wrote. "But a measure made expedient by a war, is no precedent for times of peace. It is said that the admission of West-Virginia is secession, and tolerated only because it is our secession. Well, if we call it by that name, there is still difference enough between secession against the constitution, and secession in favor of the constitution." He did not like to do it but with a wry face he signed the bill.

From month to month Lincoln had met with Seward, Welles, the Cabinet and eminent attorneys in international law on the subject of mails captured on blockade-runners and the question whether such mails should be opened and used as evidence or be forwarded without opening. Welles contended the mails should be held and opened by the prize court which disposed of the captured ships and cargoes. Seward, however, had issued a circular of instructions to the State Department that captured mails should be given up, that in effect the State Department yielded any rights to examine and break the seals of mailbags and parcels.

"By special direction of the President, unusual courtesy and concession were made to neutrals," wrote Welles in a long letter to Seward at a time when the British Minister set up the claim that naval officers in the seizure of mails on the ship *Peterhoff* had violated U.S. Government instructions. The final action in the *Peterhoff* case came when the mails were given up by a U.S. district attorney, who had applied to the prize court under direction of the Secretary of State, approved by the President. Seward, wrote Welles, having in a weak moment conceded an incontestable national right, "sought to extricate himself, not by retracing his steps, but by involving the President . . ."

Welles noted of Sumner's meeting with the President: ". . . He [the President] was confident we should have war with England if we presumed to open their mail bags, or break their seals or locks. They would not submit to it, and we were in no condition to plunge into a foreign war on a subject of so little importance . . . Of this idea of a war with England, Sumner could not dispossess him by argument, or by showing its absurdity. Whether it was real or affected ignorance, Sumner was not satisfied."

The President kept pressing his Navy Secretary and was "extremely anxious" to get at any specific cases of captured mail that had been searched. "I told him," noted Welles, "I remembered no specific mention." Perhaps the Federal district attorneys might have information. "The President said he would frame a letter to the district attorneys, and in the afternoon he brought in a form to be sent to the attorneys in Philadelphia, New York, and Boston."

Then other affairs arose and in their stride swept away the Cabinet disputes over whether Lincoln and Seward were yielding a legal right to Great Britain and if so, who was the loser by it.

Up on the border line of the wilderness settlements of the pioneers in Minnesota, five white people were murdered by Sioux red men. Federal Government agents had predicted the clash for many years because of seizures of Indian lands by white men, because of slow payment of promised funds to Indian tribes, and the trickery of white traders against individual Indians. Little Crow led the Sioux along the Minnesota River valley; they burned houses, violated women, slaughtered 490 whites, including women and children.

General Pope led his horsemen in pursuit, defeated Little Crow in battle. A military court put the Indians on trial, and partly in obedience to demands for revenge that swept the whole Northwest, the court sentenced 303 to be hanged.

Lincoln studied the record of the trial, and delayed. One by one, in his own handwriting, Lincoln listed those he would hang, 38 of them. The others, he wrote, would be held till further orders, "taking care that they neither escape, nor are subjected to any unlawful violence." On December 26, at Mankato, Minnesota, the 38 were hanged.

The President had insisted the trial record should "indicate the more guilty and influential of the culprits." In a message to Congress he pointed out that it was not definitely known who had fomented the Minnesota outbreak. "Suspicions, which may be unjust, need not to be stated." The President had learned, however, that Federal handling of Indians was not what it should be. He suggested a remodeling of the system and policy of treating Indians.

Lincoln took time to write a long letter to Miss Fanny McCullough at Bloomington, Illinois, beginning: "It is with deep grief that I learn of the death of your kind and brave Father; and, especially, that it is affecting your young heart beyond what is common." He was an older man telling her that time would teach her, the years would help. "In this sad world of ours, sorrow comes to all; and, to the young, it comes with bitterest agony, because it takes them unawares. The older have learned to ever expect it." She could not realize it now, but sometime she would be happy again. "The memory of your dear Father, instead of an agony, will yet be a sad sweet feeling in your heart, of a purer, and holier sort than you have known before."

Many times Lincoln had met and talked with her father, a Black Hawk War veteran, a Republican party man, circuit clerk and then sheriff of McLean County—a man who with one eye of no use and his left arm gone had at 51 helped organize the 4th Illinois Cavalry, commanding it in battles under Grant till far down in Mississippi he fell bullet-riddled, having shouted his last command.

Fanny McCullough could remember when she was a little girl and Lincoln used to hold her and her sister Nanny on his knees, telling their father, "These girls are not too old to be kissed."

On New Year's Eve, 1862, telegrams to the War Department reported one of the bloodiest battles of the war opening at Murfreesboro, Tennessee, along Stone's River, the Union army of Rosecrans fighting the Confederates under Bragg. The Confederates drove the right wing of the Union army back two miles, and Bragg sent a telegram of victory to Richmond on New Year's Eve: "God has given us a happy New Year." Lincoln went to bed that night with news of men marching in rain, sleeping on wet ground, fighting through mud, the South having made the gains of the day. Two days more of maneuvering and grappling went on between 41,000 under Rosecrans and 34,000 under Bragg. They fought in the rain and fog of raw winter days of short twilights. On the second day willing horses and cursing drivers couldn't get cannon moved over the soaked and slippery ground. One out of four men on the field was shot down, killed, wounded or taken prisoner; the Union army lost 12,906, the Confederates 11,739. Bragg retreated south.

And this huggermugger of smoke and steel, flame and blood, in Tennessee meant to the President far off in the White House one episode. The Union men of Tennessee would have easier going. The manpower of the South was cut down by so many figures. The war would never be ended by any one event, any single battle; the war might go on 20 or 30 years, ran the warning of Lincoln, Sherman and others.

Lincoln telegraphed Rosecrans: "God bless you, and all

with you! Please tender to all, and accept for yourself, the Nation's gratitude for yours, and their, skill, endurance, and dauntless courage."

Chapter 13

Final Emancipation Proclamation, '63

On January 1, 1863, the day set for the second and final Emancipation Proclamation, many doubted the President would issue the edict. Rumors ran in Washington that Lincoln on January 1 would withdraw, not issue, the proclamation. His courage, they were saying and writing, required bolstering, "puffing," as Greeley put it. John Murray Forbes of Boston wrote to Sumner that perhaps "a mixed deputation of laymen and clergy" could "try and influence" Lincoln to issue the document.

Harriet Beecher Stowe did not join with friends, nor with her brother Henry Ward Beecher, in suspicions that Lincoln would put off or evade the proclamation. The pioneer abolitionist agitator, William Lloyd Garrison, at the yearly meeting of the Anti-Slavery Society of Massachusetts, had rebuked the slurs of Wendell Phillips on the President's motives, holding "it is not wise for us to be too microscopic" in finding fault with the President.

Browning on December 31 wrote: "Some days ago I said to Judge Thomas [B. F. Thomas of the Massachusetts Supreme Court, 1853-59] that I thought he ought to go to the President and have a full, frank conversation with him in regard to the threatened proclamation of emancipation—that in my opinion it was fraught with evil, and evil only." Browning lamented: "The President was fatally bent upon his course, saying that if he should refuse to issue his proclamation there would be a rebellion in the north, and that a dictator would be placed over his head within the week.

There is no hope. The proclamation will come—God grant it may [not] be productive of the mischief I fear."

Uprisings of Negro slaves would surely follow the impending proclamation, with murder and worse visited on the Southern people, several English journals predicted.

Congressman John Covode the last week of December found the President in his office walking back and forth with a troubled face. As to whether he would issue the proclamation, he said: "I have studied that matter well; my mind is made up . . . *It must be done. I am driven to it.* There is no other way out of our troubles. But although my duty is plain, it is in some respects painful, and I trust the people will understand that I act not in anger but in expectation of a greater good."

Copies of the proclamation were handed Cabinet members December 30. Next morning at ten they went into session. Seward and Welles suggested minor changes. Chase argued that the slaves should be declared free in entire states, with no parts or fractions stipulated as not being included. Also Chase had brought along a complete draft of a proclamation he had written himself. He suggested to Lincoln a closing sentence to read: "And upon this act, sincerely believed to be an act of justice warranted by the Constitution, and an act of duty demanded by the circumstances of the country, I invoke the considerate judgment of mankind, and the gracious favor of Almighty God." Said Chase, "I thought this, or something like it, would be appropriate." Lincoln adopted this sentence; he left out one clause and added that "military necessity" dictated the action.

Thirteen parishes in Louisiana and counties in Virginia around Norfolk were specifically excepted by Lincoln in the proclamation. Tennessee and the nonseceded Border Slave States of Missouri, Kentucky, Maryland and Delaware were not mentioned in the proclamation. In all these areas the slaves were not to be declared free. Blair argued that people long after would read and wonder why the Louisiana parishes and Virginia counties were excepted; they were in the very heart and back of slavery, and unless there was some good reason, unknown to him, he hoped they would not be excepted. Seward remarked, "I think so, too; I think they should not be excepted."

John P. Usher, First Assistant Secretary of the Interior, who was a week later appointed to take the place of Caleb B. Smith, resigning to take a judgeship in Indiana, noted Lincoln's reply: "Well, upon first view your objections are clearly good, but after I issued the proclamation of September 22, Mr. Bouligny of Louisiana, then here, came to see me. [John Edward Bouligny, elected to Congress as a National American from a New Orleans district, served from December 5, 1859, to March 4, 1861, the only Representative from a seceding state who did not leave his seat in Congress.] He was a great invalid, and had scarcely the strength to walk upstairs. He wanted to know of me if these parishes in Louisiana and New Orleans should hold an election and elect members of Congress whether I would not except them from this proclamation. I told him I would.

"No, I did not do that in so many words," continued Lincoln. "If he was here now he could not repeat any words I said which would amount to an absolute promise. But I know he understood me that way, and that is just the same to me. They have elected members, and they are here now, Union men, ready to take their seats, and they have elected a Union man from the Norfolk district."

Blair said, "If you have a promise out, I will not ask you to break it." Seward added: "No, no. We would not have you do that." Chase interposed, "Very true, they have elected Hahn and Flanders, but they have not yet got their seats, and it is not certain that they will." Chase was voicing the fear of Northern antislavery men that Southern Union men, sympathetic to slavery, would win added strength in Congress; he believed Congress might refuse to seat Hahn and Flanders.

Michael Hahn was Bavarian-born, a New Orleans high-school graduate, a lawyer who in politics had fought the Slidell faction in Louisiana, had done his best for Douglas for President in 1860, and favored gradual compensated abolishment of slavery. Benjamin Franklin Flanders was

New Hampshire-born, a Dartmouth graduate, a high-school principal, and an editor and published in New Orleans; being an outspoken Union man, he had to leave that city early in '62, returning when the Union Army and Navy captured it that year.

On Chase's saying it was not certain that Hahn and Flanders would be seated, Lincoln rose from his chair. He was not easy about the matter. Usher noted that he walked rapidly back and forth across the room; looking over his shoulder at Chase, he burst out: "There it is, sir! I am to be bullied by Congress, am I? If I do I'll be durned." This ended the discussion.

That afternoon and next morning, as Lincoln rewrote the entire draft of the proclamation, he took his time, went to pains to have the penmanship plain, clear, unmistakable, in a manner solemn and testamentary. He had told Sumner, "I know very well that the name connected with this document will never be forgotten." The text was dry, strict, brief. Its sentences stood alone and sent out red runners against deep purple.

On the morning of New Year's Day the high officers of the Government, the civil, military and naval departments, the diplomatic corps in gold braid and official hats, arrived at the White House for the annual presidential reception. The carriages drove in the half-oval roadway, the horses champed, the important guests were delivered at the door; the long porch of the White House, the sidewalk and part of the lawn filled up with bystanders and beholders. The President began handshaking and greeting and went on for three hours.

That afternoon Seward and his son Fred walked over to the White House carrying Lincoln's own draft of the Emancipation Proclamation. Lincoln had left it with them for the State Department duly to engross. To be a complete document, the President must sign it. They found Lincoln alone in his office. The broad sheet was spread out before him on a table. He dipped his pen in an inkstand, held the pen in the air over the paper, hesitated, looked around, and said: "I never, in my life, felt more certain that I was doing right, than I do in signing this paper. But I have been receiving calls and shaking hands since nine o'clock this morning, till my arm is stiff and numb. Now this signature is one that will be closely examined, and if they find my hand trembled they will say, 'he had some compunctions.' But anyway, it is going to be done."

And with that he slowly and carefully wrote the name of Abraham Lincoln at the bottom of the Emancipation Proclamation, a bold, clear signature, though "slightly tremulous," Lincoln remarked. The others laughed, for it was better than he or they expected from fingers squeezed and wrenched by thousands that day. Then Seward signed, the great seal was affixed, and the document went into the archives of the State Department. The document—the most exciting news matter telegraphed, mailed, published, heralded over the world that day and month, for all that it was dry and formal—read:

BY THE PRESIDENT OF THE UNITED STATES OF AMERICA

A Proclamation.

Whereas, on the twentysecond day of September, in the year of our Lord one thousand eight hundred and sixty two, a proclamation was issued by the President of the United States, containing, among other things, the following, towit:

"That on the first day of January, in the year of our Lord one thousand eight hundred and sixty-three, all persons held as slaves within any State or designated part of a State, the people whereof shall then be in rebellion against the United States, shall be then, thenceforward, and forever free; and the Executive Government of the United States, including the military and naval authority thereof, will recognize and maintain the freedom of such persons, and will do no act or acts to repress such persons, or any of them, in any efforts they may make for their actual freedom.

"That the Executive will, on the first day of January aforesaid, by proclamation, designate the States and parts of States, if any, in which the people thereof, respectively, shall then be in rebellion against the United States; and the fact that any State, or the people thereof, shall on that day be, in good faith, represented in the Congress of the United States by members chosen thereto at elections wherein a majority of the qualified voters of such State shall have participated, shall, in the absence of strong countervailing testimony, be deemed conclusive evidence that such State, and the people thereof, are not then in rebellion against the United States."

Now, therefore I, Abraham Lincoln, President of the United States, by virtue of the power in me vested as Commander-in-Chief, of the Army and Navy of the United States in time of actual armed rebellion against authority and government of the United States, and as a fit and necessary war measure for suppressing said rebellion, do, on this first day of January, in the year of our Lord one thousand eight hundred and sixty three, and in accordance with my purpose so to do publicly proclaimed for the full period of one hundred days, from the day first above mentioned, order and designate as the States and parts of States wherein the people thereof respectively, are this day in rebellion against the United States, the following, towit:

Arkansas, Texas, Louisiana, (except the Parishes of St. Bernard, Plaquemines, Jefferson, St. Johns, St. Charles, St. James, Ascension, Assumption, Terrebonne, Lafourche, St. Mary, St. Martin, and Orleans, including the city of New-Orleans) Mississippi, Alabama, Florida, Georgia, South-Carolina, North-Carolina, and Virginia, (except the fortyeight counties designated as West Virginia, and also the counties of Berkley, Accomac, Northampton, Elizabeth-City, York, Princess Ann, and Norfolk, including the cities of Norfolk & Portsmouth); and which excepted parts are, for the present, left precisely as if this proclamation were not issued.

And by virtue of the power, and for the purpose

aforesaid, I do order and declare that all persons held as slaves within said designated States, and parts of States, are, and henceforward shall be free; and that the Executive government of the United States, including the military and naval authorities thereof, will recognize and maintain the freedom of said persons.

And I hereby enjoin upon the people so declared to be free to abstain from all violence, unless in necessary self-defence; and I recommend to them that, in all cases when allowed, they labor faithfully for reasonable wages.

And I further declare and make known, that such persons of suitable condition, will be received into the armed service of the United States to garrison forts, positions, stations, and other places, and to man vessels of all sorts in said service.

And upon this act, sincerely believed to be an act of justice, warranted by the Constitution, upon military necessity, I invoke the considerate judgment of mankind, and the gracious favor of Almighty God.

Abraham Lincoln

Lincoln's signature to Emancipation Proclamation—rarely he wrote his full name

Salutes of a hundred guns were fired in Pittsburgh, Buffalo, Boston, after newspapers published the proclamation. At night in Tremont Temple, Boston, it was read before an abolitionist crowd including the Negro members of the Union Progressive Association. Antislavery crowds held jubilation meetings, though some of the extremists said the document should have gone further, was too moderate. Meetings in some Northern cities lasted all night, with song, laughter, prayer, Negroes greeting the dawn kneeling and crying.

Critics took much the same view as they did of the preliminary proclamation in September. The London *Times* and the antiadministration press in general agreed with the New York *Herald:* "While the Proclamation leaves slavery untouched where his decree can be enforced, he emancipates slaves where his decree cannot be enforced. Friends of human rights will be at a loss to understand this discrimination." The Richmond *Examiner* spoke for much of the South in declaring the proclamation to be "the most startling political crime, the most stupid political blunder, yet known in American history," aimed at "servile insurrection," with the result that "Southern people have now only to choose between victory and death."

The proclamation struck at property valued on tax books at nearly $3,000,000,000. If not retracted and if finally sustained by the Union armies in the field, the newly issued document would take from Southerners, by force and without compensation, livestock classified and assessed with horses, cattle and mules, more than 3,900,000 head.

To those who shrank in horror, Lincoln later made his argument: ". . . I think the Constitution invests its commander-in-chief with the law of war in time of war. The most that can be said—if so much—is that slaves are property. Is there—has there ever been—any question that by the law of war, property, both of enemies and friends, may be taken when needed? . . Civilized belligerents do all in their power to help themselves or hurt the enemy, except a few things regarded as barbarous or cruel."

Henry Adams in London wrote: "The Emancipation Proclamation has done more for us here than all our former victories and all our diplomacy. It is creating an almost convulsive reaction in our favor all over this country. The London Times furious and scolds like a drunken drab. Certain it is, however, that public opinion is very deeply stirred here and finds expression in meetings, addresses to President Lincoln, deputations to us, standing committees to agitate the subject and to affect opinion, and all the other symptoms of a great popular movement peculiarly unpleasant to the upper classes here because it rests on the spontaneous action of the laboring classes."

Foreign Minister Earl Russell in London, in a note to

British Minister Lyons in Washington, saw no precedents to guide either as to the proclamation or in the matter of two public letters of the President of the United States, one addressed "To the Workingmen of Manchester," the other "To the Workingmen of London." It was not a custom for the ruling heads of nations to address letters to "workingmen" in other countries. Lincoln, however, had received addresses from bodies of workingmen in those cities giving him the hand of fellowship, and he replied: "I know and deeply deplore the sufferings which the workingmen at Manchester and in all Europe are called to endure in this crisis . . . Under these circumstances, I cannot but regard your decisive utterance upon the question as an instance of sublime Christian heroism which has not been surpassed in any age or in any country."

Around the world and into the masses of people whose tongues and imaginings create folk tales out of fact, there ran this item of the Strong Man who arose in his might and delivered an edict, spoke a few words fitly chosen, and thereupon the shackles and chains fell from the arms and ankles of men, women and children born to be chattels for toil and bondage.

The living issues coiled and tangled about Lincoln's feet were not, however, to be set smooth and straight by any one gesture, or a series of them, in behalf of freedom. His authority, worn often as a garment of thongs, was tied and knotted with responsibilities. Nailed with facts of inevitable fate was his leadership. The gestures of stretching forth his hand and bestowing freedom on chattel slaves while attempting to enforce his will by the violence of armies subjugating the masters of slaves on their home soil, the act of trying to hold a just balance between the opposed currents of freedom and authority, raised a riddle that gnawed in his thought many nights.

"A great day," wrote Longfellow that New Year's Day of '63. "The President's Proclamation for Emancipation of Slaves in the rebel States, goes into effect. A beautiful day, full of sunshine, ending in a tranquil moonlight night. May it be symbolical."

The argument over the President's authority to set up military governments in conquered areas went on in Congress, in the press, on platform and stump, on sidewalks, in homes and saloons. Thaddeus Stevens declared in February '63 that the President had ordered men to be elected to take their seats in Congress, had also directed what kind of men should be elected, "which, perhaps, was right enough, or we might have been overrun by secessionists." The two Congressmen elected from Louisiana, however, were objectionable to Stevens. He had said so when they were seated; he said so again and pressed for rejection of their credentials. He did not wish to be discourteous, but would expel them; they were from a conquered province that had not extinguished slavery.

The hope of the President that he might find 10 per cent of people in the Southern States who would take the oath of loyalty to the Union, and form a basis for reconstruction, was named "Lincoln's ten-per-cent plan."

Foreign and domestic affairs of a wide and kaleidoscopic character came under Lincoln's eye during early '63, toward the close of two years of war. In letters and speeches of the time were many guesses that the war would not end during Lincoln's administration.

Chapter 14

"More Horses Than Oats" — Office Seekers

As months wore on and the offices were filled, the White House was overrun by young men who wanted commissions in the Army, credentials for raising regiments; officers seeking promotions or new assignments; men seeking contracts for supplies to the Army and Navy, commendations for newly invented rifles, cannon, munitions.

"Those around him strove from beginning to end to erect barriers to defend him against constant interruption," wrote Hay, "but the President himself was always the first to break them down. He disliked anything that kept people from him who wanted to see him." Senator Henry Wilson said he counseled, "You will wear yourself out," at which Lincoln smiled sadly. "They do not want much; they get but little, and I must see them."

The Republicans, new to power, were breezy about their errors in procedure, quick to ask why this or that could not be done. Lincoln usually heard state delegations, Senators and Congressmen, party leaders, before making appointments of importance for their states. Always, too, the governors of the states must have respectful hearing.

George Luther Stearns, Frank Bird and other Boston radicals came away from a session in which they had failed to budge Lincoln, Stearns saying, "There we were, with some able talkers among us, and we had the best position too; but the President held his ground against us." "I think he is the shrewdest man I ever met," said Frank Bird. "But not at all a Kentuckian. He is an old-fashioned Yankee in a western dress."

Donn Piatt wrote of once hearing Seward say that in the ability to manage saying No to office seekers, the President "had a cunning that was genius." In a care-laden hour, according to Schurz, the President pointed out to a friend an eager throng of office seekers and Congressmen in an anteroom and spoke these words: "Do you observe this? The rebellion is hard enough to overcome, but there you see something which, in the course of time, will become a greater danger to the republic than the rebellion itself."

General Egbert L. Viele, while military governor of Norfolk, spent many hours with the President in relaxed moods. He said, as Viele noted, "If I have one vice, and I can call it nothing else, it is not to be able to say 'No.' Thank God for not making me a woman, but if He had, I suppose He would have made me just as ugly as He did, and no one would ever have tempted me."

A young Ohioan, appointed to a South American consulate, came dressed as a dandy, "fit to kill." But he was gloomy. "Mr. President, I can't say I'm so very glad of this appointment after all. Why, I hear they have bugs down there that are liable to eat me up inside of a week." "Well, young man, if they do, they'll leave behind them a mighty good suit of clothes." Cabinet members protesting an appointment of a Democrat once received the reply: "Oh, I can't afford to punish every person who has seen fit to oppose my election. We want a competent man in this office." Cameron called in behalf of a young man who had been a pest in applying for a consulate. "Where do you want to have him sent?" asked the President. The Pennsylvania leader stepped to a large globe of the earth, put an arm around it as far as he could reach, and said, "I do not know what my finger is on, but send him there." And, it was told, he was accommodated.

A New England woman on a hospital errand entered the President's office unnoticed. A man was handing Lincoln a paper. Lincoln read it carelessly and said, "Yes, that is a sufficient endorsement for anybody; what do you want?" The woman did not hear the man's reply but later heard his sarcastic remark, "I see there are no vacancies among the brigadiers, from the fact that so many colonels are commanding brigades." At this, the President threw himself forward in his chair in such a way that she saw his "curious, comical expression." He was looking the man squarely in the face; and, with one hand softly patting the other, and the funny look pervading every line of his face, he said: "My friend, let me tell you something about that. You are a farmer, I believe; if not, you will understand me. Suppose you had a large cattle yard, full of all sorts of cattle—cows, oxen, and bulls—and you kept killing and selling and disposing of your cows and oxen, in one way and another, taking good care of your bulls. By and by you would find out that you had nothing but a yard full of old bulls, good for nothing under heaven. Now it will be just so with the army, if I don't stop making brigadier-generals." The man tried to laugh, but the effort was feeble. The woman caller noticed, however, that Lincoln "laughed enough for both"; in fact, laughed the man out of the room.

From a line of people at an informal reception came a shout: "Hello, Abe, how are ye? I'm in line and hev come for an orfice too." Lincoln recognized an old Sangamon County friend and told him "to hang onto himself and not kick the traces." They shook hands and after the reception Lincoln had to explain that his old friend could not handle the transactions in the office he wanted. With lips trembling, the friend sketched a world of personal history for Lincoln's understanding in saying, "Martha's dead, the gal is married, and I've guv Jim the forty." He moved closer and half whispered, "I knowed I wasn't eddicated enough to get the place but I kinder want to stay where I ken see Abe Linkern." And for a time he worked on the White House grounds.

Lincoln had to refuse an office sought by an old friend who was not fit for it, remarking to Noah Brooks, "I had rather resign my place and go away from here, if I considered only my personal feelings, but refuse him I must." The almost forgotten Denton Offutt turned up in a letter: "I hope you will Give me the Patten office or the office of Agricultural Department or the Commissary for Purchais of Horses Mules Beef for the Army or Mail agent . . . I have to be looking out to live . . ."

He remembered good friends of New Salem days—the goodhearted "Uncle Jimmy" Short and the shrewd Bill Greene—with offices at nice salaries. He remembered his brother-in-law, Ninian W. Edwards, no longer well off, with an appointment to quartermaster at $1,800 a year, and John A. Bailhache, an editor of the *Illinois State Journal,* with an appointment as a commissary. Illinois party men brought the President reports of the two men being free with money beyond salaries and making scandalous appointments of administration enemies. Lincoln transferred Edwards to Chicago and Bailhache to New York.

When Lincoln gave his good friend Lamon an appointment, Senator James Grimes of Iowa arose in the Senate to remark, "The President of the United States saw fit, in the plenitude of his wisdom, to import to this District from the State of Illinois Mr. Ward H. Lamon, and to appoint him the marshal!" Grimes charged that "this foreign satrap, Mr. Lamon, made a peremptory order, that no person—not even members of Congress—should be admitted to the [District] jail without first supplicating and securing a written permission to do so from him." Then Grimes went to the White House: "When, for the first time in six months, I attempted to approach the foot-stool of the power enthroned at the other end of the avenue, I was told that the President was engaged." Thus there was sarcasm, and men of importance played peanut politics. Nevertheless there was the factor that Lamon was not particularly antislavery and there were complaints that jailed Negroes were not really fugitive slaves, but free Negroes kidnaped by white ruffians.

A Senator, on learning from Lincoln that Halleck had negatived proposed military changes, asked the President why he didn't get Halleck out of the way. "Well—the fact is—the man who has no friends—should be taken care of."

A private poured out his complaints one summer afternoon as Provost Marshal Fry came in and heard Lincoln's reply, "That may all be so, but you must go to your officers about it." The private told his story two or three times more as Lincoln sat and gazed out the south window on the Potomac. At last the President turned. "Now, my man, go away, *go away!* I can not meddle in your case. I could as easily bail out the Potomac River with a teaspoon as attend to all the details of the army."

One soldier letter to Lincoln pleaded, "I am near starved if I get much thinner it will take two of us to make one shadder."

One pest of a politician came often asking offices, suggesting removals and creation of new offices, and Lincoln, reviewing his day's routine to a friend, said that at night as the closing act of the day "I look under the bed to see if So-and-So is there, and if not, I thank Heaven and bounce in."

A dispute over a high-salaried Ohio postmastership brought several delegations to the White House, and papers piled high in behalf of two men about equally competent. One day, bored by still another delegation, more arguments, even more petitions, the President called to a clerk: "This matter has got to end somehow. Bring me a pair of scales." They were brought. "Now put in all the petitions and letters in favor of one man and see how much they weigh, and then weigh the other fellow's pile." One bundle weighed three-quarters of a pound more than the other. "Make out an appointment," said the President, "for the man who has the heavier papers."

Senators and Congressmen came with letters begging offices for relatives soon to be married, for friends who were sick and had dependents. "I need the position for a living," wrote one to Sumner. "I have been unfortunate and poor." To Chase and other department heads, as to the President, came letters crying personal poverty as a basis for public office, in the tone of one: "God knows no one needs the appointment more than I do." The President liked to tell of a seedy fellow asking Seward for a consulate in Berlin, then Paris, then Liverpool, coming down to a clerkship in the State Department. Hearing these places were all filled, he said, "Well, then, will you lend me 5 dollars?"

The President needed reminders to make sure he would do a thing he was inclined to do. Thus Carl Schurz in a letter to Sumner: "I think he is inclined to send in my nomination tomorrow if he is reminded of it . . . I want to press you to do this reminding. Will you? It will cost you only five minutes."

Lincoln telegraphed S. B. Moody at Springfield, Illinois: "Which do you prefer Commissary or Quarter master? If appointed it must be without conditions." The matter was personal; when a Congressman later wished to name a postmaster in Springfield, Lincoln said, "I think I have promised that to old Mrs. Moody for her husband." The Congressman demurred: "Now, Mr. President, why can't you be liberal?" "Mrs. Moody would get down on me."

Personal sentiments would govern. William Kellogg, Jr., quit West Point under demerit; if he had not resigned he would have been dismissed. His father, an Illinois Congressman, reappointed the boy. A report by General Joseph G. Totten disapproved. Lincoln wrote the Secretary of War that the father was a friend of 20 years' standing. "This matter touches him very deeply—the feelings of a father for a child—as he thinks, all the future of his child. I can not be the instrument to crush his heart. According to strict rule he has the right to make the re-nomination. Let the appointment be made. It needs not to become a precedent." Thereafter Lincoln would have the rule that no resignation should be handed in by a cadet without express stipulation in writing that the resigning cadet would not take a re-nomination.

Murat Halstead of the Cincinnati *Commercial* sought men close to the President and tried to land a postmastership for a friend. As a poor loser, Halstead wrote his friend: "I use the mildest phrase when I say Lincoln is a weak, a miserably weak man; the wife is a fool—the laughing stock of the town, her vulgarity only the more conspicuous in consequence of her fine carriage and horses and servants in livery and fine dresses and her damnable airs . . . Lincoln is very busy with trifles, and lets everybody do as they please. He is opposed to stealing, but can't see the stealing that is done." Halstead retailed further information: "The way Chase manages Lincoln is to make him believe that he [Lincoln] is doing all things. The poor silly President sucks flattery as a pig sucks milk."

Chase did not bring to Lincoln a letter of February 19, 1863, from Halstead advising: "Can't you take him [Lincoln] by the throat and knock his head against a wall until he is brought to his senses on the war business? I do not speak wantonly when I say there are persons who feel that it was doing God service to kill him, if it were not feared that Hamlin is a bigger fool than he is." To John Sherman, Halstead wrote February 8, 1863, "If Lincoln was not a damned fool, we could get along yet. He is an awful, woeful ass."

A woman kept at Lincoln with letter after letter begging her husband's appointment. An extra long letter brought his question, ". . . what is it but an evidence that you intend to importune me for one thing, and another, and another, until, in self-defence, I must drop all and devote myself to find a place, even though I remove somebody else to do it, and thereby turn him & his friends upon me for indefinite future importunity, and hindrance from the legitimate duties for which I am supposed to be placed here?"

David R. Locke, Ohio editor, under the pen name of Petroleum V. Nasby, was writing sketches that had a national audience laughing at issues of the day. He flattened pompous patriots with his comic pot shots:

> 1st. I want a offis.
> 2d. I need a offis.
> 3d. A offis wood suit me; there4
> 4th. I shood like to hev a offis.

Beneath Locke's mockery shone affection, and the President wrote to the satirist: "Why don't you come to Washington and see me? Is there no place you want? Come on and I will give you any place you ask for—that you are capable of filling—and fit to fill." Locke was interested. The President had read some of his writings and was so pleased that in a generous outburst he wrote that Locke could have "any place he asked for."

Then, as Locke analyzed it, the President saw he was offering too much to a man he knew only through newspaper sketches, so the saving clause was added, "that you are capable of filling," and, to guard himself entirely, "that you are fit to fill." Locke did go to see Lincoln, but not to ask for a place. "He gave me an hour of his time," said the humorist, "and a delightful hour it was."

A well-dressed man asked merely that the President allow the use of his name for advertising a project in view. "No!" flashed the President. "No! I'll have nothing to do with this. Do you take the President of the United States to be a commission broker? You have come to the wrong place. There is the door!" The caller slunk away.

A governor of a state entered Lincoln's office bristling

with complaints as to his state quota and enforcement. He had seen Fry and then Stanton for a session of loud angry words with each. Now it was Lincoln's turn. Fry for hours expected orders from the White House or at least a special summons. He was surprised to see the governor come in with a pleasant smile. Fry soon was saying to Lincoln: "I suppose you found it necessary to make large concessions to him."

"Oh, no, I did not concede anything," Fry noted the President's explanation. "You know how that Illinois farmer managed the big log that lay in the middle of his field! To the inquiries of his neighbors one Sunday, he announced that he had got rid of the big log. 'Got rid of it!' said they, 'how did you do it? It was too big to haul out, too knotty to split, and too wet and soggy to burn; what did you do?' 'Well, now, boys,' replied the farmer, 'if you won't divulge the secret, I'll tell you how I got rid of it—I ploughed around it.' Now," said Lincoln to Fry, "don't tell anybody, but that's the way I got rid of the governor. I ploughed around him, but it took me three mortal hours to do it, and I was afraid every minute he'd see what I was at."

How Lincoln could coax, argue and persuade, was in the adroit Thurlow Weed writing him, "I do not, when with you, say half I intend. Partly because I don't like to be a crank and partly because you talk me out of my convictions and apprehensions, so bear with me please now till I free my mind."

A letter to Postmaster General Blair in the summer of '63 went far in newspaper publication and discussion of it. The Lincoln opposition howled about it from many places; thousands of soldiers read it, forward and backward, for assurance. In two cases of postmasterships sought for widows whose husbands had fallen in battle, the President had endorsed them and now wrote: "These cases occurring on the same day, brought me to reflect more attentively than I had before done, as to what is fairly due from us here, in the dispensing of patronage, towards the men who, by fighting our battles, bear the chief burthen of saving our country. My conclusion is that, other claims and qualifications being equal, they have the better right; and this is especially applicable to the disabled soldier, and the deceased soldier's family."

A man came wearing a colonel's uniform, though no longer a colonel, dismissed for drunkenness on duty. Lincoln knew him. The man had a record for valor in battle. Lincoln heard the story. The man wanted back his old rank and place. Lincoln stood up, too moved and uneasy to stay in his chair. He took the soldier's right hand in both his own. Then slowly, tears in his voice, he told the man: "Colonel, I know your story. But you carry your own condemnation in your face." They were hard words to say, Judgment Day words. Later in referring to the case Lincoln told James M. Scovel, "I dare not restore this man to his rank and give him charge of a thousand men when he 'puts an enemy into his mouth to steal away his brain.' "

A one-legged soldier on crutches asked for some kind of a job; he had lost his leg in battle. "Let me look at your papers," said Lincoln. The man had none; he supposed his word was good. "What! no papers, no credentials, nothing to show how you lost your leg! How am I to know that you lost it in battle, or did not lose it by a trap after getting into somebody's orchard?" The President's face was droll. The honest-looking German workingman, turned soldier, earnestly muttered excuses. Lincoln saw this was no regular place seeker. Most of them came with papers too elaborately prepared. The chances were entirely in favor of any one-legged man having lost his leg in battle. "Well, it is dangerous for an army man to be wandering around without papers to show where he belongs and what he is, but I will see what can be done." Then he wrote a card for the man to take to a quartermaster who would attend to his case.

Once a humble man came asking to be made doorkeeper to the House and Lincoln let him down and out without hurting his feelings. Their conversation, as reported, ran: "So you want to be Doorkeeper to the House, eh?" "Yes, Mr. President." "Well, have you ever been a doorkeeper? Have you ever had any experience in doorkeeping?" "Well, no—no actual experience, sir." "Any theoretical experience? Any instructions in the duties and ethics of doorkeeping?" "Um—no." "Have you ever attended lectures on door-keeping?" "No, sir." "Have you read any textbooks on the subject?" "No." "Have you conversed with anyone who has read such a book?" "No, sir, I'm afraid not, sir." "Well, then, my friend, don't you see that you haven't a single qualification for this important post?" "Yes, I do." And he took his hat and left humbly, seeming rather grateful to the President.

When Judge Baldwin of California asked for a pass through army lines to visit a brother in Virginia, the President inquired, "Have you applied to General Halleck?" "Yes, and met with a flat refusal." "Then you must see Stanton." "I have, and with the same result." "Well, then," drawled Lincoln, "I can do nothing; for you must know I have very little influence with this administration." In this case it was a pleasantry with Lincoln. The same remark to a soldier's widow, who asked for a sutler's appointment, was a sorry fact.

One day, going over applications and recommendations, Lincoln said he concurred in about all that Stanton proposed. "The only point I make is, there has got to be something done that will be unquestionably in the interest of the Dutch, and to that end I want Schimmelfennig appointed." "Mr. President, perhaps this Schimmel-what's-his-name is not as highly recommended as some other German officers." "No matter about that. His name will make up for any difference there may be, and I'll take the risk of his coming out all right." Then with a laugh he spoke each syllable of the name distinctly, accenting the last: "Schim-mel-fen-*nig* must be appointed."

A speculator pressed for a pass through army lines and a Treasury license to buy cotton. He was steadily refused. "Few things are so troublesome to the government," Lincoln had remarked, "as the fierceness with which the profits in trading are sought." This particular trader brought influence to bear on Lincoln, who signed the permit requested and told the man, "You will have to take it over to Stanton for countersigning." Later the trader came back, in a heat, saying Stanton had torn to pieces and stamped his feet on the paper signed by the President. Lincoln put on a surprised look and asked the man to tell exactly how the Secretary had acted. Then, pausing a moment, he told the speculator, "You go back and tell Stanton that I will tear up a dozen of his papers before Saturday night."

A plan for mingling eastern and western troops was urged on Lincoln by a committee headed by Lovejoy. Lincoln wrote a note to Stanton suggesting a transfer of regiments. "Did Lincoln give you an order of that kind?" asked the Secretary. "He did, sir," replied Lovejoy. "Then he is a damned fool!" said Stanton. "Do you mean to say the President is a damned fool?" "Yes, sir, if he gave you such an order as that." At the White House Lovejoy told what happened. "Did Stanton say I was a damned fool?" asked Lincoln. "He did, sir, and repeated it." The President was thoughtful. "If Stanton said I was a damned fool then I must be one. For he is nearly always right, and generally says what he means. I will step over and see him."

Thurlow Weed told Leonard Swett that Lincoln kept "a regular account book" of his appointments in New York, "dividing favors so as to give each faction more than it could get from any other source, yet never enough to satisfy its appetite." In giving out offices or favors, the President had one guiding principle, as Swett saw it: "An adhesion of all forces was indispensable to his success and the success of the country; hence he husbanded his means with nicety of calculation . . . He never wasted anything, and would always give more to his enemies than he would to his friends; and the reason was, he never had anything to spare, and in the close calculation of attaching the factions to him, he counted upon the abstract affection of his friends as an element to be offset against some gift with which he must appease his enemies. Hence, there was always some truth in the charge of his friends that he failed to reciprocate their devotion with his favors. The reason was, that he had only just so much to give away. 'He always had *more horses than oats.*' "

Late at night after a long talk on the quarreling political factions in Missouri and Kentucky, Swett was saying good-by and at the door Lincoln said, "I may not have made as great a President as some other man, but I believe I have kept these discordant elements together as well as anyone could."

When Justice McLean of the Supreme Court died late in '61, friends of Davis moved to place him on the high bench. Old Eighth Circuit lawyers became active. Swett spoke for him personally to Lincoln. Months passed, a year, a year and a half—and Judge Davis saw no move of Lincoln to appoint him. On the last day of the October term of court in '62 Davis notified the members of the McLean County bar to meet him in the old courthouse at Bloomington. He spoke to them: "My official connection with the people and bar of this circuit is about to terminate. The President has tendered me an appointment as Associate Justice of the Supreme Court of the United States which I shall accept, although distrustful of my abilities to discharge the duties of the office."

Davis called the roll on the little group of lawyers who during so many years had been boon companions. Three had become judges, two U.S. Senators, one wounded and two killed in battle, one President of the United States. Davis went on to Washington, where he wrote in a letter, "Mr. Lincoln is very kind, but care worn."

Chapter 15

Hooker — Chancellorsville — Calamity

The Army of the Potomac in early '63 had lost—on the peninsula, twice at Bull Run, and again in the slaughter at Fredericksburg. It had, however, kept enemy bayonets out of Washington and the Free States. And other Northern armies, with naval co-operation, had captured all the Confederate strongholds—except Forts Sumter and Morgan—on the seacoast from Fortress Monroe in Virginia to points in Texas. Rosecrans was marching close to the Alabama line, Grant was in Mississippi, Curtis in Arkansas, Banks in New Orleans.

The Richmond *Examiner*, reviewing the scene January 20, 1863, said, "The pledge once deemed foolish by the South, that he would 'hold, occupy and possess' all the forts belonging to the United States Government, has been redeemed almost to the letter by Lincoln."

A renewed play of commentary, a sharpened political activity, rose from extremist Democrats wholly against the war. Sumner wrote Franz Lieber in January: "These are dark hours. There are senators full of despair,—not I. The President tells me that he now fears 'the fire in the rear'—meaning the Democracy—especially at the Northwest—more than our military chances." When Burnside wrote for publication a letter taking all blame on himself for the Fredericksburg disaster, Lincoln told him he was the first man found who was willing to relieve the President of a particle of responsibility.

Burnside planned a night attack on Lee's army. On the night of January 20 as the army started, rain began slowly, a wind came up, the rain turned to sleet. Horses and wagons sank in the mud and were stuck all night. Men and mules failed to make headway with the pontoons, also with the unhitched cavalry steeds and the early morning ration of whisky ordered by Burnside for every man.

After breakfast at staff headquarters next morning General Hooker talked with a newspaperman about how the commanding general was incompetent, the President and Government at Washington were imbecile and "played out," a dictator was needed and the sooner the better.

Burnside resigned, was persuaded to withdraw his resignation, was relieved of duty, and January 25, 1863, the President ordered Hooker to the command of the Army of the Potomac. Chase was pleased; so were members of the Committee on the Conduct of the War; so were many people attracted by his fighting quality and a touch of the dramatic and impetuous about Hooker. "Now there is Joe Hooker," Nicolay heard the President say. "He can fight. I think that is pretty well established—but whether he can 'keep tavern' for a large army is not so sure."

Lamon urged Lincoln to look well to the fact that there was a scheme on foot to depose him, and to appoint a military dictator in his place. Lincoln laughed and said, as Lamon quoted him: "I think, for a man of accredited courage, you are the most panicky person I ever knew; you can see more dangers to me than all the other friends I have . . . now you have discovered a new danger; now you think the people of this great government are likely to turn me out of office. I do not fear this from the people any more than I fear assassination from an individual. Now, to show you my appreciation of what my French friends would call a *coup d'état,* let me read you a letter I have written to General Hooker." He opened the drawer of a table and took out and read a letter he sent to Hooker, dated January 26, 1863, later published and widely discussed:

> General. I have placed you at the head of the Army of the Potomac. Of course I have done this upon what appear to me to be sufficient reasons. And yet I think it best for you to know that there are some things in regard to which, I am not quite satisfied with you. I believe you to be a brave and skilful soldier, which, of course, I like. I also believe you do not mix politics with your profession, in which you are right. You have confidence in yourself, which is a valuable, if not an indispensable quality. You are ambitious, which, within reasonable bounds, does good rather than harm. But I think that during Gen. Burnside's command of the Army, you have taken counsel of your ambition, and thwarted him as much as you could, in which you did a great wrong to the country, and to a most meritorious and honorable brother officer. I have heard, in

such a way as to believe it, of your recently saying that both the Army and the Government needed a Dictator. Of course it was not *for* this, but in spite of it, that I have given you the command. Only those generals who gain successes, can set up dictators. What I now ask of you is military success, and I will risk the dictatorship. The government will support you to the utmost of it's ability, which is neither more nor less than it has done and will do for all commanders. I much fear that the spirit which you have aided to infuse into the Army, of criticising their Commander, and withholding confidence from him, will now turn upon you. I shall assist you as far as I can, to put it down. Neither you, nor Napoleon, if he were alive again, could get any good out of an army, while such a spirit prevails in it.

And now, beware of rashness. Beware of rashness, but with energy, and sleepless vigilance, go forward, and give us victories.

Not long after receiving the letter, Hooker stood with his back to a cozy fireplace in his log-and-canvas army hut. And looking quizzically at his only companion, Noah Brooks, newspaper correspondent, he said, "The President tells me that you know all about the letter he wrote to me when he put me in command of this army." Mr. Lincoln had read the letter to him, admitted Brooks. "Wouldn't you like to hear it again?" asked Hooker, drawing it from a pocket.

Hooker read, pausing to demur at one point: "The President is mistaken. I never thwarted Burnside in any way, shape or manner." Resuming the reading, Hooker's tone softened, and he finished the reading almost with tears in his eyes as he folded the letter, put it back in the breast of his coat, saying: "That is just such a letter as a father might write to his son. It is a beautiful letter, and, although I think he was harder on me than I deserved, I will say that I love the man who wrote it." Then Hooker added, "After

I have got to Richmond I shall give that letter to you to have published."

A handsome soldier, Hooker looked warlike for those to whom war is color, dash, valor. Blond of hair, with wavy ringlets, with a flushed and rosy face, 49 years old, he was tall, blue-eyed, had a martial air. A West Point graduate, brevetted captain for bravery at Monterey in the Mexican War, he was a farmer and superintendent of military roads on the West Coast when the war began.

So often came a reservation in the judgments of Hooker. "He could play the best game of poker I ever saw until it came to the point when he should go a thousand better, and then he would flunk," said a cavalry officer. Yet time and again Hooker had led his division into slaughter where men fell by platoons and his lines held their ground. At Williamsburg on the peninsula under McClellan he had 2,228 killed and wounded. He was nicknamed "Fighting Joe" Hooker. Shot in the foot at Antietam, he stayed in the saddle on the field with his men till the fighting was over. Often the words came from him "When I get to Richmond" or "After we have taken Richmond." Lincoln was near groaning as he said in confidence to Brooks: "That is the most depressing thing about Hooker. It seems to me that he is over-confident."

After a conference in the White House, Lincoln said with his good-by to Hooker, "General, we shall expect to have some good news from you very soon." Then the President turned to a young New Jersey cavalryman, Sergeant J. L. Stradling. "What can I do for you, my young friend?" A permit was wanted to ride a steamer to Aquia Creek, and join up with the cavalry again, after furlough. John Hay had written across a card: "To any steamboat captain going to the front, please give bearer transportation," which Lincoln signed.

The young Sergeant was about to leave when Lincoln said to Senator Wade and two others: "Senator, we have had the head of the Army here a few minutes ago, and learned from him all he cared to tell. Now we have here the tail of the Army, so let us get from him how the rank and file feel about matters. I mean no reflection on you, Sergeant, when I say the tail of the Army." The President then spoke of many men deserting that winter. There must be some good cause.

Stradling, flustered at first, now felt the President wanted him to speak frankly. "Mr. President, so far as I know, the Army has the utmost confidence in your honesty and ability to manage this war. So far as I can learn, the army had no faith in the ability of General Burnside . . . He . . . fought his battles like some people play the fiddle, by main strength and awkwardness." Senator Wade asked if there was any excuse for such a blunder as Fredericksburg. Lincoln spoke up, "This is very interesting to me, so please go ahead." The Sergeant explained that the country was an open one, with no real mountains or rivers; both flanks of the Confederate army could have been turned. "Even we privates wondered why such an attack was made. General Burnside must have known of the sunken road, for we of the cavalry had been over this road with General Bayard in 1862, and he must have informed General Burnside all about it. If General Burnside had possessed any military genius, he would have flanked Lee out of that strong position, and fought him where he could have had at least an equal chance."

The President said, as Stradling wrote it: "What you have stated, Sergeant, seems very plausible to me. When General Hooker left us but a few minutes ago, he said, 'Mr. President, I have the finest army that was ever assembled together, and I hope to send you good news very soon.' That is just the language General Burnside used when he left me shortly before the battle of Fredericksburg. And such a disaster that followed still makes my heart sick." The frank Sergeant, opening his mind and heart, said: "Mr. President, even privates when on the ground cannot help seeing and wondering why certain movements are made. I refer to the charges of General Hooker on our right. [Hooker had demurred against making these assaults but Burnside had insisted.] Our duty, however, is not to criticise, but to obey even if we get our heads knocked off. I have found that soldiers are willing to obey without hesitation and take the chances when they feel that their show is equal to that of the enemy.

"Mr. President, I approach the Emancipation Proclamation with great reluctance, for I know how your heart was set on issuing that document. So far as I am personally concerned, I heartily approve of it. But many of my comrades said that if they had known the war would free the 'niggers' they would never have enlisted, so many of them deserted. Others said they would not desert, but would not fight any more, and sought positions in the wagon train; the Ambulance Corps; the Quartermaster's Department, and other places, to get out of fighting."

The President, Senator Wade and the other gentlemen must have wondered what they had before them in such a straightaway talker. So thought the Sergeant. But he went on: "I was born a Quaker, and was therefore an antislavery young man when I entered the army. The issuing of the proclamation caused many to desert, no doubt, and the presence of General Burnside at the head of the army caused many others to leave."

The President sat still a moment or two, then said: "The proclamation was, as you state, very near to my heart. I thought about it and studied it in all its phases long before I began to put it on paper. I expected many soldiers would desert when the proclamation was issued, and I expected many who care nothing for the colored man would seize upon the proclamation as an excuse for deserting. I did not believe the number of deserters would materially affect the army. On the other hand, the issuing of the proclamation would probably bring into the ranks many who otherwise would not volunteer."

The President, during all of the conversation, Stradling noted, was a "woe-begone" man. "He did not smile, and his face did not lighten up once." "I thank you very much," said Lincoln, with a handshake, "and I trust you will reach the front in the morning." And Sergeant Stradling left the White House, slept on sacks of oats aboard the same steamer that carried General Hooker in its cabin that night. He wrote home of his visit to the Executive Mansion: "I was awful glad to get out, and when I did get away I felt as though I had been to a funeral. Senator Wade did smile once or twice, and so did the other two gentlemen who were present, but Lincoln did not even show the shadow of a smile. His long, sad and gloomy face haunted me for days afterward."

Slowly across weeks of February, March, April, the gloom of the Army of the Potomac changed toward gaiety. Hooker had found at the close of January that in round numbers 3,000 officers and 82,000 men of the ranks were absent; they were on the rolls of the army, but not answering roll call. Some were sick, wounded, on furlough. Others had run away. Homesickness, gloom and a general feeling of uselessness had brought an average of 200 desertions a day during the winter; relatives and friends sent express bundles to their loved ones, citizens' clothing for escape. Under a new rule express trains were searched, all citizens' clothing burned.

A new regime operated. Steadily a sulky army became willing and eager to fight. It lay at Fredericksburg, a day's buggy ride from Washington, so that important public men came for personal inspections, accompanied by wives and daughters in crinoline.

Early in April Hooker said that under his command was "a living army, and one well worthy of the republic." He also rated it "the finest army on the planet." He had 130,000 troops against Lee across the river with 60,000. The President kept in constant touch with the forging and welding of this new weapon for smiting the Confederacy, sending Hooker such communications as "Would like to have a letter from you as soon as convenient" and "How does it look now?" On April 3 he notified Hooker he would arrive at the Fredericksburg camp on Sunday and stay till Tuesday morning.

In an April snowfall, Lincoln with Tad, Mrs. Lincoln, and a few friends arrived at Aquia Creek water front, lined with transports and Government steamers unloading supplies for 130,000 men and 60,000 horses and mules. A crowd of army people cheered the arrival of the President. Lincoln insisted on going to the nearest hospital tent, stopping to speak with nearly every one of the sick and wounded, shaking hands with many, asking a question or two here and there, and leaving a kind word as he moved from cot to cot.

"More than once," noted Brooks, "as I followed the President through the long lines of weary sufferers, I noticed tears of gladness stealing down their pale faces; for they were made happy by looking into Lincoln's sympathetic countenance, touching his hand, and hearing his gentle voice; and when we rode away from the camp tremendous cheers rent the air from the soldiers, who stood in groups, eager to see the President."

Brooks mentioned to Lincoln one evening at headquarters after a day of riding at army inspection that he was looking rested and in better health. "It is a great relief to get away from Washington and the politicians," was the President's answer. "But nothing touches the tired spot."

On another evening in Hooker's hut, according to Brooks, the President looked cautiously about, saw they were alone, and in a half-jocular way took out from a pocket a small piece of paper and handed it to Brooks. On it were written the figures "216,718—146,000—169,000." Brooks studied the numbers with puzzled wonder; the President explained the first figures represented the sum total of the men on the rolls of the Army of the Potomac; the second were those of the actual available force, and the last represented the numerical strength to which the force might be increased when the army should move.

In a chat with Hooker, Lincoln said, "If you get to Richmond, General—" and was interrupted by Hooker: "Excuse me, Mr. President, but there is no 'if' in this case. I am going straight to Richmond if I live." Later Lincoln remarked mournfully to Brooks, "It is about the worst

thing I have seen since I have been down here." By letter
and by word he had tried to impress on Hooker that the
objective was Lee's army and not Richmond.

On an eight-mile ride to a corps review, six mules pulled
the ambulance over a rough corduroy road that jolted the
passengers. At his wild mules the driver let fly volleys of
oaths. Lincoln leaned forward, touched the driver on the
shoulder, and said: "Excuse me, my friend, are you an
Episcopalian?" The surprised driver looked around. "No,
Mr. President, I am a Methodist." "Well, I thought you
must be an Episcopalian, because you swear just like Governor Seward, who is a church warden." The driver stopped
swearing. The ambulance plunged through jack oak and
scrub pine. Lincoln pointed to stumps where an axman
had done clever work, "a good butt"; or again to poor
chopping.

Tad said he must see "graybacks," Confederate soldiers.
Two staff men took Tad and his father on a frosty morning
down to the picket line opposite Fredericksburg. They saw
hills and a city war-swept, mansions and plain homes in
ruins, farms desolated. Smoke rose from enemy campfires
just above a stone wall where Burnside's men by thousands
had weltered in blood. From a house that stood whole out
of the wreckage floated a flag and Lincoln glimpsed the
Confederate Stars and Bars.

Tobacco, coffee, newspapers and jackknives were being
traded across the river between Confederate and Union
pickets. They spoke good morning and saluted each other
as "butternut" and "bluebelly."

From a reviewing stand the President, Hooker and the
staff watched 17,000 horsemen file past, the biggest army
of men on horses ever seen in the world, said Hooker, bigger even than the famous cavalry body of Marshal Murat
with Napoleon. Mud flew from the horses' feet on ground
soft with melting snow. On the fringe of the cavalry cloud
came Tad, in a mounted orderly's charge, his gray cloak
flying in the wind like a plume. The infantry filed past
the President—four corps, 60,000 men, a forest of moving
rifles and bayonets. Then came the reserve artillery force,

some 400 cannon. Zouave regiments in baggy red trousers, crack drill troops, marched and made a contrast. Lincoln asked Hooker if fancy uniforms were not undesirable because they made better targets, the General replying that these uniforms had the effect of inciting a spirit of pride and neatness among the men.

Hour on hour in platoons and in company front, the Army of the Potomac, a sad army that had seen rivers of blood and anguish to the depths, marched by for the Commander in Chief in the reviewing stand, surrounded by his generals. "It was noticeable," recorded Brooks, "that the President merely touched his hat in return salute to the officers, but uncovered to the men in the ranks."

In the moving platoons that day were regulars, volunteers, conscripts, bounty men. From Boston, New York, Philadelphia, were sons of Daughters of the Revolution whose ancestors had fought ragged and shivering under George Washington from Valley Forge to Yorktown, and they were mingled in divisions with German, English, Scotch, Irish, Scandinavian, Jewish, Polish immigrants or children of immigrants, whose forefathers had fought with or against Bonaparte, Frederick the Great, Marlborough, Gustavus Adolphus, in decisive battles that had hammered out historic texts of the destiny of man.

In the 2d division of the 11th corps, Brigadier General Adolph von Steinwehr had in his command Colonel Adolphus Buschbeck, Major Alex von Schluembach, Colonel Patrick H. Jones and Lieutenant Colonel Lorenz Cantador. At the head of the 3d division rode Major General Carl Schurz with Brigadier General Alexander Schimmelfennig, leading Illinois, Ohio, New York and Pennsylvania regiments. Colonel W. Krzyzanowski, whose nomination by Lincoln to brigadier had failed of approval in the Senate, headed a New York regiment. Youths who had left their classes at Harvard, Kenyon, Oberlin, Knox and many other colleges were in the ranks; wild Irish from the sidewalks of New York; Bavarians and Prussians from St. Louis and Milwaukee. Green Mountain plowboys were there; farm hands from the cornfields and orchards of Michigan.

These platoons of regulars, volunteers, conscripts, bounty men, were marching for adventure and glory; for the country and the flag; for a united nation from coast to coast; for the abolition of chattel slavery; or because they were drafted and there was no escape; or because they were paid a bounty of cash. In a hundred soldiers picked at random might be a hundred different explanations of why they had gone to war and become individual, mobile units of the Army of the Potomac. They were young, most of them in their early twenties, some in their teens—soft-haired youths, yet many of them fierce cubs of war ready to earn with pride and abandon the badge of courage.

Mrs. Lincoln wore, wrote the New York *Herald* man, "a rich black dress with narrow flounces, a black cape with broad trimming of velvet around the border and a plain hat of the same hue composed her costume. A shade of weariness, doubtless the result of her labors in behalf of the sick and wounded in Washington, rested upon her countenance but the change seemed pleasant to her. The President wore a dark sack overcoat and a fur muffler."

Instead of a lean cob with a docked tail, the President should have sat "a fair-sized cavalry horse of which there were plenty," wrote William F. Goodhue of Company C, 3d Wisconsin Infantry, to his home folks. "Mr. Lincoln sat his cob perfectly straight, and dressed as he was in dark clothes, it appeared as if he was an exclamation point astride of the small letter *m*."

General Darius N. Couch wrote: "Mr. Lincoln, sitting there with his hat off, his head bent, and seemingly meditating, suddenly turned to me and said, 'General Couch, what do you suppose will become of all these men when the war is over?' And it struck me as very pleasant that somebody had an idea that the war would sometime end."

In the Confederate army across the river horses were gaunt from lack of forage. Scurvy had begun to appear among troops lacking balanced rations. Cattle had arrived so thin that Lee asked to have them kept to fatten in the spring and salt meat issued instead. Through an unusually bleak and frigid winter some of Lee's troops had no blankets. Many wore coats and shoes in tatters. An evangelistic revival through the winter, in which religious leaders from Southern cities joined the chaplains, had brought thousands of converts and given a religious impress to the Army of Northern Virginia.

True it was "the Yanks were licked" at Charleston, dispatches told Lincoln. A fleet of ironclad vessels, long and carefully prepared, had failed to batter down Fort Sumter, and under fire from heavy shore batteries had retired somewhat crippled with one vessel sunk and two disabled. Because Charleston was a symbol, a starting point of secession, many in the North hoped it could be taken; they had expected much; they would wait.

The failure at Charleston led to Admiral Dahlgren's relieving Admiral Du Pont in command of the South Atlantic blockading squadron. Welles recorded Lincoln as saying: "Du Pont, as well as McClellan, hesitates—has *the slows*. McClellan always wanted more regiments; Du Pont is everlastingly asking for more gunboats, more ironclads. He will do nothing with any . . . He is no Farragut, though unquestionably a good routine officer, who obeys orders and in a general way carries out his instructions." Thus Lincoln kept touch personally with fleets and squadrons at sea as well as armies and expeditions on land.

"Write me often. I am very anxious," wrote Lincoln to Hooker a week after his visit to the army. He thanked Hooker for maps, newspapers and a letter which arrived April 28. "While I am anxious, please do not think I am impatient, or waste a moment's thought on me, to your own hindrance, or discomfort." He sent two telegrams to Hooker in the first week of May querying, "What's news?" Hooker was letting no one into his secrets. "I heard him say," wrote Meade, "that not a human being knew his plans either in the army or at Washington."

On May 1 Hooker had brought most of his army across the Rappahannock River, to a crossroads named Chancellorsville. Hooker attacked, Lee counterattacked, and Hooker ordered his men to fall back. "Just as we reached the enemy we were recalled," wrote Meade, while General Couch, second to Hooker in command, said: "Hooker expected Lee to fall back without risking battle. Finding himself mistaken he assumed the defensive."

Early next morning Lee sent half his army under Stonewall Jackson on a march that took them till late in the afternoon, when they delivered a surprise attack that smashed the Union flank and rear. Next day Lee outguessed and outfought Hooker. With an army half the size of Hooker's, he so mangled and baffled the Union forces that Hooker called a council of his generals, of whom four voted to stay where they were and fight, two voted to retreat across the river. Hooker then ordered the retreat.

The white moon by night and the red sun by day had looked down on over 20,000 men who lay killed or wounded on the open farms and in the wilderness of trees, thickets and undergrowth, the figures giving Union losses at 11,000, Confederate at 10,000, not including 6,000 prisoners captured by Lee and 2,000 by Hooker. Numbers, however, could not tell nor measure the vacancy nor the Southern heartache left by the death of Stonewall Jackson, shot by his own men, it was reported, as he was inspecting positions in the zone of fire. A cannon ball had broken a mansion pillar against which General Hooker leaned, knocked him down, left him senseless a half-hour, dazed for an hour or more, while the battle lines rocked and tore on the second day.

Hooker had gone into battle with a good plan and dropped it when the enemy refused to do what he expected. He was sick with himself as he told Meade he was ready to turn over the army; he had had enough and almost wished he had never been born.

News of what happened to Hooker was slow reaching the White House. "I this P.M. met the President at the War Department," wrote Welles May 4. "He said he had a feverish anxiety to get facts; was constantly up and down, for nothing reliable came from the front." Noah Brooks found the President "anxious and harassed beyond any power of description," that while without any positive information Lincoln was certain in his own mind that "Hooker had been licked." He asked Brooks to go into the room occupied by his friend Dr. Henry, a guest, and wait for later news.

"In an hour or so, while the doctor and I sat talking, about 3 o'clock in the afternoon," wrote Brooks, "the door opened and Lincoln came into the room. He held a telegram in his hand, and as he closed the door and came toward us I mechanically noticed that his face, usually sallow, was ashen in hue. The paper on the wall behind him was of the tint known as 'French gray,' and even in that moment of sorrow and dread expectation, I vaguely took in the thought that the complexion of the anguished President's visage was like that of the wall. He gave me the telegram, and in a voice trembling with emotion, said 'Read it —news from the army.'

"The despatch was from General Butterfield, Hooker's chief of staff, addressed to the War Department, and was to the effect that the army had been withdrawn from the south side of the Rappahannock and was then 'safely encamped' in its former position. The appearance of the President, as I read aloud these fateful words, was piteous . . . broken . . . and so ghostlike. Clasping his hands behind his back, he walked up and down the room, saying 'My God! my God! What will the country say! What will the country say!' He seemed incapable of uttering any other words than these, and after a little time he hurriedly left the room."

Rumors flew over Washington that the President and Halleck had gone to the front; Hooker would be put under arrest; Halleck would command; Stanton had quit; Lee had cut Hooker to pieces and was moving on Washington; McClellan was coming by special train from New York to command, while Generals Sigel, Butler, Frémont, on the shelf, would soon arrive. The bar at Willard's was crowded; men with their feet on the brass rail drank hard liquor and conducted a war that existed in their own minds.

The President wrote May 7 to Hooker as though a good fighter had been sent reeling, wasn't hurt, and might make

a swift comeback. "An early movement would . . . help,"
he wrote, asking if Hooker had in mind a plan wholly or
partially formed. "If you have, prossecute it without interference from me . . ."

Lincoln's visit at the front was partly told in General
Meade's letter to his wife: "I was summoned to headquarters, where I found the President and General Halleck. The
former said he had come down to enquire for himself as to
the condition of affairs and desired to see corps commanders . . . The President remarked that the result was in his
judgment most unfortunate; that he did not blame any
one . . . Nevertheless he thought its effect, both at home
and abroad, would be more serious and injurious than any
previous act of the war . . . Since seeing the President, he
[Hooker] seems in better spirits . . ." Meantime as many
explanations of the repulse at Chancellorsville had been
published as were offered earlier to solve the first Bull Run
rout.

Lee was carefully screening a movement that seemed to
be aimed northward, possibly another invasion of Maryland. On June 14 Lincoln queried Hooker: "If the head of
Lee's army is at Martinsburg and the tail of it on the plank
road between Fredericksburg and Chancellorsville, the
animal must be very slim somewhere. Could you not break
him?"

Welles wrote he was puzzled that no condemnation of
Hooker came from Lincoln: "The President . . . has a personal liking for Hooker, and clings to him when others give
way." As though he had it from Sumner, Welles wrote:
"The President said if Hooker had been killed by the shot
which knocked over the pillar that stunned him, we should
have been successful." As late as June 26, nearly seven
weeks since the Battle of Chancellorsville, Hooker had
done nothing to fret or harass Lee, and Lincoln gave to
Welles the first inkling that he might have to let Hooker go.

Hearing that Lincoln was going to give him command of
the army, the able and valorous corps commander General
John F. Reynolds hurried to the White House and told Lin-

coln he did not want command of the Army of the Potomac and would not take it.

Lee rested his army, received new divisions of freshly conscripted troops, slipped away into the Shenandoah Valley, and by June 29 had crossed the Potomac, marched over Maryland, and had an army of 75,000 on Pennsylvania soil. Hooker broke camp with his army and moved it northward in scattered formation.

At Frederick, Maryland, a man in civilian clothes, riding in a buggy, begging, buying and wheedling his way through straggling parties of soldiers and wagon trains, arrived at three o'clock the morning of June 28 and went to the tent of General George Gordon Meade, was let in after wrangling. He woke Meade from sleep, saying he had come to give him trouble. Meade said his conscience was clear; he was prepared for bad news.

A letter from General in Chief Halleck was put in Meade's hands: "You will receive with this the order of the President placing you in command of the Army of the Potomac . . . You will not be hampered by any minute instructions from headquarters. Your army is free to act as you may deem proper under the circumstances as they arise." Meade argued with General James A. Hardie, chief of staff of the Secretary of War, who had brought the order. He did not want the place. But every point he made had been anticipated. Meade was ordered as a soldier to accept, which he did, issuing notice that day: "By direction of the President of the United States, I hereby assume command of the Army of the Potomac."

Lincoln met his Cabinet the Sunday morning Meade took command. "The President . . . drew from his pocket a telegram from General Hooker asking to be relieved," noted Welles. "The President said he had, for several days as the conflict became imminent, observed in Hooker the same failings that were witnessed in McClellan after the Battle of Antietam—a want of alacrity to obey, and a greedy call for more troops . . ." Chase, in a long polite letter to the President that day, intimated that trickery had been on foot in the ousting of Hooker.

A. K. McClure urged Lincoln to put McClellan again in command, which was also the wish of many business and professional men of New York and Philadelphia. Lincoln replied with two questions: "Do we gain anything by opening one leak to stop another? Do we gain anything by quieting one clamor merely to open another, and probably a larger one?"

Hooker asked Noah Brooks what the President had said about him. "I hesitated," said Brooks, "but when he pressed for a reply, I said that Lincoln had told me that he regarded Hooker very much as a father might a son who was lame, or who had some other physical infirmity. His love for his son would be even intensified by the reflection that the lad could never be a strong and successful man. The tears stood in Hooker's eyes as he heard this curious characterization of himself."

The next great battle, it seemed to many, would be a duel between Meade and Lee, somewhere in Pennsylvania, at Philadelphia, Chambersburg, Harrisburg, perhaps Gettysburg.

A soldier with both legs shot off was being carried to the rear in the recent fighting. And seeing a woman selling leathery-looking pies, he called out, "Say, old lady, are those pies sewed or pegged?" Also there was a high private at Chancellorsville who had been through several campaigns with a crockery mug, from which he was drinking coffee as his regiment awaited action. A stray bullet, just missing the coffee drinker's head, shattered the mug and left only its handle on his fingers. Turning his head toward the enemy, he growled, "Johnny, you can't do that again." Lincoln told of these to Brooks. "It seems as if neither death nor danger can quench the grim humor of the American soldier."

Now the war already had a considerable past. In a little wilderness clearing at Chancellorsville, a living soldier had come upon a dead one sitting with his back to a tree, looking at first sight almost alive enough to hold a conversation. He had sat there for months, since the battle the year before that gave him his long rest. He seemed to have a story and a philosophy to tell if the correct approach were made and he could be led into a quiet discussion. The living soldier, however, stood frozen in his foot tracks a few moments, gazing at the ashen face and the sockets where the eyes had withered—then he picked up his feet, let out a cry and ran. He had interrupted a silence where the slants of silver moons and the music of varying rains kept company with the one against the tree who sat so speechless, though having much to say.

Chapter 16

Will Grant Take Vicksburg?

One question weighed heavily on the Richmond Government in the spring of '63. Would Grant take Vicksburg? If so the Mississippi River would pass wholly into Union possession. Lincoln had talked about such a result to Commander D. D. Porter, pointing at a map and saying, as quoted by Porter: "See what a lot of land these fellows hold, of which Vicksburg is the key . . . Let us get Vicksburg and all that country is ours. The war can never be brought to a close until that key is in our pocket. I am acquainted with that region and know what I am talking about . . ."

From the fall of '62 till July 1 of '63 Grant performed with armies round-about Vicksburg, marching troops along the Yazoo River, the Yalobusha, the Tallahatchie, amid the miasma of swamps and the tangles of live oak and Spanish moss, digging ditches and canals, chopping wood, building bridges, throwing up breastworks, standing waist-deep in the mud of rifle pits, sleeping in soaked fields and slogging on through monotonous heavy rains, enduring plagues of malarial fever, measles, mumps and smallpox. They became familiars of Five Mile Creek, Deer Creek, Eagle Bend, Moon Lake, Rolling Fork, the Big Sunflower, Muddy Bayou, the inlets and curves of the Mississippi River with its great sudden twist at the bluffs of Vicksburg, a city of 5,000 people, 250 feet above the river.

Grant's home-town Congressman, E. B. Washburne, wrote to Lincoln of Grant: "On this whole march for five days he has had neither a horse nor an orderly or servant, a blanket or overcoat or clean shirt. His entire baggage consists of a tooth brush." For weeks the army lived on the country, took the cattle, hogs, grain, supplies, from the farming sections where they were fighting.

Grant slogged 'and plodded, trying a plan to find it fail, devising another plan, hanging to his one purpose of taking Vicksburg. At one time Lincoln and Stanton had no word from him in ten days. His men marched 180 miles; fought five battles; killed more than the enemy; took 6,000 prisoners, 90 cannon, in 20 days. Porter's ironclad gunboats ran the fire of the heavy shore batteries around the long U bend of the Mississippi, took terrific pounding, lost coal barges and one transport, but came through with the armored flotilla safe. Two other flotillas were put on the Vicksburg operation, cutting off that city from all lines of communication in three directions. Twice Grant had tried to storm his way into Vicksburg, and failing, had settled down to pick and shovel, advancing trenches, stopping food and supplies for the city.

The commander of Vicksburg, John C. Pemberton, was a favorite of President Davis. A West Pointer, Mexican War veteran, Indian fighter, Pennsylvania-born and raised, a descendant of three generations of Quakers, his Northern birth was held against him. After Grant's second storming attempt, Pemberton spoke to his troops: "You have heard that I was incompetent and a traitor; and that it was my intention to sell Vicksburg. Follow me and you will see the cost at which I will sell Vicksburg. When the last pound of beef, bacon and flour, the last grain of corn, the last cow and hog and horse and dog shall have been consumed, and the last man shall have perished in the trenches, then, and only then, will I sell Vicksburg."

For six months and more Grant, to many people in the North, seemed to be wandering around, stumbling and bungling on a job beyond him. So crazily intricate became the layout that in early June Sherman wrote home: "I don't believe I can give you an idea of matters here. You will read so much about Vicksburg and the people now gathered about it that you will get bewildered." In March he had written, "No place on earth is favored by nature with natural defense such as Vicksburg, and I do believe the whole thing will fail"; another plan would have to be worked on.

Thus often the very spectators on the spot felt desperate, and newspaper correspondents had good reason, at times, to send the North stories of gloom and despair. Sherman arrested Thomas W. Knox, New York *Herald* correspondent, tried him by court-martial on the charge of writing letters for publication without submitting them to the commanding general. Knox was sentenced to stay outside of army lines. In Washington a committee of newspapermen laid the papers in the Knox case before Lincoln, who told the committee he couldn't embarrass his generals in the field, though he would be glad to serve Mr. Knox or any other loyal journalist. He began writing, with pauses, a statement to whom it might concern, that Knox's offense was "technical, rather than wilfully wrong" and the sentence should be revoked. "Now therefore said sentence is hereby so far revoked as to allow Mr. Knox to return to Gen. Grant's Head-Quarters, and to remain, if Gen. Grant shall give his express assent; and to again leave the Department, if Gen. Grant shall refuse such assent." This satisfied the committee.

Sherman stuck on with the army, held by affection and admiration for Grant, writing to his Senator brother that Grant was honest, able, sensible and a hero, which sentiments reached Lincoln. He was redheaded, lean, scrawny, this Sherman, with a mind of far wider range than usual in the army. One of the 11 children of a lawyer who served as judge of the Supreme Court of Ohio, he was taken into the home of Thomas Ewing, lawyer and famous Whig, when his father died. An 1840 West Pointer, Sherman saw Indian fighting in Florida, studied law, was an adjutant general in California during the Mexican War, managed a bank in San Francisco, operated a New York office for a St. Louis firm, practiced law in Leavenworth, Kansas, and at the opening of the war was superintendent of the Louisiana State Military Academy at Alexandria. He had seen the United States and anxiety rode him about it; newspapers, politicians, the educated classes, were corrupt, blind, selfish, garrulous, to the point of tragedy.

Early in the war it had racked Sherman's mind that there was to be wholesale and organized slaughter by prolonged combat between his Northern people against others "as good as ourselves." He had paced to and fro in the hall of a hotel in Cincinnati mumbling to himself, and his high-pitched commentaries had earned him the nickname of "Crazy" Sherman among those who misunderstood. For what seemed to him a just cause he would invoke terror. "To secure the navigation of the Mississippi River I would slay millions; on that point I am not only insane, but mad." Lincoln was yet to get acquainted with this lean, restless, hawk-eyed rider of war and apostle of conquest.

Charles A. Dana, once of the New York *Tribune*, had revolted at Greeley's muddled, equivocal support of Lincoln, had resigned, later was given full credentials to travel with Grant's army, see everything, and report to the President and the Secretary of War. Dana reported three remarkable men heading the campaign, Grant, Sherman and James B. McPherson, all Ohio-born, and between them "utmost confidence," no jealousy or bickering. "In their unpretending simplicity they were as alike as three peas." John A. Logan, the Douglas Democrat from far south in Illinois, Dana reported, was proving a heroic, brilliant, sometimes unsteady brigadier general.

Grant's home-town lawyer friend, now Assistant Adjutant General John A. Rawlins, Dana noted, gave himself no indulgence over Grant, "watches him day and night, and whenever he commits the folly of tasting liquor hastens to remind him that at the beginning of the war he gave him [Rawlins] his word of honor not to touch a drop." On a steamer trip up the Yazoo, Grant drank wine till he was too fuddled to make a decision as to how far upriver the boat should go, Dana ordering the steamer to return. "The next morning," wrote Dana, "Grant came out to breakfast fresh as a rose, clean shirt and all, quite himself." So faithful was the watch kept by Rawlins over Grant that no distinct occasion ever arose that scandal-bearers could point to and say that drink had brought disaster.

A steady stream of letters in the mail, and persistent callers at the White House, brought Lincoln the advice that for the sake of the country he must get rid of Grant. The tone of many ran like that of a letter of Murat Halstead, editor of the Cincinnati *Commercial*, to Secretary Chase. "How is it that Grant, who was behind at Fort Henry, drunk at Donelson, surprised and whipped at Shiloh, and driven back from Oxford, Miss., is still in command? Governor Chase, these things are true. Our noble army of the Mississippi is being wasted by the foolish, drunken, stupid Grant. He cannot organize or control or fight an army. I have no personal feeling about it; but I know he is an ass. There is not among the whole list of retired major-generals a man who is not Grant's superior."

On this letter Chase wrote an endorsement for Lincoln to read: "Reports concerning General Grant similar to the statements made by Mr. Halstead are too common to be safely or even prudently disregarded." In another letter in much the same vein, Halstead referred to Grant as "a jackass in the original package . . . a poor drunken imbecile . . . a poor stick sober and he is most of the time more than half drunk, and much of the time idiotically drunk."

Among White House callers one day came John M. Thayer, a brigadier from Grant's army, who was for special reasons making a trip east. Fixing an earnest and somewhat quizzical look on Thayer, Lincoln asked, "Well, what kind of a fellow is Grant?" Thayer replied that Grant was a real commander, popular with the army, making plans and throwing all his energies into their execution. Thayer said he had had opportunities to observe Grant during two years of service. "It has been charged in northern newspapers that Grant was under the influence of liquor on the fields of Donelson and Shiloh. The charge is atrocious, wickedly false. I saw him repeatedly during the battles of Donelson and Shiloh on the field, and if there were any sober men on the field, Grant was one of them."

"It is a relief to me to hear this statement from you," said Lincoln, "for though I have not lost confidence in Grant, I have been a good deal annoyed by reports which have reached me of his intemperance . . . Delegation after delegation has called on me with the same request, 'Recall Grant from command' . . . One day a delegation headed by a distinguished doctor of divinity from New York, called on me and made the familiar . . . protest against Grant being retained in his command. After the clergyman had concluded his remarks, I asked if any others desired to add anything to what had already been said. They replied that they did not. Then looking as serious as I could, I said: 'Doctor, can you tell me where General Grant gets his liquor?' The doctor seemed quite nonplussed, but replied that he could not. I then said to him: 'I am very sorry, for if you could tell me I would direct the Chief Quartermaster of the army to lay in a large stock of the same kind of liquor, and would also direct him to furnish a supply to some of my other generals who have never yet won a victory.' " Lincoln handed Thayer a friendly slap on the leg, lay back in his chair, had a laugh.

Nicolay and Hay noted that when overzealous people had accused Grant of intemperance, Lincoln's reply was, "If I knew what brand of whiskey he drinks I would send a barrel or so to some other generals." At one time, Nicolay noted, Grant's standing had sunk so low with newspapers, politicians and a large public that Lincoln remarked, "I think Grant has hardly a friend left, except myself."

During June, Grant's army, earlier numbering only about 40,000, was reinforced to 70,000 and more. The plantations of Jefferson Davis and his brother Joseph had been captured and supplies from them lent aid to the Union cause. A world audience was looking on and wondering how many days or months the siege might last.

The marching of Lee with 80,000 Confederate troops up into Pennsylvania, with Meade and the Army of the Potomac trailing him for battle, hoping to stop him, was a bold movement, partly made on the chance that the danger to Northern cities would cause Lincoln and Halleck to draw off troops from Grant to fight Lee. In such event it was believed Pemberton might cut his way out of the seven miles of Union trenches encircling Vicksburg.

In hundreds of caves dug in the clay hillsides of the besieged city, women and children wondered how long till the end. One eyewitness told of seeing a woman faint as a shell burst a few feet from her. He saw three children knocked down by the dirt flung out from one explosion. "The little ones picked themselves up, and wiping the dust from their eyes, hastened on." Said another, "I saw one bright young bride whose arm shattered by a piece of shell had been amputated." Yet these were minor incidents to the thousands whose daily monotonous menu of mule and horse meat with parched corn had run out in latter June. Pemberton, as he had said he would, killed the last dog for food. Then he fed the men of his garrison on rats, cane shoots and bark. Some of the men standing in the firing trenches were wobbly on their legs. Pemberton was obeying instructions from President Davis to hold Vicksburg at all costs.

Chapter 17

Deep Shadows — Lincoln in Early '63

In the months between Fredericksburg and Chancellors-ville, events swirled round the peculiar pivot where Lincoln moved, and put him into further personal isolation. So often daylight seemed to break—and it was a false dawn—and it was as yet night. When hope came singing a soft song, it was more than once shattered by the brass laughter of cannon and sudden bayonets preceding the rebel yell.

Said Howell Cobb of Georgia in early '63: "Only two things stand in the way of an amicable settlement of the whole difficulty: the Landing of the Pilgrims and Original Sin."

The first combat of Negro troops against white had taken place in the Vicksburg area when 1,000 enlisted Union black men defended Milliken's Bend from an attack of some 2,000 Confederates. The fighting was mainly hand-to-hand. General Elias S. Dennis said, "White and black men were lying side by side, pierced by bayonets. Two men, one white and the other black, were found side by side, each with the other's bayonet through his body." As such news spread North it intensified agitation for and against the use of more Negro regiments. In the deepening bitterness General John M. Thayer and others heard Lincoln say his main anxiety was in the North. "The enemy behind us is more dangerous to the country than the enemy before us."

The Richmond Government could not have planted a readier spokesman in Congress at Washington than it had in Clement L. Vallandigham saying that more than 1,000,000 had been called to arms: "Seventy-five thousand first . . . then eighty-three thousand more were demanded;

and three hundred and ten thousand responded . . . The President next asked for four hundred thousand, and Congress . . . gave him five hundred thousand; and, not to be outdone, he took six hundred and thirty-seven thousand. Half of these melted away in their first campaign." Should the war go on? "I answer no—not a day, not an hour," shouted Vallandigham. He outlined a plan for the soldiers of both armies to fraternize and go home, while the governments at Washington and Richmond should not even negotiate a treaty of peace.

A peace man of shaded sincerity, Vallandigham of Dayton, Ohio, had the country's eye. His father, a Presbyterian minister, traced directly to a Huguenot driven out of France for religious convictions, settling in Virginia in 1690. His mother was Scotch-Irish. Teaching school at Snow Hill, Maryland, he studied at night; he practiced law in Columbus, Ohio, served in the state legislature and, known as an extreme proslavery man, lost several campaigns for judge, lieutenant governor, member of Congress. Tall, bearded, sonorous, his self-righteousness gave him a personal exaltation: "I had rather that my right arm were plucked from its socket, and cast into eternal burnings, than, with my convictions, to have . . . defiled my soul with the guilt of moral perjury . . . I would that my voice could penetrate the most impenetrable of all recesses, the precincts of the White House." He became specific. "Stop fighting. Make an armistice—no formal treaty . . . Buy and sell . . . Open up railroads . . . Visit the North and West . . . the South. Exchange newspapers. Migrate. Intermarry. Let slavery alone. Hold elections at the appointed times. Let us choose a new President in sixty-four."

More adroit was Wilbur Fisk Storey, publisher of the Chicago *Times*, a broken-down newspaper he had vitalized and made the voice of the extremist enemies of the Lincoln administration. A Vermont boy, he had been printer's devil, typesetter in New York, and drifting west had edited Democratic newspapers at La Porte and Mishawaka, Indiana. In Michigan he was postmaster at Jackson under President Polk, in two cities had run drugstores, had given eight years to building up the Detroit *Free Press,* earning $30,000 for himself, and in 1861 at 42 had begun to give Chicago and the Middle West a morning paper that was gossipy, sensational, fearless, devious.

A tight-lipped, short-spoken man, his face whiskered except for the upper lip, Storey cultivated suspicion as a habit. During March '63 the Chicago *Times* printed items about "the impeachment of the President at the opening of the next session of Congress . . . the crimes committed by the Executive . . . have furnished ample grounds for his impeachment; and every true patriot will rejoice to learn that he is to be brought to punishment . . ."

Without basis or explanation, the New York *Day Book,* the Chicago *Times* and like party organs printed the one sentence: "The President's son, 'Bob,' as he is called, a lad of some twenty summers, has made half a million dollars in government contracts." That was the item entire. How or where the President's son made his money, by what particular contracts, was not told or hinted at.

Old Sam Medary was a philosopher, a natural dissenter and fanatic protestant, whose weekly newspaper, the *Crisis* at Columbus, Ohio, presented the ancient Anglo-Saxon case for personal liberty. Born of a Quaker mother, he was in his editorials eloquently antiwar and consistently held Lincoln all wrong, on the premise that all wars are all wrong.

Bluff, gray-bearded, sincere Sam Medary, 62 years old, could sit at his desk and keep up a running conversation with any visitor as his pen chased along writing an editorial. "Abe Linkin reminds us of a little anecdote we once heard, very foolish and no nub to it," he wrote. Or "If Abe Lincoln is the Government, with his army of official thieves, would it not be an act of patriotism to notify such a Government to skedaddle as soon as possible?" The President's course was "serpentine," said the *Crisis.*

A mob one night wrecked the print shop, smashed the editorial desks, and Editor Medary issued a number blaming soldiers from Camp Chase, egged on by the *Ohio State Journal* editor, whom he characterized as "dirty pup," "hired pimp," "daily associate of burglars," "gloating hyena"; the Republicans concerned were "idiots and knavish asses."

One morsel of utterance from Lincoln was seized on. Editors and orators of the opposition hurled their strength at Lincoln's fragment in his inaugural address: "Suppose you go to war, you cannot fight always; and when, after much loss on both sides, and no gain on either, you cease fighting, the identical old questions, as to terms of intercourse, are again upon you." They demurred to Lincoln's progressions in styling the Negroes in 1859 "negroes"; in 1860, "colored men"; in 1861, "intelligent contrabands"; in 1862, "free Americans of African descent."

In New York City, Samuel F. B. Morse, inventor of the electric telegraph, headed the Society for the Diffusion of Political Knowledge, sending forth showers of Peace Democrat pamphlets. To a brother-in-law Morse wrote that Lincoln was "weak," "vacillating," "illiterate," "a President without brains."

Northern fleets and armies had shattered and desolated Southern cities with houses mute as dried skulls. This, while in the North many streams of life flowed on as if the war had never been heard of.

Lincoln was "the Baboon President," "a low-bred obscene clown," if you believed the Atlanta *Intelligencer* while Robert E. Lee had with his own hands flogged a slave girl and poured brine on her bleeding wounds, if you believed the Boston *Transcript*. Each side played for hate.

New York Peace Democrats took fresh vigor from their new governor, Horatio Seymour, 53, a man of inherited fortune who had served as mayor of Utica, speaker of the state assembly, lieutenant governor, delegate to national conventions. Seymour shaved his face, liked a muffler of whiskers under his jaws; ringlets of hair circled his bald pate. He called for an end to "the incompetents" at Washington who would never save the nation; he said compromise measures could have prevented the war. The Emancipation Proclamation, Seymour said on taking office, violated the Constitution; to free 4,000,000 Negro slaves, the North would require a military despotism.

Lincoln wrote to Seymour in March '63 a letter so openly friendly that Seymour was suspicious as he read: "You and I are substantially strangers; and I write this chiefly that we may become better acquainted. I, for the time being, am at the head of a nation which is in great peril; and you are at the head of the greatest State of that nation . . . In the performance of my duty, the co-operation of your State, as that of others, is needed—in fact, is indispensable. This alone is a sufficient reason why I should wish to be at a good understanding with you. Please write me at least as long a letter as this—of course, saying in it, just what you think fit." Seymour sent a brother to Washington to convey assurances of loyal support and to protest against arbitrary arrests.

A New York *Tribune* editorial March 25, 1863, noted that politically the war issue dwarfed all others: " 'Tell your brother,' said President Lincoln lately to the brother of a prominent Democratic aspirant to the Presidency, 'that he can not be the next President of the United States unless there shall *be* a United States to preside over.' "

On the last day before a new Congress with new Democratic members would take their seats, a Conscription Act was passed empowering the Government to divide the country into districts with provost marshals and enrollment boards authorized to raise troops by drafting all able-bodied citizens between 20 and 45.

Debate raged on what the Constitution meant in saying "The . . . writ of habeas corpus shall not be suspended, unless when in cases of rebellion or invasion the public safety may require it." Had the President alone the power to suspend the writ, or did he need Congress to tell him when? This issue would not down. English history and law seemed to favor Parliament as against the King, and Congress as against the President. Lincoln himself had seldom directly ordered arrests of the sort complained of. But Stanton and Seward had, and Lincoln had not interfered.

Seward telegrams would read, "Arrest Leonard Sturtevant and send him to Fort La Fayette," or, "Send William Pierce to Fort La Fayette." Stanton would notify a U.S. marshal that John Watson was in Boston at No. 2 Oliver Place. "Watch him, look out for the clothes and letters, and seize them and arrest him when it is the right time. Don't let him see or communicate with anyone, but bring him immediately to Washington." Men arrested were charged with treason, disloyalty, inciting or participating in riot, aiding and abetting rebels, defrauding the Government, stealing Government property, robbing the U.S. mail, blockade-running, smuggling, spying, enticing soldiers to desert, aiding and harboring deserters, defrauding recruits of bounty, horse-stealing. The charges went into the records or again they did not.

The terror of secret and arbitrary arrests was softened somewhat by the Habeas Corpus bill of March 3, 1863. The Secretaries of State and of War were directed to furnish courts with names of all persons held as prisoners by authority of the Secretaries or the President. Congress made it clear that control over the habeas corpus writ rested with Congress, yet it directly authorized the President to suspend the writ. This was carefully done so that no appearance was presented of any conflict of authority between the President and Congress.

From house to house enrollers in the spring of '63 took the names of men and boys fit for the Army. Cripples, the deaf and dumb, the blind and other defectives were exempt. So were the only son of a widowed mother, the only son of aged and infirm parents, others having dependents. In a family where two or more sons of aged and infirm parents were drafted, the father if living, or if dead the mother, must say which son would stay home and which go to war. Also anyone having $300 cash, and willing to pay it as "bounty" to a substitute, was exempt and could stay at home and laugh at the war.

Western governors reported the secret Knights of the Golden Circle as disguising itself under various names, with oaths, passwords, rituals and rifles, aiming to encourage desertion, defeat the draft, and protect its members by force. In a few weeks 2,600 deserters had been arrested. Seventeen deserters fortified a log cabin and, provisioned by neighbors, defied siege. Two draft-enrollers were murdered in Indiana; women threw eggs, men rioted with clubs, guns, bricks. In a Pennsylvania county one enroller was forced to quit taking names, another was shot, the sawmill of another was burned. The Molly Maguires, an Irish miners' secret society in Pénnsylvania, made resistance; coal operators refused to give the names of leaders to the Government in fear their breakers might be burned; Stanton sent troops to quell the disturbers.

In St. Louis, the Reverend Dr. McPheeters refused to declare himself for the Union; he baptized a baby with the name of a Confederate general. A provost marshal arrested McPheeters and took control of the church. Lincoln studied the matter and wrote to General Curtis: "I tell you frankly, I believe he does sympathize with the rebels; but the question remains whether such a man, of unquestioned good moral character . . . can, with safety to the government be exiled, upon the suspicion of his secret sympathies . . . I must add that the U.S. government must not . . . undertake to run the churches . . . It will not do for the U.S. to appoint Trustees . . . or other agents for the churches."

Illinois had 2,001 deserters arrested in six months. In January the wholesale desertions and fraternizing with the enemy among troops of the 109th Illinois regiment began to look so much like a mutiny that the entire regiment was arrested, disarmed and put under guard at Holly Springs, Mississippi; these were recruits from southern Illinois, from a triangle of land wedged between the Slave States of Kentucky and Missouri. They were disgusted with Lincoln and the Emancipation Proclamation; they had enlisted to fight for the Union, "not to free the niggers." The Democratic majority in the Illinois Legislature prepared bills to restore the habeas corpus writ, to bar Negroes from entering Illinois, and otherwise to oppose the Federal Government. Then for the first time in the history of Illinois a governor prorogued the legislature, disbanded them, ordered them to go home.

Governor Morton telegraphed Lincoln he expected the Indiana Legislature in January '63 to acknowledge the Southern Confederacy. Though the legislature did not go that far it did return the Governor's message with insults and a resolution saying the policies of Governor Seymour of New York were a better model. Also this Indiana Legislature tried to take military power from the Governor, with the result that the Republican members stayed away, there was no quorum, and the legislature adjourned without appropriations of money to run the state government. Needing $250,000, Governor Morton went to Washington and got it from a fund of $2,000,000 set aside for munitions of war, to be used where rebellion existed or was threatened.

The Knights of the Golden Circle claimed 1,000,000 members. At its height it probably had thousands on its rolls. The army secret service penetrated it, one private soldier joining and becoming Grand Secretary for the State of Kentucky. The Government kept informed, guarded against upheavals, arrested ringleaders, and convicted them whenever possible. Naturally, too, some of the spies and informers reported men they personally hated, paid off old grudges. Also some officials credentialed from Washington used their powers like fools and petty tyrants.

The Sons of Liberty, the Circle of Hosts, the Union Relief Society, the Order of American Knights and other oath-bound secret societies of like aims progressed in size. They sometimes bought a storekeeper's stock entire of Colt revolvers, rifles and ammunition. Union men horsewhipped by masked committees in lonesome woodlands at night, Union men shot down in their own homes by Southern sympathizers, had their friends and kin who banded and took oaths. Violence met violence.

Protests of innocence came often from men plainly guilty. They reminded Lincoln of a governor who visited a state prison. The convicts one by one had the same story of innocence and of wrongs done them. At last the governor came to one who frankly said he had committed a crime and the sentence given him was perfect justice. "I must pardon you," said the governor. "I can't have you here corrupting all these good men."

The seething of strife was not eased in the spring of '63 by Order No. 38 issued by General Burnside commanding the Department of the Ohio, with Cincinnati headquarters. Treason, of course, was forbidden, and giving aid and comfort to the enemy. Order No. 38 was positive: "The habit of declaring sympathy for the enemy will not be allowed in this department," thereby making Burnside and his officers the judges of what was "sympathy" and how many times "sympathy" had to be declared to become a habit. They would also decide whether treason hid and lurked in the words of any suspect, Order No. 38 admonishing, "It must be distinctly understood that treason, express or implied, will not be tolerated in this department."

Vallandigham, now out of Congress, went from city to city with his cry: "If it be really the design of the administration to force this issue, then come arrest, come exile, come death itself! I am ready here to-night to meet it." On May 1 at Mount Vernon, Ohio, he rode in a parade four miles long of wagons, buggies, carriages, horsemen and a six-horse float holding 34 pretty flower girls. The *Democratic Banner* of Mount Vernon reported it "a proud and glorious day." On the platform sat Congressmen Samuel S. Cox and George Hunt Pendleton. Vallandigham had practiced for his speech. He gave again his ideas that the Government at Washington was a despotism, had rejected peace offers, was waging war to liberate black slaves and enslave white men; no men deserving to be free would submit to its conscription. Order No. 38 was a base usurpation of arbitrary power; he despised it, spat upon it and trampled it under his feet. The President was "King Lincoln," and he would advise the people to come together at the ballot box and hurl the tyrant from his throne. Applause came often. Vallandigham faced acres of people, thousands beyond reach of his voice. They led him on. His defiance and scorn of the Government ran further than in any previous hour in his career.

Three army captains from Cincinnati in plain clothes, up close to the platform, took notes and reported to Burnside. Three nights later soldiers arrived and went to Vallandigham's home at three in the morning. Fire bells tolled while soldiers with axes battered down doors, reached Vallandigham, gave him a few minutes to dress, then took him to the train for Cincinnati. A crowd of some 500 moved to the Dayton *Journal*, a Republican newspaper, broke the office windows with bricks and stones, smashed the doors, fired revolvers, put a torch to the building, gutted it.

Vallandigham from a jail cell in Cincinnati issued, without censorship, an address: "I am a Democrat—for the Constitution, for law, for the Union, for liberty—this is my only 'crime.' In obedience to the demand of Northern abolition disunionists and traitors, I am here in bonds today." A military commission tried Vallandigham and sentenced him to Fort Warren, Boston Harbor, till the war was over.

Anger, indignation and high crying rose from many newspapers and partisan Democrats. Burnside telegraphed the President he would resign if so desired. The President replied: "When I shall wish to supersede you I will let you know. All the cabinet regretted the necessity of arresting, for instance, Vallandigham, some perhaps, doubting, that there was a real necessity for it—but, being done, all were for seeing you through with it."

Lincoln's choice now seemed to lie between approval of the sentence or annulment of it. He chose still another course. The order was telegraphed to Burnside: "The President directs that without delay you send C. L. Vallandigham under secure guard to the headquarters of General Rosecrans, to be put by him beyond our military lines; and in case of his return within our lines, he be arrested and kept in close custody for the term specified in his sentence."

Vallandigham issued, without censorship, another address: "Because despotism and superior force so will it, I go within the Confederate lines . . . in vain the malice of enemies shall thus continue to give color to the calumnies and misrepresentations of the past two years." To his wife Vallandigham wrote: "I am as calm and unmoved as ever. Bear it all like a woman—a heroine. Take care of my dear, dear boy till I return. All goes well for the cause."

In Murfreesboro, Tennessee, General Rosecrans gave the prisoner a lecture ending, ". . . do you know that unless I protect you with a guard my soldiers will tear you to pieces in an instant?" Vallandigham replied: "Draw your soldiers up in a hollow square to-morrow morning . . . I will guarantee that when they have heard me through they will be more willing to tear Lincoln and yourself to pieces than they will Vallandigham."

At a house near the farthest outlying Confederate picket line, Vallandigham was left in the early morning by Union officers. At noon an ambulance took him to Bragg's headquarters; messages arrived inviting him to the hospitality of the South. He went to Wilmington, North Carolina, reporting on parole.

Meantime on June 1 General Burnside ordered the Chicago *Times* suppressed. Soldiers from Camp Douglas left the work of guarding Confederate prisoners, marched downtown and seized the newspaper plant. Copperheads made speeches that night to a Chicago crowd of 20,000 people on Court House Square. Mobs threatened to sack and burn the Chicago *Tribune* in retaliation. Senator Lyman Trumbull, Congressman Isaac N. Arnold and other Republicans held a conference with leading Democrats and telegraphed resolutions to the President asking him to revoke Burnside's order.

Lincoln wrote Stanton that many dispatches had been received June 4 "which, with former ones, induce me to believe we should revoke or suspend the order suspending the Chicago Times, and if you concur in opinion, please have it done." And the order which had brought Chicago close to mob war was revoked. The Chicago *Times* again appeared as usual with its customary columns of curses on Lincoln and all his works.

Meantime the state convention of the Democratic party of Ohio solemnly nominated the exiled Vallandigham for governor while tongues raged at Lincoln who had "banished" their leader. On June 12, 1863, Lincoln gave to the country a letter addressed to "Hon. Erastus Corning & others," the resolutions committee of the Albany Democratic convention which had blasted at the administration and demanded Vallandigham's return to freedom. Lincoln's letter covered the main points brought against him as to personal liberty, jails, gags, handcuffs.

As a Chief Magistrate he saw a distinction between peacetime arrests and the jailing of men during a gigantic rebellion. "The former is directed at the small per centage of ordinary and continuous perpetration of crime; while the latter is directed at sudden and extensive uprisings against the government, which, at most, will succeed or fail, in no great length of time. In the latter case, arrests are made, not so much for what has been done, as for what probably would be done . . . In such cases the purposes of men are much more easily understood, than in cases of ordinary crime."

Would a search of history reveal one civil war where the prevailing government had not used individuals with violence and injustice in cases where civil rights were involved? "Nothing is better known to history than that courts of justice are utterly incompetent to such cases. Civil courts are organized for trials of individuals . . . in quiet times . . . Even in times of peace, bands of horse-thieves and robbers frequently grow too numerous and powerful for the ordinary courts of justice. But what comparison, in numbers, have such bands ever borne to the insurgent sympathizers even in many of the loyal states? Again, a jury too frequently have at least one member, more ready to hang the panel than to hang the traitor. And yet again, he who dissuades one man from volunteering, or induces one soldier to desert, weakens the Union cause as much as he who kills a union soldier in battle. Yet this dissuasion, or inducement, may be so conducted as to be no defined crime of which any civil court would take cognizance."

Pointing to the death penalty as a requisite of military organization, he inquired: "Must I shoot a simple-minded

soldier boy who deserts, while I must not touch a hair of
a wiley agitator who induces him to desert? This is none the
less injurious when effected by getting a father, or brother,
or friend, into a public meeting, and there working upon
his feelings, till he is persuaded to write the soldier boy,
that he is fighting in a bad cause, for a wicked administration of a contemptible government, too weak to arrest and
punish him if he shall desert. I think that in such a case,
to silence the agitator, and save the boy, is not only constitutional, but, withal, a great mercy."

The authors of the Albany resolutions had referred to
themselves as "democrats" rather than as "American citizens" in time of national peril. "I would have preferred to
meet you upon a level one step higher than any party platform . . . But since you have denied me this, I will yet be
thankful, for the country's sake, that not all democrats
have done so." The general who arrested and tried Vallandigham, also the judge who denied the writ of habeas corpus to Vallandigham, were both Democrats. "And still more,
of all those democrats who are nobly exposing their lives
and shedding their blood on the battle-field, I have learned
that many approve the course taken with Mr. V. while I
have not heard of a single one condemning it."

The President believed that as the confusion of opinion
and action of wartime fell into more regular channels "the
necessity for arbitrary dealing" might decrease. He so desired. "Still, I must continue to do so much as may seem
to be required by the public safety."

To the foregoing a reply was made by Ohio Vallandigham Democrats who called and read it to Lincoln. They
asked, "not as a favor," that Vallandigham be given back
his rights as a citizen. Their "earnestness" about the Constitution being violated the President in his reply saw as note-
worthy and would add: "You claim that men may, if they
choose, embarrass those whose duty it is, to combat a giant
rebellion, and then be dealt with in turn, only as if there
was no rebellion. The constitution itself rejects this view."

He wrote of how "armed combinations" had resisted

arrests of deserters, had resisted draft enrollment, and "quite a number of assassinations" had occurred. "These had to be met by military force, and this again has led to bloodshed and death . . . this hindrance, of the military, including maiming and murder, is due to the course in which Mr. V. has been engaged, in a greater degree than to any other cause; and is due to him personally, in a greater degree than to any other one man . . . With all this before their eyes the convention you represent have nominated Mr. V. for Governor of Ohio; and both they and you, have declared the purpose to sustain the national Union by all constitutional means. But, of course, they and you, in common, reserve to yourselves to decide what are constitutional means . . . Your own attitude, therefore, encourages desertion, resistance to the draft and the like, because it teaches those who incline to desert, and to escape the draft, to believe it is your purpose to protect them." He closed in the tone of one at the head of a government: "Still, in regard to Mr. V. and all others, I must hereafter as heretofore, do so much as the public safety may seem to require."

Those who had relatives in the Army read the dispatch three or four times a week in the newspapers: "Two or more deserters were shot this morning." And *Harper's Weekly* inquired, "Instead of wanting Vallandigham back, ought we not rather to demand of the President, in justice and mercy, that a few more examples be made of Northern traitors?"

The President heard from the Peace Democrats in one key, the antislavery radicals in another. Said Wendell Phillips: "I believe that the President may do anything to save the Union. He may take a man's houses, his lands, his bank-stock, his horses, his slaves,—anything to save the Union . . . We need one step further,—an act of Congress abolishing slavery wherever our flag waves . . ." Whose will and wit could be trusted? "None of them—I am utterly impartial,—neither President nor Cabinet nor Senate . . ." It seemed "childish" for the President, "in bo-peep secrecy, to hide himself in the White House and launch a proclamation at us on a first day of January. The nation should have known it sixty days before."

On the slave question: "The President is an honest man; that is, he is Kentucky honest . . . the very prejudices and moral callousness which made him in 1860 an available candidate . . . necessarily makes him a poor leader,— rather no leader at all,—in a crisis like this."

An excited delegation of clergymen, troubled about the conduct of the war, came with protests. The President heard them through and, as the reading public had it from newspapers, he replied: "Gentlemen, suppose all the property you were worth was in gold, and you had put it in the hands of Blondin to carry across the Niagara River on a rope, would you shake the cable, or keep shouting out to him, 'Blondin, stand up a little straighter!—Blondin, stoop a little more—go a little faster—lean a little more to the north—lean a little more to the south'? No! you would hold your breath as well as your tongue, and keep your hands off until he was safe over. The Government is carrying an immense weight. Untold treasures are in their hands. They are doing the very best they can. Don't badger them. Keep silence, and we'll get you safe across."

The New York *Times* took as "one of the deepest sensations of the war" the order of General Grant excluding all Jews as a class from his military department. "The order, to be sure, was promptly set aside by the President but the affront to the Jews conveyed by its issue, was not so easily effaced."

Thousands of Negroes had been enlisted as soldiers in the first six months of 1863. Adjutant General Lorenzo Thomas of the War Department, in the lower Mississippi region in March, reported renewed faith in arming the blacks. He addressed 11,000 troops of two divisions, mentioning the rebels keeping at home all their slaves to raise subsistence for the armies in the field. "The administration has determined . . . to take their negroes and compel them to send back a portion of their whites to cultivate their deserted plantations. They must do this or their armies will starve."

Thomas had gone over his message thoroughly with Lincoln and Stanton. "I charge you all if any of this unfortunate race come within your lines . . . that you receive them kindly and cordially . . . They are to be received with open arms; they are to be fed and clothed; they are to be armed . . . I am here to say that I am authorized to raise as many regiments of blacks as I can. I am authorized to give commissions from the highest to the lowest."

Word had spread of the Confederate Government's order that white officers commanding Negro troops should never be taken prisoner, but put to death. Officers and men listening to the Adjutant General well knew this. "I desire only those whose hearts are in it, and to them alone will I give commissions . . . While I am authorized thus, in the name of the Secretary of War, I have the fullest authority to dismiss from the army any man, be his rank what it may, whom I find maltreating the freedmen . . . This, fellow soldiers, is the determined policy of the administration. You all know full well when the President of the United States, though said to be slow in coming to a determination, when he once puts his foot down, it is there, and he is not going to take it up." The War Department in May '63 announced a new bureau to handle Negro recruiting.

From Port Hudson on the Mississippi June 14 came word that colored troops under General Paine had led an assault, put their flag on a fort parapet amid fearful slaughter, leaving their commander wounded in front of the enemy's works as they retired. A half-mile away on a call for volunteers to go back and rescue the General, 16 stepped out from the colored regiments, moved forward in squads of four. And they brought back their general's body though only two of the 16 Negroes were alive.

A new status of the Negro was slowly taking form. In August '62 for the first time was sworn testimony taken from a Negro in a court of law in Virginia. Also Negro strikebreakers in New York were attacked by strikers, and in Chicago Negroes employed in meat-packing plants were assaulted by unemployed white men. The colored man was becoming an American citizen.

Stories arose that Confederate troops had a law to themselves: "Kill every nigger!" No distinctions would be made in battle as between free Negroes and fugitive slaves. Written petitions and spoken appeals came to Lincoln that he must retaliate: kill one Confederate white prisoner for every Negro Union soldier executed.

Negroes marching to war—with weapons—to kill—and to kill white men—it was at first a little unreal. Longfellow wrote in his diary May 28, 1863, of a visit to Boston: "Saw the first regiment of blacks march through Beacon Street. An imposing sight, with something wild and strange about it, like a dream. At last the North consents to let the Negro fight for freedom."

In an Indiana town, controlled by Copperheads, Sojourner Truth was introduced to speak at an antislavery meeting. A local physician and leading Copperhead rose and said word had spread over the community that the speaker of the evening was a man in woman's disguise; it was the wish of many present that the speaker of the evening should show his breasts to a committee of ladies. Sojourner Truth, tall, strong, unafraid, illiterate though having a natural grace of speech and body, stood silent a few moments. Then she loosed the clothing of her bosom, showed her breasts, and said in her own simple words and her deep contralto voice that these breasts she was showing had nursed black children, yes, but *more white children than black*. The audience sat spellbound. A few Copperheads slowly filed out. Toward one of them who had a look of hate and doubt on his face, Sojourner Truth shook her breasts with the melancholy query, "You want to suck?" And in this atmosphere, the gaunt black woman, the former slave, began her plea for the freedom of her race.

Strange was the play of men's thought and imagination around the Negro and his role. Antislavery journals reprinted from the Memphis *Bulletin:* "A Negro went into a menagerie, in which was a large baboon in a cage. He approached the cage closely while the baboon went through several gyrations, such as nodding and shaking his head, holding out his hands to shake, etc., to the evident delight of both Negro and baboon. Finally, the baboon seemed so intelligent and knowing, the Negro addressed him some remarks, which the baboon only answered by a nod of the head. At length the Negro was still more delighted, and broke forth with the remark, 'You're right; don't open your mouth, kase if you spokes a word the white man'l have a shovel in your hand in less dan a minit.' "

There came to Lincoln the foremost of fugitive slaves. By authority of the President to Governor Andrew of Massachusetts to raise two regiments of colored men, this ex-slave had led in recruiting the 54th and 55th Massachusetts regiments, two of his own sons in the 54th. Hundreds of black men of the 54th, and their white colonel, had been killed assaulting a fort in South Carolina, the white colonel's body resting, as South Carolinians reported, "between layers of dead niggers." And Lincoln held his first conference on important business of state with a mulatto, Frederick Douglass. Born in Maryland of a black slave mother, his father a white man, Douglass had grown up as a plantation boy living through winters without shoes or stockings. He grew to a superb physical strength, worked in shipyards as a calker, and learned to read. In the red shirt and bandanna of a sailor, with papers loaned to him by a free Negro, he rode out of Baltimore on a railroad train. In New York he recognized on Broadway another escaped slave, who told him to stay away from all Negroes, as there were informers among them who would send him back where he came from for a few dollars' reward. Then Douglass met abolitionists who paid his way to New Bedford, where he worked at his trade of calker.

Antislavery men noticed he was a natural orator and sent him from city to city to tell of his life as a slave. He had sent word to a free black woman in Maryland, who came North, married him and they made a home in Rochester, New York, where in the cellar they once had 11 runaway Negroes.

Douglass read Lincoln as completely mistaken in his Negro colonization policy. "The colored race can never be respected anywhere till they are respected in America." According to Douglass, the President listened with patience and silence, was serious, even troubled. To the point that colored soldiers ought to receive the same wages as white soldiers, the President said that employment of colored soldiers at all was a great gain to the colored people; that the wisdom of making colored men soldiers was still doubted; that their enlistment was a serious offense to popular prejudice; that they had larger motives for being soldiers than white men; that they ought to be willing to enter the service upon any conditions; that the fact they were not to receive the same pay as white soldiers seemed a necessary concession to smooth the way to their employment as soldiers, but that ultimately they would receive the same pay as whites.

On the second point, that colored prisoners should receive the same protection and be exchanged as readily and on the same terms as white prisoners, and that there should be retaliation for the shooting or hanging of colored prisoners, the President said the case was more difficult. Retaliation was a terrible remedy—once begun, no telling where it would end; that if he could get hold of the Confederate soldiers who had been guilty of treating colored soldiers as felons, he could easily retaliate, but the thought of hanging men for a crime perpetrated by others was revolting to his feelings. "In all this," noted Douglass, "I saw the tender heart of the man rather than the stern warrior and Commander-in-Chief of the American army and navy, and while I could not agree with him, I could but respect his humane spirit."

On the third point, that colored soldiers who performed great and uncommon service on the battlefield should be rewarded by distinction and promotion precisely as were white soldiers, the President had less difficulty, though he did not absolutely commit himself, simply saying he would sign any commissions for colored soldiers which his Secretary of War should commend to him. "Though I was not entirely satisfied with his views," noted Douglass, "I was so well satisfied with the man and with the educating tendency of the conflict, I determined to go on with the recruiting."

In an interlude of their talk Lincoln asked, "Who is this Phillips who has been pitching into me?" adding later: "Well, tell him to go on. Let him make the people willing to go in for emancipation; and I'll go with them."

From Memphis early in '63 Charles A. Dana reported to the War Department "a mania for sudden fortunes made in cotton, raging in a vast population of Jews and Yankees." Under Federal permits they bought cotton low from Southern planters and sold high to New England textile works. Dana himself had put in $10,000, gone into partnership with a cotton expert, and was in line to make a fortune, yet he wrote to Stanton, "I should be false to my duty did I . . . fail to implore you to put an end to an evil so enormous, so insidious."

Grant agreed with Stanton; the cotton trade was corrupting in and out of the Army; the profits of it should go to the Government. Dana arrived in Washington, had many conversations with Lincoln and Stanton. The President in March issued a proclamation outlawing all commercial intercourse with insurrectionary states except under Treasury Department regulations. One public sale by an army quartermaster of 500 bales of cotton confiscated by Grant at Oxford and Holly Springs, Mississippi, brought over $1,500,000 cash, nearly paying the cost of Grant's supplies and stores burned by the enemy at Oxford.

A war prosperity was on, gold rising in price, paper money getting cheaper. Amos A. Lawrence, humanitarian millionaire merchant of Boston, wrote to Sumner: "Cheap money makes speculation, rising prices and rapid fortunes, but it will not make patriots. Volunteers will not be found for the army when paper fortunes are so quickly made at home; and drafting will be resisted . . . We must have Sunday all over the land, instead of feasting and gambling."

A New York *World* editorial writer saw a new moneyed

class attaining domination: ". . . This is the age of shoddy.
The new brown-stone palaces on Fifth Avenue, the new
equipages at the Park, the new diamonds which dazzle un-
accustomed eyes, the new silks and satins which rustle over-
loudly, as if to demand attention, the new people who live
in the palaces, and ride in the carriages, and wear the diamonds and silks—all are shoddy. From devil's dust they
sprang, and unto devil's dust they shall return. They set or
follow the shoddy fashions, and fondly imagine themselves
à la mode de Paris, when they are only à la mode de shoddy
. . . Six days in the week they are shoddy business men. On
the seventh day they are shoddy Christians."

Food prices had slowly gone up; clothes, house rent,
coal, gas, cost more. This pressure on workingmen brought
an agitation in New York that resulted in new trade-unions.
The *World* reported a mass meeting in Cooper Union with
the building crammed to capacity and hundreds waiting outside. Nearly all trades were represented, and resolutions
were adopted unanimously pointing to wage rates inadequate to the cost of living and urging all trades to organize
and send delegates to a central body.

In spite of corruption and chicanery, an economic system of new factors was getting deep rootholds. Colt's firearms factory at Hartford, Connecticut, declared a 30 per
cent dividend for 1862. Aspinwall, Vanderbilt, Drew,
Gould and others foresaw, once the war ended, an era of
money-making, speculations and developments, individual
fortunes to surpass by far any reckonings of finance in the
former generation. Immigration was bringing to American
shores a supply of workers that would result in a labor
market more than requisite to the needs of capitalist industry.

The National Bank Act of February '63 was presented as
a device to get money to run the war, while gaining stability in currency through co-operation with the bankers, bond-
holders and business interests having cash and resources.
Therefore it stipulated gold payment of interest on bonds.
Five or more persons, under the National Bank Act, could

associate and form a bank having capital of $50,000 or more. On depositing in the U.S. Treasury interest-bearing bonds to the amount of one-third of the paid-in capital of the bank, the Government would engrave money for them, National Bank certificates, to the amount of 90 per cent of the par value of the bonds deposited. The banks would use these new certificates for carrying on a regular banking business, receiving the full profit as though they were the bank's own notes. Also the banks would receive, from the Government, interest payment in gold on the bonds deposited in the Treasury.

Thus the double profit of banker's interest on Government guaranteed and supervised money issues, and the gold-paid interest on bonds, was the inducement by which Chase, with Lincoln's complete endorsement, proposed to rally cash resources to the war for the Union. Also the aim was to bring order out of chaos in currency. Across the country were in circulation more than 8,300 sorts of paper money of solvent banks, according to one financial writer, while the issues of fraudulent, broken and worthless banks brought the total up to more than 13,000.

"Shinplasters" was the nickname for much of this mongrel money; once a soldier had used them as plasters for a wounded shinbone. Bills of the banks of one state found no circulation in another. A traveler passing through several states might have to change his money several times, pay heavy discounts and sometimes commissions. Of Government greenbacks $175 would buy $100 of gold money, perhaps moving toward the time Chase had in mind when he said earlier, "The war must go on until the rebellion is put down, if we have to put out paper until it takes a thousand dollars to buy a breakfast." Chase had urged the National Bank Act as "a firm anchorage to the Union of States," which would "reconcile as far as practicable the interests of existing institutions with those of the whole people." Lincoln in his December '62 message to Congress advocated its passage.

A Republican element, holding the view of Thaddeus

Stevens that it was a moneylender's measure, unjust to the debtor class, had little to say by way of criticism, waited to see if it would bring in the war funds promised while also, as Lincoln hoped, operating to "protect labor against the evils of a vicious currency." From opposition Democrats, few in number and influence, an outcry arose that the new national banking system would create a more insidious centralization of money power than the old Bank of the United States which Andrew Jackson had destroyed.

In these financial matters, Nicolay and Hay noted, "Mr. Chase had the constant support of the President," who sometimes made suggestions but did not insist on their being adopted. When the Secretary needed his help with Congress, the President gave it ungrudgingly to the one department of the Government where he was least expert.

A committee of New Yorkers asked the President for a gunboat to protect their city. Lincoln was puzzled. The committee were introduced as "gentlemen representing $100,000,000 in their own right." Lincoln heard them through, and in his speech, as Lawrence Weldon heard it, said: ". . . It is impossible for me, in the condition of things, to furnish you a gun-boat. The credit of the Government is at a very low ebb. Greenbacks are not worth more than 40 or 50 cents on the dollar, and in this condition of things, if I was worth half as much as you gentlemen are represented to be, and as badly frightened as you seem to be, I would build a gun-boat and give it to the Government." Weldon quoted one who listened as saying he "never saw one hundred millions sink to such insignificant proportions as it did when that committee recrossed the threshold of the White House, sadder but wiser men."

The spring and early summer of '63 saw Lincoln's rating among large groups of respectable people of influence sink lower than at any time since he had become President. Richard H. Dana, author of *Two Years Before the Mast*, also an able attorney who had managed Government cases in prize courts, wrote in March to Charles Francis Adams in London: "As to the politics of Washington, the most striking thing is the absence of personal loyalty to the President. It does not exist. He has no admirers, no enthusiastic supporters, none to bet on his head . . . He has a kind of shrewdness and common sense, mother-wit, and slipshod, low-levelled honesty, that made him a good Western jury lawyer. But he is an unutterable calamity to us where he is."

One of the three Republican Congressmen—three and no more—who defended Lincoln on the floor of the House was Albert G. Riddle of Ohio. For weeks the denunciations of the President by his own party men had flowed on, mixed with clamor and sniping criticism, Riddle interposing that "the just limit of manly debate" had been "brutally outraged." The press had "caught up and reëchoed" the clamor. If the masses of people should believe what they were hearing, "no power on earth can save us from destruction, for they would shiver the only arm that must bring us safety." Riddle would have them remember: "The war is greater than the President; greater than the two Houses of Congress . . . greater than all together; and it controls them all, and dictates its own policy; and woe to the men or party that will not heed its dictation."

Amid the snarling chaos of the winter of 1862-63 there were indications of a secret movement to impeach Lincoln. Stubbornly had he followed his own middle course, earning in both parties enemies who for different reasons wanted him out of the way. There were radical Republicans who wanted a man obedient to their wishes. There were reactionaries in both parties who hoped the confusion of an impeachment would slow down the war, bring back habeas corpus and other civil rights. Long after this embryo conspiracy had failed of its aim, Cameron said to an interviewer, Howard Carroll, in guarded statements that would implicate neither dead nor living Republicans: "Late in 1862 or early in 1863 there can be no doubt that a secret effort was made to bring about the ejectment of President Lincoln from the White House . . . I received from a number of the most prominent gentlemen an invitation to visit Washington and attend a meeting . . . to be held in regard

to national affairs . . . I went to the capital, and . . . soon
discovered that their real object was to find means by which
the President could be impeached and turned out of office
. . . I was asked for my advice. I gave it, stating . . . that
it would be a little short of madness to interfere with the
Administration."

The talk of a Southern woman spy in the White House
arrived at the point where Senate members of the Committee on the Conduct of the War set a secret morning session
for attention to reports that Mrs. Lincoln was a disloyalist.
One member of the committee told of what happened. "We
had just been called to order by the Chairman, when the
officer stationed at the committee room door came in with
a half-frightened expression on his face. Before he had opportunity to make explanation, we understood the reason
for his excitement, and were ourselves almost overwhelmed
with astonishment. For at the foot of the Committee table,
standing solitary, his hat in his hand, his form towering,
Abraham Lincoln stood. Had he come by some incantation,
thus of a sudden appearing before us unannounced, we
could not have been more astounded." There was an "almost unhuman sadness" in the eyes, and "above all an
indescribable sense of his complete isolation" which the
committee member felt had to do with fundamental senses
of the apparition. "No one spoke, for no one knew what to
say. The President had not been asked to come before the
Committee, nor was it suspected that he had information
that we were to investigate reports, which, if true, fastened
treason upon his family in the White House."

At last the caller spoke slowly, with control, though with
a depth of sorrow in the tone of voice: "I, Abraham Lincoln, President of the United States, appear of my own voli-
tion before this Committee of the Senate to say that I, of
my own knowledge, know that it is untrue that any of my
family hold treasonable communication with the enemy."
Having attested this, he went away as silent and solitary as
he had come. "We sat for some moments speechless. Then
by tacit agreement, no word being spoken, the Committee

dropped all consideration of the rumors that the wife of the President was betraying the Union. We were so greatly affected that the Committee adjourned for the day."

The author of *Uncle Tom's Cabin* came to the White House, and Lincoln, as she related it, strode toward her with two outreached hands and greeted her, "So you're the little woman who wrote the book that made this great war," and as they seated themselves at the fireplace, "I do love an open fire; I always had one to home." They talked of the years of plowshares beaten into swords. Mrs. Stowe felt about him "a dry, weary, patient pain, that many mistook for insensibility." He said of the war, "Whichever way it ends, I have the impression I shan't last long after it's over."

"Rest," he said to Noah Brooks after a horseback ride. "I don't know about 'the rest' as you call it. I suppose it is good for the body. But the tired part of me is *inside* and out of reach."

Lincoln had been daily riding the three miles between the White House and Soldiers' Home, where the family lived through the hot-weather months. Lamon had been urging that the President have a military escort, the President each time laughing it off. One morning he met Lamon. While still on the horse Lincoln said, "I have something to tell you"; they went to the President's office, locked the doors. As Lamon later wrote down the talk of Lincoln, he said he would not be sure of the exact words but was giving them to the best of his recollection: "Understand me, I do not want to oppose my pride of opinion against light and reason, but I am in such a state of 'betweenity' in my conclusions that I can't say that the judgment of *this court* is prepared to proclaim a reliable 'decision upon the facts presented.'" He paused. Lamon: "Go on, go on."

"Last night, about 11 o'clock, I went out to the Soldiers' Home alone, riding *Old Abe,* as you call him (a horse he delighted in riding), and when I arrived at the foot of the hill on the road leading to the entrance of the Home grounds, I was jogging along at a slow gait . . . when suddenly I was aroused—I may say the arousement lifted me out of my saddle as well as out of my wits—by the report of a rifle, and seemingly the gunner was not fifty yards from where my contemplations ended and my accelerated transit began. My erratic namesake, with little warning . . . and with one reckless bound . . . unceremoniously separated me from my eight-dollar plug-hat, with which I parted company without any assent, expressed or implied, upon my part. At a break-neck speed we soon arrived in a haven of safety. Meanwhile I was left in doubt whether death was more desirable from being thrown from a runaway federal horse, or as the tragic result of a rifle-ball fired by a disloyal bushwhacker in the middle of the night."

This was all told in what Lamon termed "a spirit of levity," as though the little affair might be exaggerated in importance. Lincoln seemed to want to believe it a joke. "Now," he went on, "in the face of this testimony in favor of your theory of danger to me, personally, I can't bring myself to believe that anyone has shot or will deliberately shoot at me with the purpose of killing me; although I must acknowledge that I heard this fellow's bullet whistle at an uncomfortably short distance from these headquarters of mine. I have about concluded that the shot was the result of accident. It may be that someone on his return from a day's hunt, regardless of the course of his discharge, fired off his gun as a precautionary measure of safety to his family after reaching his house." This was said with much seriousness.

He then playfully proceeded: "I tell you there is no time on record equal to that made by the two Old Abes on that occasion. The historic ride of John Gilpin, and Henry Wilson's memorable display of bareback equestrianship on the stray army mule from the scenes of the battle of Bull Run, a year ago, are nothing in comparison to mine, either in point of time made or in ludicrous pageantry . . . This whole thing seems farcical. No good can result at this time from giving it publicity . . . I do not want it understood that I share your apprehensions. I never have."

Lamon sat studying a companion who to him had always

seemed prepared for the inevitable, for fate, always careless about his personal safety, and at this time not yet recovered from sorrow over the death of his son Willie. Lamon protested: "The time . . . may not be far distant when this republic will be minus a pretty respectable President."

Death was in the air. So was birth. What was dying men did not know. What was being born none could say.

Chapter 18

The Man in the White House

The White House or Executive Mansion gave a feeling of Time. The statue of Thomas Jefferson in front of the main portico stood with green mold and verdigris. The grounds during Lincoln's first year had a smooth outward serenity. Yet hidden in shrubbery were armed men and in a basement room troops with muskets and bayonets. Two riflemen in bushes stood ready to cover the movements of any person walking from the main gate to the building entry.

The Charleston *Mercury* reprinted, October 14, 1862, a New York *Herald* item: "The President's life is considered unsafe by many persons here . . . the personal safety of the commander-in-chief ought to be looked after with the utmost diligence." The President held that the only effective way to avoid all risk was to shut himself up in an iron box, where he could not possibly perform the duties of President. "Why put up the bars when the fence is down all around? If they kill me, the next man will be just as bad for them; and in a country like this, where our habits are simple, and must be, assassination is always possible, and will come if they are determined upon it."

Company K of the 150th Pennsylvania Volunteers went

on guard duty the first week in September and in a way became part of the White House family, taking care of Tad's goats and doing other chores. "He always called me Joe," said one private. The President asked about their sick, sometimes personally looked after passes and furloughs.

Of many callers and hangers-on, only one was named by Lincoln as a possible assassin, wrote Lamon. Nearing 60, side-whiskered, gray and bald as a buzzard, large of head, paunched of belly, wearing a red flannel vest, a broad-brimmed hat, a flowing blue cape from the shoulders, Adam Gurowski would come into the President's office and give advice in a sharp peremptory tone, his voice tense. Behind large green goggles one good eye glared and blazed, while a sightless one stayed mute and pitiful, as he would snort to people that Lincoln was "the great shifter, the great political shuffler," lacked energy and executive ability, was even "a beast," or "Chase is a thousand times more fit for a President than Lincoln or Seward."

Gurowski was a studied croaker. "The country is marching to its tomb, but the grave-diggers will not confess their crime . . . O God! O God! to witness how by the hands of Lincoln-Seward-McClellan, this noblest human structure is crumbled . . ." He had held a job under Greeley and been let out. His slanderous talk and published slurs on Seward had resulted in his dismissal as a translator from the State Department. As a European republican revolutionary and as a scholar and author of political volumes, Gurowski assumed that the American Republic needed his counsel and experience. At the White House Lincoln kept an eye on him. Lamon wrote he heard Lincoln more than once remark: "Gurowski is the only man who has given me a serious thought of a personal nature. From the known disposition of the man, he is dangerous wherever he may be. I have sometimes thought that he might try to take my life. It would be just like him to do such a thing."

At one of many White House functions the British Minister Lord Lyons had, as required by custom, read a long paper one morning, formally notifying the U.S. Government that a prince of the royal family in England had taken unto himself a wife. Lincoln listened gravely throughout, and the ceremony over, took the bachelor Minister by the hand, then quietly, "And now, Lord Lyons, go thou and do likewise."

The main executive office and workroom on the second floor, 25 by 40 feet, had a large white marble fireplace, with brass andirons and a high brass fender, a few chairs, two hair-covered sofas, and a large oak table for Cabinet meetings. Lighting was by gas jets in glass globes, or when needed, by kerosene lamps. Tall windows opened on a sweep of lawn to the south, on the unfinished Washington Monument, the Smithsonian Institution, the Potomac River, Alexandria, and slopes alive with white tents, beef cattle, wagons, men of the army. Between the windows was a large armchair in which the President usually sat at a table for his writing. A pull at a bell cord would bring Nicolay or Hay from the next room. A tall desk with many pigeonholes stood nearby at the south wall. Among books were the *United States Statutes*, the Bible and Shakespeare's plays. At times the table had been littered with treatises on the art and science of war. Two or three frames held maps on which blue and red pins told where the armies were moving, fighting, camping.

Once when visitors called to pay respects, a secretary placed papers on a table for signature. The President excused himself: "Just wait now until I sign some papers, that this government may go on." At the finish of an afternoon's work with the secretaries he would say: "Boys, I reckon that'll do. We'll shut up shop for the rest of the day."

The President more than once heard a crying child in the arms of a woman belowstairs and sent word asking what the woman wanted. Or again he might hear a bawling voice, "I want to see Old Abe," or a seeker of a contract orating: "The President must be made to understand, sir, that the eyes of the people are on him, sir! They are watching him, sir!"

A woman demanded a colonel's commission for her son,

not as a favor but as a right. "Sir, my grandfather fought at Lexington, my father fought at New Orleans, and my husband was killed at Monterey." She left the office and went down the stairs with a dismissal in her ears: "I guess, Madam, your family has done enough for the country. It is time to give someone else a chance."

The President was at his desk often before seven in the morning, after "sleep light and capricious," noted Hay. His White House bed, nine feet long, nearly nine feet high at the headboard, had bunches of grapes and flying birds carved in its black walnut. Nearby was a marble-topped table with four stork-shaped legs; under its center was a bird's nest of black walnut filled with little wooden bird eggs.

In the earlier days of the administration a digest of the day's news was ready for the President before breakfast at nine o'clock. Then he would usually go over to the War Office, read telegrams, discuss "the situation" with Halleck or Stanton; back at the White House, he would take up the morning mail with his secretaries. Tuesday and Friday were usually for Cabinet meetings. On other days a stack of cards from callers would be sifted for old acquaintances and persons on urgent business.

"On the other days [than Tuesday and Friday]," wrote Hay, "it was the President's custom at about that hour [noon], to order the doors to be opened and all who were waiting to be admitted. The crowd would rush in, thronging the narrow room, and one by one would make their wants known." Some came merely to shake hands, to wish Godspeed, others for help or mercy, wailing their woe. Still others lingered, stood at the walls, hanging back in hope of having a private interview.

"Late in the day," wrote Hay, "he usually drove out for an hour's airing; at six o'clock he dined. His breakfast was an egg and a cup of coffee; at luncheon he rarely took more than a biscuit and a glass of milk, a plate of fruit in its season; at dinner he ate sparingly of one or two courses. He drank little or no wine . . . and never used tobacco. He pretended to begin business at ten o'clock in the morning, but in reality the ante-rooms and halls were full long before that hour—people anxious to get the first axe ground. He was extremely unmethodical; it was a struggle on Nicolay's part and mine to get him to adopt some systematic rules. He would break through every regulation as fast as it was made. Anything that kept the people away from him he disapproved. He wrote very few letters and did not read one in fifty that he received . . . He signed, without reading them, the letters I wrote in his name. He wrote, perhaps half a dozen a week himself—not more . . . The house remained full of people nearly all day. Sometimes, though rarely, he would shut himself up and see no one. He scarcely ever looked into a newspaper unless I called his attention to an article on some special subject. He frequently said, 'I know more about it than any of them.' "

Early in the administration Seward wrote his wife, "The President proposes to do all his work." That did not last long. He learned to detail routine and to assign work to others. "At first," wrote Fred Seward, "when I would take up to the President a paper for his signature, he would spread it out and carefully read the whole of it. But this usage was speedily abandoned, and he would hastily say, 'Your father says this is all right, does he? Well, I guess he knows. Where do I put my name?' " The procedure got him into several tangled affairs. More and more, however, as the months passed the letters and documents were sifted for his attention and signature.

T. B. Bancroft stood for an hour within three feet of Lincoln's desk, waiting to ask for a pass through Army of Potomac lines to visit the son of a friend in the 3d Pennsylvania Cavalry. Bancroft had waited half an hour with about 50 others in the Blue Room belowstairs until the announcement from a colored attendant that the President was ready to receive them, when the crowd rushed pell-mell upstairs into the office. Wrote Bancroft: "Mr. Lincoln sat at the back end of the enclosure . . . a pair of short-shanked gold spectacles sat low down upon his nose, and he could easily look over them." A boy in army blue took the chair, handing his papers to the President, who read them and said, "And you want to be a captain?" "Yes, sir." "And what do you want to be captain of? Have you got a company?" "No, sir, but my officers told me that I could get a captain's commission if I were to present my case to you." "My boy—excuse my calling you a boy—how old are you?" "Sixteen." "Yes, you are a boy, and from what your officers say of you, a worthy boy and a good soldier, but commissions as captains are generally given by the governors of the States." "My officers said *you* could give me a commission." "And so I could, but to be a captain you should have a company or something to be captain of. You know a man is not a husband until he gets a wife—neither is a woman a wife until she gets a husband. I might give you a commission as captain and send you back to the Army of the Potomac, where you would have nothing to be captain of, and you would be like a loose horse down there with nothing to do and no one having any use for you."

The boy began breaking, tears in his eyes. The President put a hand on the boy's shoulder, patting while he spoke: "My son, go back to the army, continue to do your duty as you find it to do, and with the zeal you have hitherto shown, you will not have to ask for promotion, it will seek you. *I* may say that had we more like you in the army, my hopes of the successful outcome of this war would be far stronger than they are at present. Shake hands with me, and go back the little man and brave soldier that you came." The boy stepped away as if he had been home to see a wise and kindly father.

A Washington resident complained that a man with a hand organ disturbed him day and night by grinding out music in front of his house. Lincoln: "I'll tell you what to do. Speak to Stanton about it, and tell him to send Baker [secret-service head] after the man. Baker will steal the organ and throw its owner into the Old Capitol [Prison], and you'll never be troubled with his noise again."

A farmer from a border county in Virginia claimed that

Union soldiers had taken a horse and a lot of hay from his farm and he would now like the President to send him to the proper department to have his claims paid. The President referred him to a claim department, and was reminded of a steamboat running at full speed on a Western river one day when a boy tugged at the captain's coat sleeve and cried for the boat to stop: "I've lost my apple overboard."

A young chiropodist, Isachar Zacharie, an English Jew, was introduced, with the result later that Lincoln wrote a testimonial: "Dr. Zacharie has operated on my feet with great success, and considerable addition to my comfort." The satirists had their day, the New York *Herald* saying: "Dr. Zacharie has made his début on the national stage to cut the Presidential corns."

Came a full-bosomed woman of rare face and gleam. "I have three sons in the army, Mr. Lincoln." "You may well be proud of that, madam." "There were four, but my eldest boy—" and that was all she could say as she passed on with his low-spoken "God bless you, madam" in her ear.

A fleshy and dignified man, stern and homely of face, entered one day in swallow-tail coat, ruffled shirt, white cravat, orange gloves. His watch chain had a topaz seal, his cane a gold head. He looked "ominous," said Lamon, and gave the President the impression, "I'm in for it now." The conversation ran on in a chilly way. The visitor, keeping a frozen face, shocked the President with his closing remarks as he was about to leave: "Mr. President, I have no business with you, none whatever. I was at the Chicago convention as a friend of Mr. Seward. I have watched you narrowly ever since your inauguration, and I called merely to pay my respects. What I want to say is this: I think you are doing everything for the good of the country that is in the power of man to do. You are on the right track. As one of your constituents I now say to you, do in the future as you damn please, and I will support you!" Lincoln almost collapsed with glee. He took the visitor's hand: "I thought you came here to tell me how to take Richmond." They looked into each other's faces. "Sit down, my friend," said the President.

"Sit down, I am delighted to see you. Lunch with us today. I have not seen enough of you yet."

In an interlude of business he got acquainted with a new orderly, asking name, age, what place he called home, and "Is your mother living? Do you send her money regularly?" —then meditative talk that it means much for a mother to have a good son and the mother lives a hard life with a son not trustworthy and loving. That orderly only a few days before had been offered $100 for dispatches he carried from the President. He held off till $200 was paid him, then whipped out a revolver and took the briber prisoner, later finding out the briber was a secret-service operative and he as an orderly was being tested.

Congressman A. W. Clark of Watertown, New York, pleaded for a constituent who had one boy killed in battle, another dying in prison and a third son sick at Harpers Ferry—the mother at home having gone insane. The father sat by and wept while the Congressman begged for him to take the sick boy home, as it might help bring back the wandering reason of the mother. Lincoln listened, asked no questions, and wrote "Discharge this man."

Thus ran a few specimens of the stream of thousands who wore the thresholds of the White House, nicked its banisters, smoothed the doorknobs, and spoke their wants and errands. When told this procedure was wearing on him, Lincoln said these were his "public opinion baths."

In a day's clamor and confusion, Nicolay noted the President saying: "I'll do the very best I can, the very best I know how. And I mean to keep doing so till the end. If the end brings me out all right what is said against me won't amount to anything. If the end brings me out wrong, ten angels swearing I was right would make no difference."

An old Springfield friend after an evening in the White House drawled: "How does it feel to be President of the United States?" "You have heard about the man tarred and feathered and ridden out of town on a rail? A man in the crowd asked him how he liked it, and his reply was that if it wasn't for the honor of the thing, he would much rather walk."

"Who has been abusing me in the Senate today?" he asked Senator Morrill in his office one day. The Senator hoped none of them were abusing him knowingly and willfully. "Oh, well," said Lincoln, "I don't mean that. Personally you are all very kind—but I know we do not all agree as to what this administration should do and how it ought to be done . . . I do not know but that God has created some one man great enough to comprehend the whole of this stupendous crisis from beginning to end, and endowed him with sufficient wisdom to manage and direct it. I confess I do not fully understand and foresee it all. But I am placed where I am obliged to the best of my poor ability to deal with it. And that being the case, I can only go just as fast as I can see how to go."

Seward mentioned to his son that he had known people to arrive early and sleep for hours in the hall of the White House waiting to interview the President. Writhing under the grind once, the President told General Schenck, "If to be the head of Hell is as hard as what I have to undergo here, I could find it in my heart to pity Satan himself."

The military telegraph office at the War Department was for Lincoln both a refuge and a news source. The bonds were close between Lincoln and David Homer Bates, manager of the office, and the chief of staff, Thomas T. Eckert. The President was more at ease among the telegraph operators than amid the general run of politicians and office seekers. Bates noted that Lincoln carried in his pocket at one time a well-worn copy in small compass of *Macbeth* and *The Merry Wives of Windsor*, from which he read aloud. "On one occasion," said Bates, "I was his only auditor and he recited several passages to me with as much interest apparently as if there had been a full house." Occasionally he questioned the omission of certain passages of a Shakespeare play as acted.

At a large flat-topped desk Lincoln went through flimsies of telegrams received. When he got to the bottom of the new telegrams, and began again reading important ones he had sifted out for second and more careful reading, he often said, "Well, I guess I have got down to the raisins." Operator A. B. Chandler asked what this meant, which brought the story of a little girl who often overate of raisins, and one day followed the raisins with many other goodies. It made her sick; she began vomiting, and after a time the raisins began to come up. She gasped and looked at her mother. "Well, I will be better now, I guess, for I have got down to the raisins."

In this telegraph room Lincoln had first heard of the killing of Ellsworth, of the first and second Bull Run routs, of the Seven Days' battles and McClellan's cry for help at Harrison's Landing, of the *Monitor* crippling the *Merrimac*, of the Antietam shaded victory, of Burnside and Hooker failing at Fredericksburg and Chancellorsville, of blood "up to the bridles of horses," of Lee moving his army far up in Pennsylvania toward Gettysburg. Here Lincoln received a telegram about a skirmish in Virginia where "opposing troops fought the enemy to a standstill," which reminded him of two dogs barking through a fence, continuing their barking until they came to a gate, when both ran off in opposite directions. Here he quoted from Petroleum V. Nasby: "Oil's well that ends well"; and after one of McClellan's peninsular defeats, from Orpheus C. Kerr: "Victory has once again perched upon the banners of the conquerors."

An official letter on one desk had the signature of John Wintrup, operator at Wilmington, written with extraordinary and sweeping flourishes; Lincoln's eye caught it. "That reminds me of a short-legged man in a big overcoat, the tail of which was so long that it wiped out his footprints in the snow."

A dispatch from General Schenck reported a skirmish in Virginia and 30 prisoners taken, all armed with Colt's revolvers. Lincoln read it and with a twinkle of eye said to the operator that with customary newspaper exaggeration of army news they might be sure in the next day's prints that "all the little Colt's revolvers would have grown into horse-pistols."

A message from a part of McClellan's command once

reported that Union pickets still held Ball's Cross Roads and "no firing had been heard *since* sunset." The President asked if any firing had been heard *before* sunset, and the answer being that none was reported, he laughed about the man who spoke of a supposed freak of nature, "The child was *black* from his hips *down*," and on being asked the color from the hips *up*, replied, "Why, *black*, of course."

Mrs. Lincoln had, inevitably, become a topic. "I went to the reception at Mrs. Eames'," wrote Charles Francis Adams, Jr. "If the President caught it at dinner, his wife caught it at the reception. All manner of stories about her were flying around; she wanted to do the right thing, but not knowing how, was too weak and proud to ask; she was going to put the White House on an economical basis, and, to that end, was about to dismiss 'the help' as she called the servants; some of whom, it was asserted, had already left because 'they must live with gentlefolks'; she had got hold of newspaper reporters and railroad conductors, as the best persons to go to for advice and direction. Numberless stories of this sort were current."

Her hand was in squabbles over who should have post offices and West Point cadetships. While the President was steering a delicate course trying to hold his Cabinet together, she wrote October 4, 1862, to James Gordon Bennett, whose editorials were clamoring for a Cabinet shakeup: "From all parties the cry for a 'change of cabinet' comes. I hold a letter, just received from Governor Sprague [of Rhode Island], in my hand, who is quite as earnest as you have been on the subject."

She had been pleased rather than troubled that the New York *Herald* printed two and three columns a day about her arrival at the Long Branch beach resort, her baggage, accommodations, companions, visits, amusements, toilets, gowns, seclusions. "Mrs. Lincoln, looking like a queen in her long train and magnificent coronet of flowers, stood near the centre of the room, surrounded by a brilliant suite, bowing as the ladies were presented to her . . . Before her, forming a sort of semi-circle, were a number of gentlemen, dressed *en règle,* in all the glory of fine black suits and heavy white neckties."

Bonnet gossip by a correspondent who signed merely "Burleigh" ran in several newspapers. "A number of cities are contending for the honor of furnishing a hat for the head that reclines on Abraham's bosom . . . In New York from Canal to Fourteenth, from Philadelphia to Bangor, can be seen on exhibition a 'Bonnet for Mrs. President Lincoln.' These establishments send on and notify Mrs. Lincoln that they have a love of a bonnet, which they are desirous to present to her as a testimonial of their loyalty and great regard for her personally. The amiable and kindhearted lady of the White House (for such she is) condescends to accept the gift, and at once 'Mrs. Lincoln's Hat' is on exhibition and crowds flock to see it. And such a hat! a condensed milliner's stock in trade, arched high enough to admit a canal boat under it, scalloped, fluted and plaited."

"Her manner was too animated, her laugh too frequent," wrote a woman. Congressman Washburne, entirely friendly to Lincoln, wrote to his wife, "Mrs. Lincoln came last night; I shall not express my opinion of her until I see you." John Lothrop Motley wrote to Mrs. Motley that he found her "youngish, with very round white arms, well dressed, chatty enough, and if she would not, like all the South and West, say 'Sir' to you every instant, as if you were a royal personage, she would be quite agreeable." Welles wrote in his diary: "Mrs. Lincoln has the credit of excluding Judd of Chicago from the Cabinet."

On New Year's Day, 1863, Browning rode in her carriage. "Mrs. Lincoln told me she had been, the night before, with Old Isaac Newton, out to Georgetown, to see a Mrs. Laury, a spiritualist and she had made wonderful revelations to her about her little son Willy who died last winter, and also about things on the earth. Among other things she revealed that the cabinet were all enemies of the President, working for themselves, and that they would have to be dismissed."

Her conversation and letters had much to do with executive details, as in writing, "Nicolay told me, that Caleb Smith said to him, a few days since that he had just received a letter from Kellogg, of Cincinnati that he did not know why he had received his appointment as consul. Is not the idea preposterous?" To Murat Halstead, the Cincinnati editor who in private letters referred to her as silly and vain, she sent information: "I write you in great haste to say that after all the excitement General Banks is to be returned to his command at New Orleans, and the great Nation will be comforted with the idea that he *is* not to be in the Cabinet."

When she took her boys to Niagara Falls and returned, when she stopped at the Metropolitan Hotel in New York and shopped at the big stores, it was chronicled from day to day. *Leslie's Weekly* gave brief items: "Mrs. Lincoln held a brilliant levee at the White House on Saturday evening. She was superbly dressed." Once *Leslie's* had the one-sentence item: "The reports that Mrs. Lincoln was in an interesting condition are untrue."

The run of press items about Southern relatives was steady. One day: "New Orleans papers state that D. H. Todd, brother-in-law of Mr. Lincoln, has been appointed a lieutenant in the Confederate army." Another day: "The Rebel officer who called the roll of our prisoners at Houston is Lieutenant Todd, a brother of the wife of President Lincoln. He is tall, fat, and savage against the 'Yankees.'" Or again: "Eleven second cousins of Mrs. Lincoln are members of the Carolina Light Dragoons of the Confederate forces."

One summer day in '63 Mrs. Lincoln's carriage horses ran away. "She threw herself out of her carriage," reported a newspaper. "Fortunately no bones were broken, and after some restoratives she was taken to her residence." The husband and father telegraphed Robert at Harvard: "Don't be uneasy. Your mother very slightly hurt by fall."

Mrs. Lincoln visited hospitals, gave time and care to sick and wounded. She interceded with General McClellan, won pardon for a soldier ordered shot. McClellan in letters re-

ferred to her as "Mrs. President." From several dressmakers
who applied she had chosen the comely mulatto woman,
Mrs. Elizabeth Keckley, who once had been dressmaker to
the wife of Jefferson Davis. The first spring and summer
15 new dresses were made, and as time passed Mrs. Lincoln felt a rare loyalty and spirit of service in Elizabeth
Keckley, giving her trust and confidence not offered to
others.

Away on frequent shopping trips to New York or Philadelphia, she had telegrams from her husband: "Do not
come on the night train. It is too cold. Come in the morning." Or: "Your three despatches received. I am very well,
and am glad to hear that you and Tad are so." Or the domestic news that he was "tolerably well" and "have not rode
out much yet, but have at last got new tires on the carriage
wheels, and perhaps shall ride out soon now." Gossip once
had it that when they first entered a White House carriage
he had grinned. "Well, mother, this is just about the slick-
est glass hack in town, isn't it?"

In diary and letters John Hay used the nicknames "Tycoon" and "The Ancient" for Lincoln. Mrs. Lincoln was
"Madame," and occasionally the "Hellcat" who could become more "Hell-cattical day by day." The secretaries
could not always agree with her opinion that wages specified for an unfilled position in the White House might be
handed to her directly. She questioned whether the Government or the secretaries should pay for the grain of the secretaries' horses in the White House stables. The two secretaries eventually were to find it more comfortable to move
from the White House and lodge at Willard's.

The boy Tad meant more to Lincoln than anyone else.
They were chums. "Often I sat by Tad's father reporting to
him about some important matter that I had been ordered
to inquire into," wrote Charles A. Dana, "and he would
have this boy on his knee; and, while he would perfectly
understand the report, the striking thing about him was his
affection for the child." Tad usually slept with him, wrote

John Hay. Often late at night the boy came to the President's office: "He would lie around until he fell asleep, and Lincoln would shoulder him and take him off to bed."

"Tad" was short for Tadpole, a wriggler, nervous, active. With a defective palate, his occasional "papa dear" sounded more like "pappy day." He could burst into the President's office and call out what he wanted. Or again Tad would give three sharp raps and two slow thumps on the door, three dots and two dashes he had learned in the war telegraph office. "I've got to let him in," Lincoln would say, "because I promised never to go back on the code."

A party of Boston ladies one day admired the velvet carpet, plush upholstery, mahogany furniture and pompous chandeliers of the East Room. The air was quiet, dignified. Then a slam-bang racket, a shrill voice, "Look out there!" —and young Tad came through flourishing a long whip, driving two goats hitched tandem to a kitchen chair. These goats figured in telegrams to Mrs. Lincoln, away with Tad on a visit: "Tell Tad the goats and father are very well, especially the goats." To "My dear Wife" in August '63 Lincoln wrote of weather and politics and to "tell dear Tad" of his "Nanny Goat" lost. "The gardener kept complaining that she destroyed the flowers, till it was concluded to bring her down to the White House. This was done, and the second day she had disappeared, and has not been heard of since. This is the last we know of poor 'Nanny.'"

The boy did things with a rush. "I was once sitting with the President in the library," wrote Brooks, "when Tad tore into the room in search of something, and having found it, he threw himself on his father like a small thunderbolt, gave him one wild, fierce hug, and without a word, fled from the room before his father could put out a hand to detain him." Tutors came and went, Brooks noted. "None stayed long enough to learn much about the boy; but he knew them before they had been one day in the house." Of this the father would say: "Let him run. There's time enough yet for him to learn his letters and get poky."

A Kentucky delegation was held off, couldn't get in. For

political reasons Lincoln did not want to meet them. They
were half-cursing among themselves when Tad laughed to
them, "Do you want to see Old Abe?" They laughed "Yes,"
and the boy scooted in to his father. "Papa, may I introduce some friends to you?" "Yes, son." And Tad brought
in the men whom the President had carefully avoided for
a week, introduced them with formality—and the President
reached for the boy, took him on his lap, kissed him and
told him it was all right and that he had gone through the
introductions like a little gentleman.

Tad enjoyed strutting along with Captain Bennett inspecting the cavalry on White House guard duty. The Captain one morning saw the men getting lax and bawled them
out. "The condition of the quarters is disgraceful," his
voice rasped. "Instead of being kept as they should be kept,
they look like—" and while he hesitated Tad shrilled "hell!"
For the rest of that day discipline was not so good. Nor again
one cold night when the corporal of the guard every half-
hour blew a police whistle signaling sentinels to walk their
horses fast and change places. This lessened monotony and
helped warm men and horses. Tad that night went to the
corporal of the guard, asked to see the whistle, took it and
ran for the White House. From a second-story window he
leaned out and blew it. The men and horses shifted places.
Again the whistle and again the shod horses sounding on
the cobblestones. For a half-hour Tad kept this up till he
had had his fun and then came out and handed back the
whistle to the corporal of the guard, along with a bowl of
Roman punch from the reception room, where the diplomatic corps was having a party. Thus Robert W. McBride
of the guard detail, and others, told of it.

Julia Taft was small and slight for her 16 years, wore
long curls, flew from one room to another in a ruffled white
frock and blue sash. Lincoln called her "Jew-ly," told her
she was a "flibbertigibbet." Once he held a handful of
small photographs over her head. "Do you want my picture,
Jewly?" She danced on her tiptoes, saying, "Please," and
heard, "Give me a kiss and you can have it." The shy girl

reached up, he leaned over, and she gave him a peck on the cheek. Into his arms he swept her with, "Now we will pick out a good one."

Another girl playing with Lincoln's big heavy watch asked him if it could be broken. "Of course it can't. Why, little girl, you hit it as hard as you can with a bunch of wool and even that won't break it." He asked a little boy some questions the lad enjoyed answering, patted the fellow on the shoulder, and sent him away with the pleasant but puzzling remark in his ears, "Well, you'll be a man before your mother yet."

Charles A. Dana spoke to Lincoln of his little girl, who wanted to shake hands. Lincoln walked over, took up the girl, kissed her and talked to her. Dana considered it worth mentioning. Important men of high office usually lacked a natural and easy grace in handling a child. With Lincoln, Dana noticed, the child felt easy, as if in the arms of Santa Claus or at home as with some friendly, shaggy big animal dependable in danger.

No child shrank from his presence, it was noted, and the little ones enjoyed him as they might a trusted horse. His face lighted when a little girl walked away after he had bent and kissed her, calling out, "Why, he is only a man after all!" And he knew what was in the heart of another he took on his lap in his office; as he chatted with her she called to her father, "Oh, Pa! he isn't ugly at all; he's just beautiful!"

Robert T. Lincoln, his press nickname "the Prince of Rails," away at Harvard, never saw his father, even during vacations, for more than ten minutes of talk at a time, so he said. Stepping up to his father at one reception and bowing with severe formality, "Good evening, Mr. Lincoln," his father handed Robert a gentle open-handed slap across the face. The two of them in a carriage one day were halted at a street corner by marching troops. "Father was always eager to know which state they came from. And in his eagerness to know from where they hailed, father opened the door and stepping half way out, shouted to a group of workmen standing close by, 'What is that, boys?' meaning where did they come from. One short, little red-haired man fixed him with a withering glance and retorted, 'It's a regiment, you damned old fool.' In a fit of laughter father closed the door, and when his mirth had somewhat subsided, turned to me and said, 'Bob, it does a man good sometimes to hear the truth.' A bit later, somewhat sadly he added, 'And sometimes I think that's just what I am, a damned old fool.' "

Mrs. Lincoln's afternoon receptions and the President's public levees were held regularly during the winters. Usually twice a week, on Tuesday evenings at so-called dress receptions and on Saturday evenings at a less formal function, the President met all who came. "A majority of the visitors went in full dress," wrote Noah Brooks, "the ladies in laces, feathers, silks, and satins, without bonnets; and the gentlemen in evening dress . . . Here and there a day-laborer, looking as though he had just left his work-bench, or a hard-working clerk with ink-stained linen, added to the popular character of the assembly . . . So vast were the crowds, and so affectionate their greetings, that Mr. Lincoln's right hand was often so swollen that he would be unable to use it readily for hours afterward. The white kid glove of his right hand, when the operation of handshaking was over, always looked as if it had been dragged through a dust-bin." Much of the time the President went through the handshaking sort of absent-minded. "His thoughts were apt to be far from the crowds of strangers that passed before him."

The query came, Why not take a vacation and rest? "I sincerely wish war was a pleasanter and easier business than it is, but it does not admit of holidays." At his desk one day his casual word on the hour was, "I wish George Washington or some of the old patriots were here in my place so that I could have a little rest."

Noah Brooks, somewhat scholar and dreamer, a failure as merchant in Illinois and farmer in Kansas, correspondent of the Sacramento *Union*, writing under the pen name of

"Castine" news letters widely reprinted on the West Coast, often had close touch with Lincoln, and wrote of one phase: "I have known impressionable women, touched by his sad face and his gentle bearing, to go away in tears. Once I found him sitting in his chair so collapsed and weary that he did not look up or speak when I addressed him. He put out his hand, mechanically, as if to shake hands, when I told him I had come at his bidding. It was several minutes before he was roused enough to say that he 'had had a hard day.'"

In one news letter the third year of the war Noah Brooks wrote, "The President is affable and kind, but his immediate subordinates are snobby and unpopular." What Nicolay and Hay had done to Brooks, and why he disliked them, Brooks didn't say beyond writing, "These secretaries are young men, and the least said of them the better, perhaps."

The friendship of the President and Noah Brooks steadily deepened. Brooks wrote in one news letter: "It does appear to me that it is impossible to designate any man in public life whose character and antecedents would warrant us in the belief that we have anyone now living whose talents and abilities would fit him to administer this Government better than it has been conducted through the past stormy years by the honesty, patriotism, and far-sighted sagacity of Abraham Lincoln . . ." Brooks was tired of the mud-slinging. Scandalous stories, slanders innumerable, he had heard of Mrs. Lincoln and the President's family, from "loyal people, more shame to them, not knowing the truth of what they repeat . . . Shame upon these he-gossips and envious retailers of small slanders. Mrs. Lincoln, I am glad to be able to say from personal knowledge, is a true American woman."

Out at Soldiers' Home were trees and cool shade, long sweeps of grassy land. In its 500 acres were drives that overlooked the city, the Potomac and wide landscapes. In the birds and the flowers Lincoln had only a passing interest. But there were trees—oak, chestnut, beech—maple and cypress and cedar—and they gave rest and companionship. He was still a kinsman of these growths that struggled out of the ground and sprawled and spread against the sky and kept their rootholds till storm, disaster, or time and age brought them down.

On the way to Soldiers' Home the Lincoln carriage passed through a city where one traveler had commented that everything worth looking at seemed unfinished. In March '63 the public grounds around the unfinished Washington Monument held droves of cattle, 10,000 beeves on the hoof. Shed hospitals covered acres in the outlying suburbs; one of the better they named the Lincoln Hospital.

Into churches, museums, art galleries, public offices and private mansions had arrived from battlefields the wounded and dying. The passing months saw more and more of wooden-legged men, men with empty sleeves, on crutches, wearing slings and bandages.

From a population of 60,000 the city had gone above 200,000. Among the newcomers were contractors, freed Negroes, blockade-runners, traders, sutlers, office seekers, elocutionists, gamblers, keepers of concert saloons with waiter girls, liquor dealers, candy-criers, umbrella-menders, embalmers, undertakers, manufacturers of artificial limbs, patent-medicine peddlers, receivers of stolen goods, pickpockets, burglars, sneak thieves.

Of the new arrivals of footloose women it was noted they ranged "from dashing courtesans who entertained in brownstone fronts to drunken creatures summarily ejected from army camps." One observer wrote: "Houses of ill fame are scattered all through the city. With rare exceptions, however, they have not yet ventured to intrude into respectable neighborhoods. A few of these houses are superbly furnished, and are conducted in the most magnificent style. The women are either young, or in the prime of life, and are frequently beautiful and accomplished. They come from all parts of the country, and they rarely return more than two seasons in succession, for their life soon breaks down their beauty. The majority of the 'patrons' of the better class houses are men of nominal respectability, men high in public life, officers of the army and navy, Governors of States, lawyers, doctors, and the very best class of the city population. Some come under the influence of liquor, others in cool blood."

Beer, whisky, performances of nude or scantily dressed women, brought many a soldier boy into saloon concert halls to awake later on the streets with empty pockets. Into his drinks someone had slipped "knockout drops." At intervals the lower grade of houses were raided by police or provost marshals.

The Washington correspondent of the New York *Independent* wrote in '63: "In broad daylight a few days ago, in front of the Presidential mansion . . . a woman clad in . . . fashionable garments with diamonds flashing from her slender fingers, sat upon the stone balustrade, unable to proceed . . . At last she rose . . . swaying to and fro . . . The carriage of a foreign minister . . . stopped, took in the lady, and carried her to her luxurious home. For the lady is wealthy, occupies a high social position, but she was drunk in the streets of Washington."

The high-class gambling houses, located mostly on Pennsylvania Avenue, were carpeted, gilded, frescoed, garnished with paintings and statuary for the players of faro and poker. At the four leading establishments, where introductions were necessary, could be found governors, members of Congress, department officials, clerks, contractors, paymasters. In one place there was the tradition of a Congressman who broke the bank in a single night's play, winning over $100,000. The gambling places shaded off into all styles, ending at the bottom, where smooth-spoken women plied the young infantrymen with drink and played them out of their last payday greenbacks. Colonel La Fayette C. Baker reported to Stanton in the summer of '63 that 163 gaming houses in full blast required attention.

Of the gaudy and bawdy features of Washington, John Hay wrote, "This miserable sprawling village imagines itself a city because it is wicked, as a boy thinks he is a man when he smokes and swears." One diary entry of Hay in the summer of '63 gave a picture: "I rode out to Soldiers' Home with the Tycoon tonight . . . Had a talk on philology for which the T. has a little indulged inclination. Rode home in the dark amid a party of drunken gamblers & harlots returning in the twilight from [erased]."

Walt Whitman, author of *Leaves of Grass*, prophet of the Average Man, crier of America as the greatest country in the world—in the making—wrote to the New York *Times* in the summer of '63: "I see the President almost every day, as I happen to live where he passes to or from his lodgings out of town . . . He always has a company of twenty-five or thirty cavalry, with sabres drawn, and held upright over their shoulders . . . Mr. Lincoln generally rides a good-sized easy-going gray horse, is dress'd in plain black, somewhat rusty and dusty; wears a black stiff hat, and looks about as ordinary in attire, &c., as the commonest man . . . I saw very plainly the President's dark brown face, with the deep cut lines, the eyes, &c., always to me with a deep latent sadness in the expression. Sometimes the President comes and goes in an open barouche. The cavalry always accompany him, with drawn sabres . . . None of the artists have caught the deep, though subtle and indirect expression of this man's face. They have only caught the surface. There is something else there. One of the great portrait painters of two or three centuries ago is needed."

This poet at Fredericksburg saw the mutilated and languishing on blankets laid on the bare frozen ground, lucky if layers of pine or dry leaves were between the blanket and the hard clay. "No cots; seldom a mattress," he wrote. "I go around from one case to another. I do not see that I do much good to these wounded and dying; but I can not leave them. Once in a while some youngster holds on to me convulsively, and I do what I can for him . . . sit near him for hours if he wishes it."

Hearing the screams of men lifted into ambulances, among the cases of diarrhea, pneumonia, fever, typhoid, amid the mangled, among "the agonized and damned," he said they had met terrible human tests, and noted: "Here I see, not at intervals, but quite always, how certain man, our American man—how he holds himself cool and unquestioned master above all pains and bloody mutilations."

In soft weather one moonlit February night Whitman sauntered over Washington: "Tonight took a long look at the President's house. The white portico—the palace-like, tall, round, columns, spotless as snow—the tender and soft moonlight, flooding the pale marble—everywhere a hazy, thin, blue moonlace, hanging in the air—the White House of future poems, and of dreams and dramas . . . sentries at the gates, by the portico, silent, pacing there in blue overcoats." Another evening he went to the foot of Sixth Street and saw two boatloads of wounded from Chancellorsville put off during a heavy downpour, to lie in torchlight with the rain on their faces and blankets till ambulances should arrive in an hour or two at the wharves. "The men make little or no ado, whatever their sufferings."

A letter for two boys in New York went from him in March '63. "I think well of the President. He has a face like a Hoosier Michael Angelo, so awful ugly it becomes beautiful, with its strange mouth, its deep cut, criss-cross lines, and its doughnut complexion . . . I do not dwell on the supposed failures of his government; he has shown I sometimes think an almost supernatural tact in keeping the ship afloat at all."

A New York lawyer, George Templeton Strong, wrote in his diary of hearing Lincoln say "thar" for "there," "git" for "get," "ye" for "you," "heered" for "heard," "one of 'em," for "one of them," "wa-al" for "well," once hearing the sentence, "I haint been caught lyin' yet, and I don't mean to be." Strong wrote of hearing the President read to a group of men a victory telegram from Pea Ridge, Missouri, and with an undignified elation, the preface: "Here's the dispatch. Now, as the showman says, 'Ladies and gentlemen, this remarkable specimen is the celebrated he-goat of the mountings, and he makes the following noise, to wit.'" Strong wrote, too: "He is a barbarian, Scythian, yahoo, a gorilla, in respect of outward polish, but a most sensible, straightforward old codger. The best president we have had since old Jackson's time." Strong asked mercy for a seaman he believed wrongfully convicted of manslaughter and heard the President: "It must be referred to the Attorney General, but I guess it will be all right, for me and the Attorney General's very chicken hearted!"

One Englishman wrote of his meeting in Lincoln "two bright dreamy eyes that seem to gaze through you without looking at you." Hay said of Lincoln's gaze at one suspicious character, "He looked through him to the buttons on the back of his coat."

An English author, Edward Dicey, recorded an anecdote. "At the first council of war, after the President assumed the supreme command-in-chief of the army, in place of McClellan, the General did not attend, and excused himself next day by saying he had forgotten the appointment. 'Ah, now,' remarked Mr. Lincoln, 'I recollect once being engaged in a case for rape, and the counsel for the defence asked the woman why, if, as she said, the rape was committed on a Sunday, she did not tell her husband till the following Wednesday? and when the woman answered, she did not happen to recollect it—the case was dismissed at once.'" Stories like these, added Dicey, "read dull enough in print, unless you could give also the dry chuckle with which they are accompanied, and the gleam in the speaker's eye, as, with the action habitual to him, he rubs his hand down the side of his long leg."

Nicolay held there were many pictures of Lincoln; no portrait: "Graphic art was powerless before a face that moved through a thousand delicate gradations of line and contour, light and shade, sparkle of the eye and curve of the lip, in the long gamut of expression from grave to gay, and back again from the rollicking jollity of laughter to that far-away look."

Gustave Koerner wrote, "Something about the man, the face, is unfathomable." Congressman Henry Laurens Dawes of Massachusetts said early in the administration: "There is something in his face which I cannot understand. He is great. We can safely trust the Union to him." And later he would remember Lincoln's face as "a title-page of anxiety and distress." His counselors found him "calmer and clearer-sighted" than they. "The political sagacity of no other man was ever equal to that which enabled him to gather around him in earnest support of his administration, rivalries, opposing purposes, conflicting theories, and implacable enmities, which would have rent asunder any other administration. He grew wiser and broader and stronger as difficulties thickened and perils multiplied, till the end found him the wonder in our history. I could never quite fathom his thoughts. But as I saw how he overcame obstacles and escaped entanglements, it grew upon me that he was wiser than the men around him, that the nation had no other man for the place to which he was assigned by the Great Disposer."

A beaming and officious visitor slid into the office one day as Lincoln sat writing and chirruped, "Oh, why should the spirit of mortal be proud?" The President turned a noncommittal face. "My dear sir, I see no reason whatever," and went on writing.

The wearing of gloves for ceremony he regarded as "cruelty to animals," said Lamon, who witnessed Lincoln at a levee trying to give an extra hearty handshake to an old Illinois friend—when his white kids burst with a rip and a snort. The procession of guests heard: "Well, my old friend, this is a general bustification. You and I were never intended to wear these things. They are a failure to shake hands with between old friends like us." And he went on handshaking without gloves. With Mrs. Lincoln he drove to a hotel to get a man and wife, old friends from the West, to take them for a drive. As the man got into the carriage seat alongside Lincoln he was fixed out with brand-new gloves, his wife's doing. So Lincoln began pulling on his gloves—just as the other fellow shed his with the cry, "No! no! no! put up your gloves, Mr. Lincoln," and they rode along and had a good old-time visit. "He disliked gloves," said Brooks, "and once I saw him extract seven or eight pairs of gloves from an overcoat pocket where they had accumulated after having been furnished to him by Mrs. Lincoln."

Meeting a soldier six feet seven, Lincoln surveyed him

and asked, "Say, friend, does your head know when your feet get cold?" A strapping cornhusker easily three inches taller than the President had the greeting, "Really, I must look up to you; if you ever get into a deep place you ought to be able to wade out."

The honeymooning midgets, General Tom Thumb and wife, under P. T. Barnum's management, entered the Executive Mansion one evening and stood in a reception room filled with Cabinet members, Senators, generals, Congressmen, others including families unto the smallest children. The couple advanced in what Grace Greenwood saw as "pigeon-like stateliness," almost to the feet of the President: "With profound respect they looked up, up, to his kindly face. It was pleasant to see their tall host bend, and bend, to take their little hands in his great palm, holding Madame's with special chariness, as though it were a robin's egg, and he were afraid of breaking it. He made them feel from the first as though he regarded them as real folks, presented them very courteously and soberly to Mrs. Lincoln."

In the Patent Office Hospital the President, Mrs. Lincoln, Mrs. Abner Doubleday and Noah Brooks visited the patients. Lincoln and Brooks lingered at the cot of a wounded soldier who held with a weak white hand a tract just given him by a well-dressed lady performing good works. The soldier read the title of the tract and began laughing. Lincoln noticed that the lady of good works was still nearby, told the soldier undoubtedly the lady meant well. "It is hardly fair for you to laugh at her gift." The soldier: "Mr. President, how can I help laughing a little? She has given me a tract on the 'Sin of Dancing' and both of my legs are shot off."

In Halleck's office one evening in the summer of '63 Lincoln discussed plans for a joint naval and land attack on Charleston, illustrating gradual approaches of artillery and infantry with three or four lead pencils and pen handles which he arranged in parallels and shifted according to his notions of the strategy. Gustavus Vasa Fox came in, agreed with Lincoln, but Halleck could not see it, and as Lincoln walked home that evening he spoke to Brooks of his discouragement with what he termed "General Halleck's habitual attitude of demur."

Inquiries as to the physical law or mechanical principle that underlay a phenomenon or operation came frequently from Lincoln. "Unless very much preoccupied," wrote Brooks, "he never heard any reference to anything that he did not understand without asking for further information." He would ask, "What do you suppose makes that tree grow that way?" and was not satisfied until he had found out. Or he would take one of his boy's toys to pieces, find out how it was made, and put it together again. Tad had occasion more than once, said Brooks, to bewail his father's curiosity.

The politician, the Executive, the quixotic human being, were inextricable. On board the steamer *Daylight,* which had performed bravely down the Potomac, Lincoln stood where a half-dozen members of the crew brought a tarpaulin to protect him from rain while he insisted on shaking hands with the crew. A fireman in shirt sleeves was the last up, his face and hands sooty and smoked, saying, "My hand isn't fit to give you, sir, but there's not a man aboard loves you more than I do." "Put that hand in mine," cried the President. "It has been blackened by making fires for the Union." Or again on the B. & O. Railroad when a conductor asked him, "Why do you always bother shaking hands with the engineer and fireman, whose hands are always covered with soot and grease?" the answer came, "That will all wash off, but I always want to see and know the men I am riding behind."

When he could not grant a favor, he would generally make an appearance of so doing. A committee requested him to take action in certain claim cases—and he did not want to act. However, it looked like action, and partially satisfied the committee, when he wrote a formal order on Secretary Welles to send him the evidence in the cases. He told Welles later there was no other way to get rid of the callers. An old acquaintance in Illinois, having organized a bank under the new National Bank Act, wrote offering some of the stock to Lincoln, who replied with thanks, saying he recognized that stock in a good national bank would be a good thing to hold, but he did not feel that he, as President, ought to profit from a law which had been passed under his administration. "He seemed to wish to avoid even the appearance of evil," said the banker.

John Eaton was 35, had been superintendent of schools in Toledo, Ohio, had become a Presbyterian minister and as chaplain of the 27th Ohio Volunteers had seen active service in Missouri, twice being taken prisoner and more than once preaching to Confederate soldiers on request of their commanders. "The freedom with which he discussed public affairs with me often filled me with amazement," wrote Eaton. The President spoke one day "quite fully" of the opposition, expressing surprise that there should be so much antagonism to his policy in the ranks of the great abolitionists. The criticism of such men as Greeley and Wendell Phillips was "a great grief and trial" to Lincoln, Eaton believed. "Of a well-known abolitionist and orator," wrote Eaton, "the President once exclaimed in one of his rare moments of impatience, 'He's a thistle! I don't see why God lets him live!' "

Dispatches lay before the President one morning from a Northern governor who in one telegram after another was sending threats and warnings. Lincoln made a few guesses that worked out as he foretold: "Those despatches don't mean anything. The Governor is like a boy I saw once at a launching. When everything was ready they picked out a boy and sent him under the ship to knock away the trigger and let her go. At the critical moment everything depended on the boy. He had to do the job well by a direct, vigourous blow, and then lie flat and keep still while the ship slid over him. The boy did everything right, but he yelled as if he were being murdered from the time he got under the keel until he got out. I thought the hide was all scraped off his back; but he wasn't hurt at all. The master of the yard told me that this boy was always chosen for that job, that he did his work well, that he never had been hurt, but that he always squealed in that way. That's just the way with Governor Blank. Make up your minds that he is not hurt, and that he is doing his work right, and pay no attention to his squealing. He only wants to make you understand how hard his task is, and that he is on hand performing it."

A report having much useless language lay on his desk, the work of a Congressional committee regarding a newly devised gun. "I should want a new lease of life to read this through," groaned the President. "Why can't an investigating committee show a grain of common sense? If I send a man to buy a horse for me, I expect him to tell me that horse's points—not how many hairs he has in his tail."

A big cavalry raid had filled the newspapers and raised noisy enthusiasm, but failed to cut the enemy's communications. Lincoln remarked to Whitney, "That was good circus riding; it will do to fill a column in the newspapers, but I don't see that it has brought anything else to pass."

A young brigadier with a small cavalry troop strayed into Confederate lines in Virginia and was captured. Receiving the report, Lincoln said he was sorry to lose the horses. "I can make a better brigadier any day, but those horses cost the government $125 a head."

To Thomas L. James of Utica, New York, the President said, "I do not lead; I only follow." When the Prince de Joinville asked what was his policy, he replied: "I have none. I pass my life preventing the storm from blowing down the tent, and I drive in the pegs as fast as they are pulled up."

In company with Judge Jesse L. Williams of Indiana, the Reverend Mr. Livingston discussed Lincoln's letter to General Curtis about the Reverend Dr. McPheeters in St. Louis, charged with disloyalty. Said the Judge, "On the trial of Dr. McPheeters by the general assembly of the Presbyterian Church, your letter to General Curtis was read. But the curious part of the affair was this: One party read a portion of your letter and claimed the President was on their side, and the other party read another portion of the same letter and claimed the President was on their side. So it seems, Mr. President, that it is not so easy to tell where you stand."

Lincoln joined in the laughter and was reminded of an Illinois farmer and his son out in the woods hunting a sow. After a long search they came to a creek branch, where they found hog tracks, and signs of a snout rooting, for some distance on both sides of the branch. The old man said to his boy, "Now, John, you take up on this side of the branch and I'll go up t'other, for I believe the old critter is on both sides."

A sense of speech values in Lincoln registered in such degree that he could say of another, "He can compress the most words into the smallest ideas of any man I ever met." Nicolay heard him tell of a Southwestern orator who "mounted the rostrum, threw back his head, shined his eyes, and left the consequences to God."

Robert B. Nay, released from prison on Lincoln's order, came with a letter of introduction co-signed by Senator Reverdy Johnson, on which Lincoln wrote, "I will not say thee 'Nay.'" On an envelope from Salmon P. Chase he wrote, "Nix." On a note from Seward, "What do you say to sending Bradford R. Wood to the Sandwich Islands?" the President wrote, "It won't do. Must have a tip-top man there next time." On a large envelope holding the documents related to a dispute between an admiral and a general as to their crossed-up authorities, the President wrote neatly, "Submitted to Mars & Neptune." After Shiloh a colonel wrote belittling Grant and Sherman, and Lincoln wrote, "Today I verbally told Col. Worthington that I did not think him fit for a colonel; & now upon his *urgent* request I put it in writing."

When Mrs. Gideon Welles mentioned certain malignant reports in newspapers and someone present said, "The papers are not always reliable," Lincoln interjected, "That is to say, Mrs. Welles, they lie and then they *re-lie*." A

woman who had asked the President to use his authority
in her behalf at the War Department quoted him: "It's of
no use, madam, for me to go. They do things in their own
way over there, and I don't amount to pig tracks in the War
Department."

He was afraid of long speeches and had a fear of sentiment when fact and reasoning had not laid the way for it.
His effort at a flag-raising speech before the south front of
the Treasury building was one sentence only: "The part
assigned to me is to raise the flag, which, if there be no
fault in the machinery, I will do, and when up, it will be
for the people to keep it up." Suppose the war ran on three
years, four, and seemed at no end, what then? An anxious
White House visitor asked that. "Oh, there is no alternative but to keep pegging away."

He could refer to men loyal with "buts" and "ifs" and
"ands." The Mississippi Valley was "this Egypt of the
West." What was past was past; "broken eggs cannot be
mended." To Illinois sponsors of a proposed major general
he wrote that "major-generalships are not as plenty as
blackberries." The Republican party should not become "a
mere sucked egg, all shell and no meat, the principle all
sucked out."

A foreign diplomat demurred at Lincoln's condemning
a certain Greek history as tedious. "The author of that history, Mr. President, is one of the profoundest scholars of
the age. Indeed, it may be doubted whether any man of
our generation has plunged more deeply in the sacred
fount of learning." "Yes," said Lincoln, "or come up
dryer."

In an office cabinet divided into pigeonholes were com-
partments for correspondence and memoranda. Greeley
had a pigeonhole. So did each of several letter-writing generals. And one labeled "W. & W." Brooks was curious
about, Lincoln laughing: "That's Weed and Wood—Thurlow and Fernandy—that's a pair of 'em."

Because of the unwanted publicity and the interruptions
of politicians and office seekers, Lincoln arranged with

managers of two theaters that he could go in privately by
the stage door and slip into a stage box without being seen
from the audience. "Concealed by the friendly screen of
the drapery, he saw many plays without public observation," said Brooks. He saw the notable Edwin Forrest in
King Lear, and when John McCullough played Edgar, Lincoln asked Brooks, "Do you suppose he would come to the
box if we sent for him?" Brooks said the actor would undoubtedly be gratified. And McCullough came, in stage rags
and straw, and received discriminating praise and thanks
for an evening of pleasure given the President.

Into the White House one day a Congressman brought
Jean Louis Rodolphe Agassiz, the world's foremost ichthy-
ologist, authority on fishes, fossils, animal life, glaciers,
professor of geology and zoology at Harvard—sometimes
referred to as the greatest man of learning in the United
States. "Agassiz!" blurted Lincoln to Brooks. "I never met
him yet." Brooks started to leave. "Don't go, don't go. Sit
down and let us see what we can pick up that's new from
this great man."

As Agassiz and Lincoln talked, the conversation did not
seem very learned to Brooks: "Each man was simplicity
itself. Lincoln asked for the correct pronunciation and
derivation of Agassiz's name, and both men prattled on
about curious proper names in various languages." Agassiz asked Lincoln if he had ever lectured any, Lincoln having offered some of his speculations on man's discoveries
and inventions: "I think I can show, at least in a fanciful
way, that all the modern inventions were known centuries
ago." Agassiz urged him to finish the lecture. Perhaps
sometime he would, Lincoln guessed. The two men shook
hands warmly, Agassiz left, and Lincoln smiled quizzically at Brooks: "Well, I wasn't so badly scared after all,
were you?" Brooks said it seemed as though Lincoln had
expected to be weighed down by the great man's learning.
Lincoln admitted to Brooks that he had cross-examined
Agassiz on "things not in the books."

Did the President vacillate? Was he managed by others?

Men and journals shifted in view. The New York *Herald* in May '63 approved Lincoln's reversal of a court-martial order for the hanging as traitors of citizens of loyal states captured wearing uniforms of Confederate officers. Lincoln had declared them to be merely prisoners of war.

In the President's discussions of peace, said the London *Spectator,* "He expresses ideas, which, however quaint, have nevertheless a kind of dreamy vastness not without its attraction. The thoughts of the man are too big for his mouth." He was saying that a nation can be divided but "the earth abideth forever," that a generation could be crushed but geography dictated the Union could not be sundered. As to the rivers and mountains, "all are better than one or either, and all of right belong to this people and their successors forever." No possible severing of the land but would multiply and not mitigate the evils among the American states. "It is an oddly worded argument," said the *Spectator,* "the earth being treated as if it were a living creature, an Estate of the Republic with an equal vote on its destiny."

At home and abroad judgments came oftener that America had at last a President who was All-American. He embodied his country in that he had no precedents to guide his footsteps; he was not one more individual of a continuing tradition, with the dominant lines of the mold already cast for him by Chief Magistrates who had gone before.

The inventive Yankee, the Western frontiersman and pioneer, the Kentuckian of laughter and dreams, had found blend in one man who was the national head. In the "dreamy vastness" noted by the *Spectator,* in the pith of the folk words "the thoughts of the man are too big for his mouth," was the feel of something vague that ran deep in many American hearts, that hovered close to a vision for which men would fight, struggle and die, a grand though blurred chance that Lincoln might be leading them toward something greater than they could have believed might come true.

Also around Lincoln gathered some of the hope that a

democracy can choose a man, set him up high with power and honor, and the very act does something to the man himself, raises up new gifts, modulations, controls, outlooks, wisdoms, inside the man, so that he is something else again than he was before they sifted him out and anointed him to take an oath and solemnly sign himself for the hard and terrible, eye-filling and center-staged role of the Head of the Nation.

To be alive for the work, he must carry in his breast Cape Cod, the Shenandoah, the Mississippi, the Gulf, the Rocky Mountains, the Sacramento, the Great Plains, the Great Lakes, their dialects and shibboleths. He must be instinct with the regions of corn, textile mills, cotton, tobacco, gold, coal, zinc, iron. He would be written as a Father of his People if his record ran well, one whose heart beat with understanding of the many who came to the Executive Mansion.

In no one of the 31 rooms of the White House was Lincoln at home. Back and forth in this house strode phantoms—red platoons of boys vanished into the war—thin white-spoken ghosts of women who would never again hold those boys in their arms—they made a soft moaning the imagination could hear in the dark night and the gray dawn.

To think incessantly of blood and steel, steel and blood, the argument without end by the mouths of brass cannon, of a mystic cause carried aloft and sung on dripping and crimson bayonet points—to think so and thus across nights and months folding up into years, was a wearing and a grinding that brought questions. What is this teaching and who learns from it and where does it lead? "If we could first know where we are and whither we are tending, we could better judge what to do and how to do it."

The dew came on the White House lawn and the moonlight spread lace of white films in the night and the syringa and the bridal wreath blossomed and the birds fluttered in the bushes and nested in the sycamore and the veery thrush fluted with never a weariness. The war drums rolled and the telegraph clicked off mortality lists, now a thousand, now ten thousand in a day. Yet there were moments when the processes of men seemed to be only an evil dream and justice lay in deeper transitions than those wrought by men dedicated to kill or be killed.

Beyond the black smoke lay what salvations and jubilees? Death was in the air. So was birth. What was dying no man was knowing. What was being born no man could say.

Chapter 19

Gettysburg —
Vicksburg Siege — Deep Tides, '63

The Cincinnati *Gazette* correspondent with the Army of the Potomac chanced to hear Lincoln say, "I tell you I think a great deal of that fine fellow Meade." Meade's father was a merchant, shipowner, U.S. naval agent in Cadiz, Spain. Born in Cadiz in 1815, graduated from West Point, the son took a hand in fighting Seminole Indians, resigned from the Army, worked on War Department surveys, was brevetted first lieutenant for gallantry in the Mexican War, and for five years was a lighthouse-builder among Florida reefs. He married Margaretta, daughter of John Sergeant, noted Philadelphia lawyer, in 1840, and often when away on duty wrote her a letter every day; in these were many references to "Our Saviour," to "the will of God and the uncertainty of human plans and projects," and his own "innumerable sins," which he prayed would be forgiven.

After Meade's appointment as brigadier general of volunteers August 31, 1861, he had seen active and often front-line service in every battle of the Army of the Potomac—except for a short interval of recovery from a gunshot wound at New Market Road on the Peninsula. In camp at Fredericksburg he had told Lincoln he believed the army was gratified with the President's revocation of General Hunter's emancipation proclamation, writing to his wife that the President said, "I am trying to do my duty, but no one can imagine what influences are brought to bear upon me." From camp at Falmouth he wrote her of "a very handsome and pleasant dinner" with the President and Mrs. Lincoln.

Meade quietly confessed to his wife, by letter: "I have been making myself (or at least trying to do so) very agreeable to Mrs. Lincoln, who seems an amiable sort of personage. In view also of the vacant brigadier-ship in the regular army, I have ventured to tell the President one or two stories, and I think I have made decided progress in his affections." Ten weeks later, however, there crashed on Meade, against his wish, an order he could not disobey, the President's appointment of him to the command of the Army of the Potomac.

Where McClellan most often wrote to his wife that any lack of success on his part must be laid on others, Meade more often was moderate and apologetic, writing to his wife, "Sometimes I have a little sinking at the heart, when reflecting that perhaps I may fail at the grand scratch; but I try to console myself with the belief that I shall probably do as well as most of my neighbors, and that your firm faith must be founded on some reasonable groundwork."

The President on June 15, 1863, issued a call for 100,000 troops—from Pennsylvania 50,000, Maryland 10,000. West Virginia 10,000, Ohio 30,000—to serve for six months unless sooner discharged. The Secretary of War called for help from the governors of 13 states. Thirty regiments of Pennsylvania militia, besides artillery and cavalry, and 19 regiments from New York were mobilized at Harrisburg under General Couch from the Army of the Potomac.

From day to day through latter June the news overshadowing all else in the public prints was that of Lee's army. Far behind Lee now was Richmond and its small defensive force. When he had requisitioned for rations, it was said the Confederate Commissary General replied, "If General Lee wishes rations let him seek them in Pennsylvania." When Lee had been asked about a Union army taking Richmond while he was away, he smiled, it was said. "In that case we shall swap queens." He and his chief, Davis, had decided that "valuable results" might follow the taking of Harrisburg, Philadelphia, Baltimore, Washington; besides immense amounts of supplies, provisions, munitions, there would be European recognition. Men well informed believed that Lee had nearly 100,000 men and 250 cannon, so Simon Cameron at Harrisburg sent word to Lincoln.

Lee's men were in a high and handsome stride. Twice within seven months, though far outnumbered, they had routed, sent reeling, the Army of the Potomac. "There were never such men in an army before," said Lee. "They will go anywhere and do anything if properly led." The English Lieutenant Colonel Fremantle, traveling with the invading army, noted that the universal feeling in the army was "one of profound contempt for an enemy whom they have beaten so constantly."

Fremantle wrote of Hood's ragged Jacks from Texas, Alabama, Arkansas, marching through Chambersburg with cheers and laughter at the taunts of scowling, well-dressed women: "One female had seen fit to adorn her ample bosom with a huge Yankee flag, and she stood at the door of her house, her countenance expressing the greatest contempt for the barefooted Rebs; several companies passed her without taking any notice; but at length a Texan gravely remarked, 'Take care, madam, for Hood's boys are great at storming breastworks when the Yankee colors is on them.' . . . The patriotic lady beat a precipitate retreat." No repartee was flung at a gaunt woman with a face of doom who cried from a window at the passing troops: "Look at Pharaoh's army going to the Red Sea." To a woman who sang "The Star-spangled Banner" at him, General Lee lifted his hat and rode on. From another window a woman gazed at the cool and impressive Lee riding by and murmured, "Oh, I wish he was ours!"

Like a foretokening a girl in Greencastle, "sweet sixteen

and never yet kissed," came running out of a house at
Pickett's Virginians, her face flushed and her eyes blazing.
For an apron she wore the Union flag. And she hurled a
défi: "Come and take it, the man that dares!" Pickett bowed,
sweeping his hat. His soldiers gave the girl a long cheer
and a gale of bright laughter.

The Springfield *Republican* urged Lincoln himself to take
the field; he was as good a strategist as the Northern generals had proved, and his personal presence would arouse
enthusiasm. Lincoln's instructions to Meade ran that not
Richmond but Lee's army must be the objective. Meade followed Lee with orders from Lincoln "to find and fight"
the enemy. From day to day neither Meade nor Lee had
been certain where the other was. Lee would rather have
taken Harrisburg, its stores and supplies, and then battled
Meade on the way to Philadelphia.

Lee rode his horse along roads winding through bright
summer landscapes to find himself suddenly looking at the
smoke of a battle he had not ordered or planned. Some of
his own marching divisions had become entangled with
enemy columns, traded shots, and a battle had begun that
was to swirl around the little town of Gettysburg. Lee could
draw away or carry on; he decided to carry on.

The stakes were immense, the chances fair. The new
Union commander had never planned a battle nor handled
a big army in the wild upsets of frontal combat on a wide
line. Also 58 regiments of Northern veterans who had
fought at Antietam, Fredericksburg, Chancellorsville, had
gone home, their time up, their places filled by militia and
raw recruits.

One factor was against Lee: he would have to tell his
cannoneers to go slow and count their shells, while Meade's
artillery could fire on and on from an endless supply. Also
Lee was away from his Virginia, where he knew the ground
and the people, while Meade's men were fighting for their
homes, women, barns, cattle and fields against invaders
and strangers, as Meade saw and felt it.

Lee hammered at the Union left wing the first day, the
right wing the second day, Meade on that day sending

word to Lincoln that the enemy was "repulsed at all points." On the third day, July 3, 1863, Lee smashed at Meade's center. Under Longstreet's command, General George Edward Pickett, a tall arrow of a man, with mustache and goatee, with long ringlets of auburn hair flying as he galloped his horse, headed 15,000 men who had nearly a mile to go up a slow slope of land to reach the Union center. Before starting his men on their charge to the Union center, Pickett handed Longstreet a letter to a girl in Richmond he was to marry if he lived. Longstreet had ordered Pickett to go forward and Pickett had penciled on the back of the envelope, "If Old Peter's [Longstreet's] nod means death, good-bye, and God bless you, little one!" An officer held out a flask of whisky: "Take a drink with me; in an hour you'll be in hell or glory." And Pickett said No; he had promised "the little girl" he wouldn't.

Across the long rise of open ground, with the blue flag of Virginia floating ahead, over field and meadow Pickett's 15,000 marched steadily and smoothly, almost as if on a drill ground. Solid shot, grape and canister, from the Union artillery plowed through them, and later a wild rain of rifle bullets. Seven-eighths of a mile they marched in the open sunlight, every man a target for the Union marksmen behind stone fences and breastworks. They obeyed orders; Uncle Robert had said they would go anywhere and do anything. As men fell their places were filled, the ranks closed up. As officers tumbled off horses it was taken as expected in battle. Perhaps half who started reached the Union lines surmounting Cemetery Ridge. Then came cold steel, the bayonet, the clubbed musket. The strongest and last line of the enemy was reached. "The Confederate battle flag waved over his defences," said a Confederate major, "and the fighting over the wall became hand to hand, but more than half having already fallen, our line was too weak to rout the enemy."

Meade rode up white-faced to hear it was a repulse and cried, "Thank God!" Lee commented: "They deserved success as far as it can be deserved by human valor and fortitude. More may have been required of them than they were able to perform." To one of his colonels Lee said, "This has been a sad day for us, a sad day, but we cannot expect always to gain victories." As a heavy rainfall came on the night of July 4 Lee ordered a retreat toward the Potomac.

Meade was seen that day sitting in the open on a stone, his head in his hand, willing it should rain, thankful that his army had, as he phrased it, driven "the invaders from our soil." For three days and nights Meade wasn't out of his clothes, took only snatches of sleep, while he had spoken the controlling decisions to his corps commanders in the bloodiest battle of modern warfare up till that time. Tabulations ran that the Union army lost 23,000 killed, wounded and missing, the Confederate army 28,000. Pickett came out of it alive to write his Virginia girl, "Your soldier lives and mourns and but for you, he would rather, a million times rather, be back there with his dead to sleep for all time in an unknown grave."

One tree in line of fire had 250 bullets in it, another tree 110. Farmer Rummel's cow lane was piled with 30 dead horses. Farmer Rummel found two cavalrymen who had fought afoot, killed each other and fallen with their feet touching, each with a bloody saber in his hand. A Virginian and a 3d Pennsylvania man had fought on horseback, hacking each other's head and shoulders with sabers; they clinched and their horses ran out from under them; they were found with stiff and bloody fingers fastened in each other. The peg-leg Confederate General Ewell, struck by a bullet, had chirped merrily to General John B. Gordon, "It don't hurt a bit to be shot in a wooden leg."

The brave and able General John F. Reynolds, who had once peremptorily refused Lincoln's offer of command of the Army of the Potomac, felt a bullet sink into his neck, called to his men, "Forward! for God's sake, forward!" and fell into the arms of a captain with the words, "Good God, Wilcox, I am killed."

Confederate bayonets had taken Union cannon and Union bayonets had retaken the cannon. Round Top, Little Round Top, Culp's Hill, rang with the yells of men shooting and men shot. Meadows of white daisies were pockmarked by horse hoofs. Dead and wounded lay scattered in rows, in little sudden piles. The first battle of the war fought outside a Slave State was over. Lee could have managed it better. So could Meade. The arguments began.

Meade issued an order thanking the Army of the Potomac for glorious results: "An enemy superior in numbers and flushed with the pride of a successful invasion, attempted to overcome and destroy this Army. Utterly baffled and defeated, he has now withdrawn from the contest . . . The Commanding General looks to the Army for greater efforts to drive from our soil every vestige of the presence of the invader."

On the wall map in his office, Lincoln had watched the colored pins as they changed to indicate military positions. Zach Chandler came in, spoke of painful anxiety because the fate of the nation seemed to hang in the balance, noted "the restless solicitude of Mr. Lincoln, as he paced up and down the room, reading despatches, soliloquizing, and often stopping to trace positions on the map."

The President announced to the country July 4 that news had arrived up to 10 P.M. July 3 such as to cover with honor the Army of the Potomac, to promise great success to the cause of the Union, and to claim condolence for the many gallant fallen. "For this he especially desires that on this day He whose will, not ours, should ever be done be everywhere remembered and reverenced with profoundest gratitude."

Fry of the Adjutant General's office had noticed Lincoln clinging to the War Office and devouring every scrap of news as it came over the wires. "I saw him read General Meade's congratulatory order to the Army of the Potomac. When he came to the sentence about 'driving the invaders from our soil,' an expression of disappointment settled upon his face, his hands dropped upon his knees, and in tones of anguish he exclaimed, ' "Drive the *invaders* from our soil." My God! Is that all?' "

Lincoln sent from Soldiers' Home a telegram to Halleck saying he had left the telegraph office "a good deal dissatisfied." He quoted from Meade's address about driving "the invaders from our soil," saying, "You know I did not like the phrase." Since then had come word that the enemy was crossing its wounded over the Potomac.

While the Battle of Gettysburg was being fought the President had wondered what was happening to Grant. For months he had been haunted by the colossal Vicksburg affair. Grant was trying to starve out one Confederate army in Vicksburg while he held off other Confederate armies from reaching Vicksburg. Against many representations and pleadings Lincoln had kept Grant in command and was hoping for great results. But the months passed.

When Lee's van was a day's march from Harrisburg, Lincoln had issued a long letter to an Ohio Democratic committee regarding habeas corpus and the Constitution; sent General R. H. Milroy a sharp letter for losing a division of troops and blaming it on the West Pointers who were his superiors; written a note of comfort to General David Hunter that he must not grumble so much, for he was still held in respect and esteem. On the third day's fighting he took time to pardon a deserter sentenced to be shot.

Welles July 7 was just saying good afternoon to a distinguished delegation when a dispatch was handed to him with news from Admiral Porter at Vicksburg; that city, its defenses and Pemberton's army of some 30,000 troops had surrendered to Grant and the Union army. Welles excused himself and headed for the Executive Mansion; he found the President with Chase and others, pointing on a map to details of Grant's movements.

Welles gave the news of the Porter telegram. The President rose at once, said they would not discuss Vicksburg and the map any more, and, "I myself will telegraph this news to General Meade." He took his hat as if to go, suddenly stopped and looked down with a shining face at Welles, took him by the hand, put an arm around him and broke forth: "What can we do for the Secretary of the Navy for this glorious intelligence? He is always giving us good news. I cannot, in words, tell you my joy over this result. It is great, Mr. Welles, it is great!"

The two of them walked out across the White House lawn. "This," said the President, "will relieve Banks. It will inspire me." Welles thought the opportunity good to request the President to insist upon his own views, to enforce them, not only on Meade but on Halleck. Lincoln directed Halleck to send word at once to Meade that Vicksburg had surrendered to Grant July 4, and furthermore: "Now, if General Meade can complete his work, so gloriously prosecuted thus far, by the literal or substantial destruction of Lee's army, the rebellion will be over."

Over the North as the news spread were mass meetings and speeches, rejoicing, firing of guns, ringing of bells. In hundreds of cities large and small were celebrations with torchlight processions, songs, jubilation, refreshments. "The price of gold . . . fell ten or fifteen cents and the whole country is joyous," wrote Welles. A brass band and a big crowd serenaded the President at the White House. He spoke to the crowd: ". . . in a succession of battles in Pennsylvania, near to us, through three days, so rapidly fought that they might be called one great battle on the 1st, 2d and 3d of the month of July; and on the 4th the cohorts of those who opposed the declaration that all men are created equal, 'turned tail' and run. Gentlemen, this is a glorious theme, and the occasion for a speech, but I am not prepared to make one worthy of the occasion." He would praise those who had fought so bravely. "I dislike to mention the name of one single officer, lest I might do wrong to those I might forget."

The colloquial phrase "turned tail" was as old to him as his boyhood and had the graphic edge he wished to convey. But it wasn't correct English, and he would hear about such language. He closed with a breezy and careless sentence that would do him no good among the purists of diction. "Having said this much, I will now take the music."

An odd number was Grant, a long way from home, bagging an entire army, winning the greatest Union victory of the war thus far, clearing the Mississippi River of its last Confederate hold, yet failing to send word to Washington —unless he let it go at telling Admiral Porter the Navy should be first to wire the big news to Washington. This was more of Grant's careless ways. Welles wrote, "The Secretary of War and General Halleck are much dissatisfied that Admiral Porter should have sent me information of the capture of Vicksburg in advance of any word from General Grant, and also with me for spreading it at once over the country without verification from the War Office."

The detailed facts arrived at Washington of Grant receiving 31,600 prisoners, 172 cannon, 60,000 muskets. Port Hudson, a little farther south on the Mississippi, had fallen to General Banks with 6,000 prisoners, 51 cannon, 5,000 muskets. The starved Confederates filed out of Vicksburg in silence, the Union soldiers obeying Grant's instructions "to be orderly and quiet as these prisoners pass, and to make no offensive remarks." They were paroled, Grant explaining they were largely from the Southwest. "I knew many of them were tired of the war and would get home just as soon as they could." The prisoners included Lieutenant General John C. Pemberton, a favorite of President Davis, 4 major generals, 15 brigadiers, 80 staff officers.

Lincoln's eager anxiety about a military drama enacted along river bends where he had navigated flatboats, was told in a tender handshake letter of July 13, 1863, to Grant: ". . . I write this now as a grateful acknowledgment for the almost inestimable service you have done the country . . . I never had any faith, except a general hope that you knew better than I, that the Yazoo Pass expedition, and the like, could succeed. When you got below, and took Port-Gibson, Grand Gulf, and vicinity, I thought you should go down the river and join Gen. Banks; and when you turned Northward East of the Big Black, I feared it was a mistake. I now wish to make the personal acknowledgment that you were right, and I was wrong."

Meade was writing to Halleck July 8, "I think the decisive battle of the war will be fought in a few days," receiving from Halleck two days later the advice, "I think it will be best for you to postpone a general battle till you can concentrate all your forces and get up your reserves and reinforcements." On July 12 Meade reported to Halleck that he would attack next day "unless something intervenes to prevent it," recognizing that delay would strengthen the enemy and would not increase his own force. The war telegraph office operator Albert B. Chandler said that when this dispatch arrived from Meade, Lincoln paced the room wringing his hands and saying, "They will be ready to fight a magnificent battle when there is no enemy there to fight."

Next day Halleck wired Meade in words surely Lincoln rather than Halleck: "You are strong enough to attack and defeat the enemy before he can effect a crossing. Act upon your own judgment and make your generals execute your orders. Call no council of war. It is proverbial that councils of war never fight. Reinforcements are being pushed on as rapidly as possible. Do not let the enemy escape."

The night before, however, Meade had already called a council of war, finding that only two of his corps commanders wanted to fight. Meade himself was for immediate combat, but when the discussion was over decided to wait. The Monday following Meade's council of war, July 13, Hay's diary noted "the President begins to grow anxious and impatient about Meade's silence." The morning of the 14th "the President seemed depressed by Meade's despatches of last night. They were so cautiously & almost timidly worded—talking about reconnoitering to find the enemy's weak place, and other such." The President said he feared Meade would do nothing. About noon came a dispatch. The enemy had got away unhurt. The President was deeply grieved. "We had them within our grasp," he said to Hay. "We had only to stretch forth our hands & they were ours. And nothing I could say or do could make the Army move." It seemed to Hay that one of the President's dispatches to Meade of a few days before "must have cut like a scourge," but Meade returned so reasonable and earnest a reply that the President concluded Meade knew best what he was doing.

Welles recorded of July 14 that as Cabinet members were gathering, "Stanton said abruptly and curtly he knew nothing of Lee's crossing. 'I do,' said the President emphatically, with a look of painful rebuke to Stanton. 'If he has

not got all of his men across, he soon will.' " Lincoln said
he did not believe they could take up anything in the Cabinet for that day. Welles walked out slowly. The President
hurried and overtook Welles. They walked across the White
House lawn to the departments and stopped to talk a few
moments at the gate. Welles believed he could never forget
the voice and face of the President as he spoke. "And that,
my God, is the last of this Army of the Potomac! There is
bad faith somewhere. Meade has been pressed and urged,
but only one of his generals was for an immediate attack,
was ready to pounce on Lee; the rest held back. What does
it mean, Mr. Welles? Great God! what does it mean?"

On July 14 Lincoln wrote a long bitter letter to Meade:
"I do not believe you appreciate the magnitude of the mis-
fortune involved in Lee's escape. He was within your easy
grasp, and to have closed upon him would, in connection
with our other late successes, have ended the war . . . Your
golden opportunity is gone, and I am distressed immeasur-
ably because of it. I beg you will not consider this a prosse-
cution, or persecution of yourself. As you had learned that
I was dissatisfied, I have thought it best to kindly tell you
why." This letter never reached Meade, Lincoln later scrib-
bling on the envelope "never sent or signed." It lacked the
tone of Lincoln's remark to Simon Cameron in a later reference to Meade: "Why should we censure a man who has
done so much for his country because he did not do a little
more?"

Robert Lincoln said he went into his father's room to find
him "in tears, with head bowed upon his arms resting on
the table at which he sat." To the question, "Why, what
is the matter, father?" the answer came slowly, "My boy,
I have just learned that at a council of war, of Meade and
his Generals, it had been determined not to pursue Lee, and
now the opportune chance of ending this bitter struggle is
lost."

A few days having passed, he could see it was well he had
not sent Meade the letter he meant to be kindly but which
was not kindly. Having met in Meade a rare humility and
sincerity throughout their many difficult interchanges, Lin-

coln sent through Howard the salutation that Meade was more than a brave and skillful officer, was "a true man."

As the days passed Welles continued to blame chiefly General in Chief Halleck: "In this whole summer's campaign I have been unable to see, hear, or obtain evidence of power, or will, or talent, or originality on the part of General Halleck. He has suggested nothing, decided nothing, done nothing but scold and smoke and scratch his elbows."

On the last day of the Battle of Gettysburg Alexander H. Stephens, Vice-President of the Confederate States, had with one companion started down the James River from Richmond in a small steamer, aiming to reach Washington as commissioners of the Confederate Government and hold a conference with the President of the United States. Their dispatch of July 4 requested permission to pass through the blockade. The final decision after much consultation was in a telegram sent by Lincoln to the blockading admiral: "The request of A. H. Stephens is inadmissible. The customary agents and channels are adequate for all needful communication and conference between the United States forces and the insurgents." Thus did Lincoln dismiss his old-time colleague.

There was issued a "Proclamation of Thanksgiving," July 15, 1863, by the President. In diapasons of Old Testament prose, in the attitude of piety in which the name of Almighty God was invoked, Lincoln emerged as a man of faith. "It has pleased Almighty God to hearken to the supplications and prayers of an afflicted people," ran the opening chords, "and to vouchsafe to the army and the navy of the United States victories on land and on the sea so signal and so effective as to furnish reasonable grounds for augmented confidence that the Union of these States will be maintained, their constitution preserved, and their peace and prosperity permanently restored . . . It is meet and right to recognize and confess the presence of the Almighty Father and the power of His Hand equally in these triumphs and in these sorrows:

"Now, therefore, be it known that I do set apart Thurs-

day the 6th. day of August next, to be observed as a day
for National Thanksgiving, Praise and Prayer, and I invite
the People of the United States to assemble on the occasion in their customary places of worship, and in the forms
approved by their own consciences, render the homage due
to the Divine Majesty, for the wonderful things he has
done in the Nation's behalf . . ."

On the date this proclamation was issued the dignity and
majesty of the U.S. Government was being challenged, upset, smeared with insult and threatened with the disorders
and violence of revolution, in the largest city in the United
States.

During the three days of July 13, 14, 15, mobs or crowds
in New York City met by prearrangement, with a specific
design as to what points they would attack and carry, drove
out the U.S. provost marshal from his office at 43d Street
and Third Avenue, wrecked the wheel or revolving drum
from which the names of drafted men were drawn, tore
to pieces the books and papers, poured turpentine on the
floor, set the building on fire, fought off police and firemen,
and the draft office and six adjoining buildings burned.
They wrecked and burned the U.S. draft office on Broadway two doors from 29th Street, looted stores nearby, and
burned 12 buildings; they smashed windows and doors and
sacked the home of Republican Mayor Opdyke and burned
at midnight the home of U.S. Postmaster Abram Wake-
man, first stripping the premises of furniture and clothing;
they burned a ferry house, hotels, drugstores, clothing
stores, factories, saloons where they were refused free
liquor, police stations, a Methodist church, a Protestant
mission, the Colored Orphan Asylum at 43d Street and
Lexington Avenue. They drove out 40 policemen and 15
armed workmen from the state arsenal at 21st Street and
Second Avenue, trampling over five of their dead, seizing
muskets and cartridges, setting the building on fire; they
hanged a Negro from a tree on Clarkson Street and burned
the body with loud howling; they hanged three a day of Ne-

groes; they hanged to a lamppost a captain of the 11th regiment of the state guard; they hanged, shot or beat and trampled to death at least 30 Negroes and so terrorized the colored population that it disappeared upstate and across to New Jersey. They erected for protection and refuge barricades on First Avenue from 11th to 14th Streets, on Ninth Avenue from 32d to 43d Streets, with smaller barricades across intersecting thoroughfares. They sang "We'll hang old Greeley to a sour apple tree, and send him straight to hell!"; they yelled "To hell with the draft and the war!" and "Tell Old Abe to come to New York!"

The mobs were not driven in their work by mere blind wrath. Somebody had done some thinking, somebody had chosen a time when all the state guards the governor could scrape together had gone to Gettysburg. The only organized force ready against the first riots was a police department of 1,500 members. With club and revolver they had fought night and day, and their dead lay in scores, their wounded by the hundreds.

The mobs of the first day's riots aimed straight at a thing they hated: the Draft. It was a Monday, and on the previous Saturday 1,200 names had been picked by a blindfolded man out of the wheel. These 1,200 names had been published, and unless something happened to make the Government change its mind most of the men answering to these 1,200 names would be put into uniforms and sent to fight.

If they believed such newspapers as the *World*, the *Journal of Commerce*, the *Express*, the *Daily News*, the *Day Book*, the *Mercury*, they were to be the willing cannon fodder of a tyrannical and oppressive Government daily violating the Constitution and the fundamental law of the land. Said the *Daily News:* "The people are notified that one out of about two and a half of our citizens are to be brought off into Messrs. Lincoln & Company's charnelhouse. God forbid!"

The newspapers had printed the Fourth of July speech of Franklin Pierce, former President of the United States, at a great Democratic mass meeting at Concord, New Hampshire. Said Pierce, "It is made criminal for that noble martyr of free speech, Mr. Vallandigham, to discuss public affairs in Ohio—ay, even here, in time of war the mere arbitrary will of the President takes the place of the Constitution." Governor Seymour of New York told a Fourth of July audience that the country was on "the very verge of destruction" because of Government coercion, "seizing our persons, infringing upon our rights, insulting our homes . . . men deprived of the right of trial by jury, men torn from their homes by midnight intruders."

By the time the subtle arguments of the newspapers and of Pierce and Seymour had been simplified into plain words for the 400,000 foreign-born citizens of New York, of whom 203,740 were Irish, they had lost their fine philosophic distinctions. And far beyond any discussion was the terribly simple and outstanding fact that any man having $300 could buy his freedom from the draft. It was "a rich man's war and a poor man's fight," ran the talk in 5,000 saloons and 20 times as many homes.

Drafted men, their relatives and friends, reinforced by thousands of sympathizers who favored some kind of direct action, gathered early the morning of July 13 in vacant lots with clubs, staves, cart rungs, pieces of iron, and moved as if by agreement to a lot near Central Park where they organized, began patrolling the city, and put the first sign of their wrath and vengeance on the draft offices wrecked and burned. The first acts of the three days' tornado had some semblance of an uprising of the people against a Government discriminating in its conscription between the rich and the poor. The second and third days, however, saw the events come under the sway of the city's criminal and gang elements, then numbering between 50,000 and 70,000, who swarmed out for loot and the work of getting the police defied and overrun.

Governor Seymour probably set forth a sincere viewpoint in a proclamation calling for enforcement of law and order. He meant to say he might have favored a few small riots which would show a healthy Democratic opposition to the draft, but when the mobs ran wild and made war against the rich, it was time to place the emphasis on property, safety, strict law enforcement, rather than on personal liberty and the class discrimination of the Conscription Act.

Besides the many mobs carrying banners inscribed "No Draft" and "No $300 Arrangements with Us," there had been many other mobs with varied and mixed motives. Class war was the cry behind the big placards of one division: "The Poor Man's Blood for the Rich Man's Money." Eagerness for loot lay back of the stripping of houses of jewelry, plate, furniture, rugs, clothes. Primitive race antagonism, set aflame by political malevolence, underlay the hanging and beating of black men by white men. In thousands of boys the savage was unleashed; they robbed houses and set them on fire; they beat to death with fists and clubs the young Negro cripple Abraham Franklin; they tore off the clothes of Jeremiah Robinson, who was trying to escape to a ferryboat wearing his wife's dress and hood, threw him to the pavement, kicked him in the face and ribs, killed him and threw the body into the river.

Robert Nugent, assistant provost marshal in charge of conscription, received the second day of the riots a telegram from his Washington chief, James B. Fry, directing him to suspend the draft. Governor Seymour and Mayor Opdyke clamored that he should publish this order. Nugent said he had no authority, but he finally consented to sign his name to a notice: "The draft has been suspended in New York City and Brooklyn," which was published in newspapers. This had a marked quieting effect.

The storm in the streets began to slow down as though winds had changed. There was added quieting effect as infantry, cavalry, artillery, from the Army of the Potomac commenced arriving.

On July 14, the second of the three-day riots, a telegram dated at the War Department, Washington, and signed "A. Lincoln" went addressed to Robert T. Lincoln, Fifth Avenue Hotel, New York, with the query, "Why do I hear no more of you?"

After 150 Regular Army soldiers with ball cartridges had

faced a crowd of 2,000, fired in the air, and received a volley of stones in reply, and had then shot into the swarming and defiant mass, killing 12 and wounding more, the hullabaloo began to die down.

Soon afterward James R. Gilmore, who had sent Lincoln reports on the riots from the New York *Tribune* office, called on Lincoln at the White House and asked why the President could not say Yes or No to the recommendation for a special commissioner to expose the instigators of the riots. Lincoln hesitated and in a peculiar half-bantering manner, according to Gilmore, replied: "Well, you see if I had said no, I should have admitted that I dare not enforce the laws, and consequently have no business to be President of the United States. If I had said yes, and had appointed the judge, I should—as he would have done his duty—have simply touched a match to a barrel of gunpowder. You have heard of sitting on a volcano. We are sitting upon two; one is blazing away already, and the other will blaze away the moment we scrape a little loose dirt from the top of the crater. Better let the dirt alone,—at least for the present. One rebellion at a time is about as much as we can conveniently handle."

Governor Seymour wrote to the President asking for suspension of the draft, the President replying that he could not consent. "*Time* is too important." Due credit in the quota would be made for volunteers, Lincoln stipulated; he also said he would be willing to facilitate a decision from the U.S. Supreme Court on whether the draft law was constitutional. "But I can not consent to lose the *time* while it is being obtained . . ." His purpose was to be "just and constitutional; and yet practical." He was yielding nothing to the astute and persistent Governor who had so often given words of hope to New York City that the draft would be got rid of.

Lincoln did during those hectic summer weeks prepare an address to the country giving the facts and logic which dictated his actions in the draft. Having written this argument, Lincoln filed it away in a pigeonhole of personal papers and it was not heard of till long afterward. One relentlessly logical passage read: "There can be no army without men. Men can be had only voluntarily, or involuntarily. We have ceased to obtain them voluntarily; and to obtain them involuntarily, is the draft—the conscription. If you dispute the fact, and declare that men can still be had voluntarily in sufficient numbers prove the assertion by yourselves volunteering in such numbers, and I shall gladly give up the draft. Or if not a sufficient number, but any one of you will volunteer, he for his single self, will escape all the horrors of the draft; and will thereby do only what each one of at least a million of his manly brethren have already done. Their toil and blood have been given as much for you as themselves. Shall it all be lost rather than that you too, will bear your part?"

His mind had dwelt, evidently, on a law to enforce universal selective service, the Government taking all men physically fit, no man escaping by purchase or substitution. Such conscription was operating in several European monarchies and republics, but as Lincoln looked out across the American scene in 1863, he seemed to believe it could not then be put to work in the United States, even if he could find Congressmen to advocate it. Perhaps the opposition had more than a demagogue's idle phrase in the cry "The rich man's money against the poor man's blood."

His elaborately prepared address, said Nicolay and Hay, was intended more especially for the honest and patriotic Democrats of the North, "but after he had finished it, doubts arose in his mind as to the propriety or the expediency of addressing the public directly in that manner," and "with reserve and abnegation, after writing it, he resolved to suppress so admirable a paper." He laid his paper aside as a meditation that had exercised his mind and sharpened his humility and perhaps deepened his patience.

New York City saw on August 19, 1863, no less than 10,000 troops from the Army of the Potomac assisted by the 1st Division New York State Guards. Governor Seymour proclaimed that citizens should obey the law of Congress as to conscription. New draft offices went into operation. Cavalry patrols rode up and down the streets.

The draft proceeded, meeting covert instead of open resistance. Tammany, Tweed, A. Oakey Hall, Fernando Wood and his brother Ben, the *World*, the *Express*, the *Day Book*, the *Mercury*, many scurrying politicians, examining physicians, and fixers, lawyers, did their work. Upward of $5,000,000 was appropriated by the municipality of New York for draft-evasion purposes. According to the "infallible" record which Lincoln had mentioned to Seymour, of 292,441 men whose names were drawn from the wheels 39,877 failed to report for examination. Of the remaining 252,564, for good or bad reasons 164,394 were exempted. This left 88,170 available for duty, of whom 52,288 bought exemptions at $300 apiece, which yielded the Government $15,686,400. The original 292,441 names were thus cut down to 35,882 men, of whom 26,002 hired substitutes to go to war for them. This left 9,880 who lacked political pull or seemed to want to join the army and fight.

There now arose at Niagara Falls, Canada, Clement L. Vallandigham, crying that on British soil he was a freeman but if he crossed over into the U.S.A. he was a felon and would be clapped into jail. Discussion of habeas corpus and the right of free speech flared higher. The New York *World* declared that the crime of arresting Vallandigham was a Lincoln blunder and inquired why the President had not arrested Fernando Wood for remarks at New York mass meetings as treasonable as those of Vallandigham in Ohio.

Mrs. Vallandigham left her home in Dayton, Ohio, to join her husband at Windsor, Canada, opposite Detroit, to help him campaign from there. It was reported she told her friends that she never expected to return from Canada until she did so as the wife of the governor of Ohio. This reminded Lincoln of a man out in Illinois running for supervisor on the county board. On leaving home election morning he said, "Wife, tonight you shall sleep with the supervisor from the township." News came in the evening that her husband was beaten in the election, and she was all dressed up for going out when she met her defeated man at the door. "Wife, where are you going all dressed up this time of night?" he exclaimed. "Going?" she countered. "Why you told me this morning that I should sleep tonight with the supervisor of this town and as the other man was elected instead of you, I was going to his house." Whereupon the husband, as newspapers quoted Lincoln, "acknowledged the corn, she didn't go out, and he bought a new Brussels carpet for the parlor."

During those six weeks of Vallandigham's banishment Lee had been repulsed at Gettysburg; Grant had taken Vicksburg and Confederate power on the Mississippi River was gone; a violent three-day uprising in the largest city in the North, and minor revolts at other points, had been brought under control. Lincoln, pleased at the outlook, wrote a letter that James C. Conkling read at an immense mass meeting in Springfield, Illinois: "There are those who are dissatisfied with me. To such I would say: You desire peace; and you blame me that we do not have it." One way to peace was to suppress the rebellion by force of arms. "This, I am trying to do. Are you for it? If you are, so far we are agreed. If you are not for it, a second way is, to give up the Union. I am against this. Are you for it? If you are, you should say so plainly. If you are not for *force*, nor yet for *dissolution*, there only remains some imaginable *compromise*."

He promised that if any peace proposition came from those who controlled the Confederate Army, "It shall not be rejected, and kept a secret from you." There was another issue. "You are dissatisfied with me about the negro . . . I suggested compensated emancipation; to which you replied you wished not to be taxed to buy negroes. But I had not asked you to be taxed to buy negroes, except in such way, as to save you from greater taxation to save the Union exclusively by other means."

He launched into the finish of what was really a paper aimed at the masses of people in America and Europe: "The signs look better. The Father of Waters again goes unvexed to the sea . . . And while those who have cleared the great river may well be proud, even that is not all. It is hard to say that anything has been more bravely, and well done, than at Antietam, Murfreesboro, Gettysburg, and on many fields of lesser note. Nor must Uncle Sam's Web-feet be forgotten. At all the watery margins they have been present. Not only on the deep sea, the broad bay, and the rapid river, but also up the narrow muddy bayou, and wherever the ground was a little damp, they have been, and made their tracks. Thanks to all. For the great republic—for the principle it lives by, and keeps alive—for man's vast future,—thanks to all.

"Peace does not appear so distant as it did. I hope it will come soon, and come to stay; and so come as to be worth the keeping in all future time. It will then have been proved that, among free men, there can be no successful appeal from the ballot to the bullet; and that they who take such appeal are sure to lose their case, and pay the cost. And then, there will be some black men who can remember that, with silent tongue, and clenched teeth, and steady eye, and well-poised bayonet, they have helped mankind on to this great consummation; while, I fear, there will be some white ones, unable to forget that, with malignant heart, and deceitful speech, they strove to hinder it. Still, let us not be over-sanguine of a speedy final triumph. Let us be quite sober. Let us diligently apply the means, never doubting that a just God, in his own good time, will give us the rightful result."

No previous letter, address or state paper of Lincoln's received such warm-hearted comment. Many newspapers joined with the New York *Times* seeing it as having hard sense, a temper defying malice. "Even the Copperhead gnaws upon it as vainly as a viper upon a file. The most consummate rhetorician never used language more pat to the purpose and still there is not a word not familiar to the plainest plowman . . . Abraham Lincoln is today the most popular man in the Republic . . ."

The New York *World* was saying, "Nature has not endowed Mr. Lincoln with a single great or commanding quality. He has indeed a certain homely untutored shrewdness and vulgar honesty . . . but no . . . higher degree of consideration than belongs to a village lawyer . . ." The London *Times* was annoyed at Lincoln's latest letter: "The persons, if there be any such, to whom such jargon can appear impressive or even intelligible, must have faculties and tastes of which we can form no idea."

Living in the same house, seeing the chief in many moods, Hay was writing, "The Tycoon is in fine whack. I have rarely seen him more serene & busy. He is managing this war, the draft, foreign relations, and planning a reconstruction of the Union, all at once. I never knew with what tyrannous authority he rules the Cabinet, till now. The most important things he decides & there is no cavil . . . There is no man in the country, so wise, so gentle and so firm. I believe the hand of God placed him where he is."

In September '63 the Boston publisher Benjamin B. Russell issued a collection of *The Letters of President Lincoln on Questions of National Policy,* with a preface, as though the letters were literature and unique reading matter. The sheaf filled 22 pages, and sold at eight cents a copy, two copies 15 cents.

By the carefully wrought appeal in simple words aimed to reach millions of readers and by the face-to-face contact with thousands who came to the White House, Lincoln was holding to the single purpose of adding momentum to what there was of popular will for war. The late summer and early fall of '63 seemed to mark a deepening of loyalties to Lincoln and his vision of where to go and how.

The President needed anchors, needed hope. A million volunteers had answered his call and given toil and blood for the cause of which he was the mouthpiece. Soon he was to order a draft for 300,000 more conscripts. He had told Mary Livermore there was little realization of the agony and cost that yet lay ahead. The reports of Grant and Sherman far down in the intestinal center of the Confederacy told him their belief that the war had only truly begun, as it could only be ended by complete and bloody conquest. So furiously had it raged thus far that both sides had often been left no time to bury their dead.

Chapter 20

Lincoln at Storm Center

From the Big Black River in Mississippi, Sherman was writing to Lincoln: "The South must be ruled by us, or she will rule us. We must conquer them, or ourselves be conquered. They ask, and will have, nothing else, and talk of compromise is bosh; for we know they would even scorn the offer . . . I would not coax them, or even meet them halfway, but make them so sick of war that generations would pass away before they would again appeal to it . . . The people of this country in after-years will be better citizens from the dear-bought experience of the present crisis. Let them learn it now, and learn it well, that good citizens must obey as well as command."

A fierce insolence would Vallandigham, Seymour, the organization Democrats, have found in this treatise if Sherman had let it be published as Lincoln proposed. "I know what I say when I repeat that the insurgents of the South sneer at all overtures looking to their interests . . . They tell me to my face that they respect Grant, McPherson, and our brave associates who fight manfully and well for a principle, but despise the Copperheads and sneaks at the North, who profess friendship for the South and opposition to the war, as mere covers for their knavery and poltroonery."

Sherman invoked his doctrine of terror: "Our officers, marshals, and courts, must penetrate into the innermost recesses of their land, . . . that it makes no difference whether it be in one year, or two, or ten, or twenty; that we will remove and destroy every obstacle, if need be, take every life, every acre of land, every particle of property, every thing that to us seems proper; that we will not cease till the end is attained . . ."

When the vaguely furtive and definitely garrulous James R. Gilmore of the New York *Tribune* came again with a scheme, Lincoln listened. It was doubtful whether Lincoln gave Gilmore a glad hand and took him to his bosom in the easy and familiar way Gilmore wrote about it. Yet it seemed definite that Gilmore and others in the summer of '63 interested Lincoln, at least mildly and tentatively, in plans to sound out Zebulon B. Vance, the 33-year-old governor of North Carolina, on how far Vance might be willing to go toward bringing his state back into the Union.

The break between Vance and the Davis Government ran deep, the feeling bitter. The planter aristocracy, the slaveholders, the original secessionists, had no such hold in North Carolina as in the Cotton States. Her mountaineers, farmers, seacoast population, were "different." Vance spoke for his people when he served notice on the Richmond Government that his state troops would go into action against Confederate authorities who should try to override the right of any citizen to the writ of habeas corpus. Vance protested to Richmond against Confederate War Department officers "engaging in speculations of private account" in North Carolina. Vance telegraphed and wrote Davis that a Georgia regiment, its men and officers, started a riot the night of September 9, burned and destroyed the Raleigh *Standard*, and in retaliation a mob of citizens the next morning burned and destroyed the Raleigh *State Journal*. "I feel very sad in the contemplation of these outrages," Vance told Davis. "The distance is quite short to either anarchy or despotism, when armed soldiers, led by their officers, can with impunity outrage the laws of a State."

The Georgia regiment that had wrecked and burned the Raleigh *Standard* newspaper plant hated its peace tone, hated a four-column address published July 31, 1863. Governor Vance had helped, it was said, to write the address with its cry, "The great demand of the people of this part of the State is *peace;* peace upon any terms that will not enslave and degrade us."

Vance would welcome reunion of the states and "any peace compatible with honor," according to the information Gilmore brought Lincoln. He had it, he said, from Edward Kidder, a merchant of Wilmington, North Carolina. Born in New Hampshire, Kidder had gone to Wilmington in 1826 when he was 21, had lived there ever since, "accumulating a vast fortune, and having larger business transactions than any other man in the State." Lincoln read Kidder's confidential report of a talk with Governor Vance. Slavery was dead, the report ran, the Confederacy hopeless, and Vance favored a return to the Union on terms of honor and equity. Therefore Kidder hoped Gilmore would run the blockade into Wilmington, interview Governor Vance at Kidder's home, bringing to Vance Lincoln's peace terms.

In the months that followed, with further errands and with plans changing, nothing much directly came of the scheme. Whether Lincoln reached across the state lines and convinced Governor Vance that peace efforts would be worth while was not clear. It was clear as daylight, however, that a few months after Gilmore and Kidder had laid their plans before Lincoln, Governor Vance was going nearly as far as Lincoln could wish in blunt suggestions and arguments sent to Jefferson Davis. A letter of Vance to Davis in December '63 was a straight and open plea for "some effort at negotiation with the enemy."

There was a Union sentiment in North Carolina, as in several areas of the South—as in one county in Alabama having no slaves and sending no troops to the Confederate armies. Lincoln was responsive to all such Union areas. What he did in some cases might never be known. In many affairs he was careful to keep no record.

The French government advised the American Minister in Paris that the sooner the American government showed a willingness to recognize the government of Archduke Maximilian, set up in Mexico by French armies, the sooner would those armies be ready to leave Mexico. Seward replied that the determination of the President was to err on the side of neutrality, if he erred at all, as between France and Mexico.

In plainer words than the covert phrasings of diplomacy, Lincoln had answered General John M. Thayer's query, "Mr. President, how about the French army in Mexico?" He shrugged his shoulders and wrinkled his eyebrows. "I'm not exactly 'skeered,' but I don't like the looks of the thing. Napoleon has taken advantage of our weakness in our time of trouble, and has attempted to found a monarchy on the soil of Mexico in utter disregard of the Monroe doctrine. My policy is, attend to only one trouble at a time. If we get well out of our present difficulties and restore the Union, I propose to notify Louis Napoleon that it is about time to take his army out of Mexico. When that army is gone, the Mexicans will take care of Maximilian."

Heading the Military Department of Missouri was General John M. Schofield, 32 years old, cool, sober, a West Pointer, professor of physics, chief of staff for General Lyon in the fighting at Wilson's Creek. Now he was Lincoln's main buffer in a Slave State seething with civil war. To the President, he reported the return of thousands of soldiers from defeated Confederate armies at Vicksburg and elsewhere. At first organized secretly as gangs, they joined up into regiments and small armies; they had raided, foraged supplies from Unionists, stolen money and horses, burned houses and railroad bridges, looted villages and towns, shot and hanged Union men. Toward keeping order Schofield organized ten regiments of Federal troops. Once he estimated there were 5,000 armed and banded guerrillas in Missouri.

Schofield's authority often tangled with that of Missouri's provisional governor, 65-year-old Hamilton Rowan Gamble. Virginia-born of Irish immigrants, his wife from South Carolina, Gamble had been member of the legislature, secretary of state, presiding judge of the state supreme court. He had pronounced Lincoln's call for troops in April '61 unconstitutional and had leaned toward those who wished to make Missouri independent of both North and South, repelling invaders whether in blue or gray. As chairman of the committee on Federal relations in the state constitutional convention of '61, Gamble hoped for "amicable adjustment" without civil war. That same convention appointed him provisional governor of the state, replacing the regularly elected Claiborne F. Jackson, whom Unionist forces had run out of the state capital.

Gamble wrote that the radicals were "openly and loudly" threatening to overthrow the state provisional government by violence. Lincoln replied that Schofield would take care of the violence, that it was not a party but individual radicals making the threats. "I have seen no occasion to make a distinction against the provisional government because of its not having been chosen and inaugurated in the usual way. Nor have I seen any cause to suspect it of unfaithfulness to the Union."

Yet Lincoln knew that the face of Gamble was toward the past, that the emancipation ordinance passed by the conservative convention in the summer of '63 was evasive, odorous of politics, setting the year 1870 for slavery to "cease" in Missouri, but to "cease" under the peculiar conditions that all slaves over 40 would still be slaves till they died, while all slaves under 12 would be slaves until they were 23, and those of all other ages until the Fourth of July, 1876. In the atmosphere of the convention that passed this ordinance Governor Gamble felt called on to offer his resignation, but it was refused by a vote of 51 to 29.

A delegation of German radicals from Missouri called at the White House and later published their report that the President had refused their demands for dismissal of Seward, Blair and Halleck, had declined their requests that he restore Frémont, Sigel and Butler to important commands.

In Missouri excitement flared high as the radical Union Emancipation convention met, with delegates from four-fifths of the counties of the state. The high cry in Jefferson City September 1 was that Governor Gamble's "pro-slavery" provisional government was paralyzing Federal power. A Committee of Seventy, one from each county in

the state, was appointed to call on the President and lay
their cause before him. At train stops on the way to Washington this committee was hailed by brass bands, antislavery delegations and orators. At Washington they were
joined by a Committee of Eighteen from Kansas on the
same errand.

Lincoln told Hay that if they could show that Schofield
had done anything wrong, their case was made, that he believed they were against Schofield because Schofield would
not take sides with them. "I think I understand this matter
perfectly and I cannot do anything contrary to my convictions, to please these men, earnest and powerful as they
may be." Meanwhile the Missouri-Kansas committees dominated the Washington scene, took in a big reception to
themselves at the Union League Hall, where Gamble was
denounced and immediate emancipation demanded.

The delegation took two days to prepare an address to
the President. The wrongs their people had borne were
heavy. Crimes and outrages they alleged and enumerated
for Lincoln's eye. They were exasperated men whose voices
rose out of mixed motives of war and politics; public service and private revenge; the hangover of greed and corruption among Frémont's associates, of connivance and trickery by the Blairs in their animosities toward Frémont and
others, of anger that Schofield had lent detachments of
Enrolled Militia to Grant for the Vicksburg operation, of
wrath that Lincoln and members of Congress were trying
to emancipate the slaves of Missouri by gradual purchase
instead of direct bestowal of freedom by proclamation, of
indignation at Schofield's Order No. 92 prohibiting Kan-
sans from pursuing guerrillas over the state line, of dis-
gruntlement on the part of some with the apportionment
of Federal offices and favors, of suspicion on the part of
others that Lincoln's policy was Kentuckian and his lean-
ings pro-slavery.

Their prepared address to the President voiced three
demands. First, General Schofield must be relieved, and
General Butler appointed in his stead. Second, the system
of Enrolled Militia in Missouri must be broken up and

national forces substituted. Third, at elections persons must not be allowed to vote who were not entitled by law to do so.

At nine o'clock the morning of September 30, the 88 delegates walked through the great front doors into the White House. Then the great front doors were locked and stayed locked till the conference was over. At the committees' own request, all reporters and spectators were barred.

Lincoln looked along panels of faces. His eyes roved over stubborn men, in the main sincere, some with a genius of courage and sacrifice. He told John Hay later: "They are nearer to me than the other side, in thought and sentiment, though bitterly hostile personally. They are utterly lawless —the onhandiest devils in the world to deal with—but after all, their faces are set Zionwards."

The address was read to the President by the chairman, Charles Daniel Drake, a St. Louis lawyer, 52 years old, educated as a midshipman in the U.S. Navy, author of notable law treatises, member of the Missouri Legislature, an early leader against secession. His voice carried what Enos Clarke, another St. Louis delegate, described as "a deep, impressive, stentorian tone." And Enos Clarke took note that while Chairman Drake read, the President listened with patient attention, and when the reading was over rose slowly, and with a deliberation born of what they knew not, began a lengthy reply. Said Clarke: "I shall never forget the intense chagrin and disappointment we all felt at the treatment of the matter in the beginning of his reply . . . He gave us the impression of a pettifogger speaking before a justice of the peace jury. But as he talked on and made searching inquiries of members of the delegation and invited debate, it became manifest that his manner at the beginning was really the foil of a master . . ."

Enos Clarke recalled Lincoln saying: "You gentlemen must bear in mind that in performing the duties of the office I hold I must represent no one section, but I must act for all sections of the Union in trying to maintain the supremacy of the Government." This from Lincoln had been heard over and again privately, publicly, in letters and speeches.

Clarke, however, caught another expression that could not have been anticipated. "I desire to so conduct the affairs of this administration that if, at the end, when I come to lay down the reins of power, I have lost every other friend on earth, I shall at least have one friend left, and that friend shall be down inside of me."

Two hours ran on, some of it in speechmaking, some in random talk. Hay noted the President saying he could not give a hasty answer. "I will take your address, carefully consider it, and respond at my earliest convenience . . ." As President, he had uniformly refused to give the governor exclusive control of the Missouri State Militia, while on the other hand the Enrolled Militia existed solely under state laws with which he had no right to interfere. As to Schofield, Lincoln was sorry they had not made specific complaints. "I cannot act on vague impressions." He went into details as to Schofield's record. "I know nothing to his disadvantage. I am not personally acquainted with him. I have with him no personal relations. If you will allege a definite wrong-doing, and, having clearly made your point, prove it, I shall remove him." The suspension of habeas corpus by Schofield in Missouri was in obedience to the President's official decree. "You object to its being used in Missouri. In other words, that which is right when employed against opponents is wrong when employed against yourselves. Still, I will consider that."

They objected to Schofield's muzzling the press. "As to that," continued Lincoln, "I think when an officer in any department finds that a newspaper is pursuing a course calculated to embarrass his operations and stir up sedition and tumult, he has the right to lay hands upon it and suppress it, but in no other case. I approved the order in question after the 'Missouri Democrat' had also approved it." A delegate interrupted: "We thought it was to be used against the other side." And Lincoln agreed, "Certainly you did. Your ideas of justice seem to depend on the application of it."

Hay noted that as an inquisition the morning did not work out, Lincoln meeting each point, issue, grievance, "with a quick counter-statement so brief and clinching that the several volunteer spokesmen who came forward to support the main address retired, one by one, disconcerted and overwhelmed." The formal session drew to a close with Lincoln saying: "Still you appear to come before me as my friends, if I agree with you, and not otherwise. I do not here speak of mere personal friendship. When I speak of my friends I mean those who are friendly to my measures, to the policy of the Government." They knew the President was referring to loyal Union men who might even be proslavery in viewpoint when he said: "If a man votes for supplies of men and money, encourages enlistments, discourages desertions, does all in his power to carry the war on to a successful issue, I have no right to question him for his abstract political opinions. I must make a dividing line somewhere between those who are opponents of the Government, and those who only approve peculiar features of my Administration while they sustain the Government."

One of the men from Missouri felt Lincoln was not so quick in his answers, not so much at ease as Hay believed. "The President in the course of his reply hesitated a great deal," said this man, "and was manifestly, as he said, very much troubled over affairs in Missouri. He said they were a source of more anxiety to him than we could imagine. He regretted that some of the men who had founded the Republican party should now be arrayed apparently against his administration." Twice before, the Missourian had met Lincoln, and had not seen such a perplexed look on Lincoln's face. "When he said he was *bothered* about this thing he showed it. He spoke kindly, yet now and then there was a little rasping tone in his voice that seemed to say, 'You men ought to fix this thing up without *tormenting* me.' But he never lost his temper."

When all points had been covered, and there seemed nothing more to say, Chairman Drake stepped forward. "Mr. President, the time has now come when we can no longer trespass upon your attention but must take leave of you." Then came the most impressive moment of the two hours, Drake saying the men who stood before the President now would return, many of them to homes surrounded by "rebel" sentiment. "Many of them, sir, in returning there do so at the risk of their lives, and if any of those lives are sacrificed by reason of the military administration of this government, let me tell you, sir, that their blood will be upon your garments and not upon ours." This was terribly, though only partly, true and near to ghastly prophecy. Enos Clarke noted that during this address of Drake, "the President stood before the delegation with tears streaming down his cheeks, seeming deeply agitated."

One by one the delegates shook hands with the President and took leave. To Clarke it was memorable; he shook hands, walked off with others, and at the door turned for a final look. "Mr. Lincoln had met some personal acquaintances with whom he was exchanging pleasantries, and instead of the tears of a few moments before, he was indulging in hearty laughter. This rapid and wonderful transition from one extreme to the other impressed me greatly."

The next night Secretary Chase opened his home and gave the delegation a reception, told them he was heartily in sympathy with their mission. On to New York went the delegates to a rousing public meeting in Cooper Union, where William Cullen Bryant spoke for them, where the President was threatened with revolutionary action if he did not yield to their demands.

As in other cases, Lincoln now stood by his men. In a long letter October 5 to the Missouri-Kansas Committee he said that in their address of September 30, besides four supplementary ones on October 3, enough of "suffering and wrong" was stated.

> Yet the whole case, as presented, fails to convince me, that Gen. Schofield, or the Enrolled Militia, is responsible for that suffering and wrong . . . We are in civil war. In such cases there always is a main question; but in this case that question is a perplexing compound— Union and Slavery. It thus becomes a question not of two sides merely, but of at least four sides, even among

those who are for the Union, saying nothing of those who are against it. Thus, those who are for the Union *with*, but not *without* slavery—those for it *without*, but not *with*—those for it *with* or *without*, but prefer it *with*—and those for it *with* or *without*, but prefer it *without*. Among these again, is a subdivision of those who are for *gradual* but not for *immediate*, and those who are for *immediate*, but not for *gradual* extinction of slavery. It is easy to conceive that all these shades of opinion, and even more, may be sincerely entertained by honest and truthful men. Yet, all being for the Union, by reason of these differences, each will prefer a different way of sustaining the Union. At once sincerity is questioned, and motives are assailed. Actual war coming, blood grows hot, and blood is spilled. Thought is forced from old channels into confusion. Deception breeds and thrives. Confidence dies, and universal suspicion reigns. Each man feels an impulse to kill his neighbor, lest he be first killed by him. Revenge and retaliation follow. And all this, as before said, may be among honest men only. But this is not all. Every foul bird comes abroad, and every dirty reptile rises up. These add crime to confusion. Strong measures, deemed indispensable but harsh at best, such men make worse by mal-administration. Murders for old grudges, and murders for pelf, proceed under any cloak that will best cover for the occasion.

Finally, he had directed General Schofield that the request of the committee regarding elections was proper. The third demand of the Committee of Seventy was granted.

In his own serious advice to Schofield, Lincoln made it plain he had no immediate hope of peace for that region. In the young, blond, whiskered Schofield had been found an administrator who understood Lincoln once writing to him: "If both factions, or neither, shall abuse you, you will probably be about right. Beware of being assailed by one, and praised by the other."

What to do about the Negro and slavery in this Slave

State was covered in three sentences to Schofield: "Allow no part of the Military under your command, to be engaged in either returning fugitive slaves, or in forcing, or enticing slaves from their homes; and, so far as practicable, enforce the same forbearance upon the people . . . Allow no one to enlist colored troops, except upon orders from you, or from here through you. Allow no one to assume the functions of confiscating property, under the law of congress, or other wise, except upon orders from here."

A deepening trend was seen in the Cincinnati *Telegraph and Advocate,* under auspices of the Roman Catholic Archbishop of Cincinnati, in July advising its readers that Negro slavery was virtually abolished; it would oppose on moral and religious grounds all efforts to restore or re-establish it.

The new governor of Kentucky, Thomas E. Bramlette, in his September inaugural spoke against the arming of Negroes; he asked what could be done with such soldiers at the end of the war. He was speaking for those of his Slave State who knew that such soldiers would bring grave problems.

A vision was coming to many that somehow amid the confusions of emancipation proclamations, enforced conscription, habeas corpus, there belonged in the picture many regiments of black men fighting for whatever the war was about. "I want to see 200,000 black soldiers in the field," Charles Francis Adams, Jr.—no radical—wrote to his father, "and then I shall think it time to have peace." From the South now, since Gettysburg and Vicksburg, came less emphasis on the right of secession and the cry more often that the South was in a defensive war.

Habits of stealing and lying changed for the better when freed Negroes came into the contraband camps. So alleged the American Freedmen's Inquiry Commission, headed by Robert Dale Owen, in their report published in June '63, saying, ". . . one of the first acts of the Negroes, when they found themselves free, was to establish schools at their own expense." The former crime of learning to read being no longer a crime, made some of them glad. They were starting churches. Also now that they could be married and have a family life if they chose, some were taking that course. "The Negro is found quite ready to copy whatever he believes are the rights and obligations of what he looks up to as the superior race."

The pathos of mixed bloods, and the fact of a mulatto woman being in more peril from a Northern white soldier than from a black freedman, was recited by the commission. "Many colored women think it more disgraceful to be black than to be illegitimate; for it is especially in regard to white men that their ideas and habits as to this matter are perverted. A case came to the knowledge of the commission, in which a mulatto girl deemed it beneath her to associate with her half sister, a black, the daughter of her mother's husband, her own father being a white man." The commission inserted in its report sentences over which Lincoln, possibly, both laughed and cried as he read: ". . . Our Chief Magistrate would probably be surprised to learn with what reverence, bordering on superstition, he is regarded by these poor people. Recently, at Beaufort, a gang of colored men . . . at work on the wharf, were discussing the qualifications of the President—how he had dispersed their masters, and what he would undoubtedly do hereafter for the colored race—when an aged, white-headed Negro—a 'praise-man' (as the phrase is) amongst them—with all the solemnity of an old prophet, broke forth: *What do you know 'bout Massa Linkum? Massa Linkum be evrywhere. He walk de earth like de Lord.'*"

Chapter 21

Chickamauga — Elections Won, '63

After the drawn battle at Murfreesboro in January '63, General Rosecrans kept the Army of the Cumberland at that same place in Tennessee for six months, fortifying, drilling, setting no troops into motion. Late in June '63, Rosecrans marched his forces through rough and broken country, and by September 9 had, without a battle, maneuvered the Confederate army under Bragg out of Chattanooga and put his own troops into that strategic center. While on this operation, Rosecrans wrote to Lincoln early in August reciting conditions: bad roads, bad weather, cavalry weakness, long hauls for bridge material.

"I think," Lincoln replied, "you must have inferred more than Gen Halleck has intended, as to any dissatisfaction of mine with you . . ." He wrote of anxiety while Rosecrans stayed inactive as Grant was threatened at Vicksburg by Johnston's army, which might any day have been joined by Bragg's army.

In the matter of supplies, road and weather conditions, campaign requisites, what he thought he had to have before he could start fighting, Rosecrans seemed as muddled and querulous as McClellan the year before. The complaints of Rosecrans, however, did not insinuate that jealous plotters and malicious geese at Washington were trying to snare and frustrate him. Lincoln met this personal quality, and never in his letters and telegrams to Rosecrans took on the peremptory manner, the ironic tone, he had latterly used with McClellan. On one slight affair the President telegraphed Rosecrans: "In no case have I intended to censure you, or to question your ability . . . I frequently make mistakes myself, in the many things I am compelled to do hastily." It may have come to Lincoln that into Rosecrans' ear had been poured an offer, by James R. Gilmore, that Horace Greeley and others wanted to run him for President. And Rosecrans had said No, "My place is in the army."

Rosecrans, 44 years old, was born in Kingston, Ohio. Graduating fifth in the class of 1842 at West Point, he served four years as professor of natural philosophy and of engineering at the national academy. He had organized a kerosene manufacturing company just before the war began, quit coal oil and money-making, and served with credit under McClellan in West Virginia; he came through hard fighting at Corinth and Murfreesboro, rated as an able commanding officer, not lacking piety. To his brother, Bishop Rosecrans, the General wrote a letter published in the *Catholic Telegraph* at Cincinnati excoriating Northern "rebel leaders" who foment guerrilla warfare.

The Richmond War Department had arranged for Longstreet with 20,000 troops from the Army of Northern Virginia to be sent by railroad down across the Carolinas and up into far northern Georgia to the help of Bragg. This gave Bragg 70,000 troops as against Rosecrans' 57,000. The two armies grappled at Chickamauga Creek near Crawfish Spring September 19, 1863.

Hay noted: "Sunday morning, the 20th of September, the President showed me Rosecrans' despatches of the day before, detailing the first day's fighting, and promising a complete victory the next day. The President was a little uneasy over the promise."

Late that Sunday afternoon Dana at Chattanooga wired: "My report to-day is of deplorable importance. Chickamauga is as fatal a name in our history as Bull Run." The right and center were shattered. The left wing, under the Union Virginian General George H. Thomas, held. Till sunset, till darkness and night, his 25,000 men held solid on a horseshoe of a rocky hillock against twice their number. One brigade ran out of ammunition and met Longstreet's veterans with the bayonet. Next day Thomas began moving in good order to Chattanooga, Bragg failing to make another attack.

A heavy day's work had been done that Sunday, with Union killed, wounded and missing reckoned at 16,000, Confederate at 18,000, a larger affair in blood loss than Antietam.

Enough news of the battle reached Lincoln that Sunday night so he could not sleep. Welles noted on Monday: "The President came to me this afternoon with the latest news. He was feeling badly. Tells me a dispatch was sent to him at the Soldiers' Home shortly after he got asleep, and so disturbed him that he had no more rest, but arose and came to the city and passed the remainder of the night awake and watchful."

Hay's diary read: "The next morning [September 21] he [the President] came into my bedroom before I was up, & sitting down on my bed said, 'Well, Rosecrans has been whipped, as I feared. I have feared it for several days. I believe I feel trouble in the air before it comes.'" To Rosecrans that day Lincoln sent a telegram: "Be of good cheer. We have unabated confidence in you, and in your soldiers and officers. In the main you must be the judge as to what is to be done . . ."

On the evening of September 23 John Hay rode out by moonlight to Soldiers' Home to bring the President to Washington for a night council of war; Stanton with dark news from Chattanooga was shaken by one of his frenzies of excitement. Hay found the President abed. "I delivered my message to him as he robed himself & he was considerably disturbed. I assured him as far as I could that it meant nothing serious, but he thought otherwise, as it was the first time Stanton had ever sent for him." According to Chase's memorandum of the meeting, much conversation followed, the President and Halleck disinclined to weaken Meade, Seward and Chase decisive for reinforcing Rosecrans.

At 2:30 A.M. September 24, Meade was ordered by telegraph to prepare two army corps, under General Hooker, ready for transport, with five days' cooked provisions, with baggage, artillery, ammunition, horses, to follow. Further appeals came from Rosecrans and Dana; soon the enemy might cut off their communications and supplies. Stanton told Eckert to work out a rail schedule to Chattanooga. At 8 A.M. Eckert reported the troop transport could be done in 15 days. Stanton jumped for joy. "The plan was so well laid and withal so sensible," wrote Bates, "that Lincoln and Stanton both indorsed it." Superintendent Thomas A. Scott of the Pennsylvania Railroad and officers of the Baltimore & Ohio and other railroads were called to Washington, and arrangements completed. Scott went to Louisville, a midway

point, kept the wires hot with brief messages; from Beale-
ton, Virginia, to Chattanooga, Tennessee, 1,233 miles,
23,000 men were transported in 11½ days.

To Mrs. Lincoln at the Fifth Avenue Hotel in New York,
the President September 24 telegraphed as to Chickamauga
that the Union army was worsted mainly in yielding ground.
"According to rebel accounts . . . they lost six killed, and
eight wounded. Of the killed, one Major Genl. and five Brigadiers, including your brother-in-law, Helm." Now Lincoln
wrote for his wife's stepmother at Lexington, Kentucky:
"Allow Mrs. Robert S. Todd, widow, to go south and bring
her daughter, Mrs. General B. Hardin Helm, with her children, north to Kentucky."

Every day while Rosecrans had operated around Chattanooga that month the President had been keeping an
anxious watch on East Tennessee, a region of mountaineers
and hill people who owned no slaves and whose hearts,
many of them, Lincoln knew were with the Union cause. In
that region kinfolk of his had lived and died.

While Rosecrans marched toward Chattanooga, and Lincoln was urging Burnside with the Army of the Ohio to take
Knoxville and occupy East Tennessee, once more a delegation from that region called at the White House to lay their
wrongs before the President. And the President did not have
the heart to face them and talk with them. He wrote them
a groaning and bitter letter, saying he knew well what they
had been waiting for when on successive days they sent
cards and notes asking an interview which he refused. "I
knew it was the same true, and painful story, which Gov.
Johnson, Mr. Maynard, Dr. Clements and others have been
telling me for more than two years. I also knew that meeting you could do no good; because I have all the while
done, and shall continue to do the best for you I could, and
can. I do as much for East Tennessee as I would, or could,
if my own home, and family were in Knoxville." He mentioned the difficulties of getting an army into the region and
keeping it there. No one could fail to see those difficulties
"unless it may be those who are driven mad and blind by
their sufferings."

Then in three weeks, early in September, Burnside and the Army of the Ohio had crossed the Tennessee line, entered Kingston, and marched into Knoxville to be met by cheering crowds. Flags long hidden were flashed out into sunlight, officers and soldiers welcomed into homes.

Though repeatedly ordered to join Rosecrans, Burnside delayed, and September 25 Lincoln wrote him: ". . . On the 19th. you telegraph once from Knoxville, and twice from Greenville, acknowledging receipt of order, and saying you will hurry support to Rosecrans. On the 20th. you telegraph again from Knoxville, saying you will do all you can, and are hurrying troops to Rosecrans. On the 21st. you telegraph from Morristown, saying you will hurry support to Rosecrans; and now your despatch of the 23rd. comes in from Carter's Station, still farther away from Rosecrans."

The letter was a patient and weary framing of the query to Burnside "How can you be so stupid?" Having written it, Lincoln delayed sending it. Then he decided not to send it at all. Instead he sent Burnside two telegrams suggesting that troops be rushed to Rosecrans at Chattanooga.

Meantime came charges that three major generals, McCook, Crittenden, Negley, had, during the Chickamauga battle, sought personal safety or had mismanaged their forces. The President issued orders for a court of inquiry. The court met, heard evidence and cleared the generals of conduct unbecoming to officers.

Rosecrans under strain was cracking, putting into telegrams to Lincoln many complaints of poor communications and subsistence, and such generalties as "Our future is not bright." In a telegram October 12 Lincoln tried heartening Rosecrans: "You and Burnside now have him [the enemy] by the throat, and he must break your hold, or perish . . . Sherman *is* coming to you."

The Confederates had a hold on the Tennessee River by which they blocked water transport of food and supplies for Rosecrans' army; and the long rough wagon route that met rail connections with Nashville was threatened. The Dana reports ran gloomier that second week in October; Rosecrans was "dawdling" while catastrophe hung close, starvation or disorderly retreat. And on October 16: "The incapacity of the commander is astonishing, and it often seems difficult to believe him of sound mind. His imbecility appears to be contagious."

The same day Halleck wrote to Grant at Cairo, Illinois: "You will receive herewith the orders of the President of the United States placing you in command of the Departments of the Ohio, Cumberland and Tennessee." Thus Lincoln put Grant at the head of all military operations west of the Alleghenies. "It is left optional with you to supersede General G. H. Thomas or not."

After a personal conference at Indianapolis with Stanton, Grant, by a rail route and a final horseback trip of 55 miles, arrived at Chattanooga October 23. Rosecrans had left October 20 to report at Cincinnati for further orders. To Hay October 24 the President said that ever since Chickamauga Rosecrans had been "confused and stunned like a duck hit on the head."

George Henry Thomas, "the Rock of Chickamauga," was a peculiar instance, a Virginia-born West Pointer who stayed with the Union. Appointed a colonel in April '61, and with others required to renew his oath of allegiance to the U.S. Government, Thomas replied, "I don't care; I would just as soon take the oath before each meal during my life if the department saw fit to order it." Thomas, now 47, saw service in Indian wars and in the Mexican War, was an artillery instructor at West Point, a cavalry major. At Mill Springs Thomas had shown a flash, at Murfreesboro fire and flint, at Chickamauga granite steadiness and volcanic resistance. Slowly in the trampling and grinding of events George Henry Thomas was arriving at his own.

A laconic streak underlay the sluggish outside of him. In a council of generals at Murfreesboro, when asked by Rosecrans to protect a proposed retreat, he woke from a nap to say, "This army can't retreat." In a like council at Chickamauga he dozed, and only came out of the doze to mutter repeatedly, "Strengthen the left," almost as though he read in a crystal ball the terrible necessity of the next day, when everything crumbled except himself and the left wing. This

brevity functioned again when after a battle he was asked
whether the dead should be buried in the order of the states
they came from. "No, no," said Old Pap Thomas. "Mix
them up. I am tired of State rights."

Now Thomas was joined with Sherman and other tried
commanders, with Grant as chief of the West, with forces
massed at Chattanooga near the Alabama and Georgia state
lines, wedging toward the Deep South as if hoping to cut it
in two.

Meade September 24 was writing his wife: "I was summoned to Washington and informed that the President considered my army too large for a merely defensive one . . .
The President is the best judge of where the armies can be
best employed, and if he chooses to place this army strictly
on the defensive, I have no right to object or murmur . . .
There still existed a feverish anxiety that I should try and
do something."

One staff man wrote that though the newspapers were
mentioning "the fine autumn weather" for fighting, Meade
was not going to risk another Fredericksburg. Lincoln, however, was willing to take that risk, and October 16 wrote to
Halleck his guess that Lee, overestimating the number of
soldiers stripped from Meade for Western duty, might fight
in the open. The President made a proposal for Meade to
consider, an offer at no time previously made to a general in
the field: "If Gen. Meade can now attack him [Lee] on a
field no worse than equal for us, and will do so with all the
skill and courage, which he, his officers and men possess,
the honor will be his if he succeeds, and the blame may be
mine if he fails."

The offer of Lincoln to Meade reached the press and was
published. Lincoln evidently wished it made known that, as
the newspapers said, he had ordered Meade "to pursue after
Lee's army, to find the enemy, and to fight him wherever
found; and that he [the President] would be responsible for
Meade's defeat, if he should be defeated." It seemed as
though Lincoln took this step so there could be no possible
mistake in the public mind that he wanted fighting, had

ordered fighting, and would blame no commander if there was fighting that brought more useless slaughter. A hostile and defeatist press poured its scorn on "this silly and most unmilitary order," as the Chicago *Times* termed it in an article headed "Exposure of Lincoln's Folly."

But Lee had again outguessed Meade, as Meade humbly and frankly confessed to his wife in a note from Warrenton, Virginia, four days later: "Lee has retired across the Rappahannock, after completely destroying the railroad on which I depend for my supplies. His object is to prevent my advance, and in the meantime send more troops to Bragg. This was a deep game, and I am free to admit that in the playing of it he has got the advantage of me."

When Lincoln groaned to Hay or Welles, or to himself alone, over the inaction of the Army of the Potomac, it was not because of any trickery, evasion or politics of that army's commander. For Meade had not asked command. It had been thrust on him. And always with the gravest courtesy he made it plain to Lincoln, Halleck and Stanton that if they believed he was "too slow or prudent," as he phrased it, he would willingly fight under someone else. On October 23 he wrote to Mrs. Meade: "Yesterday I received an order to repair to Washington, to see the President. I ... was detained so late that I remained there all night ... The President was, as he always is, very considerate and kind. He found no fault with my operations, although it was very evident he was disappointed that I had not got a battle out of Lee. He coincided with me that there was not much to be gained by any farther advance; but General Halleck was very urgent that something should be done, but what that something was he did not define."

From the Southern press and home strategists, Lee was receiving the same sort of criticism as that heaped on Meade in the North. Like Meade, he was too slow and too prudent, ran many an editorial. They were both Christian gentlemen, Meade and Lee, clean, reverent and pious, each strict in the observance of Episcopal forms, praying regularly to the same God while they led their hosts seeking to mangle and eviscerate each other.

In promoting Admiral Dahlgren, Lincoln gave his approval to aggressive tactics at Charleston, whatever the increased cost. During six days in August, a fleet of monitors and gunboats bombarded Charleston; an army of 18,000 troops waited while 12 batteries of heavy rifled cannon opened fire at a two-mile distance; in one 40-minute period they dropped 120,000 pounds of projectiles into the defending forts. A storming column of Negro soldiers led by the white Colonel Robert Gould Shaw, of an old and distinguished Boston family, captured Fort Wagner. Shaw, "the blue-eyed child of fortune," crying, "Onward, boys!" fell dead from bullets, and became an enshrined memory and a symbol to the antislavery forces of the North.

Lincoln read the news telegraphed by the commanding general, August 24: "Fort Sumter is today a shapeless and harmless mass of ruins." As later news trickled in it turned out that the much-hated city still serenely held her own. And though Fort Sumter seemed to be a ruin, it kept a garrison. For many months Charleston was let alone.

From cities and towns of the North a steady stream of men and boys in blue moved south, always south, month by month filling gaps in the ranks. The machinery of the draft was working. Among generals it was commented that the substitutes, bounty men, human material pressed into service by the enrolling officers, were not as good soldier stuff as the earlier recruits of the war.

To the President came many instances of Federal judges releasing drafted men through habeas corpus proceedings. The Cabinet September 14 saw Lincoln in a warlike mood, going so far as to say he might have to arrest a few Federal judges. "The President was very determined," noted Welles, "and intimated that he would not only enforce the law, but if Judge Lowry [Lowrie] and others continued to interfere and interrupt the draft he would send them after Vallandigham."

Of another Cabinet session next morning Chase recorded it came out that two U.S. court judges in Pennsylvania—Cadwalader at Philadelphia and McCandless at Pittsburgh—had released more drafted men by far than all the state courts put together. Stanton's view was that these two Federal judges had taken a hand in "some very gross proceedings, under color of judicial authority, manifestly intended to interfere with the recruiting and maintenance of the army."

On September 15 was issued a proclamation as finally drafted by Seward. Solemnly it was made known by the President that "the privilege of the writ of *habeas corpus* is suspended throughout the United States" and this suspension would continue till modified or revoked by a later proclamation. A sonorous pronouncement it would be when read by a provost marshal, in support of the marshal's saying in effect to the judge, "I'm going to take this drafted man away with me and put him in the army and your court can't stop me because I have the United States Army and Navy backing me."

Hay wrote to Nicolay August 7 of Washington being "dismal now as a defaced tombstone." Part of the dismal air came from the conscription. On Executive Mansion stationery Hay wrote: "The draft fell pretty heavily in our end of town. William Johnston (cullud) was taken while polishing the Executive boots . . . A clerk in the War Department named Ramsey committed suicide on hearing he was drafted."

While the President in early October was dealing with habeas corpus, with the committee of radicals from Missouri and Kansas, with Burnside in Tennessee, Rosecrans at Chattanooga and Meade in Virginia, besides many routine matters, Seward took on the work of writing a Thanksgiving proclamation, which the President signed. Over the signature of A. Lincoln came the pronouncement, "I do therefore invite my fellow citizens in every part of the United States, and also those who are at sea and those who are sojourning in foreign lands, to set apart and observe the last Thursday of November next, as a day of Thanksgiving and Praise to our beneficent Father who dwelleth in the Heavens."

The changed air of expectation that the Union cause would yet win, the shift from the gloom of the first half of

'63, made the basis for thanksgiving. With the Gettysburg and Vicksburg victories, one of them ending Confederate hopes of winning by invasion of the North, the other sending the Mississippi "unvexed to the sea," many considered the war at an end or nearly so. Intangible psychic factors played on both sides. The North wondered why the South didn't quit.

The South dug deeper into itself for new motives and began fighting with despair for honor, for a mystic pennant, for a lost cause that could eventually be looked back on as having had a clean death. "The drums that beat for the advance into Pennsylvania seemed to many of us to be beating the funeral march of the dead Confederacy," later wrote General Daniel H. Hill, one of Lee's ablest lieutenants, now in the West with Bragg. "Duty, however, was to be done faithfully and unflinchingly to the last . . . The waning fortunes of the Confederacy were developing a vast amount of 'latent unionism' in the breasts of the original secessionists, those fiery zealots who in '61 proclaimed that 'one Southern could whip three Yankees.' The negroes and the fire-eaters with 'changed hearts' were now most excellent spies."

Both Lee and Davis, after the July defeats, issued appeals to soldiers to come back to the army. Davis offered pardons to officers and men absent without leave who would return in 20 days. Wives, mothers, sisters, daughters of the Confederacy were beseeched by the Richmond head of their Government, "If all now absent return to the ranks you will equal in numbers the invaders."

Thousands of Confederate deserters in the mountains of Alabama fought off cavalry sent to arrest them. The Confederate Bureau of Ordnance asked for the church bells of Georgia to be melted and remolded for war. One gold dollar bought ten paper Confederate dollars. A Louisiana father, beginning to doubt the Southern orators, was writing his son in the Confederate Army, "This war was got up drunk but they will have to settle it sober."

In a call for 300,000 more troops October 16, 1863, Lincoln said the new men were wanted to follow up and clinch the winning streak of Union armies that summer.

The document stipulated that quotas would be *required* from the various states. In reality it was another executive order for a draft. Between provost marshals and various state officials, particularly Governor Seymour of New York, there began discussions and quarrels as to methods of drafting. The war, the draft, habeas corpus suspension, had been denounced at five overflow meetings in and around Cooper Union in New York City June 3, 1863, at a Peace Convention. "God did not intend that we should succeed in this war," said the convention's address to the public. "Had He intended it He would not have placed in command a Lincoln with such coadjutors as Butler or Burnside." As the address was read to the convention, "the groans and hisses for the President, and the cheers for Vallandigham and peace were specially vigorous," said the New York *Times*. Bartenders in saloons roundabout served patrons with "Jeff Davis cocktails," "Stonewall punches," "Sumter bumpters."

Under the heading "Lincoln to Be Declared Perpetual President," the *Crisis* October 7 said, "It is now stated that a bill has been prepared and will be placed before the next Congress declaring Lincoln President while the war lasts."

The fast and furious fall campaign in the Buckeye State revolved around Lincoln. Ohio mass meetings at which orators excoriated the President, and with metaphors nailed his hide to the barn door, drew thousands of people. Crowds did not number 30,000 and 40,000 as often as the Democratic press claimed, yet the Copperhead clans did gather in tens of thousands. And the Union party meetings drew tens of thousands. Not since the Lincoln-Douglas debates had the prairie electorate gathered in such numbers and with so high an excitement. George E. Pugh, candidate for lieutenant governor, shouted from the campaign platform that if his running mate, Vallandigham, were elected governor there would be "fifty thousand fully armed and equipped freemen of Ohio to receive their Governor-elect at the Canadian line and escort him to the State House to see that he takes the oath of office."

On October 13, Election Day in Ohio and Pennsylvania, Welles called at the White House, and noted, "The President says he feels nervous." The wires that night clicked off news that the Ohio Copperhead ticket had the votes of 185,000 citizens and 2,200 soldiers of Ohio. However, John Brough of the Union party was elected governor by a majority of 61,920 in the citizen vote and 39,179 in the soldier ballots, a total of over 101,000. Pennsylvania returns gave Governor Curtin re-election by a 41,000 majority. A letter from General McClellan endorsing Curtin's opponent had had little effect.

Welles on October 14 found Lincoln relieved of the gloom of the day before. "He told me he had more anxiety in regard to the election results of yesterday than he had in 1860 when he was chosen. He could not, he said, have believed four years ago that one genuine American voter would, or could be induced to, vote for such a man as Vallandigham."

At the Maryland election the Governor's party, Conservative Union, was sunk with a vote of 15,984 as against 36,360 for the candidates of the Unconditional Union or Emancipation party. Four on the latter ticket were among the five new Congressmen elected, and the Emancipationists won a majority in both houses of the legislature.

In the Border Slave States of Delaware and Kentucky the Union party also won, while in Missouri the Union Emancipationist radicals swept into so many legislative seats that the two U.S. Senatorships were divided between Union party factions, one to B. Gratz Brown, a leading radical, the other to John B. Henderson, a conservative. Lincoln was pleased. The event fitted the turmoil. He wired friends at Jefferson City, Missouri: "Yours saying Brown and Henderson are elected Senators, is received. I understand, this is one and one. If so, it is knocking heads together to some purpose."

In all the Northern States except New Jersey, the Union party ticket swept the field. A Chicago newspaper exulted: "Everywhere it has been a slaughter of Copperheads. Springfield, Ill., went Union by 138, a gain of 440 since 1862." In the State House at Springfield sat Governor Dick Yates, who when lit up was a blunt and familiar talker. In

the campaign he had made a speech to a Methodist conference at Springfield and was quoted: "I have visited Old
Abe and urged him to use more radical measures and he
has said to me, 'Never mind, Dick, it will be all right yet.
Hold still and see the salvation of the Lord!' (Loud and
prolonged cheering, stamping of feet, etc.)" The speech
had something, and was argued about in the tall-grass
weeklies, even the New York *Herald* saying that immense
applause from the people had greeted "the above Cromwel-
lian phrase."

Chapter 22

Lincoln Speaks at Gettysburg

A printed invitation notified Lincoln that on Thursday, November 19, 1863, exercises would be held for the dedication of a National Soldiers' Cemetery at Gettysburg.

The duties of orator of the day had fallen on Edward
Everett. Born in 1794, he had been U.S. Senator, governor
of Massachusetts, member of Congress, Secretary of State
under Fillmore, Minister to Great Britain, Phi Beta Kappa
poet at Harvard, professor of Greek at Harvard, president
of Harvard. His wife was Charlotte Gray Brooks, daughter
of Peter Chardon Brooks, first of American marine and
life-insurance millionaires. Serene stars had watched over
their home life and children until Everett's wife was sent to
a private retreat, incurably insane. A lifelong friendship
took root between him and her father; they shared a sorrow.

The Union of States was a holy concept to Everett, and
the slavery issue secondary, though when president of Harvard from 1846 to 1849 he refused to draw the color line,
saying in the case of a Negro applicant, Beverly Williams,
that "If this boy passes the examinations, he will be admitted." Not often was he so provocative. Suave, hand-

somely venerable in his 69th year, Everett was a natural choice of the Pennsylvania commissioners. He notified them that he would appear for the Gettysburg dedication November 19.

Lincoln meanwhile, in reply to the printed invitation, sent word to the commissioners that he would be present at the ceremonies. The commissioners then considered whether the President should be asked to deliver an address. Clark E. Carr of Galesburg, Illinois, representing his state on the Board of Commissioners, noted that the decision of the board to invite Lincoln to speak was "an afterthought."

David Wills of Gettysburg, as the special agent of Governor Curtin and also acting for the several states, by letter informed Lincoln, ". . . I am authorized by the Governors of the various States to invite you to be present and participate in these ceremonies . . . It is the desire that after the oration, you, as Chief Executive of the nation, formally set apart these grounds to their sacred use by a few appropriate remarks." "The invitation," wrote Carr, "was not settled upon and sent to Mr. Lincoln until the second of November, more than six weeks after Mr. Everett had been invited to speak, and but little more than two weeks before the exercises were held."

Lamon noted that Lincoln wrote part of his intended Gettysburg address in Washington, covered a sheet of foolscap paper with a memorandum of it, and before taking it out of his hat and reading it to Lamon he said it was not at all satisfactory to him. He had been too busy to give it the time he would like to.

The armies of Meade and Grant required attention. And there were such unforeseen affairs as the marriage of Kate Chase, daughter of the Secretary of the Treasury, at the most brilliant wedding the new Northern regime had as yet put on in Washington. The bridegroom was Governor William Sprague of Rhode Island, handsome of figure, an heir of wealth, iron and textile manufacturer, railroad and bank president, artillery officer with a record of a horse shot from under him at Bull Run, U.S. Senator by election in the spring of '63. He was 33 years old, had paid $11,000 for one of his string of horses, and his bride of 28 had beauty plus wit and a gift for politics. Lincoln, attending alone, and bringing a dainty fan as a present for the bride, probably went because that was better than to let talk run as to why he did not go. He dropped in and left early.

Two men, in the weeks just before the Gettysburg ceremonies, had done their best to make him see himself as a world spokesman of democracy, popular government, the mass of people as opposed to aristocrats, classes and special interests. John Murray Forbes, having read Lincoln's lively stump-speech letter to the Springfield, Illinois, mass meeting, wrote to Sumner September 3, "I delight in the President's plain letter to plain people!" Forbes followed this five days later with a letter which Sumner carried to the White House and handed to Lincoln.

An aristocracy ruled the South and controlled it for war, believed Forbes, pointing to "the aristocratic class who own twenty negroes and upwards" as numbering "about 28,000 persons, which is about the 178th part of 5,000,000" whites. So Forbes urged, "Let the people North and South see this line clearly defined between the people and the aristocrats, and the war will be over! Bonaparte, when under the republic, fighting despots of Europe, did as much by his bulletins as he did by his bayonets. You," Forbes urged the President, "have the same opportunity . . . My suggestion, then, is that you should seize an early opportunity and any subsequent chance, to teach your great audience of plain people that the war is not the North against the South, but the people against the aristocrats."

This same idea Forbes wrote to William Evans, an English liberal, who was to call on the President. "I wish you could make him see and feel," said Forbes, "that you and Bright and others represent the democratic element in Great Britain, and that you look upon him as fighting the battle of democracy for all the world! I wish our people understood this as well as yours do!" And William Evans after seeing Lincoln wrote Forbes November 3: "Your suggestions were duly attended to."

Thus while Lincoln shaped his speech to be made at Gettysburg he did not lack specific advice to stand up and be a world spokesman. Some newspapers now had it that the President was going to make a stump speech over the graves of the Gettysburg dead as a political play. Talk ran in Washington that by attending Governor Curtin's "show" the President would strengthen himself with the Curtin faction without alienating the opposing Cameron clique.

Though the Gettysburg dedication was to be under interstate auspices, it had tremendous national significance for Lincoln; on the platform would be the state governors whose co-operation with him was of vast importance. Also widely mouthed and printed had been the slander and libel that on his visit to the battlefield of Antietam nearly a year before he had laughed obscenely at his own funny stories and called on Lamon to sing a cheap comic song. Perhaps he might go to Gettysburg and let it be seen how he demeaned himself on a somber landscape of sacrifice.

His personal touch with Gettysburg, by telegraph, mail, courier and by a throng of associations, made it a place of great realities to him. Just after the battle there, a woman had come to his office, the doorman saying she had been "crying and taking on" for several days trying to see the President. Her husband and three sons were in the army. On part of her husband's pay she had lived for a time, till money from him stopped coming. She was hard put to scrape a living and needed one of her boys to help.

The President listened to her, standing at a fireplace, hands behind him, head bowed, motionless. The woman finished her plea. Slowly and almost as if talking to himself alone the words came and only those words: "I have two, and you have none." He crossed the room, wrote an order for the military discharge of one of her sons. On a special sheet of paper he wrote full and detailed instructions where to go and what to say in order to get her boy back.

In a few days the doorman told the President the same woman was again on hand crying and taking on. "Let her in," was the word. She had found doors opening to her and officials ready to help on seeing the President's written words she carried. She had located her boy's camp, regiment, company. She had found him, yes, wounded at Gettysburg, dying in a hospital, and had followed him to the grave. And, she begged, would the President now give her the next one of her boys?

As before he stood at the fireplace, hands behind him, head bent low, motionless. Slowly and almost as if talking to himself alone the words came and as before only those words: "I have two, and you have none." He crossed the room to his desk and began writing. As though nothing else was to do she followed, stood by his chair as he wrote, put her hand on the President's head, smoothed his thick and disorderly hair with motherly fingers. He signed an order giving her the next of her boys, stood up, put the priceless paper in her hand as he choked out the one word, "There!" and with long quick steps was gone from the room with her sobs and cries of thanks in his ears.

Thus the Kentuckian, James Speed, gathered the incident and told it. By many strange ways Gettysburg was to Lincoln a fact in crimson mist.

Thaddeus Stevens said in November '63 that Lincoln was a "dead card" in the political deck. He favored Chase as a more thoroughgoing antislavery man for the next President, and hearing that Lincoln and Seward were going to Gettysburg, but not Chase, he clipped his words, "The dead going to eulogize the dead."

On November 17 the President issued a little proclamation fixing a township line "within the City of Omaha" as the starting point for the Union Pacific Railway. Congress had made it his duty to do this.

The Gettysburg speech was shaping at the same time that Lincoln was preparing his annual message to Congress, assembling it in less than three weeks. In that message he would point to "actual commencement of work upon the Pacific railroad," his own act of fixing an initial point being the most tangible part of the commencement.

When Lincoln boarded the train for Gettysburg November 18, his best chum in the world, Tad, lay sick abed and the doctors not sure what ailed him. The mother still mourned for Willie and was hysterical about Tad. But the President felt imperative duty called him to Gettysburg.

Provost Marshal General Fry as a War Department escort came to the White House, but the President was late in getting into the carriage for the drive to the station. They had no time to lose, Fry remarked. Lincoln said he felt like an Illinois man who was going to be hanged and as the man passed along the road on the way to the gallows the crowds kept pushing into the way and blocking the passage. The condemned man at last called out, "Boys, you needn't be in such a hurry to get ahead, there won't be any fun till I get there."

Flags and red, white and blue bunting decorated the four-car special train. Aboard were three Cabinet members, Seward, Usher and Blair, Nicolay and Hay, Army and Navy representatives, newspapermen, the French and Italian Ministers and attachés. The rear third of the last coach had a drawing room, where from time to time the President talked with nearly everyone aboard as they came and went. Approaching Hanover Junction, he arose and said, "Gentlemen, this is all very pleasant, but the people will expect me to say something to them tomorrow, and I must give the matter some thought." He then returned to the rear room of the car.

An elderly gentleman got on the train and, shaking hands, told the President he had lost a son at Little Round Top at Gettysburg. The President answered he feared a visit to that spot would open fresh wounds, and yet if the end of sacrifice had been reached "we could give thanks even amidst our tears." They quoted from his unburdening to this old man: "When I think of the sacrifices of life yet to be offered, and the hearts and homes yet to be made desolate before this dreadful war is over, my heart is like lead within me, and I feel at times like hiding in deep darkness." At one stop a little girl lifted to an open window thrust a bunch of rosebuds into the car. "Flowerth for the President." Lincoln stepped over, bent down, kissed her face. "You are a little rosebud yourself."

At sundown the train pulled into Gettysburg and Lincoln was driven to the Wills residence. A sleepy little country town of 3,500 was overflowing with human pulses again. Private homes were filled with notables and nondescripts. Hundreds slept on the floors of hotels. Military bands blared till late in the night serenading whomsoever. The weather was mild and the moon up for those who chose to go a-roaming. Serenaders called on the President and heard him: "In my position it is sometimes important that I should not say foolish things. [A voice: "If you can help it."] It very often happens that the only way to help it is to say nothing at all. Believing that is my present condition this evening, I must beg of you to excuse me from addressing you further."

At dinner in the Wills home that evening Lincoln met Edward Everett, Governor Curtin and others. About 11 o'clock, he gathered his sheets of paper and went next door for a half-hour with his Secretary of State. Whether Seward made slight or material alterations in the text was known only to Lincoln and Seward. It was midnight or later that Lincoln went to sleep. He slept better for having a telegram from Stanton reporting there was no real war news and "On inquiry Mrs. Lincoln informs me that your son is better this evening."

Fifteen thousand, some said 30,000 or 50,000, people were on Cemetery Hill for the exercises next day when the procession from Gettysburg arrived afoot and horseback—members of the U.S. Government, the Army and Navy, governors of states, mayors of cities, a regiment of troops, hospital corps, telegraph company representatives, Knights Templar, Masonic Fraternity, Odd Fellows and other benevolent associations, the press, fire departments, citizens of Pennsylvania and other states. At ten o'clock Lincoln in a black suit, high silk hat and white gloves came out of the Wills residence, mounted a horse, and held a reception on horseback. At 11 the parade began to move. Clark

E. Carr, just behind the President, believed he noticed that the President sat erect and looked majestic to begin with and then got to thinking so that his body leaned forward, his arms hung limp, his head bent far down.

A long telegram from Stanton at ten o'clock had been handed him. Burnside seemed safe though threatened at Knoxville, Grant was starting a big battle at Chattanooga, and "Mrs. Lincoln reports your son's health as a great deal better and he will be out today."

The march began. "Mr. Lincoln was mounted upon a young and beautiful chestnut horse, the largest in the Cumberland Valley," wrote Lieutenant Cochrane. This seemed the first occasion that anyone had looked at the President mounted with a feeling that just the right horse had been picked to match his physical length.

The march was over in 15 minutes. But Mr. Everett, the orator of the day, had not arrived. Bands played till noon. Mr. Everett arrived. On the platform sat Governors Curtin of Pennsylvania, Bradford of Maryland, Morton of Indiana, Seymour of New York, Parker of New Jersey, Dennison of Ohio, with ex-Governor Tod and Governor-elect Brough of Ohio, Edward Everett and his daughter, Major Generals Schenck, Stahel, Doubleday and Couch, Brigadier General Gibbon and Provost Marshal General Fry, foreign Ministers, members of Congress, Colonel Ward Hill Lamon, Secretary Usher, and the President of the United States with Secretary Seward and Postmaster General Blair immediately at his left.

The U.S. House chaplain, the Reverend Thomas H. Stockton, offered a prayer while the thousands stood with uncovered heads. Benjamin B. French, officer in charge of buildings in Washington, introduced the Honorable Edward Everett, who rose, bowed low to Lincoln, saying, "Mr. President." Lincoln responded, "Mr. Everett."

The orator of the day then stood in silence before a crowd that stretched to limits that would test his voice. Beyond and around were the wheat fields, the meadows, the peach orchards, long slopes of land, and five and seven miles further the contemplative blue ridge of a low mountain range. His eyes could sweep all this as he faced the audience. He had taken note of it in his prepared address. "Overlooking these broad fields now reposing from the labors of the waning year, the mighty Alleghanies dimly towering before us, the graves of our brethren beneath our feet, it is with hesitation that I raise my poor voice to break the eloquent silence of God and Nature . . . As my eye ranges over the fields whose sods were so lately moistened by the blood of gallant and loyal men, I feel, as never before, how truly it was said of old that it is sweet and becoming to die for one's country."

He gave an outline of how the war began, traversed decisive features of the three days' battles at Gettysburg, discussed the doctrine of state sovereignty and denounced it, drew parallels from European history, and came to his peroration quoting Pericles on dead patriots: "The whole earth is the sepulchre of illustrious men." He had spoken for one hour and 57 minutes, some said a trifle over two hours, repeating almost word for word an address that occupied nearly two newspaper pages.

Everett came to his closing sentence without a faltering voice: "Down to the latest period of recorded time, in the glorious annals of our common country there will be no brighter page than that which relates THE BATTLES OF GETTYSBURG." It was the effort of his life and embodied the perfections of the school of oratory in which he had spent his career. His poise, and chiefly some quality of inside goodheartedness, held most of his audience to him.

The Baltimore Glee Club sang an ode written for the occasion by Benjamin B. French. Having read Everett's address, Lincoln knew when the moment drew near for him to speak. He took out his own manuscript from a coat pocket, put on his steel-bowed glasses, stirred in his chair, looked over the manuscript, and put it back in his pocket. The Baltimore Glee Club finished. Ward Hill Lamon rose and spoke the words "The President of the United States," who rose, and holding in one hand the two sheets of paper at which he occasionally glanced, delivered the address in his high-pitched and clear-carrying voice. The Cincinnati *Commercial* reporter wrote, "The President rises slowly, draws from his pocket a paper, and, when commotion subsides, in a sharp, unmusical treble voice, reads the brief and pithy remarks." Hay wrote in his diary, "The President, in a firm, free way, with more grace than is his wont, said his half dozen words of consecration." Charles Hale of the Boston *Advertiser*, also officially representing Governor Andrew of Massachusetts, had notebook and pencil in hand, took down the slow-spoken words of the President:

Fourscore and seven years ago, our fathers brought forth upon this continent a new nation, conceived in liberty and dedicated to the proposition that all men are created equal.

Now we are engaged in a great civil war, testing whether that nation—or any nation, so conceived and so dedicated—can long endure.

We are met on a great battle-field of that war. We are met to dedicate a portion of it as the final resting place of those who have given their lives that that nation might live.

It is altogether fitting and proper that we should do this.

But, in a larger sense, we cannot dedicate, we cannot consecrate, we cannot hallow, this ground. The brave men, living and dead, who struggled here, have consecrated it, far above our power to add or to detract.

The world will very little note nor long remember what we say here; but it can never forget what they did here.

It is for us, the living, rather, to be dedicated, here, to the unfinished work that they have thus far so nobly carried on. It is rather for us to be here dedicated to the great task remaining before us; that from these honored dead we take increased devotion to that

cause for which they here gave the last full measure
of devotion; that we here highly resolve that these dead
shall not have died in vain; that the nation shall, under
God, have a new birth of freedom, and that government of the people, by the people, for the people, shall
not perish from the earth.

In the written copy of his speech from which he read
Lincoln used the phrase "our poor power." In other copies
of the speech which he wrote out later he again used the
phrase "our poor power." So it was evident that he meant
to use the word "poor" when speaking to his audience, but
he omitted it. Also in the copy held in his hands while facing the audience he had not written the words "under God,"
though he did speak those words and include them in later
copies which he wrote. Therefore the words "under God"
were decided upon after he wrote the text the night before
at the Wills residence.

The New York *Tribune* and many other newspapers indicated "(Applause.)" at five places in the address and
"(Long continued applause.)" at the end. The applause,
however, according to most of the responsible witnesses,
was formal, a tribute to the occasion. Ten sentences had
been spoken in less than three minutes. A photographer had
made ready to record a great historic moment, had bustled
about with his dry plates, his black box on a tripod, and
before he had his head under the hood for an exposure,
the President had said "by the people, for the people" and
the nick of time was past for a photograph.

The New York *Tribune* man and other like observers
merely reported the words of the address with the one preceding sentence: "The dedicatory remarks were then delivered by the President." Strictly, no address as such was
on the program from him. He was down for a few "dedicatory remarks." Lamon wrote that Lincoln told him just
after delivering the speech that he had regret over not having prepared it with greater care. "Lamon, that speech
won't *scour*. It is a flat failure and the people are disap-

pointed." On the farms where Lincoln grew up, when wet soil stuck to the mold board of a plow they said it didn't "scour."

The nearby *Patriot and Union* of Harrisburg took its fling: "The President succeeded on this occasion because he acted without sense and without constraint in a panorama that was gotten up more for the benefit of his party than for the glory of the nation and the honor of the dead . . . We pass over the silly remarks of the President; for the credit of the nation we are willing that the veil of oblivion shall be dropped over them and that they shall no more be repeated or thought of."

The Chicago *Times* held that "Mr. Lincoln did most foully traduce the motives of the men who were slain at Gettysburg" in his reference to "a new birth of freedom," adding, "They gave their lives to maintain the old government, and the only Constitution and Union . . . The cheek of every Ameircan must tingle with shame as he reads the silly, flat, and dish-watery utterances of the man who has to be pointed out to intelligent foreigners as the President of the United States."

The Chicago *Tribune* had a reporter who telegraphed (unless some editor who read the address added his own independent opinion) a sentence: "The dedicatory remarks of President Lincoln will live among the annals of man." The Cincinnati *Gazette* reporter added after the text of the address, "That this was the right thing in the right place, and a perfect thing in every respect, was the universal encomium."

The American correspondent of the London *Times* wrote that "the ceremony was rendered ludicrous by some of the sallies of that poor President Lincoln . . . Anything more dull and commonplace it would not be easy to produce." Count Gurowski wrote in his diary, "Lincoln spoke, with one eye to a future platform and to re-election."

The Philadelphia *Evening Bulletin* said thousands who would not read the elaborate oration of Mr. Everett would read the President's few words "and not many will do it

without a moistening of the eye and a swelling of the heart."
The Providence *Journal* reminded readers of the saying that
the hardest thing in the world is to make a good five-minute
speech: "We know not where to look for a more admirable
speech than the brief one which the President made at the
close of Mr. Everett's oration."

Lincoln had spoken of an idea, a proposition, a concept,
worth dying for, which brought from a Richmond newspaper a countering question and answer, "For what are we
fighting? An abstraction."

The Springfield *Republican* comment ran: "Surpassingly
fine as Mr. Everett's oration was in the Gettysburg consecration, the rhetorical honors of the occasion were won by
President Lincoln. His little speech is a perfect gem; deep in
feeling, compact in thought and expression, and tasteful
and elegant in every word and comma. Then it has the merit
of unexpectedness in its verbal perfection and beauty. We
had grown so accustomed to homely and imperfect phrase
in his productions that we had come to think it was the
law of his utterance. But this shows he can talk handsomely
as well as act sensibly. Turn back and read it over, it will
repay study as a model speech."

"The Lounger" in *Harper's Weekly* inquired why the
ceremony at Gettysburg was one of the most striking events
of the war. "The President and the Cabinet were there,
with famous soldiers and civilians. The oration by Mr. Everett was smooth and cold . . . The few words of the President were from the heart to the heart. They can not be read,
even, without kindling emotion. 'The world will little note
nor long remember what we say here, but it can never forget what they did here.' It was as simple and felicitous and
earnest a word as was ever spoken."

Everett's opinion was written to Lincoln the next day:
"I should be glad if I could flatter myself that I came as
near to the central idea of the occasion in two hours as you
did in two minutes." Lincoln's immediate reply was: "In
our respective parts yesterday, you could not have been excused to make a short address, nor I a long one. I am

pleased to know that, in your judgment, the little I did say was not entirely a failure."

At Everett's request Lincoln wrote with pen and ink a copy of his Gettysburg Address, and the manuscript was auctioned at a Sanitary Fair in New York for the benefit of soldiers. On request of George Bancroft, the historian, he wrote another copy for a Soldiers' and Sailors' Fair at Baltimore. He wrote still another to be lithographed as a facsimile in a publication, *Autographed Leaves of Our Country's Authors*. For Mr. Wills, his host at Gettysburg, he wrote another. The first draft, written in Washington, and the second one, held while delivering it, went into Hay's hands to be eventually presented to the Library of Congress.

The ride to Washington took until midnight. Lincoln was weary, talked little, stretched out on one of the side seats in the drawing room and had a wet towel laid across his eyes and forehead.

He had stood that day, the world's foremost spokesman of popular government, saying that democracy was yet worth fighting for. What he meant by "a new birth of freedom" for the nation could have a thousand interpretations. The taller riddles of democracy stood up out of the address. It had the dream touch of vast and furious events epitomized for any foreteller to read what was to come. His cadences sang the ancient song that where there is freedom men have fought and sacrificed for it, and that freedom is worth men's dying for. For the first time since he became President he had on a dramatic occasion declaimed, howsoever it might be read, Jefferson's proposition which had been a slogan of the Revolutionary War—"All men are created equal"—leaving no other inference than that he regarded the Negro slave as a man. His outwardly smooth sentences were inside of them gnarled and tough with the enigmas of the American experiment.

Back at Gettysburg the blue haze of the Cumberland Mountains had dimmed till they were a blur in a nocturne. The moon was up and fell with a bland golden benevolence on the new-made graves of soldiers, on the sepulchers of old settlers, on the horse carcasses of which the onrush of war had not yet permitted removal. The New York *Herald* man walked amid them and ended the story he sent his paper: "The air, the trees, the graves are silent. Even the relic hunters are gone now. And the soldiers here never wake to the sound of reveille."

In many a country cottage over the land, a tall old clock in a quiet corner told time in a tick-tock deliberation. Whether the orchard branches hung with pink-spray blossoms or icicles of sleet, whether the outside news was seedtime or harvest, rain or drouth, births or deaths, the swing of the pendulum was right and left and right and left in a tick-tock deliberation.

The face and dial of the clock had known the eyes of a boy who listened to its tick-tock and learned to read its minute and hour hands. And the boy had seen years measured off by the swinging pendulum, had grown to man size, had gone away. And the people in the cottage knew that the clock would stand there and the boy would never again come into the room and look at the clock with the query, "What is the time?"

In a row of graves of the Unidentified the boy would sleep long in the dedicated final resting place at Gettysburg. Why he had gone away and why he would never come back had roots in some mystery of flags and drums, of national fate in which individuals sink as in a deep sea, of men swallowed and vanished in a man-made storm of smoke and steel.

The mystery deepened and moved with ancient music and inviolable consolation because a solemn Man of Authority had stood at the graves of the Unidentified and spoken the words "We can not consecrate—we can not hallow—this ground. The brave men, living and dead, who struggled here, have consecrated it far above our poor power to add or detract . . . from these honored dead we take increased devotion to that cause for which they gave the last full measure of devotion."

To the backward and forward pendulum swing of a tall

old clock in a quiet corner they might read those cadenced words while outside the windows the first flurry of snow blew across the orchard and down over the meadow, the beginnings of winter in a gun-metal gloaming to be later arched with a star-flung sky.

Chapter 23

Epic '63 Draws to a Close

A week after Lincoln's return from Gettysburg, Hay wrote to Nicolay: "The President is sick in bed. Bilious." Still later came definite information. The President had varioloid, a mild form of smallpox. Owen Lovejoy sent in his name, waited in the reception room, saw a door open just enough to frame Lincoln in a dressing gown saying, "Lovejoy, are you afraid?" "No, I have had the small-pox." And walking in, he heard Lincoln: "Lovejoy, there is one good thing about this. I now have something I can give everybody." Press items told of office seekers suddenly fleeing the White House on hearing what ailed the President.

An epic of action around Chattanooga came to its high point and Lincoln on a sickbed could read a Grant telegram: "Lookout Mountain top, all the rifle-pits in Chattanooga Valley, and Missionary Ridge entire, have been carried and now held by us," and a dispatch from Thomas: "Missionary Ridge was carried simultaneously at six different points . . . Among the prisoners are many who were paroled at Vicksburg." And again from Grant on November 27: "I am just in from the front. The rout of the enemy is most complete . . . The pursuit will continue to Red Clay in the morning, for which place I shall start in a few hours."

For the first time in a large-scale combat, Confederate

soldiers had been routed, had run away. They had valor, as they had shown at Chickamauga. What explained their panic? The usual answer was Bragg, upright, moral, irascible, disputatious, censorious, dyspeptic, nervous, so harsh with his corrections and criticisms that the discipline of his army had gone to pieces. Grant had studied Bragg, knew him as Lee knew McClellan, and gauged his plans accordingly. Bragg had cornered Grant, put his army within gunshot range overlooking the Union army, making retreat for Grant "almost certain annihilation," said Grant. Then the rank and file of Grant's army had thrown orders to the wind and taken mountains away from an army holding the top ridges with cannon and rifle pits.

Anger at Jeff Davis, and mistrust of him, arose among some of his best aides because of his not knowing Bragg was second-rate. And Jeff Davis answered by appointing his friend Bragg Chief of Staff of the Confederate armies, with headquarters in Richmond. Newspapers of the North spread the story before their readers the last Thursday of November, the Day of Thanksgiving proclaimed by the President weeks earlier.

Now Sherman could be released with an army to march on Knoxville and relieve Longstreet's siege of Burnside there—which Sherman did in a clean, fast operation. Now Grant and Sherman could lay their plans to move farther south—on Atlanta—perhaps drive a wedge and split the Confederacy that lay east of the Mississippi.

The President's annual message to Congress began with "renewed, and profoundest gratitude to God" for another year "of health, and of sufficiently abundant harvests." Efforts to stir up foreign wars had failed. The treaty between the United States and Great Britain for suppression of the slave trade was working. The national banking law passed by Congress had proved a valuable support to public credit. The troops were being paid punctually. And the people? The President saluted them. "By no people were the burdens incident to a great war ever more cheerfully borne."

The report of the Secretary of War, "a document of great interest," was too valuable to summarize. The Union Navy was tightening its blockade of the enemy. More than 1,000 vessels had been captured; prizes amounted to $13,000,000. New navy yards were wanted. Enlisted seamen in 1861 numbered 7,500, now 34,000. The post office had taken in nearly as much money as it had spent and might soon become self-sustaining. Though a great war was on, 1,456,514 acres of land had been taken up under the new Homestead Law. The President agreed that the law should be modified to favor soldiers and sailors of Federal service.

The breath of a new and roaring age, intricate with man's new-found devices, rose at intervals throughout the message. A continuous line of telegraph from Russia to the Pacific Coast was being wrought under arrangements effected with the Russian Emperor. The proposed international telegraph across the Atlantic Ocean, and a telegraph line from Washington to the seaboard forts and the Gulf of Mexico, deserved reasonable outlay from Congress.

The Executive invited a backward look at the war. The "rebel" borders were pressed still farther back, the Mississippi opened, Tennessee and Arkansas cleared of insurgent control, slaveowners "now declare openly for emancipation," Maryland and Missouri disputing only as to the best mode of removing slavery within their own limits. Of former slaves 100,000 were in the U.S. military service, half of them bearing arms. "So far as tested, it is difficult to say they are not as good soldiers as any."

Looking to the present and future, the President had thought fit to issue a Proclamation of Amnesty and Reconstruction, a copy of it being transmitted to Congress. To those who wanted it the Union Government would give amnesty, forget what had been. Reconstruction, the bringing together again of the departed brothers into the Union, would begin with amnesty. This was the theory and the hope, not explicitly formulated, that underlay the proclamation and the oath Lincoln discussed for Congress in his message. He cited his constitutional pardoning power: through the rebellion many persons were guilty of treason; the President was authorized to extend pardon and amnesty on conditions he deemed expedient. Full pardon would be granted with restoration of property, except as to slaves and where rights of third parties intervened, and on condition that every such person took an oath:

> . . . in presence of Almighty God, that I will henceforth faithfully support, protect and defend the Constitution of the United States, and the union of the States thereunder; and that I will, in like manner, abide by and faithfully support all acts of Congress . . . and . . . abide by and faithfully support all proclamations of the President made during the existing rebellion having reference to slaves . . . So help me God.

The proclamation had no reference to states that had kept loyal governments, never seceded—meaning Missouri, Kentucky, Maryland, Delaware. The intention of the proclamation was to give a mode by which national authority and loyal state governments might be re-established. The President's message reasoned for the amnesty proclamation. "The form of an oath is given, but no man is coerced to take it. The man is only promised a pardon in case he voluntarily takes the oath . . ."

The Executive set at rest all talk that the Emancipation Proclamation would be revoked. "While I remain in my present position I shall not attempt to retract or modify the emancipation proclamation; nor shall I return to slavery any person who is free by the terms of that proclamation, or by any of the acts of Congress." Before this sentence the silence in the hall was "profound," noted Noah Brooks, but with its reading "an irresistible burst of applause" swept the main floor and galleries.

Movements for emancipation in states not included in the Emancipation Proclamation were "matters of profound gratulation." He still favored gradual emancipation by Federal purchase of slaves. "While I do not repeat in detail what I have heretofore so earnestly urged upon this subject, my general views and feeling remain unchanged."

Noah Brooks in his news letter two days later found Senator Sumner "irate because his doctrine of State suicide finds no responsive echo" in the President's message. As a "vent to this half-concealed anger," wrote Brooks, "during the delivery of the Message the distinguished Senator from Massachusetts exhibited his petulance to the galleries by eccentric motions in his chair, pitching his documents and books upon the floor in ill-tempered disgust." Sumner still held that the seceded states had by secession committed suicide and should be governed as territories, conquered provinces on trial and under compulsion.

Lincoln spoke of the newborn fury of some of the Missouri radicals. Hay wrote December 13 of the President "very much displeased" at fresh reports from Missouri. Congressman Washburne had been in Missouri and saw, or thought he saw, that Schofield was overplaying his hand in factional politics; when Washburne spoke of electing Gratz Brown and J. B. Henderson as U.S. Senators, one from each faction, Schofield had replied he would not consent to the election of Brown. Also Brown had told the President that Schofield had refused to consent to a state constitutional convention, even though Brown had promised in that event he would as U.S. Senator vote to confirm Schofield as a major general. "These things," wrote Hay, "the President says, are obviously transcendent of his instructions to Schofield and must not be permitted. He has sent for Schofield to come to Washington and explain these grave matters."

Schofield in the White House heard Lincoln and replied the facts were that the desired union of conservatives and radicals in Missouri was impossible; they were more bitterly opposed to each other than either was to the Democrats. According to Schofield, Lincoln promptly dismissed the subject, "I believe you, Schofield; those fellows have been lying to me again." Later, from Congressman James S. Rollins, Schofield heard that one group of Missouri politicians had called on the President and given a version of Missouri affairs. The President had opened a little right-hand drawer of his desk, taken out a letter from Schofield, read it to them and said, *"That* is the truth about the matter; you fellows are lying to me."

To the Secretary of War, Lincoln wrote: "I believe Gen.

Schofield must be relieved from command of the Department of Missouri; otherwise a question of veracity, in relation to his declarations as to his interfering, or not, with the Missouri Legislature, will be made with him, which will create an additional amount of trouble, not to be overcome by even a correct decision of the question." Lincoln sent to the Senate a nomination of Schofield for major general. There a majority favored it. But by a small minority, controlling the Military Committee, it was hung up against the President's wishes for weeks.

Then came word from Grant that General Foster, heading the Department and Army of the Ohio, was leaving on account of ill-health. On being asked whom to appoint in Foster's place, Grant wired, "Either McPherson or Schofield." Halleck handed Grant's dispatch to Schofield, who carried it to Lincoln saying he would take all chances on the new job. Lincoln: "Why, Schofield, that cuts the knot, don't it? Tell Halleck to come over here, and we will fix it right away." Then Schofield was appointed and transferred, with Rosecrans taking his place in Missouri.

The New York *Times* was saying that Lincoln's refusal to identify himself with either side in Missouri exhibited broad-souled patriotism, singleness of purpose. "Mr. Lincoln never forgets he is President of the nation and his prime duty is to save the nation from the rebellion which has threatened to destroy it. He . . . consequently can not be drawn into any petty strife."

This month of December '63 seemed to mark the beginning of a period in which, North and South, extremists more often referred to Confederate leaders ending on the gallows. Hanging with rigor, system, ceremonial, lay in the imaginings of the more fiery Republican radicals.

The Richmond *Examiner* editorial writer, Edward A. Pollard, in December quoted from Lincoln's Amnesty Proclamation and set down his judgment as a historian: "In proposing these utterly infamous terms, this Yankee monster of inhumanity and falsehood, had the audacity to declare that in some of the Confederate States the elements of re-

construction were ready for action . . . This insulting and
brutal proposition of the Yankee Government was the apt
response to those few cowardly factions which in North
Carolina, and in some parts of Georgia and Alabama,
hinted at 'reconstruction.' "

The New York *Metropolitan Record* queried: "Ye war
Democrats, what do you think of being told that the black
soldier is just as good as the white, for this is the amount
of the President's message? What next? Shall we look
among the black race for the President's successor?" The
Record had no patience "with the great criminal who now
occupies the Presidential chair."

In the week of the President's message, and while he yet
lay sick, a New York *World* editorial reprinted in the Detroit *Free Press* joined in a remarkably human commentary.
From those extremist opposition organs came generous
wishes:

> We believe we but echo the feelings of the whole
> country, without distinction of party, in sincerely hop-
> ing that the President will soon be restored to health
> and strength . . . His death at this time would tend to
> prolong the war . . .
>
> Mr. Lincoln has oftentimes acted wrongly, unwisely,
> arbitrarily; but still he hesitates before he takes an
> extreme position, and is willing to obey, although not
> always quick to perceive, the drift of public opinion.
> Without elevation of character, he has a self-poise, a
> reticence, an indisposition to commit himself, which
> in many a trying crisis has saved him from being the
> utter tool of the madmen whose folly brought on the
> war . . .
>
> So heaven help Abraham Lincoln, and restore him
> to his wonted health and strength.

A history rather than a biography would be required for
recording the life of Lincoln, wrote James Russell Lowell,
of the *North American Review,* in an article on Lincoln in

January '64. An eminent Bostonian, author of Yankee dialect verse, poet, essayist, critic, Harvard professor in the chair of modern languages and belles-lettres—Lowell sketched Lincoln as ". . . so gently guiding public sentiment that he seems to follow it, by so yielding doubtful points that he can be firm without seeming obstinate in essential ones." People come in time to see that such a political leader has shaken himself loose and is free from temper and prejudice. ". . . perhaps none of our Presidents since Washington has stood so firm in the confidence of the people as he does after three years of stormy administration . . . At first he was so slow that he tired out all those who see no evidence of progress but in blowing up the engine; then he was so fast, that he took the breath away from those who think there is no getting on safely while there is a spark of fire under the boilers . . . Mr. Lincoln . . . has always waited . . . till the right moment brought up all his reserves."

Lowell months before had written in a private letter: "Lincoln may be right, for aught I know, but I guess an ounce of Frémont is worth a pound of long Abraham. Mr. Lincoln seems to have the theory of carrying on the war without hurting the enemy. He is incapable, of understanding that they *ought* to be hurt." Lowell now enfigured Lincoln as a logger in a crazy river snatching his way on a shaky raft and trying to hold to the main current through rapids. "He is still in wild water, but we have faith that his skill and sureness of eye will bring him out right at last." The very homeliness of Lincoln's genius was its distinction, thought Lowell. "His kingship was conspicuous by its workday homespun. Never was ruler so absolute as he, nor so little conscious of it; for he was the incarnate commonsense of the people."

The new Congress in December '63, by the New York *Tribune Almanac*, had in the House 102 Republicans and unconditional Unionists, 75 Democrats, 9 Border State men; in the Senate 36 Republicans and unconditional Unionists, 9 Democrats and 5 conditional Unionists.

One set of reports about himself that year the President did not bother to answer. Over and again the opposition newspapers large and small said that his salary was to be raised from $25,000 to $100,000 a year, as he wished, that he was drawing his salary in gold while the soldiers were paid in greenbacks, that his length of time in office was to be fixed by Congress for a life term, as he wished.

Day after day the question of the Negro and his destiny crossed the events of each hour. He was "the inevitable Sambo," "the everlasting nigger," the living interrogation point. To one side he incarnated the slavery issue, to the other the race-equality problem. The trend of feeling against slavery went on deepening. Francis George Shaw of Boston wrote to the President, "My only son, Colonel Robert Gould Shaw of the 54th Regiment Massachusetts Volunteers (colored troops) was killed on the parapet of Fort Wagner in South Carolina, and now lies buried in its ditch among his brave and devoted followers." To the request of Colonel Shaw's friends for his corpse came a reply it was "buried under a layer of niggers." The father urged the President to take immediate measures for protection to colored troops. "If our son's services and death shall contribute in any degree towards securing to our colored troops that equal justice which is a holy right of every loyal defender of our beloved country, we shall esteem our great loss a blessing."

Antislavery Roman Catholics declared their convictions in a more positive tone. The Christmas issue of the *Catholic Telegraph*, December 24, 1863, published: "It seems that there is a Priest in Kentucky who is still holding forth in favor of slavery. He ought to hide in the Mammoth Cave and associate with the fossils . . . A Catholic Priest, in the holy times of Christmas, advocating slavery! Handing over women and children into infamous bondage with one hand and offering incense with the other to the infant Saviour— THE REDEEMER OF ALL! What a subject for meditation before the altar on Christmas morning! If slavery must have its advocates let them be found amongst the laity, and not amongst the Priests." The sermon on the war given by

Archbishop John Hughes August 17, 1862, was resented by Southern Catholics, by Northern antiwar groups; he replied to criticisms of his course printed in the Baltimore *Catholic Mirror*. He broke his connection with the fiercely antiwar and anti-Lincoln *Metropolitan Record*.

That the year of '63 was coming to an end with not one Negro slave revolt, not one scene of killing and plunder, as a result of the Emancipation Proclamation, made the going easier for Lincoln.

But for the New Year's season the *Crisis* reprinted a lamentation from the Zanesville, Ohio, *Aurora:* "The people of the North owe Mr. Lincoln but eternal hatred and scorn. There are 500,000 new made graves; there are 500,000 orphans; there are 200,000 widows . . . thieves in the Treasury, provost marshals in the seats of justice, butchers in the pulpit—and these are the things which we owe Mr. Lincoln. As the Lord liveth, we shall pay him all we owe him some day—him, and all the bloody band of traitors, plunderers and knaves."

That Christmas Lincoln wrote a letter of thanks for a solid gold watch to James H. Hoes, Esq., a Chicago jeweler. Hoes had donated the watch to the first Sanitary Commission Fair held in Chicago, as a token to be awarded the one person making the largest contribution of funds to the fair. Lincoln donated his original hand-written draft of the Emancipation Proclamation; it sold at auction for $3,000. A Chicago publisher was assigning territory to canvassers selling lithographed copies of "The Emancipation Proclamation, Genuine Facsimile in President Lincoln's Handwriting."

To Usher F. Linder, Douglas Democrat and storytelling lawyer of the old "orgmathorial" Eighth Circuit, Lincoln sent a Christmas gift. Linder's boy had joined the Confederate Army, had been taken prisoner, and his father sent letters to Lincoln asking a pardon. Weeks passed and Linder received a note dated December 26, 1863: "Your son Dan. has just left me, with my order to the Sec. of War, to administer to him the oath of allegiance, discharge him & send him to you."

The year of 1863 saw glimmering of the last hopes of the Richmond Government for European recognition. The despair of Jefferson Davis as to overseas help, as to ships or money from England was set forth in his December message to the Confederate Congress. Davis dwelt at such length and so bitterly on the point that he was rebuked by some of the Southern newspapers for overemphasis of it. Rhett and Yancey among civilians, and the former slave trader General Bedford Forrest, a military leader perhaps as great in his own field as Stonewall Jackson, had said, "If we are not fighting for slavery, then what are we fighting for?" They were told that the outlawing of the African slave trade by the Confederacy in '61 was a gesture for European good will with a hope of recognition as a World Power among nations. Yet that recognition had not come. All maneuvers and prayers for it had failed.

As early as '61, Archbishop John Hughes had come to Washington, met Lincoln and the Cabinet, indicated that he could not take official appointment. At the President's request, however, joined to that of his old friend Seward, the Archbishop became one of the President's personal agents with full powers to set forth the Union cause in Europe. The Archbishop had interviewed the French Emperor, attended a canonization of martyrs in Rome, laid the cornerstone of a new Catholic university in Dublin built partly from moneys collected in America. In this tour of eight months over Europe the Archbishop spoke the pro-Northern views which he gave in a published letter to the pro-Southern Archbishop of New Orleans.

Meanwhile the war, the Emancipation Proclamation, the messages of Lincoln, the antislavery propaganda, had sharpened the instinct against slavery among masses of people in all countries. In homes and at work millions in Europe had asked, "What is this slavery in America?" the simplest answer being, "It is where a white man owns a black man like he owns a horse, a cow or a dog," the talk going farther, "What about the black women and children?" "The white man owns them too." "He can breed them, beat them, sell them?" "Yes." "Oh! oh!"

Uncle Tom and Simon Legree, Little Eva, and Eliza crossing the ice pursued by bloodhounds, had been presented on stages of world capitals and in hundreds of smaller cities. A thousand folk tales had gone traveling of the mixed bloods of white and Negro races, of fathers selling their children, of lusts and sins and concubines, of fantastic tricks of fate involving those legally proved to have one drop of Negro blood.

A long letter to the Loyal National League of New York came from "friends of America" in France. Among signers were the Count de Gasparin, Protestant, former Minister of Public Instruction; Augustin Cochin, Catholic, author of *The Abolition of Slavery;* Henri Martin, Catholic, Republican, author of a history of France; Edouard Laboulaye, professor in the Collège de France, "moderate Catholic, moderate Republican." They gave Lincoln and his administration complete approval in a propaganda document of 17 pages dated October 31, 1863, and reprinted some weeks later in America.

Italian republican liberals sent to Lincoln a cadenced address lavish with Latin gestures, its first signer the famous fighting patriot Giuseppe Garibaldi. Señor Don Matias Romero, envoy of the Republic of Mexico, presented his credentials at the White House. An army of some 25,000 French soldiers and a fleet were holding a large part of Mexico. But the fugitive President Juarez had in the field perhaps 27,000 troops. Lincoln read a response to Señor Romero: ". . . Thanking you for the liberal sentiments you have expressed for the United States, and congratulating you upon the renewed confidence which your government has reposed in you, it is with unaffected pleasure that I bid you welcome to Washington."

In Great Britain, with the "mother-tongue," were cross-currents as complex and varied as in the United States, as muddled as Missouri. The Emancipation Proclamation, mass meetings of workingmen formulating resolutions and addresses to Lincoln, had roused the active friends of the South, who organized Southern Clubs, gathered in men and influence, and carried on propaganda favoring the Confederacy. In April, three days' subscriptions in London to a Confederate loan amounted to 9,000,000 pounds sterling; later it ran to a total of 16,000,000 pounds, subscribers paying 15 per cent down. The last week in June '63 a motion in the House of Commons for recognition of the Southern Confederacy as a sovereign state was shelved by adjournment and by the speeches and tactics of John Bright and a handful of liberals. When, a little later, news arrived of the victories of Gettysburg and Vicksburg, the motion had lost what chance it ever had.

A *North British Review* writer came to the nub of the matter for many of the British. He quoted from pamphlets and personal letters of Americans showing their almost barbaric faith that "the hand of God" was shaping America. "Citizens of the United States are born with a giant ambition in their brains; and almost the first syllables they lisp have a sort of trumpet twang, as thus, 'Here I come, ready to grasp a sceptre and to rule the world.' "

For all the quaffing of toasts to the British Queen and her people, Lincoln and Seward saw that their only dependable well-wisher in Europe, except republican Switzerland, was the land of absolutist monarchy, Russia, the farthest of European extremes from "government of the people, by the people, for the people." Seward arranged secret understandings with Russia so momentous that he must have consulted with Lincoln about them. In America perhaps only Seward and Lincoln knew what conditional assurances were given the Russian government as to the purchase of the peninsula of Alaska. Not to Nicolay nor Hay nor Noah Brooks, nor to others to whom the President sometimes revealed secrets of state, did he give any inklings. And not even to his bosom friend Thurlow Weed did Seward give clues. Estimates ran that it was worth from $1,400,000 to $10,000,000. The United States was to buy it as soon as convenient, the purchase price to include certain naval expenses of the Russian government—some such understanding was worked out between the Washington and St. Petersburg governments.

Early in October '63 one Russian fleet lay in San Francisco harbor, another at New York with five first-class war vessels. Stalwart Muscovites in gay uniforms, outlandish whiskers, in excellent Russian, indifferent French and worse English, added merriment wherever they went. They sat for Brady photographs. They visited Meade's headquarters in Virginia, fell from the upper decks of cavalry horses, ate heartily, carried their liquor well.

Special writers filled many newspaper columns with tales of the Russian naval visitors, giving an extra spread to one shipboard reception where U.S. military officers and Mrs. Lincoln drank to the health of the Czar. The Richmond *Examiner* drew a parallel: "The Czar emancipates the serfs from their bondage of centuries, and puts forth the whole strength of his empire to enslave the Poles. Lincoln proclaims freedom to the African, and strives at the same time to subjugate free born Americans."

The essential viewpoint of Seward and Lincoln was probably hit off by *Harper's Weekly:* "England and France have recognized the belligerent rights of the rebels . . . Russia has not."

To Bayard Taylor, author of travel books, who had served as secretary of the American Legation at St. Petersburg under Minister Cameron, Lincoln wrote in December '63; "I think a good lecture or two on 'Serfs, Serfdom, and Emancipation in Russia' would be both interesting and valuable. Could not you get up such a thing?" Not long after, Taylor was addressing lyceum audiences on "Russia and the Russians." And Hay mentioned in his diary that the President went one evening to hear Taylor's lecture.

A Southern Union man, James Louis Petigru of Charleston, South Carolina, 74 years old, had gone as worn and infirm oaks fall; even Rhett said he could not find words to tell what a man this had been. At the first gun of the war Petigru had said, "I never believed that slavery would last a hundred years, now I know it won't last five." His name for appointment to the U.S. Supreme Court to replace Justice McLean or Justice Campbell was seriously laid before Lincoln and by him gravely considered.

Of Lincoln, Petigru had no high opinion, writing in March '62, "The *Mercury* has thrown off all reserve and proclaims J. D. [Jefferson Davis] is unfit for his place. I am myself afraid that he is but little better qualified for it than Lincoln is for his." Now Petigru was beyond the war and his daughter was to write in his epitaph, "In the great Civil War he withstood his People for his Country, but his People did homage to the Man who held his conscience higher than their praise."

Both sides had laid under earth brigadiers and major generals, the South mourning Stonewall Jackson, Van Dorn, Helm, Paxton, Tracy, Tilghman, Pender, both Garnetts, Barksdale, Preston Smith; the North its Reynolds, Berry, Sill, Lytle, Bayard, Sanders, Buford, Corcoran. The Union commissions had come to Lincoln's desk and he had signed them; the War Department reports had come to his desk that they were through with commissions. Colleges, societies, lodges, clubs, were treasuring in creped rosters the names of their dead who had not availed themselves of the $300 clause.

When General Michael Corcoran, who had proved his valor often under fire, died from the fall of a horse on him, a comrade of the Fenian Brotherhood in New York intoned a requiem: "Deep in the green sod let him rest under the starry arch of the Republic he so nobly served and within sight of that city where his name will never sound strange."

Major General John A. Logan, on furlough from Grant's army, had spoken to the people of Du Quoin, Illinois: "How do they know we are all abolitionists, regular straight-outs? Did we tell them so? Did we say so? Why is it? Well, I will tell you. It is because we are in the army and Abraham Lincoln is President. That is the reason. These men don't know enough or don't want to know that Abraham Lincoln, because he is President don't own the Government. This is our Government. This war ain't fighting for Mr. Lincoln. It is fighting for the Union, for the Government . . . I have seen Democrats shot down and buried in the same grave with the Republican and the Abolitionist. They are all fighting for the same country, the same ground . . .

You will again see the great railroads running from the North to the South, from the East to the West."

The human causes operating in America were many and varied and moving, requiring the brush of chaos to do a mural of the crossed interests of climate and geography, of native and foreign blood streams, of bread-and-butter necessity, of cultural environment, of mystic hopes. As they passed before Lincoln in their many guises and dialects, he considered, decided, waited, looked often abstracted, seemed more often to have his mind elsewhere than in Washington.

Lincoln was at the vortex of the revolution to break the power of the Southern planter aristocracy and usher in the dominance of the financial and industrial interests centered in New York City. He may have seen Paris correspondence of the New York *Times* at the year's end: "The popularity of Mr. Lincoln has much advanced abroad by his late acts . . . I heard a leading French politician say lately: 'You Americans don't appreciate Mr. Lincoln at his proper value. No monarch in Europe could carry on such a colossal war in front while harassed by so many factions and fault-finders behind . . . On every side I hear people begin to say that Mr. Lincoln will merit more than a biography—he will merit a history.' "

Newspapers were printing a strangely worded psalm of praise for Lincoln the man, spoken in the 1863 Thanksgiving sermon at the Second Presbyterian Church of Auburn, New York, by its pastor, the Reverend Henry Fowler. The progress of the President kept pace with the progress of the people, Fowler believed, comparing it with the time in Jewish history when the prophet Samuel was the mediator between a passing and a coming epoch. "Such an epoch of perplexity, transition, change, is not often witnessed. In every such passage of a nation there ought to be a character like that of Samuel. Misunderstood and misrepresented at the time; attacked from both sides; charged with not going far enough and with going too far; charged with saying too much and saying too little, he slowly, conscientiously and honestly works out the mighty problem. He was not a founder of a new state of things like Moses, he was not a champion of the existing order of things like Elijah. He stood between the two; between the living and the dead; between the past and the present; between the old and the new; with that sympathy for each which at such a period is the best hope for any permanent solution of the questions which torment it. He has but little praise from partisans, but is the careful healer binding up the wounds of the age . . .

"His awkward speech and yet more awkward silence, his uncouth manners, his grammar self-taught and partly forgotten . . . doing nothing when he knows not what to do; hesitating at nothing when he sees the right; lacking the recognized qualification of a party leader, and yet leading his party as no other man can; sustaining his political enemies in Missouri to their defeat, sustaining his political friends in Maryland to their victory; conservative in his sympathies and radical in his acts . . . his religion consisting in truthfulness, temperance, asking good people to pray for him and publicly acknowledging in events the hand of God, he stands before you as the type of 'Brother Jonathan,' a not perfect man and yet more precious than fine gold." The President took such outpourings to heart. As prose it had a touch of his own flavor.

New Year's Day of 1864 came, and Benjamin Perley Poore noted at the morning reception in the White House: "Mr. Lincoln was in excellent spirits, giving each passer-by a cordial greeting and a warm shake of the hand, while for some there was a quiet joke." Mrs. Lincoln stood at his right hand, wearing purple silk trimmed with black velvet and lace, a lace necktie fastened with a pearl pin, a white plume topping her headdress. At noon the doors were thrown open for the people to pour through in a continuous stream for two hours. "A living tide which swept in, eddied around the President and his wife, and then surged into the East Room which was a maelstrom of humanity, uniforms, black coats, gay female attire, and citizens generally." Noah Brooks' eye took in Mrs. Lincoln lacking mourning garb for the first time in the more than twenty months since Willie Lincoln died.

While the President had lain abed with varioloid, an immense crowd had streamed down Pennsylvania Avenue to the Capitol grounds looking skyward toward the Capitol dome. The bronze legs and torso of the massive heroic figure of a helmeted woman representing Armed Freedom, after years of lying helpless and forlorn on the ground below, had been lifted to the top of the dome. And on this day, precisely at noon, the last section of this 19½-foot high bronze statue, consisting of the head and shoulders of the incomplete goddess, left the mass of material at the foot of the dome and moved serenely upward, drawn by a slender wire cable.

From a chaos of timbered scaffolding the head and shoulders emerged and swung lightly and calmly into place joined to her torso. A workman drove a ringing sledge hammer three times. The Union banner ran up a flagstaff. Artillery roared a salute.

To one onlooker, Noah Brooks, the prolonged and loud shout of the crowd seemed to say to the azure that day: "Take her, oh, heavens blue and gay, take her to thy protecting arms, with all her bronze and all her charms."

John Eaton of Toledo, Ohio, had talked with Lincoln one day about the statue of Armed Freedom to be hoisted over the Capitol dome, new marble pillars to be installed on the Senate wing, a massive and richly embellished bronze door being made for the main central portal. People were saying it was an extravagance during wartime, Eaton remarked. Lincoln answered, "If people see the Capitol going on, it is a sign we intend the Union shall go on."

Chapter 24

Grant Given High Command, '64

As a former Douglas Democrat now for the war and the Union, Grant was accepted and endorsed by an element that could never see Lincoln as their leader. The powerful New York *Herald* spoke for a miscellany of interests when through the winter of '63 and '64 it kept up a cry for Grant for President, "Grant, the People's Candidate." Many other newspapers joined in.

Lincoln had never seen Grant. He knew Grant only from what he read and what he heard in talk about his best fighter. To Congressman Washburne, Lincoln said: "About all I know of Grant I have got from you. I have never seen him. Who else besides you knows anything about Grant?" Washburne: "I know very little about him. He is my townsman but I never saw very much of him. The only man who really knows Grant is Jones. He has summered and wintered with him." Washburne referred to a Galena man, J. Russell Jones, a U.S. marshal at Chicago who had visited with Grant in Mississippi.

Lincoln wired Jones to come on to Washington. Jones picked up his mail on the way to the depot and opened it on the train. In it was a letter from Grant answering one Jones had written urging the General to pay no attention to the newspapers trying to run him for President. Grant was saying that he had as big a job as one man could ask, that he was out to suppress the "rebellion," and everything that reached him trying to push him into politics went into the wastebasket. Arriving in Washington, Jones sent word he would be glad to call when convenient and the President set eight o'clock that evening. Then as Jones told it: "The

President gave directions to say to all that he was engaged for the evening . . . opened the conversation by saying that he was anxious to see somebody from the West with whom he could talk upon the general situation . . . Mr. Lincoln made no allusion whatever to Grant. I had been there but a few minutes, however, when I fancied he would like to talk about Grant. 'Mr. President, if you will excuse me for interrupting you, I want to ask you kindly to read a letter that I got from my box as I was on my way to the train.' Whereupon I gave him Grant's letter. He read it with evident interest. When he came to the part where Grant said that it would be impossible for him to think of the presidency as long as there was a possibility of retaining Mr. Lincoln in the office, he read no further, but arose and, approaching me, put his hand on my shoulder and said: 'My son, you will never know how gratifying that is to me. No man knows, when that presidential grub gets to gnawing at him, just how deep it will get until he has tried it; and I didn't know but what there was one gnawing at Grant.' The fact was that this was just what Mr. Lincoln wanted to know."

Among the first acts of Congress that winter was the voting of a medal of thanks to Grant for his victories. The country had its first word from Grant, as to running for President, in January '64: "I aspire only to one political office. When this war is over, I mean to run for Mayor of Galena [his Illinois home town], and if elected, I intend to have the sidewalk fixed up between my house and the depot." Some comment ran like that of *Leslie's Weekly:* "If General Grant should go on joking in this dry style, he will soon joke Lincoln out of the next nomination."

To his father February 20 Grant wrote cautioning the old man not to believe all he read in the public prints. "I am not a candidate for any office. All I want is to be left alone to fight this war out." America had its chuckle over Mrs. Grant's saying to a New York *Herald* interviewer, "I have no doubt Mr. Grant will succeed, for he is a very obstinate man." Lincoln thereafter occasionally spoke of "Mr. Grant, as Mrs. Grant calls him."

Bills in House and Senate to revive the rank of lieutenant general of the armies of the United States on February 26 passed both houses. On February 29 the President signed the bill, named Grant for the newly created office and the Senate confirmed it.

And now Halleck at last was to go. Lincoln had told Hay and others on various occasions, "I am Halleck's friend because he has no others." Also to Hay, Lincoln had said that Halleck was "little more . . . than a first-rate clerk."

Grant at Nashville wrote to Sherman that his personal success in the war was due to the energy and skill of his subordinates, above all to Sherman and McPherson. "I feel all the gratitude this letter can express, giving it the most flattering construction." Sherman groaned over the prospect of Grant's leaving. "For God's sake and your country's sake, come out of Washington . . . Come West; take to yourself the whole Mississippi Valley." Sherman knew that for Grant, as for himself, the war was for a river and whether that river should belong to one or several nations. Also both knew that political forces in Washington could hamstring the best of commanders.

Grant traveled toward Washington with his 14-year-old boy Fred, and his chief of staff John Rawlins. Crowds and cheers met Grant as the train moved on to Washington. There on the evening of March 8 he walked into Willard's and asked for a room. The clerk said he had only a top-floor room. Grant said that would do—and signed the register. The clerk took a look at the name and then jumped fast to assign Grant the best in the house. Grant walked into the dining room and was ordering food when word passed among the guests, "It's Grant," and questions: "Where is he?" "Which is he?" Someone stood on a chair and called for three cheers for Grant. Three cheers rang out. The diners pounded on tables, waved napkins, threatened the glassware, yelled the name of Grant, Grant, Grant!

After a few minutes, as Noah Brooks noted it, "General Grant, looking very much astonished and perhaps annoyed, rose to his feet, awkwardly rubbed his mustache with his napkin, bowed, resumed his seat and attempted to finish his dinner." The diners then seemed slowly to get the idea that Grant had come to the dining room for a meal. And they let him eat in peace.

Soon Grant was on his way with Senator Cameron to report to the President at the White House, in a tarnished uniform with a major general's stars on the shoulder straps. "He had no gait, no station, no manner, rough, light-brown whiskers, rather a scrubby look," wrote Richard Henry Dana. "He had a cigar in his mouth, and rather the look of a man who did, or once did, take a little too much to drink . . . a slightly seedy look, as if he was out of office and on half pay, nothing to do but hang around, a clear blue eye and a look of resolution, as if he could not be trifled with, and an entire indifference to the crowd about him . . . He does not march, nor quite walk, but pitches along as if the next step would bring him on his nose."

It was the night of the President's weekly reception. A buzz and a murmur ran round the big East Room, reaching the President with news that Grant would soon step into the room. As the General entered, a hush fell on the crowd. They moved back and made a pathway. Lincoln saw him coming, put out his long bony hand for the shorter and smaller one of Grant's. "I'm glad to see you, General." The two men stood a moment with struck hands.

Lincoln introduced the General to Seward, who escorted him toward Mrs. Lincoln in the East Room. The buzz of talk became a hullabaloo. The crowd swirled around the short bullet-shaped man who embodied Donelson, Shiloh, Vicksburg, Chattanooga, in his rough frame. They cheered and yelled, jammed toward him, men and women wanting to touch his hands. He "blushed like a schoolgirl," shook hands till sweat poured down his face. Veins on his forehead bulged red. He dropped a remark later that it was a hotter spot than he had ever known in battle.

"Stand up so we can all have a look at you!" came cries. And the shrinking war hero stepped up on a sofa and stood where they could look at him. Then he made a tour of the room with Mrs. Lincoln's arm in his. Lincoln, with a lady on his arm, followed, his fissured face lighted, taking in all the contrasts that appealed to his sense of humor. Ladies caught in the crush had their laces torn and crinolines mashed; many got up on chairs, tables, sofas, to be out of harm's way or to get a better view.

"It was the only real mob I ever saw in the White House," wrote Noah Brooks. "For once at least the President of the United States was not the chief figure in the picture. The little scared-looking man who stood on a crimson-covered sofa was the idol of the hour. He remained on view for a short time, then he was quietly smuggled out by friendly hands."

Grant returned when the crowd was gone and met Lincoln with Stanton and Nicolay in a small drawing room. And Lincoln did nearly all the talking—all of it on the point that the next day, when he was to hand formally to Grant the new commission, each of them should say little, but what they did say should be pat to the occasion. Grant put in his inside coat pocket a copy of the President's speech and, saying good night, left the room with Stanton. Next day at one o'clock the Cabinet, Halleck, Grant's son Fred, Rawlins, Owen Lovejoy and Nicolay assembled to hear two little speeches that were telegraphed to the wide world.

Lincoln, facing Grant, read four sentences: "General Grant, The nation's appreciation of what you have done, and it's reliance upon you for what remains to do, in the existing great struggle, are now presented with this commission, constituting you Lieutenant General in the Army of the United States. With this high honor devolves upon you also, a corresponding responsibility. As the country herein trusts you, so, under God, it will sustain you. I scarcely need to add that with what I here speak for the nation goes my own hearty personal concurrence."

Grant held a half-sheet of note paper, on it a hurried lead-pencil scrawl. "His embarrassment was evident and extreme," noted Nicolay. "He found his own writing very difficult to read." The speech, however, fitted Grant as he read, facing Lincoln, his three-sentence response: "Mr. President: I accept this commission with gratitude for the high honor confered. With the aid of the noble armies that have fought in so many fields for our common country, it will be my earnest endeavor not to disappoint your expectations. I feel the full weight of the responsibilities now devolving on me and know that if they are met it will be due to those armies, and above all to the favor of that Providence which leads both Nations and men."

The news of Lincoln and Grant meeting, their two simple little speeches, was at once a universal press and sidewalk topic. The North brightened a little. The South saw Northern morale changed, at least slightly, for the better.

Grant rode by rail to the Army of the Potomac headquarters at Brandy Station, talked with Meade, felt out the spirit of the officers and men, said nothing much. Of intrigue and wirepulling in Washington he had heard and seen not a little in this week. Senators Wade and Chandler had been to the President and called for removal of Meade from command of the Army of the Potomac. Grant found Meade sincere, generous, open-minded, and told Meade he had no thought of a substitute for him.

No other man of high command in Washington had been so completely noncommittal regarding future plans as Grant. He was a good listener, and of his first interview with Lincoln alone, Grant wrote: "He stated to me that he had never professed to be a military man or to know how campaigns should be conducted, and never wanted to interfere in them: but that procrastination on the part of commanders, and the pressure from the people at the North and Congress, *which was always with him,* forced him into issuing his series of 'Military Orders'—one, two, three, etc. He did not know but they were all wrong, and did know that some of them were. All he wanted or had ever wanted was someone who would take the responsibility and act . . . I did not communicate my plans to the President, nor did I to the Secretary of War or to General Halleck."

After four days in Washington Grant told Lincoln he

would go west, be gone about nine days, then return and direct operations from eastern headquarters. Of his four-day stay in Washington he said to Lincoln, "This has been rather the warmest campaign I have witnessed during the war."

Before starting west, Grant ordered Sherman in command of all Western armies, McPherson to take Sherman's department, John A. Logan being given McPherson's corps. He rode to Nashville, talked with Sherman on a campaign plan, huge but simple. As Sherman put it: Grant "was to go for Lee and I was to go for Joe Johnston." That was all. The two of them believed they would start a never-ending hammering, a pressure of irresistible pincers—and close out the war.

Returning to Washington, Grant found himself hailed as the most popular man in the United States. "He hardly slept on his long journey east," said the New York *Tribune*, "yet he went to work at once." Grant ordered so many troops away from Washington for service with the Army of the Potomac that Stanton showed anxiety, even nervousness, about the small garrisons that would be left to man the forts around the capital. "I have already sent the men to the front," Grant replied to Stanton's questions. Stanton held this contrary to his plans; he would order the men back, saying, "We will see the President about that. I will have to take you to the President." Grant: "That is right. The President ranks us both." Then Stanton, in Lincoln's office facing the seated President, "Now, General, state your case." Grant: "I have no case to state. I am satisfied as it is." And Lincoln, after hearing Stanton's argument that Grant was exceeding his authority and putting Washington in danger by stripping the garrison, spoke: "Now, Mr. Secretary, you know we have been trying to manage this army for nearly three years and you know we haven't done much with it. We sent over the mountains and brought Mr. Grant, as Mrs. Grant calls him, to manage it for us; and now I guess we'd better let Mr. Grant have his own way." And there the matter rested. The incident was told and published, many believing it had a quality of the three men partaking.

Lincoln's own way of telling Grant to call on the administration for troops, but not too many, took the form of an ancient fable. "He said he thought he could illustrate what he wanted to say by a story," wrote Grant. "At one time there was a great war among the animals, and one side had great difficulty in getting a commander who had sufficient confidence in himself. Finally, they found a monkey, by the name of Jocko, who said that he thought he could command their army if his tail could be made a little longer. So they got more tail and spliced it on to his caudal appendage. He looked at it admiringly, and then thought he ought to have a little more still. This was added, and again he called for more. The splicing process was repeated many times, until they had coiled Jocko's tail around the room, filling all the space. Still he called for more tail, and, there being no other place to coil it, they began wrapping it around his shoulders. He continued his call for more, and they kept on winding the additional tail about him until its weight broke him down."

Phil Sheridan arrived in Washington early in April. Grant had appointed him to head the combined cavalry of the Army of the Potomac. Five feet five inches high, less than 130 pounds in weight—a total stranger to Washington and service in the east—young-looking, 33 years old, cool and guarded he was, refusing to tell anybody how to win the war. Halleck took him to Stanton and it was a meeting with no compliments. Halleck took him to the White House. Lincoln offered Sheridan both his hands, and he hoped Sheridan would fulfill Grant's expectations, and added that the cavalry of the Army of the Potomac had not gone so far as it might have.

At Culpeper Court House with Grant next day Sheridan again felt at home. A black-haired Irish Catholic boy who went from Perry County, Ohio, to West Point, Sheridan had followed soldiering ever since. As a fighter leading men against odds he had proved his wild and stubborn ways at Murfreesboro, Chickamauga and Chattanooga. Grant heard doubts spoken in Washington about Sheridan. They would soon find out whether Sheridan could fight, answered Grant. Lincoln about this time was asked for an opinion of Sheridan and limited himself to saying: "I will tell you just what kind of a chap he is. He is one of those long-armed fellows with short legs that can scratch his shins without having to stoop over."

In snow and rain of the last week in March, Grant and Rawlins set up headquarters at Culpeper Court House with the Army of the Potomac. Into their hands came daily reports and dispatches from troops on a line that ran 1,200 miles from the Atlantic to the Rio Grande, 21 army corps, 18 departments, with 800,000 men enrolled, 533,000 present and fit for duty. On a day soon to come the armies were to move, Butler up the James River, Grant and Meade across the Rapidan, Sigel up the Shenandoah, Averell in West Virginia, Sherman and Thompson from Chattanooga, and Banks up the Red River toward Texas.

Hitherto armies had acted independently, "like a balky team, no two ever pulling together," said Grant, as he explained to Lincoln that each army was to hammer away at enemy armies, railroads and supplies, "until by mere attrition, if in no other way, there should be nothing left to him." Grant and Meade in the east, and Sherman and Thomas in the west, were to be a giant nutcracker having the South crushed when they should finally meet. Thus Grant outlined the grand strategy to Lincoln.

"The President has been powerfully reminded," wrote Hay in his diary, "by General Grant's present movements and plans, of his [the President's] old suggestion so constantly made and as constantly neglected, to Buell & Hooker, et al., to move at once upon the enemy's whole line so as to bring into action . . . our great superiority of numbers . . . This idea of his own, the Pres[t] recognized with especial pleasure when Grant said it was his intention to make all the line useful—those not fighting could help the fighting. 'Those not skinning can hold a leg,' added Lincoln."

Grant was to hit Lee so hard in Virginia that Lee could send no help to Johnston in Georgia. Sherman was to hit Johnston so heavily in Georgia that Johnston would never shift troops to Lee in Virginia. So they hoped and planned. Grant's orders to his scattered subcommanders were relayed through Halleck at Washington. Burnside was taking his orders from Grant.

The Burnside corps had mobilized at Annapolis, its veterans of Roanoke, the Peninsula, Antietam, Fredericksburg, Chancellorsville and Knoxville being joined by new recruits that included several Negro regiments. They passed in review before the President standing on the balcony of Willard's. The black troops cheered, laughed, threw their caps in the air, marching past the signer of the Emancipation Proclamation. A rain blew up and soaked the marchers. Bystanders urged Lincoln to go in out of the rain. "If *they* can stand it, I guess I can," he answered as burnt and shot-riddled flags swept by on Pennsylvania Avenue.

Grant took a six-mile ride to see Meade, talking as he rode with Colonel Horace Porter of his favorable impression of Lincoln, of how frankly Lincoln had said he did not want to know Grant's plans. A delegation of "crossroads wiseacres," as Lincoln told it to Grant, criticized Grant for paroling Pemberton's army at Vicksburg and Lincoln gave the delegation a story with a moral:

> Sykes had a yellow dog he set great store by, but there were a lot of small boys around the village, and that's always a bad thing for dogs, you know. These boys didn't share Sykes's views, and they were not disposed to let the dog have a fair show. Even Sykes had to admit that the dog was getting unpopular; in fact, it was soon seen that a prejudice was growing up against that dog that threatened to wreck all his future prospects in life. The boys, after meditating how they could get the best of him, finally fixed up a cartridge with a long fuse, put the cartridge in a piece of meat, dropped the meat in the road in front of Sykes's door,

and then perched themselves on a fence a good distance off, holding the end of the fuse in their hands. Then they whistled for the dog. When he came out he scented the bait, and bolted the meat, cartridge and all. The boys touched off the fuse with a cigar, and in about a second a report came from that dog that sounded like a clap of thunder. Sykes came bouncing out of the house, and yelled, "What's up? Anything busted?" There was no reply, except a snicker from the small boys roosting on the fence; but as Sykes looked up he saw the whole air filled with pieces of yellow dog. He picked up the biggest piece he could find, a portion of the back with a part of the tail still hanging to it, and after turning it round and looking it all over, he said, "Well, I guess he'll never be much account again —as a dog." And I guess Pemberton's forces will never be much account again—as an army. The delegation began looking around for their hats before I had quite got to the end of the story, and I was never bothered any more after that about superseding the commander of the Army of the Tennessee.

Lincoln adopted a set form to meet one question and, according to the Chicago *Journal*, the dialogue ran:

VISITOR: When will the army move?

LINCOLN: Ask General Grant.

VISITOR: General Grant will not tell me.

LINCOLN: Neither will he tell me.

END OF VOLUME II

AMERICAN HERITAGE
SHORT HISTORY OF
THE CIVIL WAR

BY BRUCE CATTON

A concise presentation of the Civil War by its most
famous living student. This fast moving narrative
covers both the political and military aspects of the
war and succeeds in capturing the feelings of a nation during the years of its greatest peril.

Here too is the ordinary soldier who, speaking for
all America, North and South, says something this
country can never forget.

LAUREL LEAF LIBRARY   50c

JOHN RANSOM'S DIARY

INTRODUCTION BY BRUCE CATTON

This straightforward and unique diary of a 20-year-old Civil War soldier was written during his long, desperate months in Confederate prisons. Though surrounded by cruelty, death and disease, his unwavering courage and hopeful spirit helped him to survive the horror and suffering that claimed so many lives.

This book is a vivid and valuable record of the appalling conditions of Civil War prison life as well as an eloquent testimony to man's indomitable spirit.

"A tale of adventure, of suspense from beginning to end, of fierce hate and great love . . . with the added knowledge that *it really happened.*" —Bruce Catton

AN ORIGINAL LAUREL EDITION   50c

OTHER LAUREL ❧ EDITIONS IN AMERICAN HISTORY AND BIOGRAPHY

THE LAUREL SERIES OF GREAT SHORT STORIES

MAN AND WAR

EDITED BY M. JERRY WEISS

What does war mean to you ... to a family ... to a nation?

A brilliant collection of fiction and non-fiction offering a greater understanding of the nature of war, its emotions ... its everlasting fear and hell ... its brutal futility ...

Writers represented range from Tom Paine and Henry Wadsworth Longfellow to William Saroyan and Karl Shapiro, from Abraham Lincoln and Walt Whitman to John Dos Passos and Bertrand Russell.

LAUREL LEAF LIBRARY 50c